Paleonutrition

Center for
Archaeological Investigations

Southern Illinois University
at Carbondale

Visiting Scholar Conference Volumes

Paleonutrition

The Diet and Health of Prehistoric Americans

Edited by
Kristin D. Sobolik

Center for Archaeological Investigations
Southern Illinois University at Carbondale
Occasional Paper No. 22

Edited by Donna Whitfield Butler
Designed by Linda Jorgensen-Buhman
Word processing by Brenda Blythe Wells
Graphics layout by Thomas Gatlin

Contents

Figures

Tables

Foreword

The 19 chapters in the body of this volume present paleonutritional information resulting from virtuoso analyses of a wide variety of archaeological materials. The book exemplifies modern interdisciplinary archaeology at its best. Yet that often-used phrase, "interdisciplinary archaeology," is redundant because archaeology is interdisciplinary by definition. The archaeological enterprise as a whole, whether practiced as a kind of history, as a social science, and/or as one of the humanities, has always required substantive contributions from many different arts and sciences to the process of actually getting to know something about the past (Watson 1991). A large portion of archaeological recovery is earth science, whereas analyses and interpretation of archaeological materials draw upon archeometry (i.e., physics, chemistry, statistics), anthropology, cartography and geography, art history and the history of architecture, botany and zoology, ecology, economics, psychology, and sociology.

Rafael Pumpelly, himself a geologist, assembled the earliest, well-documented, explicitly interdisciplinary archaeological field and laboratory staff. In 1904, he brought together a geomorphologist (his son) and a cultural geographer as well as four archaeologists to carry out fieldwork in Central Turkestan and enlisted a zoologist, a chemist, two human paleontologists, and a botanist to help analyze the finds (Pumpelly 1908).

It was 50 years before Pumpelly's example was followed by another archaeologist working in Asia, Robert J. Braidwood. Braidwood's interdisciplinary approach to the origins of food production in the Near East established a new research focus and mode in archaeology (Braidwood 1952, 1979; Braidwood and Braidwood 1950; Braidwood et al. 1983; Braidwood and Howe 1960) that has been the object of a great deal of work by many scholars since then (e.g., individual chapters in Cowan and Watson [1992]; Gebauer and Price [1992]; and Harris and Hillman 1989).

In North America, in the recent past (i.e., 30 to 40 years ago and earlier) archaeologists prided themselves on their multivalent skills as excavators; photographers; cartographers; lithic, ceramic, floral, and faunal analysts; statisticians; scholars, authors, and editors. But as this volume makes abundantly clear, the lone archaeologist functioning as jack- or jill-of-all-trades is thoroughly obsolete. Increasing specialization is now the rule and the necessity in North America as elsewhere. Even small archaeological projects require many collaborators. The recovery, analysis, and interpretation of one human paleofecal specimen from a dry cave, for example, necessitate the cooperation of the field archaeologists with—minimally—one or more radiocarbon dating laboratories, paleoethnobotanists, palynologists and phytolith analysts, parasitologists, zooarchaeologists, DNA analysts, and biochemists. Similarly, the recovery, analysis, and interpretation of the fragmentary skeletal remains left by one ancient individual necessitate—minimally—cooperation of archaeologists, radiocarbon dating laboratories, several physical anthropologists/ biological anthropologists/bioarchaeologists, geologists, DNA analysts, and bone chemists.

Further developments in interdisciplinary archaeology in the United States are being impelled by the Native American Graves Protection and Repatriation Act passed in 1990. Archaeological research projects in the United States now often include Native American advisors, consultants, and liaisons. I think this trend will increase and that more extensive and intensive collaboration between Euramerican archaeologists and Native American cultural heritage representatives will ensue. Such collaboration is difficult, and even more demanding of great mutual trust (as well as great patience) than is traditional interdisciplinary research, but the results are amply worth the costs. And the costs should be lessened as more Native Americans and members of other indigenous groups become archaeologists, natural scientists, and other kinds of scholars. Ideally, a neo-archaeology that combines "Western" analytical and scientific theories and methods with diverse indigenous values and wisdom will ultimately be shaped into a comprehensive and sensitive interdisciplinary discipline whose practitioners address the full potential of not only the economic but also the social and ideological records left through the millennia by ancient and premodern human groups.

Patty Jo Watson

References

Braidwood, L., R. Braidwood, B. Howe, C. Reed, and P. Watson (editors)
    1983   *Prehistoric Archeology along the Zagros Flanks*. Oriental Institute Publication 105. Oriental Institute, Chicago.
Braidwood, R. J.
    1952   *The Near East and the Foundations for Civilization*. Condon Lectures, Oregon State System of Higher Education. University of Oregon, Eugene.
    1979   The Agricultural Revolution. Reprinted in *Hunters, Farmers, and Civilizations: Old World Archaeology*, edited by C. Lamberg-Karlovsky, pp. 91–99. Originally published 1960, *Scientific American* 203:130–148. W. H. Freeman, San Francisco.
Braidwood, R. J., and L. Braidwood
    1950   Jarmo: A Village of Early Farmers in Iraq. *Antiquity* 24:189–195.
Braidwood, R. J., and B. Howe (editors)
    1960   *Prehistoric Investigations in Iraqi Kurdistan*. Oriental Institute, University of

Chicago, Studies in Ancient Oriental Civilization No. 31. University of Chicago Press, Chicago.

Cowan, C. W., and P. J. Watson (editors)
   1992   *The Origins of Agriculture: An International Perspective.* Smithsonian Institution Press, Washington, D.C.

Gebauer, A. B., and T. D. Price (editors)
   1992   *Transitions to Agriculture in Prehistory.* Monographs in Old World Archaeology No. 4. Prehistory Press, Madison, Wisconsin.

Harris, D. R., and G. C. Hillman (editors)
   1989   *Foraging and Farming: The Evolution of Plant Exploitation.* One World Archaeology No. 13. Unwin Hyman, London.

Pumpelly, R. (editor)
   1908   *Explorations in Turkestan, Expedition of 1904. Prehistoric Civilizations of Anau: Origins, Growth, and Influence of Environment,* vols. 1 and 2. Carnegie Institution of Washington, Washington, D.C.

Watson, P. J.
   1991   Origins of Food Production in Western Asia and Eastern North America: A Consideration of Interdisciplinary Research in Anthropology and Archaeology. In *Quaternary Landscapes,* edited by C. Shane and E. Cushing, pp. 1–37. University of Minnesota Press, Minneapolis.

Preface

This volume consists of papers presented at the Ninth Annual Visiting Scholar Conference, *Paleonutrition: The Diet and Health of Prehistoric Americans*, at Southern Illinois University at Carbondale, March 27–28, 1992. The conference was jointly sponsored by the Center for Archaeological Investigations and the SIUC Division of Continuing Education. Financial support was provided by the Center, the SIUC Office of Research Development and Administration, the SIUC chapter of Sigma Xi, SIUC Women's Studies, and by the institutions with which the participants are affiliated and the participants themselves. I would like to thank Don Rice, Kim Smiley, Patrice Teltser, Brian Butler, and George Gumerman for their support of both the conference and this volume; Donna Butler, Brenda Wells, and Tom Gatlin for their long, hard work on the volume itself; and Joan Corse and Carolyn Taylor for their patience and smiles during my year at SIUC. As always, I thank Scott D. Peterson for his patience and understanding. Student volunteers at the conference were Kelly Cichy, Charles Hagebusch, David Leavens, Bob McCullough, and Liming Zhou.

The conference was designed to bring together scholars (both as speakers and as audience) working in all aspects of dietary and health reconstruction to discuss the advances that have been made in understanding the nutrition of prehistoric Americans and how those studies have helped define the integrative nature of paleonutrition. Wing and Brown's introduction to paleonutrition in 1979, *Paleonutrition: Method and Theory in Prehistoric Foodways*, provided a basis for what studies of nutrition could achieve in archaeological contexts, but the volume stopped short of providing case examples and of exploring the strengths and weaknesses of paleonutritional studies.

As was the Visiting Scholar Conference, this volume is a forum for participants to discuss their research and its contribution to an understanding of paleonutrition, of the limitations of discrete dietary and health data assemblages, and of how those limitations can be overcome. Past and present research on the nutrition of prehistoric Americans is analyzed through case studies, and the future of paleonutrition as a discipline is defined. It is hoped that this volume, which brings together researchers interested in diet, health, and nutrition, will demonstrate the techniques of paleonutritional study, will expose researchers and readers to the limitations involved in conducting dietary and health-status research, and will provide the knowledge needed to overcome those limitations.

The volume is divided into four main parts according to the types of data important in the process of understanding paleonutrition. The last paper in each part includes comments by a discussant about the papers in that section and ideas about the importance, problems, new research, and future of their particular areas of interest to paleonutritional studies. I have provided comments on Part IV in my introduction. The volume's concluding paper (Part V) is written by Elizabeth S. Wing who comments on the past, present, and future of paleonutritional analyses, with particular emphasis on what has been achieved since Wing and Brown's original text on the subject and on what remains to be achieved in the future.

Indirect Studies (Part I) presents papers on the faunal and floral remains from archaeological sites. They are labeled "indirect," not because they do not provide essential dietary information but because it is difficult to sort out which remains are actually dietary in nature. *Coprolite Studies* (Part II) and *Bioarchaeology* (Part III) are considered "direct" studies because their data sets actually reflect either direct dietary ingestion or a lifetime accumulation of dietary information. *Integrative Studies* (Part IV) offers case studies in which researchers have attempted to combine a variety of dietary and health data assemblages and techniques. Such analyses are becoming more prominent in dietary and health reconstruction as researchers are becoming aware of the importance of integrating a diversity of data from different resources. These case studies illustrate some of the problems of integrating a wide range of dietary and health information and their possible solutions.

We hope that this volume will be the impetus needed to launch paleonutritional studies into a higher sphere, that of integrating assemblages and information in order to assess prehistoric diet, health, and nutrition. The interaction provided by the setting of the conference and its subsequent publication cannot be achieved by individual scholars conducting and publishing independent research. Only through the interaction of analysts and the comprehensive review of dietary archaeological remains is a synthetic statement on the nutrition of a prehistoric population attainable.

1. Introduction

Kristin D. Sobolik

The analysis of prehistoric diets has been incorporated into archaeological studies with increasing frequency. Such dietary research includes the study of potential food items identified from the plant and animal refuse of a site (Guilday and Parmalee 1982; Minnis 1985; Pearsall 1983; Smith 1975) and the analysis of more specific samples recovered from coprolites (Bryant and Williams-Dean 1975; Fry 1980; Sobolik 1990). The analysis of human remains has further provided scholars with evidence of the long-term impact of diet on the health and mortality of individuals (Buikstra 1984; Cook 1984; Palkovich 1987). Rarely, however, are all of those disciplines incorporated into a synthetic analysis of prehistoric diet.

The history of nutritional research in archaeology indicates that each dietary and health discipline has developed as a separate field, with little integration between the disciplines. Such analyses also tend to be conducted by different researchers, and the results are reported separately. If an integration of the results is undertaken, it is the archaeologist, usually not a dietary or health expert, who integrates the conclusions. Because such synthesizers are often unaware of the scope and limitations of each data set, their interpretations frequently lack potential insight or authority. Furthermore, few archaeologists tend to raise those issues to the next higher level: reconstructing the nutritional quality of the diet.

Paleonutrition research, a relatively new area of study, combines dietary and health information gained from both archaeology and physical anthropology. Previously, scientists were content with reconstructing the diet of a prehistoric population, but paleonutritional analyses not only answer the question of what people ate but also evaluate what the effects of that diet were on overall health and nutrition. As scientists we are now becoming concerned with the applications of prehistoric diet to overall nutrition and health, asking questions that will place prehistoric information in an anthropological context.

The acquisition of food is at the core of the driving force of human evolution. Culture is constantly in flux due to various internal and external stimuli, including environmental and climatic shifts, population structure and group-

Paleonutrition: The Diet and Health of Prehistoric Americans, edited by Kristin D. Sobolik. Center for Archaeological Investigations, Occasional Paper No. 22. © 1994 by the Board of Trustees, Southern Illinois University. All rights reserved. ISBN 0-88104-078-9.

1

ings, warfare, and the more mundane decisions and compromises needed for group function and survival. The success of a cultural group can be jeopardized if the group does not adapt and respond to those stimuli.

The most basic and most immediate component of the decision-making process of an individual in a population is the acquisition of food. If the availability of food shifts, which could happen for a variety of reasons, cultural subsistence patterns need to shift in response. Cultural survival depends on obtaining sufficient food and nutrients and on the adaptation of the group to any changes that will place a constraint on that acquisition.

Food availability shifts can result from natural and cultural changes. Natural changes can include environmental and climatic fluctuations that will affect the quantity and types of resources available and seasonal changes that affect the presence and quality of resources. Cultural evolutionary changes, which may occur in at least partial response to the natural changes in food availability, include group mobility patterns and the adoption of a more reliable and productive means of obtaining food. The advent of an agricultural subsistence economy, which produces a population that usually exceeds the environmental carrying capacity for a hunter-gatherer economy, stimulates extensive changes in the cultural patterns of a population (Larsen 1982; McCorriston and Hole 1991).

Cultural ideology can also induce shifts in food availability, which would in turn affect group cultural evolution and patterns. Examples that would affect overall group health and nutrition are storage practices, food preparation techniques, and dietary diversity. How food is stored and/or prepared affects the nutritional content of the food and in turn affects group nutrition (see Rylander, Chapter 8). Cultural ideas on diversity in diet, and the importance or preferential acquisition of such diversity, will also affect group nutrition. Recent paleonutrition studies, however, have started to focus on the health and nutrition of individuals or small groups of a population (i.e., females, children, elites; see Gumerman, Chapter 6). Various food taboos and division of labor in food acquisition are examples of the cultural ideology of food availability that can affect individuals in a population.

In our analysis of the nutritional implications of the prehistoric diet and health, we can ascertain subsistence activities, pinpoint changes in food availability, and, most importantly, obtain information on evolutionary changes in prehistoric subsistence patterns and cultural responses. Research on the diet, health, and nutrition of prehistoric peoples allows us to bridge the gap between the technical determination of what they ate (analyzed from archaeological refuse remains and human skeletal material) and the determination of the behavioral and cultural changes they experienced. "Prehistoric remains can never fully reflect the true extent of the complexity of the prehistoric foodway. However, the role of nutrition is so basic to human existence, it is better to attempt to get a glimpse and accept this view as incomplete rather than to not look at all" (Wing and Brown 1979:174).

Integrative Analyses

The most important aspect of determining paleonutrition is the integration of disciplines. By combining the information gained from zoo-archaeological, paleoethnobotanical, coprolite, and bioarchaeological studies, a more complete picture of the paleonutrition of a prehistoric population can be revealed. The food refuse examined by each discipline contributes pieces to the entire paleonutrition puzzle, yet no single assemblage provides all the pieces. Each assemblage also has inherent limitations, many of which can be resolved through the analysis of the other assemblages. Only the analysis of the biological remains of the people themselves will indicate the impact the diet had on their health and mortality.

To emphasize the importance of each assemblage and discipline in evaluating the diet and nutrition of prehistoric peoples, I offer a short review of pale-oethnobotany, zooarchaeology, coprolite analyses, and bioarchaeology. The type of information that can be gained through each discipline is then reviewed and critically evaluated. The problems inherent in assessing paleo-nutrition through each assemblage alone will be discussed, as well as the importance of the other assemblages and disciplines in alleviating those limitations. A flow chart (Figure 1-1) is used to illustrate both the limitations and the positive aspects of each assemblage and the necessity for integration in determining paleonutrition.

Paleoethnobotany

Paleoethnobotany is defined as the recovery, identification, and interpretation of plant remains excavated from archaeological contexts (Ford 1979). Paleoethnobotany encompasses many subfields, coarsely divided into two groups: macroanalyses involving the study of seeds, nuts, fruits, fiber, wood, and charcoal; and microanalyses involving the study of pollen, phytoliths, and microscopic fiber particles (Bohrer 1986; Johannessen 1988; Pearsall 1989). Plant remains often represent the dietary staples for some populations (Bean and Lawton 1965; Bean and Saubel 1972; Farrington 1985; Lee 1968; Sobolik 1991), and humans are "completely dependant on plants either directly or indirectly" (Smith 1985:97). The analysis of plant remains from archaeological sites is necessary to recognize the importance of plant items to the diet and nutrition of a population. The interpretation of macro-remains from archaeological sites provides information on the dietary practices of a prehistoric population, particularly as related to that specific period in time (Pearsall 1988).

The main limitations of paleoethnobotanical material are threefold. First, plant material recovered from an archaeological site most likely underestimates the importance of smaller, more fragile dietary remains. Matrix samples are screened during excavations, and unless specific samples are taken (such as for flotation, phytoliths, or pollen), small remains may be lost. Material for flotation, phytoliths, and pollen are usually taken according to random or grid sampling and usually do not cover the entire excavated site, as normal

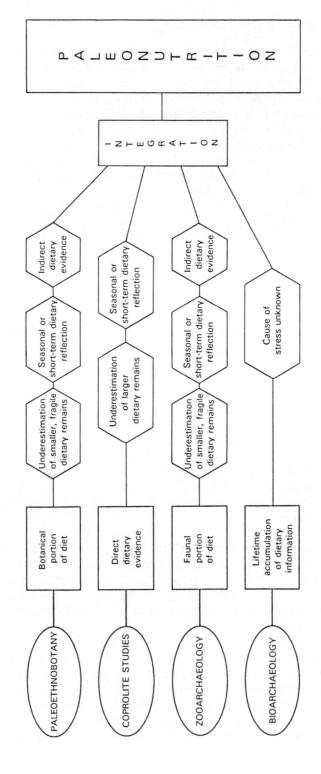

Figure 1-1. *The necessary integration of disciplines in paleonutritional studies.*

screening procedures do. Also, fragile materials will often be broken or degraded before they can be analyzed.

Second, plant material from archaeological sites may represent the diet of the occupants on a seasonal or short-term basis. This problem is particularly relevant to camps of hunter-gatherers, who tend to occupy sites seasonally (Lee and DeVore 1968), or to the short-term camps of more sedentary populations. The material recovered from those sites is biased for that particular season, or for what the occupants ate during that small period of time. Determining year-round dietary intake with such a sample is difficult if not impossible. Foods may also have been processed outside the site, and refuse in the site will not represent entire diet (Murra 1980).

Third, plant remains may be an indirect estimation of diet. Plant remains preserved from an archaeological site are deposited through many channels, so not all the botanical remains recovered in an archaeological excavation represent dietary remains, or even cultural debris (Adams and Gasser 1980; Hally 1981; Keepax 1977; Minnis 1981). Botanical items may be the main constituents of clothing, basketry, shelter, bedding material, firewood, and floors, as well as food items. Further, plant remains may be brought to sites by agents other than humans, such as burrowing rodents who may inhabit the site, or plant leaves and seeds may blow into a site or grow over it.

The analyst must decide which of the botanical remains actually represent dietary items, which represent other aspects of prehistoric life, and which represent natural deposition or contamination. The botanical remains recovered from archaeological excavations are similar "to a crumb surviving a whole loaf of bread" (Bohrer 1986:36), and the "crumb" does not represent the entire meal.

Zooarchaeology

The study of animal remains recovered from archaeological sites is undertaken by a wide variety of analysts skilled in the identification of particular faunal categories (Casteel 1976; Klippel and Morey 1986; Parmalee 1988; Rollins et al. 1990; Senior and Pierce 1989; Zimmerman et al. 1987). Although gaining skill in faunal identification is one important aspect of the analysis of faunal remains, researchers have become increasingly concerned with understanding the nature of bone assemblages and their recovery (Hill 1979; Johnson 1985; Shipman 1981). The analysis of faunal remains from archaeological sites is important because there is no comparable method for determining the significance of animals to the prehistoric diet and nutrition. The analysis of faunal remains, however, has limitations similar to those observed with plant material.

Depending upon excavational procedures, animal remains can provide types of information similar to those identified from plant remains. Animal remains are preserved at a higher frequency in many archaeological sites than plant remains, reducing problems of recovery. Distribution of animal remains can be used to determine changes in dietary practices through time, geographical differences in animal usage, and possible status differences in any people consuming the animals. Animal remains also indicate the major types of hunting practices used and possibly the main habitats exploited, both of which affect nutritional intake.

As with plant material, animal remains are an indirect source of dietary information (Grayson 1988; Lyman 1982). Because humans use animals to satisfy many needs other than subsistence (e.g., as beasts of burden, as social and hunting companions, and as resources for tools, shelter, and clothing), not all remains recovered can be assumed to represent food refuse. Further, humans share their habitations with other animals, and bone remains from sites may, in fact, reflect food debris from carnivores (Andrews and Evans 1983; Blumenschine 1988; Korth 1979; Mellett 1974), rodents (Bocek 1986; Hoffman and Hays 1987), owls (Korth 1979), and raptors (Emslie 1988; Hockett 1989). Consequently, the deposited bone assemblage must be scrutinized with care before dietary inferences are made. Foods may also have been processed outside the site, and refuse in the site will not represent entire diet (Murra 1980).

Recovered animal remains often underestimate the importance of small, fragile remains to the prehistoric diet. An accurate estimation depends on the sampling and screening techniques of the archaeologist and the nature of the material, which can vary considerably. In open sites there tends to be a smaller number of identifiable bone fragments, as compared with the faunal array from a dry cave, in which preservation can be excellent. Caves, however, serve as homes for many animals in addition to humans (e.g., rodents, birds, snakes, and many small mammalian carnivores), so it is even more problematical to assume that the bone assemblage from cave sites represents primarily human refuse (Grayson 1988; Lyman 1982, 1987).

As with paleoethnobotanical material, the faunal remains from archaeological sites may represent seasonal or short-term diet, depending upon site occupancy. The faunal remains may not reflect year-round dietary intake, and an analysis of seasonal nutrition is not complete. The analysis of dietary remains from one season may indicate a nutritionally sufficient diet, whereas during the opposite season the diet may be lacking in certain nutrients, or the people may be starving.

Coprolite Analysis

Coprolites represent such an unusual data source that their analysis is usually undertaken by specialists, most often within the subdivision of paleoethnobotany (Ford 1979). In order to conduct a thorough coprolite analysis, the researcher should be able to identify and interpret all types of botanical remains—fiber, seeds, and pollen—and nonbotanical remains—animal bone and hair, insects, fish and reptile scales, and parasites—to name a few of the many coprolitic constituents (Bryant 1974, 1986; Fry 1985; Sobolik 1993). Coprolite analysis thus involves a myriad of sciences other than strictly paleoethnobotany.

Coprolite analysis aids determination of paleonutrition in two main ways. First, analysis of plant and animal materials, as stated previously, is an indirect approach to determining paleonutrition. Coprolites, however, are a unique resource for determining prehistoric subsistence, and their analysis is a direct approach to the question of diet (Bryant 1974). The constituents of a coprolite are mainly the remains of intentionally eaten food items, representing the dietary remains of specific individuals. That type of precise sample cannot be replicated from animal or plant debris recovered from archaeological sites. Second, coprolites tend to preserve small, fragile remains that are not normally found in site matrix. Such materials are preserved mainly because of the compact nature of coprolites, which tend to keep the constituents separated from the site matrix. They are typically recovered as a result of normal coprolitic processing techniques, which involve first reconstitution and then screening with fine, micron-mesh screens rather than the coarser screens used during archaeological excavations.

The limitations of coprolite analysis are twofold. First, even though analysis directly indicates the ingestion of food items, the constituents of coprolites do not contain the entire diet of an individual or a population. The different food items ingested, such as pollen, meat, and seeds, pass through the digestive system at different rates; thus coprolite contents do not reflect one specific meal. Also, coprolites contain only the indigestible portion of foods. The actual digested portion has been absorbed by the body. For example, it is estimated that meat protein may be completely absorbed during the digestion process, often leaving few traces in the coprolite (Fry 1985), although recent research on protein residues in coprolites indicates that meat protein can be detected (Newman et al. 1993).

Also, as stated previously, plant and animal remains may reflect seasonal or short-term dietary intake. This is particularly true of coprolites. Individual coprolites often reflect items individuals ate either earlier that day (as with some bulky macromaterials) or what they may have eaten up to a month ago (as with pollen; Sobolik 1988). Determining year-round dietary intake using coprolites, even with a large sample size, becomes risky and inconclusive.

Bioarchaeology

The analysis of human skeletal remains has been conducted since scientific archaeological excavations were begun (see Armelagos et al. [1982]; Lovejoy et al. [1982]; and Ubelaker [1982] for reviews). Analyses of growth arrest lines, pathology, trace elements, and stable isotopes provide some of the information most useful for reconstructing paleonutrition. Bioarchaeological studies pertaining to paleonutrition encompass a broad area of research.

Growth arrest lines occur mainly when the health and nutrition of an individual temporarily arrests, or retards, the growth of skeletal elements, particularly long bones and teeth (Larsen 1987). Harris lines may be visible in radiographs of long bones (Goodman and Clarke 1981; Martin et al. 1985; Mensforth 1981). Enamel hypoplasias and Wilson bands, similar types of growth arrest lines that are particularly sensitive markers of nutritional stress (Larsen 1987), are visible on the teeth (Rose et al. 1978; Rose et al. 1985; Steele and Bramblett 1988). The etiology of Wilson bands appears similar to that for

Harris lines, mainly appearing during short periods of nutritional stress (Rose et al. 1985). Enamel hypoplasias, however, most likely indicate more severe and long-lasting nutritional stress (Huss-Ashmore et al. 1982; Martin et al. 1985). Both Wilson bands and enamel hypoplasias may result from a variety of environmental and cultural factors or from diseases such as syphilis, rickets, and tuberculosis (Ortner and Putschar 1985; Steinbock 1976).

Weaning (Clarke and Gindhart 1981), seasonal nutritional deprivation (Martin et al. 1985), and nutritional inadequacy in general (Goodman et al. 1980; Rose et al. 1978) have been most commonly implicated as causes of the growth arrest lines seen in archaeological samples. However, a wide variety of additional stresses have been associated with enamel hypoplasias in modern populations: overall malnutrition (Baume and Meyer 1966; Enwonwu 1973), nonspecific diarrhea (Sweeney et al. 1971), tuberculosis and maternal rubella (Stave 1965), cerebral palsy (Herman and McDonald 1963), and parasitic infection (Suckling and Thurley 1984). Neiburger (1990) has also stated that there are a variety of nondietary factors that may also produce enamel hypoplasia, although the problems with associating enamel hypoplasias and nonnutritionally related solutions have been well argued by Goodman (Chapter 11, this volume).

Caries and gum-related infections, also commonly connected to diet, are observed in the human dentition as well. Caries have been observed in archaeological samples to be particularly prevalent among agriculturalists, who consume starchy foods (Larsen 1983; Patterson 1984; Schmucker 1985). Abscessing, a gum-related disease, develops when bacteria invade the oral tissues (Ortner and Putschar 1985; Steinbock 1976) and may result from the initial infection of the tooth due to caries.

The main types of disorders impacting human bone in archaeological contexts are porotic hyperostosis and cribra orbitalia. Both disorders are most likely caused by anemia (Stuart-Macadam 1987), particularly iron deficiency anemia (El-Najjar et al. 1976; Taylor 1985), chronic disease (Kent 1986; Stuart-Macadam 1988), and a variety of other problems simultaneously affecting the individual (Merbs and Vestergaard 1985; Walker 1985; Weaver 1985).

The analysis of trace elements and carbon and nitrogen isotopes in bone, in order to determine diet as well as possible nutritional deficiencies, has only recently become an important part of paleonutrition, even though the actual research on trace elements and isotopes began during the early twentieth century (Chisholm et al. 1982; Gilbert 1985; Schoeninger 1979; Schoeninger et al. 1983; Sealey and van der Merwe 1985; Sillen et al. 1989). Trace element content of bone can be a good measure of nutritional deficiency because trace elements stored in bone are used in times of stress in order to keep the elements prevalent in organs and circulating in the blood. The most common trace element studies conducted on archaeological skeletal material are analyses of the strontium and calcium, particularly their ratios, in bone collagen (Blakely 1989; Runia 1987; Schoeninger 1979; Sealy and Sillen 1988).

Stable isotope analyses are also useful for evaluating prehistoric diet because, similar to strontium/calcium ratios, the differences in the isotopic ratios are maintained through food webs (Bumstead 1985; Chisholm et al.

1982; van der Merwe 1982). Plants use different photosynthetic pathways for the fixation of atmospheric ^{12}C and ^{13}C. Usually tropical grasses, such as corn, photosynthesize by the C^4 pathway, while other plants tend to photosynthesize by the C^3 pathway, and succulents and cacti tend to photosynthesize by the CAM, or intermediate, pathway (van der Merwe 1982). Thus differential ratios of $^{12}C/^{13}C$ are incorporated into the bones of the consumers.

Nitrogen isotopes in bone have only recently been studied, and they are the least understood (Sillen et al. 1989). It was first suggested that nitrogen isotopes would be useful to distinguish marine from terrestrial dietary intake (Schoeninger and DeNiro 1984), although it is now realized that such a relationship cannot easily be distinguished (Heaton et al. 1986; Sillen et al. 1989).

Problems with the relationship between stable isotopic ratios and prehistoric diet have been indicated (Grupe 1988; Hanson and Buikstra 1987; Runia 1987; Sillen et al. 1989). Sillen and colleagues (1989) reviewed the problems associated with both isotopic, particularly nitrogen, and strontium/calcium ratio studies. They stated that "it is becoming increasingly clear that, unless questions about the origin of the constituents of collagen are addressed fully, isotopic measurements will be limited to qualitative, rather than quantitative statements about dietary composition" (Sillen et al. 1989:506) and that strontium/calcium ratios "cannot be ascribed to the meat-to-plant ratio in the diet" (Sillen et al. 1989:508).

A skeleton represents a specific sample, an individual in a population. Such samples are unique because they contain the effects of a lifetime of nutrition (Gill-King 1988), even though bone tends to be remodeled. Consequently, only the human skeleton can clearly document intermittent periods of stress on the population such as may be seen in populations relying on seasonal foods or chronic stress such as seen in populations that are continuously undernourished or malnourished or the ultimate effect of poor nutrition, increased mortality rates.

The main problem in the analysis of human remains is that most disorders affect bone in similar ways, making it difficult to identify the specific cause of a disorder. When select disorders are present, some stress may be indicated; however, those disorders could have been caused by a variety of factors such as environmental, cultural, physiological, psychological, and nutritional stresses. Since the specific stressor may be unknown, assuming the stress is a dietary deficiency is problematic.

Syntheses

In determining paleonutrition, the analyst needs to integrate a variety of assemblages. Nutritional data derived from the analyses of plants, animals, coprolites, and human skeletons need to be simultaneously considered (Figure 1-1) for the most conclusive results. Each of these assemblages has limitations that can be solved, or at least reduced, through examination of other assemblages. Examination of plant and animal remains recovered from sites is an indirect method for determining diet; coprolites provide direct evidence of diet; and human remains furnish information about the impact of that diet.

Plant remains, animal remains, and coprolites are seasonal indicators of dietary intake, while human skeletal material reflects a lifetime accumulation of dietary information. Plant and animal assemblages, as a result of recovery techniques and matrix preservation, tend to underestimate the importance of small, fragile dietary remains or make it difficult to assume that those remains are dietary refuse. This limitation can be resolved through the analysis of coprolites, which often preserve such remains in an indisputable dietary context. Human skeletal remains can document nutritional stress on an individual, but the stress is usually nonspecific. Therefore, for the most conclusive results, the diet of the population should be reconstructed using plant remains, animal remains, and coprolites, and the nutritional content of the diet must be analyzed to determine if the stresses associated with the human material could be nutritionally caused.

Only in exceptional instances will remains from all four assemblages discussed above be obtainable in large quantities from a single site or small geographical area. For instance, analyses of hunter-gatherer habitation sites tend to produce few skeletons; coprolites are only preserved in dry or freezing conditions; and faunal materials are best preserved in conditions that are not often conducive to plant preservation. At sites where all of the paleonutritional material is not represented, a comprehensive analysis should be conducted of what remaining material is available. Later, interpretations and conclusions should indicate and reflect the limitations of those data due to seasonality of site occupation, representation of small, fragile dietary constituents, the possible incorporation of noncultural remains into dietary samples, or the lack of specific causes of nutritional stress.

The last step in determining the nutrition of a prehistoric population is assessment of nutritional adequacy. The specific dietary components should be compared and analyzed using nutrition tables that can be found in a variety of sources (i.e., Food and Agriculture Organization [FAO] 1970; FAO/World Health Organization [WHO] 1973; Gebhardt et al. 1982; Griffiths and Hare 1906; Haytowitz and Matthews 1984; Marsh et al. 1977). After the nutritional content of the food items has been determined, a comparison between the nutrients provided by the diet and the nutrients required by the population should be made. The nutritional requirements of modern American populations are easily obtainable (Committee on Dietary Allowances 1980); however, the fact that the prehistoric population being analyzed is not the same as modern American populations must be considered.

Paleonutritional studies can make exciting contributions to the understanding of prehistoric life. Under optimal conditions, a variety of assemblages should be integrated to determine the diet and nutrition of a population because individual analyses cannot stand alone (see *Integrative Studies* section). Such integration is necessary because the analysis of each assemblage in itself does not represent a complete picture. There are inherent problems with each data set, problems that can be solved only through the incorporation of other databases from other assemblages. Through the interaction of analysts and the thorough analysis of dietary archaeological remains, a comprehensive understanding of the paleonutrition of a population is attainable.

Acknowledgments

I would like to thank D. Gentry Steele, Vaughn M. Bryant, Jr., Don S. Rice, and Daniel H. Sandweiss for their insightful discussions and their editorial comments. Stephen Bicknell drafted Figure 1-1. This research is part of a dissertation funded by the National Science Foundation (BNS-9004064) and Sigma Xi.

References

Adams, K. R., and R. E. Gasser
  1980   Plant Microfossils from Archaeological Sites: Research Considerations, and Sampling Techniques and Approaches. *The Kiva* 45:293–300.
Andrews, P., and E. M. N. Evans
  1983   Small Mammal Bone Accumulations Produced by Mammalian Carnivores. *Paleobiology* 9(3):289–307.
Armelagos, G. J., D. S. Carlson, and D. P. Van Gerven
  1982   The Theoretical Foundations and Development of Skeletal Biology. In *A History of American Physical Anthropology, 1930–1980*, edited by F. Spencer, pp. 305–328. Academic Press, New York.
Baume, L. J., and J. Meyer
  1966   Dental Dysplasia Related to Malnutrition, with Special Reference to Melanodontia and Odontoclasia. *Journal of Dental Research* 45:726–741.
Bean, L., and H. Lawton
  1965   *The Cahuilla Indians of Southern California*. Malki Museum Press, Morongo Indian Reservation, Banning.
Bean, L., and K. S. Saubel
  1972   *Temalpakh: Cahuilla Indian Knowledge and Usage of Plants*. Malki Museum Press, Morongo Indian Reservation, Banning.
Blakely, R. L.
  1989   Bone Strontium in Pregnant and Lactating Females from Archaeological Samples. *American Journal of Physical Anthropology* 80:173–185.
Blumenschine, R. J.
  1988   An Experimental Model of the Timing of Hominid and Carnivore Influence on Archaeological Bone Assemblages. *Journal of Archaeological Science* 15:483–502.
Bocek, B.
  1986   Rodent Ecology and Burrowing Behavior: Predicted Effects on Archaeological Site Formation. *American Antiquity* 51:589–603.
Bohrer, V. L.
  1986   Guideposts in Ethnobotany. *Journal of Ethnobiology* 6:27–43.
Bryant, V. M., Jr.
  1974   The Role of Coprolite Analysis in Archeology. *Bulletin of the Texas Archeological Society* 45:1–28.

12 | *K. D. Sobolik*

1986   Prehistoric Diet: A Case for Coprolite Analysis. In *Ancient Texans: Rock Art and Lifeways along the Lower Pecos*, edited by H. J. Shafer, pp. 132–135. Texas Monthly Press, San Antonio.

Bryant, V. M., Jr., and G. Williams-Dean
1975   The Coprolites of Man. *Scientific American* 232:100–109.

Buikstra, J. E.
1984   The Lower Illinois River Region: A Prehistoric Context for the Study of Ancient Diet and Health. In *Paleopathology at the Origins of Agriculture*, edited by M. N. Cohen and G. J. Armelagos, pp. 217–234. Academic Press, Orlando.

Bumstead, M. P.
1985   Past Human Behavior from Bone Chemical Analysis: Respects and Prospects. *Journal of Human Evolution* 14:539–551.

Casteel, R. W.
1976   *Fish Remains in Archaeology and Paleo-environmental Studies*. Academic Press, New York.

Chisholm, B. S., D. E. Nelson, and H. P. Schwarcz
1982   Stable-Carbon Isotope Ratios as a Measure of Marine Versus Terrestrial Protein in Ancient Diets. *Science* 216:1131–1132.

Clarke, S. K., and P. S. Gindhart
1981   Commonality in Peak Age of Early-Childhood Morbidity Across Cultures and Over Time. *Current Anthropology* 22:574–575.

Committee on Dietary Allowances
1980   *Recommended Dietary Allowances*. National Academy of Sciences, Washington, D.C.

Cook, D. C.
1984   Subsistence and Health in the Lower Illinois Valley: Osteological Evidence. In *Paleopathology at the Origins of Agriculture*, edited by M. N. Cohen and G. J. Armelagos, pp. 235–269, Academic Press, Orlando.

El-Najjar, M. Y., D. J. Ryan, C. G. Turner II, and B. Lozoff
1976   The Etiology of Porotic Hyperostosis among the Prehistoric and Historic Anasazi Indians of the Southwestern United States. *American Journal of Physical Anthropology* 44:447–448.

Emslie, S. D.
1988   Vertebrate Paleontology and Taphonomy of Caves in Grand Canyon, Arizona. *National Geographic Research* 4(1):128–142.

Enwonwu, C. O.
1973   Influence of Socio-Economic Conditions on Dental Development in Nigerian Children. *Archives of Oral Biology* 18:195–207.

Farrington, I. S. (editor)
1985   *Prehistoric Intensive Agriculture in the Tropics*. BAR International Series 232. British Archaeological Reports, Oxford.

Food and Agriculture Organization (FAO), Food Policy and Food Science Service, Nutrition Division
1970   *Amino-Acid Content of Foods and Biological Data on Proteins*. Food and Agriculture Organization of the United Nations. Rome, Italy.

Food and Agriculture Organization (FAO) and World Health Organization (WHO)
1973   *Energy and Protein Requirements*. Report of a Joint FAO/WHO ad hoc Expert Committee. Food and Agriculture Organization Nutrition Meeting Series No. 52, World Health Organization Technical Report Series No. 522. Rome, Italy.

Ford, R. I.
1979   Paleoethnobotany in American Archaeology. In *Advances in Archaeological*

Method and Theory, vol. 2, edited by M. B. Schiffer, pp. 285–336. Academic Press, New York.

Fry, G. F.
1980   Prehistoric Diet and Parasites in the Desert West of North America. In *Early Native Americans,* edited by D. L. Bowman, pp. 117–141. Mouton Press, The Hague.
1985   Analysis of Fecal Material. In *The Analysis of Prehistoric Diets,* edited by R. I. Gilbert, Jr., and J. H. Mielke, pp. 127–153. Academic Press, Orlando.

Gebhardt, S. E., R. Cutrufelli, and R. H. Matthews
1982   *Composition of Foods: Fruits and Fruit Juices; Raw, Processed, Prepared.* Agriculture Handbook No. 8–9. United States Department of Agriculture, Washington, D.C.

Gilbert, R. I., Jr.
1985   Stress, Paleonutrition, and Trace Elements. In *The Analysis of Prehistoric Diets,* edited by R. I. Gilbert, Jr., and J. H. Mielke, pp. 339–359. Academic Press, Orlando.

Gill-King, H.
1988   Archeological Footnote to History. Paper presented at the 59th Annual Meeting of the Texas Archeological Society, Houston.

Goodman, A. H., G. J. Armelagos, and J. C. Rose
1980   Enamel Hypoplasias as Indicators of Stress in Three Prehistoric Populations from Illinois. *Human Biology* 52:515–528.

Goodman, A. H., and G. Clark
1981   Harris Lines as Indicators of Stress in Illinois Populations. In *Biocultural Adaptation: Comprehensive Approaches to Skeletal Analysis,* edited by D. L. Martin and M. P. Bumstead, pp. 35–46. Research Reports No. 20. University of Massachusetts, Amherst.

Grayson, D. K.
1988   Last Supper Cave. In *Danger Cave, Last Supper Cave, and Hanging Rock Shelter: The Faunas,* edited by D. K. Grayson, pp. 1–130. Anthropological Papers Vol. 66, Pt. 1. American Museum of Natural History, New York.

Griffiths, D., and R. F. Hare
1906   *Prickly Pear and Other Cacti as Food for Stock II.* New Mexico Agricultural Experiment Station Bulletin No. 60.

Grupe, G.
1988   Impact of the Choice of Bone Samples on Trace Element Data in Excavated Human Skeletons. *Journal of Archaeological Science* 15:123–129.

Guilday, J. E., and P. W. Parmalee
1982   Vertebrate Faunal Remains from Meadowcroft Rockshelter, Washington County, Pennsylvania: A Re-evaluation and Interpretation. In *Meadowcroft: Collected Papers on the Archaeology of Meadowcroft Rockshelter and the Cross Creek Drainage,* edited by R. C. Carlisle and J. M. Adovasio, pp. 163–174. Department of Anthropology, University of Pittsburgh.

Hally, D. J.
1981   Plant Preservation and the Content of Paleobotanical Samples: A Case Study. *American Antiquity* 46:723–742.

Hanson, D. B., and J. E. Buikstra
1987   Histomorphological Alteration in Buried Human Bone from the Lower Illinois Valley: Implications for Paleodietary Research. *Journal of Archaeological Science* 14:549–563.

Haytowitz, D. G., and R. H. Matthews
    1984   *Composition of Foods: Vegetables and Vegetable Products: Raw, Processed, Prepared.* Agriculture Handbook No. 8–11. United States Department of Agriculture, Washington, D.C.
Heaton, T. J. E., J. C. Bogel, G. von la Chevallerie, and G. Collett
    1986   Climatic Influence on the Isotopic Composition of Bone Nitrogen. *Nature* 322:822–823.
Herman, S., and R. McDonald
    1963   Enamel Hypoplasia in Cerebral Palsied Children. *Children's Dental Journal* 30:46–49.
Hill, A. P.
    1979   Butchery and Natural Disarticulation: An Investigatory Technique. *American Antiquity* 44:739–744.
Hockett, B. S.
    1989   Archaeological Significance of Rabbit-Raptor Interactions in Southern California. *North American Archaeologist* 10(2):123–139.
Hoffman, R., and C. Hays
    1987   The Eastern Wood Rat *(Neotoma floridana)* as a Taphonomic Factor in Archaeological Sites. *Journal of Archaeological Science* 14:325–337.
Huss-Ashmore, R., A. H. Goodman, and G. J. Armelagos
    1982   Nutritional Inference from Paleopathology. In *Advances in Archaeological Method and Theory,* vol. 5, edited by M. B. Schiffer, pp. 395–474. Academic Press, New York.
Johannessen, S.
    1988   Plant Remains and Culture Change: Are Paleoethnobotanical Data Better Than We Think? In *Current Paleoethnobotany: Analytical Methods and Cultural Interpretations of Archaeological Plant Remains,* edited by C. A. Hastorf and V. S. Popper, pp. 145–166. University of Chicago Press, Chicago.
Johnson, E.
    1985   Current Developments in Bone Technology. In *Advances in Archaeological Method and Theory,* vol. 8, edited by M. B. Schiffer, pp. 157–235. Academic Press, New York.
Keepax, C.
    1977   Contamination of Archaeological Deposits by Seeds of Modern Origin with Particular Reference to the Use of Flotation Machines. *Journal of Archaeological Science* 4:221–229.
Kent, S.
    1986   The Influence of Sedentism and Aggregation on Porotic Hyperostosis and Anaemia. *Man* 21:605–636.
Klippel, W. E., and D. F. Morey
    1986   Contextual and Nutritional Analysis of Freshwater Gastropods from Middle Archaic Deposits at the Hayes Site, Middle Tennessee. *American Antiquity* 51:799–813.
Korth, W. A.
    1979   Taphonomy of Microvertebrate Fossil Assemblages. *Annals of the Carnegie Museum of Natural History* 48:235–285. Pittsburgh.
Larsen, C. S.
    1982   *The Anthropology of St. Catherine's Island: 3. Prehistoric Human Biological Adaptation.* Anthropological Papers Vol. 51, Pt. 3. American Museum of Natural History, New York.

1983   Behavioral Implications of Temporal Change in Cariogenesis. *Journal of Archaeological Science* 10:1–8.

1987   Bioarchaeological Interpretations of Subsistence Economy and Behavior from Human Skeletal Remains. In *Advances in Archaeological Method and Theory*, vol. 10, edited by M. B. Schiffer, pp. 339–445. Academic Press, New York.

Lee, R. B.

1968   What Hunters Do for a Living, or How to Make Out on Scarce Resources. In *Man the Hunter*, edited by R. B. Lee and I. DeVore, pp. 30–48. Aldine, Chicago.

Lee, R. B., and I. DeVore (editors)

1968   *Man the Hunter*, Aldine, Chicago.

Lovejoy, C. O., R. P. Mensforth, and G. J. Armelagos

1982   Five Decades of Skeletal Biology as Reflected in the *American Journal of Physical Anthropology*. In *A History of American Physical Anthropology, 1930–1980*, edited by F. Spencer, pp. 337–356. Academic Press, New York.

Lyman, R. L.

1982   Archaeofaunas and Subsistence Studies. In *Advances in Archaeological Method and Theory*, vol. 5, edited by M. B. Schiffer, pp. 331–393. Academic Press, New York.

1987   Zooarchaeology and Taphonomy: A General Consideration. *Journal of Ethnobiology* 7:93–117.

McCorriston, J., and F. Hole

1991   The Ecology of Seasonal Stress and the Origins of Agriculture in the Near East. *American Anthropologist* 93:46–69.

Marsh, A. C., M. K. Moss, and E. W. Murphy

1977   *Composition of Foods: Spices and Herbs; Raw, Processed, Prepared*. Agriculture Handbook No. 8–2. United States Department of Agriculture, Washington, D.C.

Martin, D. L., A. H. Goodman, and G. J. Armelagos

1985   Skeletal Pathologies as Indicators of Quality and Quantity of Diet. In *The Analysis of Prehistoric Diets*, edited by R. I. Gilbert, Jr., and J. H. Mielke, pp. 227–280. Academic Press, Orlando.

Mellett, J. S.

1974   Scatological Origin of Microvertebrate Fossil Accumulations. *Science* 185:349–350.

Mensforth, R. P.

1981   Growth Velocity and Chondroblastic Stability as Major Factors Related to the Pathogenesis and Epidemiological Distribution of Growth Arrest Lines. *American Journal of Physical Anthropology* 54:253.

Merbs, C. F., and E. M. Vestergaard

1985   The Paleopathology of Sundown, a Prehistoric Site near Prescott, Arizona. In *Health and Disease in the Prehistoric Southwest*, edited by C. F. Merbs and R. J. Miller, pp. 85–103. Anthropological Research Papers No. 34. Arizona State University, Tempe.

Minnis, P.

1981   Seeds in Archaeological Sites: Sources and Some Interpretive Problems. *American Antiquity* 46:143–152.

1985   *Social Adaptation to Food Stress: A Prehistoric Southwestern Example*. University of Chicago Press, Chicago.

Murra, J. V.
    1980   *The Economic Organization of the Inka State.* JAI Press, Greenwich, Connecticut.

Neiburger, E. J.
    1990   Enamel Hypoplasias: Poor Indicators of Dietary Stress. *American Journal of Physical Anthropology* 82:231–232.

Newman, M. E., R. M. Yohe II, H. Ceri, and M. Q. Sutton
    1993   Immunological Protein Residue Analysis of Non-lithic Archaeological Materials. *Journal of Archaeological Science* 20:93–100.

Ortner, D. J., and W. G. J. Putschar
    1985   *Identification of Pathological Conditions in Human Skeletal Remains.* Smithsonian Contributions to Anthropology No. 28. Smithsonian Institution Press, Washington.

Palkovich, A. M.
    1987   Endemic Disease Patterns in Paleopathology: Porotic Hyperostosis. *American Journal of Physical Anthropology* 74:527–537.

Parmalee, P. W.
    1988   Avian Remains from Danger Cave. In *Danger Cave, Last Supper Cave, and Hanging Rock Shelter: The Faunas,* edited by D. K. Grayson, pp. 37–43. Anthropological Papers Vol. 66, Pt. 1. American Museum of Natural History, New York.

Patterson, D. K.
    1984   *A Diachronic Study of Dental Paleopathology and Attritional Status of Prehistoric Ontario Pre-Iroquois and Iroquois Populations.* Archaeological Survey of Canada No. 122. National Museum of Man Mercury Series, Ottawa.

Pearsall, D. M.
    1983   Evaluating the Stability of Subsistence Strategies by Use of Paleoethnobotanical Data. *Journal of Ethnobiology* 3:121–137.
    1988   Interpreting the Meaning of Macroremains Abundance: The Impact of Source and Context. In *Current Paleoethnobotany: Analytical Methods and Cultural Interpretations of Archaeological Plant Remains,* edited by C. A. Hastorf and V. S. Popper, pp. 97–118. University of Chicago Press, Chicago.
    1989   *Paleoethnobotany: A Handbook of Procedures.* Academic Press, New York.

Rollins, H. B., D. H. Sandweiss, and J. C. Rollins
    1990   Mollusks and Coastal Archaeology: A Review. In *Archaeological Geology Decade of North American Geology Special Volume 4,* edited by J. Donahue and N. Lasca, pp. 467–478. Geological Society of America, Boulder.

Rose, J. C., G. J. Armelagos, and J. W. Lallo
    1978   Histological Enamel Indicator of Childhood Stress in Prehistoric Skeletal Samples. *American Journal of Physical Anthropology* 48:511–516.

Rose, J. C., K. W. Condon, and A. H. Goodman
    1985   Diet and Dentition: Developmental Disturbances. In *The Analysis of Prehistoric Diets,* edited by R. I. Gilbert, Jr., and J. H. Mielke, pp. 281–306. Academic Press, Orlando.

Runia, L. T.
    1987   Strontium and Calcium Distribution in Plants: Effect on Paleodietary Studies. *Journal of Archaeological Science* 14:295–310.

Schmucker, B. J.
    1985   Dental Attrition: A Corelative Study of Dietary and Subsistence Patterns. In *Health and Disease in the Prehistoric Southwest,* edited by C. F. Merbs and R. J.

Miller, pp. 275–323. Anthropological Research Papers No. 34. Arizona State University, Tempe.

Schoeninger, M. J.
1979 Status at Chalcatzingo: Some Empirical and Technical Aspects of Strontium Analysis. *American Journal of Physical Anthropology* 52:29–310.

Schoeninger, M. J., and M. J. DeNiro
1984 Nitrogen and Carbon Isotopic Composition of Bone Collagen from Marine and Terrestrial Animals. *Geochimica et Cosmochimica Acta* 48:625–639.

Schoeninger, M. J., M. J. DeNiro, and H. Tauber
1983 Stable Nitrogen Isotope Ratios of Bone Collagen Reflect Marine and Terrestrial Components of Prehistoric Human Diet. *Science* 220:1381–1383.

Sealy, J. C., and A. Sillen
1988 Sr and Sr/Ca in Marine and Terrestrial Foodwebs in the Southwestern Cape, South Africa. *Journal of Archaeological Science* 15:425–438.

Sealey, J. C., and N. J. van der Merwe
1985 Isotope Assessment of Holocene Human Diets in Southwest Cape, South Africa. *Nature* 315:138–140.

Senior, L. M., and L. J. Pierce
1989 Domestication: Turkeys and Domestication in the Southwest: Implications from Homol'ovi III. *The Kiva* 54:245–259.

Shipman, P.
1981 *Life History of a Fossil: An Introduction to Taphonomy and Paleoecology.* Harvard University Press, Cambridge.

Sillen, A., J. C. Sealy, and N. J. van der Merwe
1989 Chemistry and Paleodietary Research: No More Easy Answers. *American Antiquity* 54:504–512.

Smith, B. D.
1975 *Middle Mississippian Exploitation of Animal Populations.* Anthropological Papers No. 57. Museum of Anthropology, University of Michigan, Ann Arbor.

Smith, C. E., Jr.
1985 Recovery and Processing of Botanical Remains. In *The Analysis of Prehistoric Diets*, edited by R. I. Gilbert, Jr., and J. H. Mielke, pp. 97–126. Academic Press, Orlando.

Sobolik, K. D.
1988 The Importance of Pollen Concentration Values from Coprolites: An Analysis of Southwest Texas Samples. *Palynology* 12:201–214.
1990 A Nutritional Analysis of Diet as Revealed in Prehistoric Human Coprolites. *Texas Journal of Science* 42(1):23–36.
1991 *Paleonutrition of the Lower Pecos Region of the Chihuahuan Desert.* Ph.D dissertation, Department of Anthropology, Texas A&M University, College Station.
1993 Direct Evidence for the Importance of Small Animals to Prehistoric Diets: A Review of Coprolite Studies. *North American Archaeologist* 14(3):227–244.

Stave, U.
1965 Prenatal Factors and Their Evaluation. *Journal of Dental Research* 44:185–196.

Steele, D. G., and C. A. Bramblett
1988 *The Anatomy and Biology of the Human Skeleton.* Texas A&M University Press, College Station.

Steinbock, R. T.
1976 *Paleopathological Diagnosis and Interpretation: Bone Diseases in Ancient Human*

Populations. Charles C. Thomas, Springfield, Illinois.
Stuart-Macadam, P.
    1987   Porotic Hyperostosis: New Evidence to Support the Anemia Theory. *American Journal of Physical Anthropology* 74:521–526.
    1988   Nutrition and Anaemia in Past Human Populations. In *Diet and Subsistence: Current Archaeological Perspectives,* edited by B. V. Kennedy and G. M. LeMoine, pp. 284–287. Proceedings of the 19th Annual Chacmool Conference, Archaeological Association of the University of Calgary, Calgary, Alberta.
Suckling, G., and D. C. Thurley
    1984   Developmental Defects of Enamel: Factors Influencing Their Macroscopic Appearance. In *Tooth Enamel IV,* edited by R. W. Fearnhead and S. Suga, pp. 121–136. Tiden-Barnangen Tryckerier AB, Stockholm.
Sweeney, E. A., A. J. Saffir, and R. de Leon
    1971   Linear Hypoplasia of Deciduous Incisor Teeth in Malnourished Children. *American Journal of Clinical Nutrition* 24:29–31.
Taylor, M. G.
    1985   The Paleopathology of a Southern Sinagua Population from Oak Creek Pueblo, Arizona. In *Health and Disease in the Prehistoric Southwest,* edited by C. F. Merbs and R. J. Miller, pp. 115–118. Anthropological Research Papers No. 34. Arizona State University, Tempe.
Ubelaker, D. H.
    1982   The Development of American Paleopathology. In *A History of American Physical Anthropology, 1930–1980,* edited by F. Spencer, pp. 329–336. Academic Press, New York.
van der Merwe, N. J.
    1982   Carbon Isotopes, Photosynthesis, and Archaeology. *Science* 149:854–855.
Walker, P. L.
    1985   Anemia among Prehistoric Indians of the American Southwest. In *Health and Disease in the Prehistoric Southwest,* edited by C. F. Merbs and R. J. Miller, pp. 139–164. Anthropological Research Papers No. 34. Arizona State University, Tempe.
Weaver, D. S.
    1985   Subsistence and Settlement Patterns at Casas Grandes, Chihuahua, Mexico. In *Health and Disease in the Prehistoric Southwest,* edited by C. F. Merbs and R. J. Miller, pp. 119–127. Anthropological Research Papers No. 34. Arizona State University, Tempe.
Wing, E. S., and A. B. Brown
    1979   *Paleonutrition: Method and Theory in Prehistoric Foodways.* Academic Press, New York.
Zimmerman, L. S., D. G. Steele, and J. Maier
    1987   A Visual Key to the Identification of Otoliths. *Bulletin of the Texas Archeological Society* 58:175–200.

I. Indirect Studies: Paleoethnobotany and Zooarchaeology

2. The Value of Archaeological Plant Remains for Paleodietary Reconstruction

Gayle J. Fritz

Abstract: Macrobotanical remains have been considered relatively poor indicators of diet because of the complexities of differential deposition and preservation. In spite of those problematic factors, paleoethnobotanical studies are crucial for understanding prehistoric subsistence. Although flotation-recovered assemblages of carbonized plant parts from open sites do not reveal proportions of specific food sources in the diet, they do allow interpretation of chronological trends and regional variations. That potential can be demonstrated by using recent studies from eastern North America, where macrobotanical remains provide key information about agricultural evolution that stable carbon isotope research has failed to detect.

Introduction

Archaeological plant remains (limited in this paper to macrobotanical remains, thereby excluding pollen and phytoliths) are a key source of information in various research pursuits. Primary applications have been in reconstructing past vegetation and climate; in investigating human impact on the environment; in studying the uses of plants for fuel, fodder, shelter, clothing, tools, medicines, and ritual substances; and, finally, in studying plants used for food. Within the general category of subsistence, the focus tends to be on broad economic trends such as the shift from generalized to specialized patterns of resource procurement. A major trend charted by the analysis of archaeobotanical remains is, of course, the transition from gathering to agriculture, including plant domestication and subsequent agricultural intensification and spread. Studies attempting to reconstruct or otherwise evaluate in detail the diets of particular ancient societies are significant, but

Paleonutrition: The Diet and Health of Prehistoric Americans, edited by Kristin D. Sobolik. Center for Archaeological Investigations, Occasional Paper No. 22. © 1994 by the Board of Trustees, Southern Illinois University. All rights reserved. ISBN 0-88104-078-9.

they do not represent the majority of paleoethnobotanical reports, even those that are primarily subsistence focused.

Weaknesses of the Archaeobotanical Record

Paleoethnobotanists steer away from quantifications of dietary constituents because of the problematic factors of differential deposition, preservation, and recovery. Much time is spent analyzing and interpreting carbonized plant remains retrieved by flotation from sites where moisture and various organisms have destroyed all uncharred macrobotanical material. Some food plants are underrepresented because they were rarely, if ever, cooked (e.g., many fleshy fruits) or because they possess no dense structural parts that would survive fire in a recognizable state (e.g., greens and some tubers). Some are consistently overrepresented because they have dense and distinctive structural parts. In eastern North America, hickory nutshell is a classic example of residue from food processing that may be especially abundant archaeologically because of its density and its use for fuel.

Many authors have discussed the complex factors confounding efforts to interpret actual human consumption as opposed to production (Dennell 1976, 1979; Dimbleby 1978; Hastorf 1988; Munson et al. 1971; Pearsall 1989; Yarnell 1982). In North America, we may overestimate the importance of maize in particular sites where cob-filled smudge pits were excavated, since those pits signify hide smoking or some other activity not directly related to eating. The archaeobotanical record in the Old World and in the Andes is further complicated by the common practice of burning seed-filled animal dung for fuel, thereby introducing edible plant parts that in those situations were not consumed by people (Miller and Smart 1984; Pearsall 1988).

The inescapable conclusion is that archaeobotanical assemblages from most sites are incomplete, indirect, and skewed records of the vegetal component of past human diet. Pearsall has recently stressed this limitation of the data. She concludes that researchers attempting to "evaluate nutrition of prehistoric populations, to indicate importance of different plant foods in the diet, or by comparison to faunal remains, to uncover the distinct contributions of plant and animal resources" often have "unrealistic goals" (1989:447). This lack of realism is especially true when one is dealing with flotation-recovered samples of carbonized material. Pearsall states unequivocally, "In settings where only accidently charred material is preserved, too many complications are introduced to attempt reconstructing food values from macroremains" (1989:210). Furthermore, she has reservations about conversions of macroremains into food value estimates by using data from dry sites such as rockshelters or waterlogged sites where preservation may appear more complete.

MacNeish (1967), for example, calculated relative dietary contributions of wild and domesticated types of foods, both animal and vegetable, for the various phases represented in the Tehuacan Valley rockshelters. His pioneering effort is open to methodological criticism (Pearsall 1989:208–210, 450–452), and it has not become a model for many subsequent studies (but see Pozorski

[1983] and Flannery [1986]). As Pearsall notes, even in dry rockshelters or permanently waterlogged sites, "It would be a mistake to assume that deposited remains represent the sum total of plant food consumed by site inhabitants" (1989:210).

Strengths of the Archaeobotanical Record

I will not dwell further on the limitations of archaeobotanical data. Although the many archaeologists who recognize those constraints are absolutely correct, I believe there has been a tendency to downplay or to neglect the overall strengths of macrobotanical remains. The fact that the data are indirect and unsuitable for quantification of nutrient components in paleodiets does not make them poor sources of subsistence data in general. I argue that they remain a key source of subsistence information, sometimes the best source available. Interpretations of paleonutrition and health may in such cases be limited to rather general statements, but broad interpretations can be attempted and serious mistakes can be avoided.

The most significant contributions are studies monitoring subsistence trajectories through time in one region and those that document variations among contemporaneous societies in different regions or subregions. When archaeobotanical remains have been recovered and reported using comparable methods, they can contribute either the core database or one key analytical constituent for research addressing dietary change. Aspects of subsistence can be integrated with paleoepidemiological issues, paleodemography, technology, ideology, and sociopolitical evolution.

By focusing on several case studies from the Southwest and from eastern North America, I hope to illustrate the potential of macrobotanical remains for supplying general information about paleodiet. These particular studies address ongoing concerns with the development of agricultural systems and the cultural as well as biological causes and consequences of that shift.

Case Study 1: Basketmaker Agriculture on the Colorado Plateau

The prehistoric Anasazi sequence on the Colorado Plateau is divided into Basketmaker and Pueblo periods, with a temporal boundary of approximately A.D. 700 between the earlier, Basketmaker pithouse villages and the later, Pueblo sites with above-ground room blocks. Intensification of agriculture has been cited as a major economic shift accompanying the Basketmaker-to-Pueblo transition (Gilman 1987). I would not dispute some form of agricultural intensification but, as an outsider, have puzzled over the characterization of Basketmakers as essentially modified hunter-gatherers with a relatively low dependence on maize (Zea mays) and other cultigens (e.g., Plog 1979). Compared with the incipient farming societies of the Late Woodland period in eastern North America, maize is relatively abundant at Basketmaker sites. Conditions favoring better than average preservation exist in dry rockshelter sites, but even so, the robust cobs and diversity of maize types indicate a well-developed and successful agricultural system before the Pueblo period (see Jones and Fonner 1954).

Recent considerations of macrobotanical remains from paleofeces by Paul Minnis (1989) force us to reassess the significance of maize in the Basketmaker III diet in the Four Corners area. Rather than demonstrating a shift toward higher maize consumption in Pueblo times, the paleofecal record indicates "a basic continuity from Basketmaker III to Pueblo III periods in the consumption of plant foods" (Minnis 1989:557). Maize was already the dominant plant food in the Basketmaker III diet, and economically valuable ruderal plants— goosefoot *(Chenopodium* spp.), purslane *(Portulaca retusa)*, ground cherry *(Physalis* spp.), beeweed *(Cleome serrulata)*, and amaranth *(Amaranthus* spp.)— were present in the same general proportions as later, indicating that agricultural ecosystems were well established before the Basketmaker-to-Pueblo transition (Minnis 1989).

Further documentation for pre-Pueblo period maize dependency in the Four Corners area has been published by Matson (1991) and by Matson and Chisholm (1991). These authors push the date for serious Anasazi agriculture back to at least 2000 B.P., if not earlier, by integrating the evidence from settlement patterning, stable carbon isotopes, paleofeces (including both pollen and macrobotanical remains), and flotation-recovered remains. Matson and Chisholm (1991), like Minnis, stress that the earlier dietary evidence—in this case Basketmaker II—indicates higher levels of maize consumption than expected and little difference when compared to Pueblo II and III databases. Maize occurs in 25 of 28 Basketmaker II human fecal deposits, accounting for between 50% and 100% of total macrofossil weight in 17 of them. Matson and Chisholm assert, "Clearly the most important resource in the coprolites is maize followed by pinyon pine and Indian rice grass" (1991:450).

Stable carbon isotope ratios from four Basketmaker II burials are similar to those from three Pueblo II/III burials, with the Basketmaker samples yielding $\delta^{13}C$ values ranging between -7.3 and -7.9 ‰ and the Pueblo samples between -7.1 and -7.4 ‰: "It is here that we can most firmly make our statement about change, or rather, the lack of change. Both the Pueblo and the Basketmaker people on Cedar Mesa show similar reliance on C_4 plants, which must mean primarily maize in this case, in the absence of substantial other C_4 plants in the Cedar Mesa coprolite and bulk sample analysis" (Matson and Chisholm 1991:454).

Flotation-recovered plant remains from Turkey Pen Cave are consistent with the more direct Cedar Mesa dietary data sets. Maize and squash *(Cucurbita* sp.) both have 100% ubiquity values in the flotation samples. The total weight of maize fragments is 16.2 g, and that of squash is 2.2 g, followed by 1.4 g of pinyon nuts *(Pinus edulis)*, 1 g of Indian ricegrass seeds *(Oryzopsis hymenoides)*, and .9 g of banana yucca *(Yucca baccata)*. The authors conclude that the nonfecal macrobotanical evidence "supports the inference about the dominance of maize and squash horticulture based on the coprolite analysis" (Matson and Chisholm 1991:451–452).

Implications for Colorado Plateau prehistory are far-reaching. These two studies obviously counter the view of Basketmaker populations as basically food collectors who grew some crops as a risk-reduction measure. The non-fecal macrobotanical remains are in basic agreement with direct data sources and might be treated as more representative in future investigations.

Case Study 2: Premaize Food Production in Eastern North America

Similar studies in eastern North America have increased the understanding of agricultural evolution. As in the Southwest, stable isotopic data and paleofecal information have made it possible to evaluate the significance of cultigens in the diets of various past societies. For the most part, as in the Southwest, archaeobotanical assemblages recovered by flotation are congruent to the more direct data sources. Assemblages with little or no maize come from time periods for which the stable isotope values, at least those from the same subregion, are extremely negative ($\delta^{13}C$ values of -20 ‰ or more). Conversely, I can think of no assemblage with high maize frequencies and high ubiquity values where these data conflict with the available stable carbon isotope record (compare, for example, Asch and Asch [1985] and Johannessen [1988] with Buikstra and Milner [1991]), although we need more paired isotopic and macrobotanical information from single sites.

Researchers in most of the East have the advantage of not needing to worry about native C_4 grasses moving up the food chain with grazing animals or about economically important CAM pathway succulents such as cacti. The single notable C_4 plant, amaranth *(Amaranthus spp.)*, is well documented as *not* being a member of eastern agricultural systems except in the southwest Ozark region, where it seems to be a relatively minor crop *(Amaranthus hypochondriacus)* introduced from the Southwest late in prehistory along with maize (Fritz 1986, 1990). The economically significant chenopod species is *Chenopodium berlandieri,* a C_3 plant. Direct isotopic assays on prehistoric cultigen chenopod specimens from southwest Ozark rockshelters (Fritz 1986) and on archaeological material from Illinois (Buikstra et al. 1988) leave no doubt about this.

Archaeologists working in eastern North America do have a disadvantage in applying stable carbon isotopic analysis, however, because the earliest food production systems there did not include maize or any other C_4 or CAM pathway plant. Evaluations of the dietary significance of premaize cultigens such as sumpweed *(Iva annua* var. *macrocarpa)*, sunflower *(Helianthus annuus* var. *macrocarpus)*, and chenopod *(C. berlandieri* ssp. *jonesianum)* are therefore generally quasi-quantitative or highly impressionistic. Paleoethnobotanists with firsthand experience sorting flotation samples dominated by those cultigen seed types and associated, probable crop taxa including knotweed *(Polygonum erectum)*, maygrass *(Phalaris caroliniana)*, and little barley *(Hordeum pusillum)* tend to infer that they were increasingly important in some parts of the Midsouth (e.g., eastern Tennessee), as early as 1000 B.C. and probably even more important across a general midlatitudinal zone in the Midwest (roughly from northwestern Arkansas to eastern Ohio) during the first millennium A.D. (Asch and Asch 1985; Fritz 1990; Johannessen 1988; Yarnell 1974b, 1993; Yarnell and Black 1985). These assessments are based on high ubiquity values (percentage of flotation samples in which the taxa are present), dramatically increased seed:nutshell ratios, many more seeds recovered per liter of soil floated (i.e., higher density), and much higher percentages of total seed counts contributed by the crop types. These measures go along with increased occurrences of carbonized masses of the relevant seed taxa in pits dating between the Middle Woodland and Early Mississippian periods at open sites (Asch and Asch 1981; Johannessen 1984; Lopinot et al. 1991), as well as occurrences of uncarbonized seed masses in storage context at rockshelter sites (Fritz 1986; Fritz and Smith 1988).

Not all archaeologists are impressed by these indirect data, however, and the view of pre-Mississippian (i.e., pre-maize) societies as essentially hunter-gatherers is persistent (Fiedel 1987; Lynott et al. 1986; Steponaitis 1986). Therefore, while informed archaeologists today do not challenge the evidence for indigenous crops by the early first millennium B.C., centuries before maize is documented in the East, they continue to disagree about the dietary significance and potential overall biological and social impact of native seed crop production.

The integrated, multidisciplinary studies at Salts Cave and Mammoth Cave in Kentucky have contributed the most direct evidence for consumption of significant proportions of pre-maize cultigens in eastern North America. Analyses of more than 100 human fecal and intestinal samples from Salts and Mammoth caves were integrated with analyses of flotation-recovered carbonized plant remains from the Salts Cave vestibule (Gardner 1987; Marquardt 1974; Watson 1974; Watson and Yarnell 1986; Yarnell 1969, 1974a, 1974b). This is the one case I know of in eastern North America where estimates of native seed crop consumption were attempted (Yarnell 1969, 1974b). The estimates were based on the paleofecal contents alone—not on amounts of flotation-recovered seeds. The two most significant results of the Salts-Mammoth Cave research are, first, that native crops (sunflower, sumpweed, chenopod, and maygrass) comprised 69% of the estimated diet of the Salts Cavers based on proportions of identified food remains, and, second, that percentages of carbonized seeds in vestibule midden deposits correspond closely to those in the fecal assemblage. *Chenopodium* is overrepresented in flotation samples from the vestibule midden, but even so, it comprises an impressive 25% average food value in the paleofeces.

The data from Salts Cave document production and heavy consumption of native cultigens during the first millennium B.C. In the late 1960s and early 1970s, however, when the Salts Cave results were reported, appreciation was hindered by uncertainty about the time span represented and the cultigen status of chenopod. Even with those questions resolved (Fritz and Smith 1988; Gardner 1987; Gremillion 1990; Kennedy 1990; Smith 1984, 1985a, 1985b; Watson and Yarnell 1986), the special-activity nature (i.e., deep cave mineral mining) of the Salts Cave diet has made some people reluctant to generalize that they or any other Early Woodland populations were regularly ingesting such large quantities of native seed crops.

From this point on, inferences must be based on *indirect* macrobotanical evidence, the best available of which comes from large-scale projects in Tennessee, Illinois, and Alabama. Flotation sampling strategies have been intensive, with individual soil sample volumes averaging 10 liters or more. Total weights of analyzed plant remains are in the thousands or tens of thousands of grams per project, and total quantities of seeds are typically in the thousands or tens of thousands per site, occasionally in the millions. Distinct trends are observable by comparing ratios, frequencies, and ubiquity and density values. Bolstered primarily by seed-rich features at sites in eastern and central Tennessee, the mean number of identified seeds per 100 g of nutshell in the Southeast region as a whole rises from 8, 15, and 19 in the Early, Middle, and Late Archaic periods, respectively, to 85 in the Early Woodland and 171 in the Middle Woodland period (Yarnell and Black 1985). Percentages of native small grain taxa in these seed assemblages increase from less than 30% before the Late Archaic to 90% during the Middle Woodland period (Yarnell and Black 1985:99).

The same general trend is revealed both in the lower Illinois River valley and in the American Bottom area of westcentral Illinois (Asch and Asch 1985; Johannessen 1984, 1988; Lopinot 1991). Density (mean number of seeds per 10-liter sample) and frequency values of the seed crop taxa rise dramatically throughout the Middle and Late Woodland periods (ca. 300 B.C. to A.D. 800) and remain high in Emergent Mississippian (A.D. 800–1000) and Early Mississippian components (A.D. 1000–1250). Nutshell density values decline, as do the ratios of nutshell:wood. Maize is absent or rare before the Late Woodland period, and it remains uncommon in components predating the Emergent Mississippian (A.D. 800–1000), at which point it becomes ubiquitous. Sissel Johannessen has written, "It is clear that these trends reflect major changes in patterns of behavior" and that "we know . . . diet has changed over this time span" (1988:160). She (1988:161–162) describes Archaic populations as living in nut groves, Woodland period people as living in gardens, and Mississippian populations as living in maize fields.

Most eastern North American paleoethnobotanists and many of our archaeological colleagues are convinced that production of native crops was more than a minor concern for many Woodland and early Mississippian period societies (Asch and Asch 1985; Fritz 1990; Johannessen 1988; Smith 1987, 1989; Yarnell 1993). However, we refrain from speculating in print as to percentages of calories or nutrient components derived from these crops, and personally, I am unwilling to go on record with a speculation of that sort. In spite of this limitation, I believe that the biological and social consequences of pre-maize agriculture were significant. Possible effects of increased availability of storable carbohydrates for fertility, mortality, and general health status have been discussed by bioarchaeologists such as Buikstra and colleagues (1986) and Rose and colleagues (1991). It is obviously important to know whether pre-Mississippian societies were pure hunter-gatherers, hunter-gatherers who may have occasionally supplemented their diets with small amounts of native seed crops, or people already committed to an annual cycle of gardening or small-scale field agriculture.

Case Study 3: The Introduction of Maize into Eastern North America

Stable carbon isotope analysis is now being used to monitor the incorporation of maize into the mixed seed cropping systems of the Midwest and Midsouth. Comparative archaeobotanical analyses in other subregions indicate that the adoption of maize signals the first farming efforts in the Deep South, the Great Lakes region, New England, and the Atlantic seaboard. In general, carbon isotope series correspond to macrobotanical assemblages, as mentioned earlier. However, in parts of the East, there is a lag between the earliest occurrences of carbonized maize fragments in the archaeological record and rises in ^{13}C enrichment.

We now have direct AMS radiocarbon dates on maize from three Middle Woodland sites—Holding in Illinois, Icehouse Bottom in Tennessee, and Edwin Harness in Ohio—ranging from approximately 50 B.C. to A.D. 200 (Chapman and Crites 1987; Ford 1987; Riley and Walz 1992), several centuries before any evidence for ^{13}C enrichment in human burials. Slight increases in the ubiquity of macrobotanical maize occur in some subregions between A.D. 500 and 800 (Asch and Asch 1985; Parker 1991), the time frame for the earliest detectable ^{13}C enrichment. Carbon isotope ratios, however, remain highly negative for the most part until after A.D. 1000 (Buikstra et al. 1988; Buikstra and Milner 1991; Lynott et al. 1986; Schwarcz et al. 1985).

In southeast Missouri and northeast Arkansas, for example, maize was recovered in relatively low frequencies from several Late Woodland and Early Mississippian sites including Zeebree (Harris 1976), Toltec (Fritz 1988), Owls Bend, and Gooseneck (Voigt 1986). Human burials from these sites, however, do not exhibit elevated ^{13}C levels (Lynott et al. 1986; Nassaney 1991). Rose and associates (1991) hypothesize that this pattern reflects ceremonial significance of maize—the ritual handling of a plant whose fruit was not consumed by many members of the society. This scenario is plausible, and it may reflect the mechanism by which maize was introduced into some subregions of the Eastern Woodlands. Before ruling out alternatives, however, I would question the sensitivity of isotopic analysis for detecting very low levels of C_4 plant consumption.

If early agriculturalists had high-quality diets in general, with protein available from meat, nuts, and cultivated C_3 pathway plants, and if they were consuming maize seasonally, for a total of less than 10% to 15% of their diet as averaged through the year, could we detect it in many assays? Bone chemists (Tieszen 1991), biological anthropologists (Buikstra and Milner 1991), and archaeologists (Parkington 1991) have recently published cautionary statements leading me to doubt our capability of isotopically recognizing initial stages of maize consumption. Buikstra and Milner, for example, discuss the "unresolved issue" of "the amount of C_4 plant-derived carbon necessary to shift δ^{13}C values in the omnivorous consumer," suggesting that "the collagen of human groups consuming significant amounts of animal protein, along with a broad spectrum of C_3 plants may not register an observable impact of minor increments of C_3 plant-derived carbon" (1991:322).

The point of this discussion is to emphasize that the limitations of indirect paleodietary data—in this case carbonized corncob and kernel fragments—are not unlike the limitations of direct data such as bone chemistry. We are constrained by thresholds of visibility and by the small amount of sampling conducted so far. I speculate that low frequencies of maize in flotation samples reflect a small contribution of maize to the diet of more people than just budding chiefs and priests. Especially in the initial stages of eastern North American maize agriculture, then, the flotation-recovered macrobotanical remains do not appear to be an inferior source of dietary information.

Conclusions

These three case studies underscore the need to recover, analyze, and integrate as many types of subsistence information as possible. While nonfecal macrobotanical remains impose limitations for paleodietary reconstruction, they have the potential for illuminating long-term subsistence trends and regional variability in plant use. We would be seriously handicapped by a lack of the more direct data sources, but fortunately we can use the other sources to assess the biases in the archaeobotanical record. Integrative studies on the Colorado Plateau and, in Kentucky, at Salts and Mammoth caves show general agreement between fecal remains and nonfecal, flotation-derived plant assemblages. Comparisons of stable carbon isotope series with records for archaeobotanical maize again show basic consistency. In eastern North America, however, the archaeobotanical record may currently be more informative than bone chemistry about low levels of maize consumption. My answer, then, to the question in Sissel Johannessen's (1988) subtitle "Are Paleoethnobotanical Data Better Than We Think?" would be, when used judiciously, *yes*.

References

Asch, D. L., and N. B. Asch
  1985   Prehistoric Plant Cultivation in West-Central Illinois. In *Prehistoric Food Production in North America*, edited by R. I. Ford, pp. 149–203. Anthropological Papers No. 75. Museum of Anthropology, University of Michigan, Ann Arbor.
Asch, N. B., and D. L. Asch
  1981   Archeobotany of Newbridge, Carlin, and Weitzer Sites—the White Hall Components. In *Faunal Exploitation and Resource Selection: Early Late Woodland Subsistence in the Lower Illinois Valley*, by B. W. Styles, pp. 275–291. Scientific Papers No. 3. Northwestern University Archeological Program, Evanston.
Buikstra, J. E., W. Autry, E. Breitburg, L. Eisenberg, and N. van der Merwe
  1988   Diet and Health in the Nashville Basin: Human Adaptation and Maize Agriculture in Middle Tennessee. In *Diet and Subsistence: Current Archaeological Perspectives*, edited by B. V. Kennedy and G. M. LeMoine, pp. 243–259. Proceedings of the 19th Annual Chacmool Conference, Archaeological Association of the University of Calgary, Calgary, Alberta.

Buikstra, J. E., L. W. Konigsberg, and J. Bullington
    1986   Fertility and the Development of Agriculture in the Prehistoric Midwest. *American Antiquity* 51:528–546.
Buikstra, J. E., and G. R. Milner
    1991   Isotopic and Archaeological Interpretations of Diet in the Central Mississippi Valley. *Journal of Archaeological Science* 18:319–329.
Chapman, J., and G. D. Crites
    1987   Evidence for Early Maize *(Zea mays)* from the Icehouse Bottom Site, Tennessee. *American Antiquity* 52:352–354.
Dennell, R.
    1976   The Economic Importance of Plant Resources Represented on Archaeological Sites. *Journal of Archaeological Science* 3:229–247.
    1979   Prehistoric Diet and Nutrition: Some Food for Thought. *World Archaeology* 11:121–135.
Dimbleby, G.
    1978   *Plants and Archaeology: The Archaeology of the Soil.* Humanities Press, Atlantic Highlands, New Jersey.
Fiedel, S. J.
    1987   *Prehistory of the Americas.* Cambridge University Press, Cambridge.
Flannery, K. V.
    1986   Food Procurement Area and Preceramic Diet at Guila Naquitz. In *Guila Naquitz: Archaic Foraging and Early Agriculture in Oaxaca, Mexico,* edited by K. V. Flannery, pp. 303–317. Academic Press, New York.
Ford, R. I.
    1987   Dating Early Maize in the Eastern United States. Paper presented at the 10th Ethnobiology Conference, Gainesville.
Fritz, G. J.
    1986   *Prehistoric Ozark Agriculture: The University of Arkansas Rockshelter Collections.* Ph.D. dissertation, University of North Carolina at Chapel Hill. University Microfilms, Ann Arbor.
    1988   Adding the Plant Remains to Assessments of Late Woodland/Early Mississippi Period Plant Husbandry. Paper presented at the 53rd Annual Meeting of the Society for American Archaeology, Phoenix.
    1990   Multiple Pathways to Farming in Precontact Eastern North America. *Journal of World Prehistory* 4:387–435.
Fritz, G. J., and B. D. Smith
    1988   Old Collections and New Technology: Documenting the Domestication of *Chenopodium* in Eastern North America. *Midcontinental Journal of Archaeology* 13:3–27.
Gardner, P. S.
    1987   New Evidence Concerning the Chronology and Paleoethnobotany of Salts Cave, Kentucky. *American Antiquity* 52:358–367.
Gilman, P. A.
    1987   Architecture as Artifact: Pit Structures and Pueblos in the American Southwest. *American Antiquity* 52:538–564.
Gremillion, K. J.
    1990   Morphological Variation in *Chenopodium* from Kentucky. Paper presented at the 47th Southeastern Archaeological Conference, Mobile.
Harris, S. E.
    1976   Botanical Remains, Recovery Techniques, and Preliminary Subsistence Results. In *A Preliminary Report of the Zeebree Project: New Approaches in Contract*

Archeology in Arkansas, edited by D. F. Morse and P. A. Morse, pp. 60–64. Research Report No. 8. Arkansas Archeological Survey, Fayetteville.

Hastorf, C. A.
1988   The Use of Paleoethnobotanical Data in Prehistoric Studies of Crop Production, Processing, and Consumption. In *Current Paleoethnobotany: Analytical Methods and Cultural Interpretations of Archaeological Plant Remains,* edited by C. A. Hastorf and V. S. Popper, pp. 119–144. University of Chicago Press, Chicago.

Johannessen, S.
1984   Paleoethnobotany. In *American Bottom Archaeology,* edited by C. J. Bareis and J. W. Porter, pp. 197–214. University of Illinois Press, Urbana.
1988   Plant Remains and Culture Change: Are Paleoethnobotanical Data Better Than We Think? In *Current Paleoethnobotany: Analytical Methods and Cultural Interpretations of Archaeological Plant Remains,* edited by Christine A. Hastorf and Virginia S. Popper, pp. 145–166. University of Chicago Press, Chicago.

Jones, V. H., and R. L. Fonner
1954   Plant Remains from Sites in the Durango and LaPlata Areas, Colorado. In *Basketmaker II Sites near Durango, Colorado,* edited by E. Morris and R. Burgh, pp. 93–115. Carnegie Institution of Washington Publication 604. Washington, D.C.

Kennedy, M. C.
1990   *An Analysis of the Radiocarbon Dates from Salts and Mammoth Caves, Mammoth Cave National Park, Kentucky.* Unpublished Master's thesis, Department of Anthropology, Washington University, St. Louis.

Lopinot, N. H.
1991   Archaeobotanical Remains. In *The Archaeology of the Cahokia Mounds ICT-II: Biological Remains,* by N. H. Lopinot, L. S. Kelly, and G. R. Milner, and R. Paine, pp. 1–268. Illinois Cultural Resources Study No. 13. Illinois Historic Preservation Agency, Springfield.

Lopinot, N. H., G. J. Fritz, and J. E. Kelly
1991   The Archaeological Context and Significance of *Polygonum erectum* Achene Masses from the American Bottom Region. Paper presented at the 14th Ethnobiology Conference, St. Louis.

Lynott, M. J., T. W. Boutton, J. E. Price, and D. E. Nelson
1986   Stable Carbon Isotopic Evidence for Maize Agriculture in Southeast Missouri and Northeast Arkansas. *American Antiquity* 51:51–65.

MacNeish, R. S.
1967   A Summary of Subsistence. In *The Prehistory of the Tehuacan Valley: I, Environment and Subsistence,* edited by D. S. Byers, pp. 290–309. University of Texas Press, Austin.

Marquardt, W. H.
1974   A Statistical Analysis of Constituents in Human Paleofecal Specimens from Mammoth Cave. In *Archeology of the Mammoth Cave Area,* edited by P. J. Watson, pp. 193–202. Academic Press, New York.

Matson, R. G.
1991   *The Origins of Southwestern Agriculture.* University of Arizona Press, Tucson.

Matson, R. G., and B. Chisholm
1991   Basketmaker II Subsistence: Carbon Isotopes and Other Dietary Indicators from Cedar Mesa, Utah. *American Antiquity* 56:444–459.

Miller, N. F., and T. L. Smart
1984   Intentional Burning of Dung as Fuel: A Mechanism for the Incorporation of Charred Seeds into the Archaeological Record. *Journal of Ethnobiology* 4:15–28.

Minnis, P. E.
    1989   Prehistoric Diet in the Northern Southwest: Macroplant Remains from Four
            Corners Feces. *American Antiquity* 54:543–563.
Munson, P. J., P. W. Parmalee, and R. A. Yarnell
    1971   Subsistence Ecology of Scovill, a Terminal Middle Woodland Village.
            American Antiquity 36:410–431.
Nassaney, M. S.
    1991   Spatial-Temporal Dimensions of Social Integration During the Coles Creek
            Period in Central Arkansas. In *Stability, Transformation, and Variation: The Late
            Woodland Southeast*, edited by M. S. Nassaney and C. R. Cobb, pp. 177–220.
            Plenum Press, New York.
Parker, K. E.
    1991   Sponemann Phase Archaeobotany. In *The Sponemann Site: The Formative
            Emergent Mississippian Sponemann Phase Occupations (11-Ms-517)*, by A. C.
            Fortier, T. O. Maher, and J. A. Williams, pp. 377–419. American Bottom Archae-
            ology FAI-270 Site Reports, vol. 23. University of Illinois Press (for the Illinois
            Department of Transportation), Urbana.
Parkington, J.
    1991   Approaches to Dietary Reconstruction in the Western Cape: Are You What
            You Have Eaten? *Journal of Archaeological Science* 18:331–342.
Pearsall, D. M.
    1988   Interpreting the Meaning of Macroremain Abundance: The Impact of
            Source and Context. In *Current Paleoethnobotany: Analytical Methods and Cultural
            Interpretations of Archaeological Plant Remains*, edited by C. A. Hastorf and V. S.
            Popper, pp. 97–118. University of Chicago Press, Chicago.
    1989   *Paleoethnobotany: A Handbook of Procedures*. Academic Press, New York.
Plog, F. T.
    1979   Prehistory: Western Anasazi. In *Southwest*, edited by Alfonzo Ortiz, pp.
            108–130. Handbook of North American Indians, vol. 9, W. G. Sturtevant, general
            editor. Smithsonian Institution, Washington, D.C.
Pozorski, S.
    1983   Changing Subsistence Priorities and Early Settlement Patterns on the North
            Coast of Peru. *Journal of Ethnobiology* 3:15–38.
Riley, T. J., and G. Walz
    1992   AMS Dating of Maize from the Middle Woodland Holding Site (11MS118)
            in the American Bottom of Illinois. Paper presented at the 49th Southeastern
            Archaeological Conference, Little Rock.
Rose, J. C., M. K. Marks, and L. L. Tieszen
    1991   Bioarchaeology and Subsistence in the Central and Lower Portions of the
            Mississippi Valley. In *What Mean These Bones? Studies in Southeastern Bioarchae-
            ology*, edited by M. L. Powell, P. S. Bridges, and A. M. Wagner Mires, pp. 7–21.
            University of Alabama Press, Tuscaloosa.
Schwarcz, H. P., J. Melbye, M. A. Katzenberg, and M. Knyf
    1985   Stable Isotopes in Human Skeletons of Southern Ontario: Reconstructing
            Palaeodiet. *Journal of Archaeological Science* 12:187–206.
Smith, B. D.
    1984   *Chenopodium* as a Prehistoric Domesticate in Eastern North America:
            Evidence from Russell Cave, Alabama. *Science* 226:165–167.
    1985a   *Chenopodium berlandieri* ssp. *jonesianum*: Evidence for a Hopewellian
            Domesticate from Ash Cave, Ohio. *Southeastern Archaeology* 4:107–133.
    1985b   The Role of *Chenopodium* as a Domesticate in Pre-Maize Garden Systems of

the Eastern United States. *Southeastern Archaeology* 4:51–72.

1987   The Independent Domestication of Indigenous Seed-Bearing Plants in Eastern North America. In *Emergent Horticultural Economies of the Eastern Woodlands*, edited by W. F. Keegan, pp. 3–47. Occasional Paper No. 7. Center for Archaeological Investigations, Southern Illinois University, Carbondale.

1989   Origins of Agriculture in Eastern North America. *Science* 246:1566–1571.

Steponaitis, V. P.

1986   Prehistoric Archaeology in the Southeastern United States, 1970–1985. *Annual Review of Anthropology* 15:363–404.

Tieszen, L. L.

1991   Natural Variations in the Carbon Isotope Values of Plants: Implications for Archaeology, Ecology, and Paleoecology. *Journal of Archaeological Science* 18:227–248.

Voigt, E. E.

1986   Late Woodland and Emergent Mississippian Plant Use. In *New World Paleoethnobotany: Collected Papers in Honor of Leonard W. Blake*, edited by E. E. Voigt and D. M. Pearsall, pp. 197–232. *The Missouri Archaeologist* 47.

Watson, P. J.

1974   Prehistoric Horticulturists. In *Archeology of the Mammoth Cave Area*, edited by P. J. Watson, pp. 233–238. Academic Press, New York.

Watson, P. J., and R. A. Yarnell

1986   Lost John's Last Meal. In *New World Paleoethnobotany: Collected Papers in Honor of Leonard W. Blake*, edited by E. E. Voigt and D. M. Pearsall, pp. 241–255. *The Missouri Archaeologist* 47.

Yarnell, R. A.

1969   Contents of Human Paleofeces. In *The Prehistory of Salts Cave, Kentucky*, edited by Patty Jo Watson, pp. 41–54. Reports of Investigation No. 16. Illinois State Museum, Springfield.

1974a   Intestinal Contents of the Salts Cave Mummy and Analysis of the Initial Salts Cave Flotation Series. In *Archeology of the Mammoth Cave Area*, edited by P. J. Watson, pp. 109–112. Academic Press, New York.

1974b   Plant Food and Cultivation of the Salts Cavers. In *Archeology of the Mammoth Cave Area*, edited by P. J. Watson, pp. 113–122. Academic Press, New York.

1982   Problems of Interpretation of Archaeological Plant Remains of the Eastern Woodlands. *Southeastern Archaeology* 1:1–7.

1993   The Importance of Native Crops During the Late Archaic and Woodland. In *Foraging and Farming in the Eastern Woodlands*, edited by C. M. Scarry, pp. 13–26. University of Florida Press, Gainesville.

Yarnell, R. A., and M. J. Black

1985   Temporal Trends Indicated by a Survey of Archaic and Woodland Plant Food Remains from Southeastern North America. *Southeastern Archaeology* 4:93–106.

3. The Value of Archaeological Faunal Remains for Paleodietary Reconstruction: A Case Study for the Midwestern United States

Bonnie W. Styles

Abstract: Faunal remains from archaeological sites provide critical data
for paleodietary reconstructions. They do not represent a complete inventory of animal foods, much less the exact quantities of meat and
nutrients; however, they provide dietary evidence unattainable through
studies of paleofeces and human skeletons. Archaeological faunal
records are abundant, and analyses have yielded evidence for strong
regional patterning in faunal exploitation practices. Studies of archaeological sites from the lower Illinois and central Mississippi River valleys
of Illinois document temporal shifts in Holocene faunal assemblages.
Late prehistoric (Late Woodland and Mississippian) and protohistoric
(Oneota) sites may show a reduction in white-tailed deer and other
terrestrial mammals, the primary sources of red meat. Linear programming models provide a framework for examining the potential
importance of those subsistence shifts to human nutrition. The declining
representation of sources of red meat corresponds to increased reliance
on cultivated plants, including corn after A.D. 600–800, by relatively
sedentary populations. Bioanthropological data provide corroborating
evidence for the reduction of red meat in the form of pathologies related
to iron deficiency anemia and other evidences of malnutrition and
diseases that are ultimately linked to a reliance on maize.

Introduction

Faunal remains from archaeological sites provide indirect but
primary data for paleodietary reconstructions. Although they do not provide
a complete inventory of all the animal foods, much less the quantities of meat

Paleonutrition: The Diet and Health of Prehistoric Americans, edited by Kristin D. Sobolik. Center
for Archaeological Investigations, Occasional Paper No. 22. © 1994 by the Board of Trustees,
Southern Illinois University. All rights reserved. ISBN 0-88104-078-9.

and nutrients, consumed at a site, they do provide dietary evidence for the faunal component of the diet that is unattainable through studies of paleofeces and human skeletons alone. Bioanthropological studies provide evidence for nutritional deficiencies but cannot specify which animals were consumed. The combination of zooarchaeological, archaeobotanical, and bioanthropological data provides the best opportunity to characterize the species composition and nutritional impact of the faunal portion of the diet.

Archaeological faunal records for the midwestern United States are abundant, and analyses have yielded evidence of strong regional patterning in faunal exploitation strategies and ample evidence for dietary change through time. This study tracks some of the major subsistence changes documented for the resource-rich lower Illinois and central Mississippi River valleys of Illinois and examines the implications of those changes for human nutrition.

Keene is correct to point out that the study of prehistoric diet has largely been "limited to enumeration of resources utilized by the prehistoric population and description of the associated modes of production" (1985:155). He notes some exceptions in the works of Earle and Christenson (1980), Reidhead (1976), and Wing and Brown (1979) who look at diet from economic and biological perspectives. I will use the results of previous economically based linear programming models to examine the nutritional importance of recorded shifts in faunal exploitation.

A number of seminal studies have examined the reconstruction of prehistoric diets. Wing and Brown's *Paleonutrition: Method and Theory in Prehistoric Foodways* (1979) advocates an integrated approach that incorporates studies of human, plant, animal, and other cultural remains from sites, with broader studies of biological requirements for human growth and development, the availability of food resources, the development of subsistence technology and strategy, and cultural attitudes. Gilbert and Mielke's *Analysis of Prehistoric Diets* (1985) covers topics of preservation and analysis of plant and animal remains, paleofeces, and human skeletons from archaeological sites, as well as dietary modeling based on nutritional and nonfood constraints and the role of ethnographic inference. The two books cover analytic methods for zooarchaeology, and I will not repeat this information. Some of the greatest recent advances in zooarchaeological methods are in consideration of (1) the taphonomy of deposits (e.g., Grayson 1991), (2) the potential role of bone destruction (e.g., Lyman 1984, 1991), (3) the role of paleoecological change (Klippel and Turner 1991; Styles 1986), (4) issues related to quantification and sample size effects (Grayson 1984), and (5) the importance of settlement function and mobility strategies (e.g., Styles and Purdue 1991). Advances in recovery, quantification, and assessments of taphonomy and bone destruction have improved the ability to interpret fauna from archaeological contexts and—in conjunction with interdisciplinary research on changes in climate, geology, resource availability, plant use, human demography, and settlement strategies—have led to a better understanding of subsistence shifts.

Environmental Setting

The lower Illinois and central Mississippi River valleys of Illinois are resource-rich settings. Both valleys are historically characterized by the rich aquatic habitats of the large rivers, tributary streams, and backwater lakes and sloughs. Those habitats were rich in fish (e.g., catfish, suckers, sunfish, bowfin, and gar), geese, ducks, and other water birds, semiaquatic mammals (e.g., beaver [*Castor canadensis*], muskrat [*Ondatra zibethicus*], river otter [*Lutra canadensis*), and mink [*Mustela vison*]), aquatic turtles, and freshwater mussels. The productivity of those aquatic habitats increased through time with post-Pleistocene and mid-Holocene climatic change and floodplain evolution (Styles 1986; Styles et al. 1983). The ecological changes had impacts on human subsistence as did changes in mobility and settlement strategies.

Terrestrial floodplain environments historically supported deciduous forest (e.g., cottonwood, willow, elm, ash, hackberry, oak, and hickory), wet and dry prairies, and marshes. The uplands supported oak-hickory forest, savanna or barrens, and prairie habitats. The terrestrial environments were also rich in plant and animal foods. Nineteenth-century terrestrial environments included a variety of mammals of potential economic importance such as white-tailed deer *(Odocoileus virginianus)*, elk *(Cervus elaphus)*, black bear *(Ursus americanus)*, raccoon *(Procyon lotor)*, and numerous small mammal species (Hoffmeister 1989; Hoffmeister and Mohr 1972; Purdue and Styles 1986, 1987). Those environments also supported turkey *(Meleagris gallopavo)*, prairie chicken *(Tympanuchus cupido)*, passenger pigeon *(Ectopistes migratorius)*, and box turtle *(Terrapene* sp.). Of the large mammals, elk and black bear were apparently not abundant in prehistory, and the bison *(Bison bison)* was a late entrant to the state (after A.D. 1400; Purdue and Styles 1986, 1987).

A number of studies have demonstrated that there was climatic, geomorphic, and vegetative change during the mid-Holocene, from approximately 8500 to 5000 B.P. (e.g., Hajic 1990; King 1981; King and Allen 1977; Smith 1985; Styles 1985). During that period the Prairie Peninsula extended into Illinois. The terrestrial environments, like the aquatic environments, of the Illinois and Mississippi River valleys changed through time, and all of those changes had impacts on human subsistence, settlement, and mobility strategies (e.g., Brown 1985; Styles et al. 1983).

Trends in Midwestern Faunal Exploitation

Methods

For the purposes of this study, I summarize Holocene faunal data from 45 components from 10 archaeological sites in the lower Illinois and central Mississippi River valleys that range in age from 8,500 to 200 years before the present (Table 3-1; Figure 3-1). The long-term trends in faunal exploitation have been discussed in a variety of papers (e.g., Styles et al. 1984; Styles et al. 1982), and a number of publications summarize shorter-term shifts

Table 3-1. *Faunal Data Selected for This Study*

Site	Period	Source
Lower Illinois River Valley		
Koster		
Horizon 11	Early Archaic (8500–8450 B.P.)	Neusius 1982
Horizons 10B, 10A, 9C/D, 9A/B, 8F, 8E	Middle Archaic 1 (8200–7600 B.P.)	Neusius 1982
Horizons 8D, 8C, 8B, 8A	Middle Archaic 2 (7300–6850 B.P.)	Neusius 1982
Horizons 6 lower, 6 main	Middle Archaic 3 (5700–4900 B.P.)	Hill 1975
Smiling Dan	Middle Woodland (2000 B.P.)	Styles et al. 1985
Newbridge	Early Late Woodland (1500 B.P.)	Styles 1981
Hill Creek	Mississippian (758 B.P.)	Colburn 1985
Central Mississippi River Valley		
Modoc Rock Shelter		
Strata 30–31, 28, 23/26, 20/21, 15–19, 14	Early Archaic (8500–8200 B.P.)	Styles and White 1991
Strata 12/13, 11, 10, 9 7/8, 6	Early Middle Archaic (8000–7200 B.P.)	Styles and White 1991
Strata 5, 4, 3, 2, 1	Middle Middle Archaic (6800–6200 B.P.)	Styles and White 1991
Strata A, A2	Late Middle Archaic (5600–ca. 5200 B.P.)	Styles and White 1991
Strata B, 9E, 8 E/C	Early Late Archaic (4700–4300 B.P.)	Styles and White 1991 Thorson and Styles 1992
Florence Street		
Florence phase	Early Woodland (2400–2300 B.P.)	Cross 1983b
Mund		
Mund phase	Early Late Woodland (1470 B.P.)	Cross 1983a
Range		
Patrick phase	Late Late Woodland (1250 B.P.)	Kelly 1987

Table 3-1.—*Continued*

Site	Period	Source
Dohack phase	Emergent Mississippian (1150–1100 B.P.)	Kelly 1990a
Range phase	Emergent Mississippian (1100–1050 B.P.)	Kelly 1990b
Julien Stirling phase	Mississippian (900–800 B.P.)	Cross 1984
Waterman	Historic (230–200 B.P.)	Parmalee and Bogan 1980

(e.g., Kelly and Cross 1984; Neusius 1982; Styles 1981; Styles et al. 1983). This is the first study that attempts to quantitatively compare shifts in the two river valleys and examine the shifts from a nutritional perspective.

I include faunal data only from components that are relatively comparable in faunal preservation and recovery techniques and for which the settlement function is reported. I group small components that show similar faunal patterns at the Koster and Modoc Rock Shelter sites to expand sample sizes and simplify summary diagrams. Some reported faunal assemblages for sites in the region are not included in this study because of problems related to recovery techniques, sample sizes, or specialized settlement function. In the case of settlement function, I do not include sites that appeared to be too specialized to characterize faunal exploitation for a particular cultural period (e.g., a mortuary camp and a winter hunting camp).

Vertebrate faunal taxa are divided into eight categories on the basis of economic importance and gross habitat preference: fish, aquatic turtles, terrestrial turtles, aquatic birds (waterfowl and other water birds), all other birds, white-tailed deer, other terrestrial mammals, and semiaquatic mammals. The other terrestrial mammal category primarily includes small mammals like squirrel (*Sciurus* spp.), raccoon, cottontail rabbit (*Sylvilagus floridanus*), and rodents. Quantitative summaries use the number of identified specimens (NISP). Although comparisons based on NISP suffer from differences between taxa such as in the numbers of elements that can be identified and the density and fracturing of bone, these data are not biased by differences in how the faunal remains are grouped for calculations of minimum numbers of individuals (MNI). Grayson (1984:66–67) points out that aggregation procedures affect MNI calculations and detract from the value of MNI as a measure of taxonomic abundance. After analyzing the relationship between NISP and MNI, Grayson concludes that "for any given fauna, MNI values can normally be tightly predicted from NISP counts. . . . As a result, the information on relative abundance that resides in MNI counts generally resides as well in

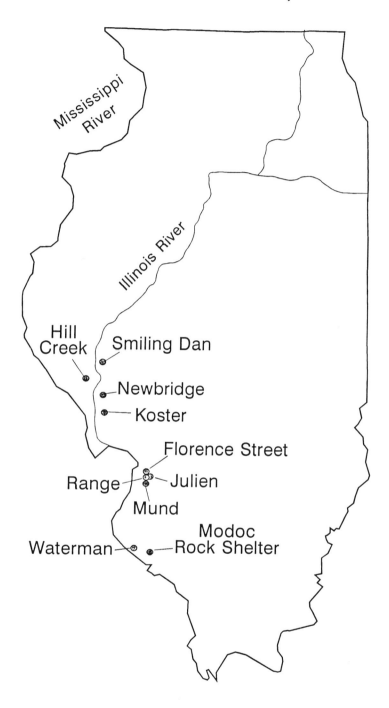

Figure 3-1. *Locations of archaeological sites in the lower Illinois and central Mississippi River valleys.*

NISP counts, and if relative abundance is the target of analysis, there would seem to be little reason to spend the time and effort to calculate minimum numbers of individuals" (1984:63–64). Given that the goal of this analysis is to examine broad changes in the proportional representation of faunal taxa, the use of NISP is appropriate. To assess relative abundance, the proportion of each taxon to the vertebrate NISP is calculated. In the case of mussels, I plot the mussel NISP against the total NISP. Mussel data were not systematically reported for the central Mississippi River valley sites and thus are not included for that region. The diachronic comparisons may be more meaningful than synchronic interpretations of the relative importance of taxa for one period of time.

Quantitative summaries are based on macro-recovered remains recovered in quarter-inch (0.64 cm) or half-inch (1.27 cm) mesh screens for the lower Illinois River valley; quarter-inch mesh screens for Modoc Rock Shelter in the central Mississippi River valley; and published counts for Woodland and Mississippian sites in the American Bottom of the central Mississippi Valley, which combined hand-picked fauna and fauna collected from flotation samples (0.42 mm mesh screens). Variation in recovery techniques contributes to potential biases in faunal representation. Addition of flotation data to the lower Illinois River valley sites would increase the representation of fish (e.g., Styles 1981); however I chose not to combine flotation and screened fauna because of the vastly different sample sizes and sediment volumes that they represent. The inclusion of some fauna from flotation samples from the Woodland and Mississippian sites for the American Bottom faunal tallies could result in a higher proportional representation of small-bodied taxa such as fish, amphibians, rodents, and passerine birds. However, general recovery of macrofauna through handpicking rather than systematic screening could result in an underrepresentation of small-bodied taxa for those time periods. Given the realities of how faunal remains were recovered and reported and the desire to examine relative abundances, the primary focus on macro-recovered remains is the most reasonable approach.

Results

Trends in faunal representation are readily apparent in the lower Illinois River valley (Figure 3-2). The bars in each column show changes in proportional representation through time. More precise listings of the time intervals and associated cultural periods are provided in Table 3-1. There is a marked increase in the proportional representation of freshwater mussels around 7300 B.P. during the Middle Archaic period (Styles 1986). Use of mussels during the Archaic period is greater than during the late prehistoric period. The proportional representation of fish increases in late Middle Archaic components that date between 5700 and 4900 B.P. The increase corresponds to increases in quiet-water taxa and has been linked to the development of shallow flood-basin lakes (Styles 1986). Relative use of fish is greatest in the late prehistoric period, represented here by Middle Woodland, early Late Woodland, and Mississippian components. The same time periods also

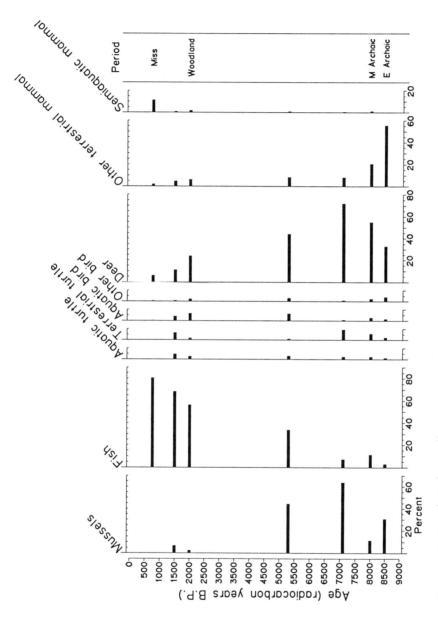

Figure 3-2. *Trends in lower Illinois River valley faunal assemblages. Percentage of total NISP is presented for freshwater mussels; percentage of vertebrate NISP is presented for other taxa.*

show relatively high utilization of other aquatic resources such as aquatic turtles, aquatic birds, and semiaquatic mammals. There may be a slight increase in the use of aquatic turtles and aquatic birds through time. Increased use of aquatic resources in the Woodland and Mississippian periods has been linked to localized exploitation of renewable resources by relatively sedentary horticultural populations (e.g., Styles 1981).

Use of terrestrial resources shows an overall decline through time. Representation of white-tailed deer climbs and peaks in the Middle Archaic and then declines in the Woodland and Mississippian periods. The increase in deer between the Early and Middle Archaic at the Koster site has been linked to changes in settlement and mobility strategies. According to Neusius (1982), increased patchiness because of Hypsithermal climatic effects led to logistical exploitation strategies for white-tailed deer during the Middle Archaic period. The use of other terrestrial mammals, predominately small mammals, shows an overall decline through time. The high proportion of small mammals, specifically squirrels in the Early Archaic deposits (8500–8450 B.P.) at Koster, has been attributed to opportunistic exploitation of locally abundant small mammals at mobile residential camps (Neusius 1982). Although Woodland and Mississippian peoples were cultivating a variety of plant foods, there does not appear to be an increase in the representation of small mammals that would have been attracted to the fields.

Trends for the prehistoric period of the Mississippi River valley (Figure 3-3) are similar, albeit more complicated. There is an increase in the representation of fish in prehistoric times. As noted for the lower Illinois River valley, use of fish increases during the Middle Archaic period. A dramatic increase occurs at Modoc Rock Shelter around 8000 B.P., which is earlier than noted for the lower Illinois River valley. However, that shift is recorded for the first base-camp occupation (Stratum 12/13) and is attributed in part to the change in settlement function and mobility. Early Archaic occupations at Modoc Rock Shelter, like those at Koster, are attributed to residential camps (Styles and White 1991). Patterns for other aquatic taxa differ somewhat from those in the lower Illinois River valley, although there may be a similar increase through time in the use of semiaquatic mammals. Use of aquatic birds does not vary systematically through time.

The patterns for white-tailed deer and other terrestrial mammals are similar to those noted for the lower Illinois River valley. Early Archaic deposits at Modoc Rock Shelter show relatively high proportions of squirrels and low proportions of white-tailed deer when compared to later time periods (Styles and White 1991). The Early Archaic components at Modoc Rock Shelter are short-term residential camps, while the Middle Archaic components represent more long-term base-camp occupations. The increased use of white-tailed deer at Modoc Rock Shelter has been attributed to increased availability of white-tailed deer during the mid-Holocene and to changes in settlement function with the establishment of long-term base-camp occupations (Styles et al. 1983). The general trend of a relatively high proportion of small mammals to increasing representation of white-tailed deer has been noted for a number of sites. At Rodgers Shelter in Missouri, small mammals predominated over deer

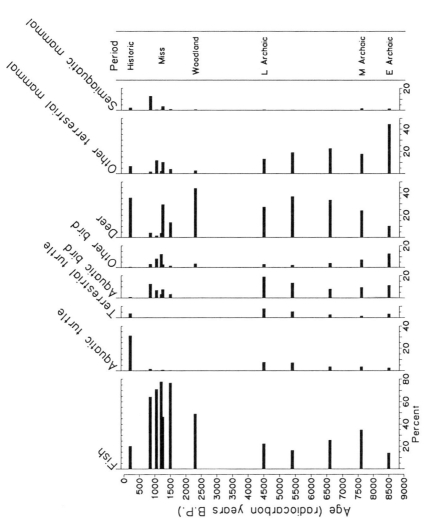

Figure 3-3. *Trends in central Mississippi River valley faunal assemblages. Percentage of vertebrate NISP is presented.*

from about 8500 to 6300 B.P. (McMillan and Klippel 1981:227–230). At Graham Cave in Missouri, small forest animals were more abundant in strata dating from 10,000 to 9000 B.P., and deer increased after 8500 B.P. (McMillan and Klippel 1981:238). The greater representation of small mammals, primarily squirrels, in the early Holocene has been attributed to a greater abundance of gray squirrels (Sciurus carolinensis) and a lower abundance of white-tailed deer prior to the opening of the forest during the Hypsithermal (McMillan and Klippel 1981). Representation of white-tailed deer in the late prehistoric period (especially in the Emergent Mississippian and Mississippian periods) in the central Mississippi River valley is relatively low. As was noted for the lower Illinois River valley we do not see a dramatic increase in the representation of small mammals during the latter part of the prehistoric period when gardening would have reached its peak.

The historic Michigamea and Kaskaskia occupation at the Waterman site does not follow the trends indicated for the prehistoric period. The representation of fish is lower than noted for Woodland and Mississippian sites. The proportion of aquatic turtles is higher than for any of the prehistoric periods. Use of birds in general appears low. Use of deer is higher than in the Woodland and Mississippian periods, possibly reflecting trade initially with the French and later with the British. The assemblage included a few bones from domestic cow, pig, and horse, but Parmalee and Bogan (1980:49) suggest that those remains may have been intrusive from a later American homestead.

The Nutritionally Optimal Diet

Three previous linear programming studies developed for the midwestern United States provide a framework for examining the nutritional value of prehistoric diets. Reidhead's (1980) optimization model is based on an assumption of least effort. He also considered seasonal availability and nutritional value of food resources and average person-hour costs based on prehistoric technology. Optimal diets were predicted for Late Woodland (ca. A.D. 500–1000) and Fort Ancient (ca. A.D. 1000–1300) occupants of the Leonard Haag site in southeastern Indiana. Keene (1981) developed a linear programming model that predicts optimal subsistence strategies for Late Archaic (ca. 4000–1000 B.C.) hunter-gatherers of the Saginaw Valley of southern Michigan. Keene emphasizes nutrition and nonfood needs rather than a more traditional focus on energetic efficiency; however, a major assumption of his model is that hunter-gatherers attempted to satisfy their basic needs at the lowest possible cost. Thus, the program produces a schedule of resource use that minimizes cost subject to the constraining factors of resource availability and nutrient and nonfood needs. Hewitt (1983) produced optimal foraging models for the Middle Archaic occupants of the Koster site in the lower Illinois River valley. His models are based on estimates of the nutritional value and amounts and distribution of foods through space and time, and they also assume that "foraging behavior would tend to minimize the amount of effort expended to provide sufficient foods" (Hewitt 1983:355). Optimal models were created for the historic nineteenth-century environment and the mid-Holocene Hypsithermal (ca. 8500–5000 B.P.) environment.

My goal here is not to evaluate the validity of these models (see Hawkes and O'Connell [1992]; Jochim [1988]; Keene [1983]; Reidhead [1979]; and Styles [1984] for critiques of optimal foraging models) but to use them to examine the nutritional value of animal foods, the interplay with plant foods, and the potential nutritional impacts of changes in animal exploitation. All three optimal foraging studies consider 10 nutritional needs for energy (calories), protein, calcium, phosphorous, iron, vitamin A, thiamin, riboflavin, niacin, and ascorbic acid. Those nutrients were selected by the researchers because they are important to human nutrition and because quantified data are available and are presented for animal foods. Only Keene considers a nonfood need, that is the need for hides for clothing manufacture.

The models yield relatively similar predictions for the faunal portion of the diet (Table 3-2). The optimal solution for Late Archaic in Michigan includes fish, deer, turtle, beaver, and raccoon. The optimal solutions for Late Woodland and Fort Ancient in Indiana include fish, turtle, freshwater mussels, and deer. The optimal solution for the Hypsithermal (Middle Archaic) in the lower Illinois River valley includes deer, raccoon, and turtle and for the historic period model includes deer, squirrel, raccoon, muskrat, waterfowl, fish, turtle, and freshwater mussel. The focus on terrestrial resources in the Hypsithermal model results from the use of the "smallest area within which all nutrient requirements can be satisfied" (Hewitt 1983:285) and an overly negative view of aquatic resource availability during the Hypsithermal. Geomorphic and paleoecological research (Styles 1986) suggests that aquatic resource availability in the lower Illinois River valley improved during the mid-Holocene.

Keene argues that energy, not protein, is the limiting factor for temperate hunters and gatherers. The sensitivity of the models to calcium needs is responsible for the strong and perhaps surprising emphasis on turtles in all of the models and freshwater mussels in Reidhead's models and Hewitt's historic model. If mussels were abundant, then they would have figured into the optimal solution for Michigan as well (Keene 1981:171).

All of the researchers recognize that secondary resources would also be utilized. For example, Reidhead (1980:167) suggests that other resources such as turkey, elk, raccoon, beaver, waterfowl, bear, opossum, squirrel, and muskrat could have been exploited without a big increase in labor costs. On the basis of his analysis of opportunity costs, Hewitt (1983:284, 285) indicates that attractive resources during the Hypsithermal would probably have included waterfowl, wolf, coyote, freshwater mussels, turkey, and muskrat. Attractive resources for the historic period would have also included wolf, river otter, fox, coyote, beaver, and turkey.

Some of the differences in models result from differences in reconstructions of faunal availability between the three regions; others result from differences in plant foods included in the models based on reconstructed availability and temporal subsistence change. Keene (1981) considers greens, bush fruit, tree fruits, tubers, hickory nuts, acorns, hazelnuts, black walnuts, and beechnuts; only greens and bush fruit occur in the optimal solution for the Late Archaic.

Table 3-2. *Optimal Solutions for Faunal Exploitation Based on Linear Programming Models*

Fauna	Model				
	Middle Archaic Illinois	Late Archaic Michigan	Late Woodland Indiana	Fort Ancient Indiana	Historic Illinois
Mussel			*	*	*
Fish		*	*	*	*
Turtle	*	*	*	*	*
Waterfowl					*
Deer	*	*	*	*	*
Beaver		*			
Raccoon	*	*			*
Squirrel					*
Muskrat					*

Sources: Keene (1981:157, 169)—Late Archaic in Michigan; Reidhead (1980:158, 173, 1981:87, 97)—Late Woodland and Fort Ancient in Indiana; Hewitt (1983:284–285)—Middle Archaic (Hypsithermal) and historic in Illinois .
* = appears in optimal solution.

Hewitt (1983) considers greens, fruits, tubers, hickory nuts, acorns, hazelnuts, walnuts, and weed seeds. All of those plant foods, except weed seeds, occur in his optimal solution for the Hypsithermal. Reidhead's (1980, 1981) optimal solution for the Late Woodland consists of acorns, fruits, greens, hickory nuts, tubers, maple sugar, squash, and weed seeds. The optimal solution for Fort Ancient plants includes maize, fruits, greens, maple sugar, squash, tubers, and weed seeds. According to Reidhead, the introduction of maize into the Fort Ancient model "results in an important restructuring of nutrient demands. . . . With the introduction of corn, which is a relatively low cost source of energy with poor quality protein, a new dimension in nutrient demands is added. In the fall, protein emerges as the major limiting nutrient (of the Fort Ancient model)" (1980:174). The shift to maize agriculture results in a shift from energy to protein as a limiting factor in the diet.

Nutritional Significance of Shifts in Midwestern Faunal Exploitation

The greatest variation in archaeological faunal records occurs in the representation of fish, deer, and other terrestrial mammals. Assessments of the nutritional value of animal foods are summarized by Keene (1981:136–137) and Reidhead (1981:54–56). Fish are important sources of food energy and protein. Use of fish generally increases through time and must have carried some nutritional benefits. Fish meat is a good source of calcium, and entrails are relatively high in vitamin A (Keene 1981:136). Keene (1981:171) notes that a strong emphasis on fish in his model was based on the model's sensitivity to calcium requirements. Proportional use of white-tailed deer generally decreases throughout prehistory. White-tailed deer meat was an important source of food energy and protein. Organ meet from deer is an important source of iron, vitamin A, and niacin. Meat from other terrestrial animals provided good sources of food energy and protein (Keene 1981:136–137). Their overall use also declines through time.

Some temporal variation in the use of freshwater mussels, aquatic birds, and semiaquatic mammals was also noted. Freshwater mussels are poor sources of food energy and protein; however, they are excellent sources of calcium, iron, and phosphorous (Keene 1981:136). Use of mussels appears to decline in the late prehistoric period in the lower Illinois River valley. The loss of calcium from mussels may have been offset to a degree by increased use of fish. Aquatic birds such as waterfowl are good sources of food energy and protein, but they are not extraordinary for other nutrients (Keene 1981:137). Use may increase slightly through time in the lower Illinois River valley but doesn't change much in the central Mississippi River valley. Use of semiaquatic mammals may show a slight increase through time. Semiaquatic mammals such as beaver and muskrat are also good sources of protein and food energy. Beaver meat is an excellent energy source and is also high in vitamin A and riboflavin. Muskrat is also a good source of riboflavin (Keene 1981:136).

Certainly plant foods offer alternative sources for many of these nutrients. For example, nuts, oily and starchy seeds, maize, and maple syrup are all good sources of food energy (see Asch and Asch [1978:307]; Keene [1981:138]; Reidhead [1981:57–58] for nutritional values of plant foods). Some nuts and oily seeds are high in protein, although the protein is not as balanced as animal protein. In general, wild plant foods do not provide as much calcium as freshwater mussels, but hazelnuts and chenopods are better sources than turtles (Keene 1981:138). Marsh elder, or sumpweed (*Iva annua*), is an excellent source of calcium (Asch and Asch 1978:306). Some plant foods including chenopods, black walnuts, marsh elder, and squash seeds are good sources of iron but may not be as easy for humans to utilize (Asch and Asch 1978:306). The oily seeds provide the best source of phosphorous available (Asch and Asch 1978:307). Black walnuts provide more than freshwater mussels. Acorns, nuts, chenopods, and maize are also good sources of phosphorous. Greens are the best sources of vitamin A (Keene 1981:138). Marsh elder and sunflower seeds are good sources of thiamin. None of the plant foods are good sources of riboflavin. Greens, bush fruit, tubers, and squash flesh are the best sources of ascorbic acid. Marsh elder is an excellent source of niacin; other plant foods are poorer sources than many animal foods.

Use of these plant foods also varied through time in the lower Illinois River valley (Asch and Asch 1985). Nuts—especially hickory nuts—dominate in Archaic period botanical assemblages. Starchy and oily seeds from goosefoot

(Chenopodium berlandieri) and marsh elder *(Iva annua)* respectively increase in abundance during the Late Archaic period of the lower Illinois River valley, and those plants were probably cultivated by 4,000 years ago. Other early cultigens may have included squash *(Cucurbita sp.)*, bottlegourd *(Lagenaria siceraria)*, and sunflower *(Helianthus annuus)*. Squash first appears in the lower Illinois River valley around 7000 B.P., but its representation increases in Middle Woodland contexts around 2000 B.P. By the Middle Woodland period, the list of cultigens includes squash, bottlegourd, marsh elder, sunflower, and the four plants of the starchy seed complex (goosefoot, knotweed [*Polygonum erectum*], maygrass [*Phalaris caroliniana*], and little barley [*Hordeum pusillum*]). Maize *(Zea mays)* was introduced in the Midwest by A.D. 600 in the late Late Woodland period but was not common until after A.D. 800 (Asch and Asch 1985:199). Common bean *(Phaseolus vulgaris)* has been recovered at several Mississippian sites (ca. 760 B.P.) in the lower Illinois River valley but is sparsely represented (Asch and Asch 1985:199). Trends in plant utilization recorded for the American Bottom (Johannessen 1984) are similar. Nutshell roughly declines through time and corresponds to an increase in starchy and oily seeds. Maize first appears in the Late Woodland period with a dramatic increase in the Emergent Mississippian period. The earliest squash remains from the American Bottom are from the Early Woodland period (2500 B.P.; Johannessen 1984:207). However, two blossom scars from squash *(Cucurbita cf. pepo)* are recorded for early Late Archaic contexts (Stratum 9E, ca. 4700 B.P.) at Modoc Rock Shelter in the central Mississippi Valley (King 1992:83).

The most significant change relative to human health and nutrition would be the overall decline in the representation of deer and other terrestrial mammals during the late prehistoric period. The reduced proportion of deer is noted for early Late Woodland sites (ca. 1500 B.P.) in the lower Illinois and central Mississippi River valleys and continues through the Mississippian period in both areas. Those sites also show relatively low proportions of other terrestrial mammals. The potential reduction in the proportion of red meat in the diet is even more pronounced for protohistoric Oneota populations such as the one represented in the A.D. 1300 component at the Morton site in the central Illinois River valley (Styles and King 1990).

As noted by Reidhead (1980, 1981), the introduction of maize—a good source of energy but a poor source of protein—resulted in a shift from energy to protein as a limiting factor in the diet. As noted above, maize was introduced into the midwestern United States by A.D. 600 but was not common until after A.D. 800. The reduction in red meat is initially associated with early Late Woodland sites that predate reliance on maize. Those sites however show abundant evidence for the cultivation of squash and oily and starchy seeds by sedentary horticulturists. The reduction in the use of terrestrial sources of red meat is linked with increased reliance on cultivated plants and increasingly sedentary occupations.

Bioanthropological studies provide some support and evidence for the impact of the dietary shifts. On the basis of studies of Middle and late Late Woodland populations in the lower Illinois River valley, Buikstra (1977) reported that the late Late Woodland population showed a decrease in acute stress markers (Harris lines and enamel hypoplasia), which she related to the greater reliability and storability of agricultural food products. However, the late Late Woodland population showed greater evidence for chronic stress markers (slower maturation rate and decreased cortical thickness of femora), acute infectious disease, and stable strontium content in bone. She ultimately linked those shifts to increased reliance on maize that resulted in a greater carbohydrate load and malnutrition, which in turn contributed to decreased resistance to infectious disease. Milner's (1982) analysis of nonelite Mississippian populations from peripherally located sites in the American Bottom revealed the presence of cribra orbitalia and porotic hyperostosis, which indicated that many young children suffered from chronic iron deficiency anemia. Following Cook (1979), Milner (1982:233) suggested that weaning age children may have been fed maize gruel, which was deficient in protein and iron. Heavy use of maize in conjunction with a reduction in red meat would have promoted problems associated with malnutrition and iron deficiency anemia, specifically among young children. The infant mortality rate was high for Mississippian populations of the American Bottom (Milner 1984). However, if infants and children survived, then their diets appeared to improve. He found evidence for irregularly spaced Harris lines, which suggested that stress occurred, but not on a regular seasonal basis. Dental decay was rampant in Mississippian period adults (Milner 1984:238) and has also been linked to high carbohydrate intake. The trend toward poor nutrition appears to intensify in the latest prehistoric occupations in the midwestern United States. For example, the Oneota population (A.D. 1300) associated with the Morton site in the central Illinois River valley provided abundant evidence for iron deficiency anemia and various infectious diseases (Milner and Smith 1990).

Conclusion

As illustrated by this case study, faunal remains from archaeological sites can provide critical data for paleodietary reconstructions, especially when potential biases resulting from recovery techniques, preservation, taphonomy, and settlement function are considered. Because of the desire to examine temporal subsistence trends, an important element of this comparative study was the selection and comparison of faunal assemblages from components and sites for which recovery techniques, preservation, and settlement function were broadly comparable.

Analyses of faunal data from carefully selected archaeological sites in the lower and central Mississippi River valleys document differences in Holocene faunal assemblages that reflect temporal changes in aboriginal subsistence and settlement practices. With increasingly sedentary occupations in the river valleys, the emphasis on renewable aquatic resources, especially fish, increased. Overall use of terrestrial resources, especially mammals, declined. The decline in the use of red meat correlates with increased emphasis on cultivation and ultimately with evidence for malnutrition and related increases in infectious disease. The major shifts in faunal exploitation correspond to shifts in overall subsistence and settlement and mobility strategies as occupations changed from short-term residential camps to relatively more sedentary base-camp occupations to even more sedentary homesteads, villages, and towns. As indicated by the nutritional analyses and bioanthropological data, the subsistence choices made by prehistoric peoples clearly were not always optimal for nutrition.

Acknowledgments

I would like to thank Kristin Sobolik for her invitation to participate in the conference on paleonutrition and for her constructive comments on early drafts of this paper. The paper also benefited from suggestions provided by Bruce McMillan of the Illinois State Museum and three anonymous reviewers. The faunal data from Modoc Rock Shelter that is incorporated in this study was synthesized by Karli White, Illinois State Museum, and me with support from the National Endowment for the Humanities (Research Grant: RO-21430). Erich Schroeder, Illinois State Museum, prepared Figure 3-1 using Harvard Graphics. Figures 3-2 and 3-3 were generated with assistance from Eric Grimm, Illinois State Museum, using Tilia, a computer program designed by him for the summarization of pollen data.

References

Asch, D. L., and N. B. Asch
    1978   The Economic Potential of *Iva annua* and Its Prehistoric Importance in the Lower Illinois Valley. In *The Nature and Status of Ethnobotany*, edited by R. I. Ford, pp. 301–341. Anthropological Papers No. 67. Museum of Anthropology, University of Michigan, Ann Arbor.
    1985   Prehistoric Plant Cultivation in West-Central Illinois. In *Prehistoric Food Production in North America*, edited by R. I. Ford, pp. 149–203. Anthropological Papers No. 75. Museum of Anthropology, University of Michigan, Ann Arbor.
Brown, J. A.
    1985   Long-term Trends to Sedentism and the Emergence of Complexity in the American Midwest. In *Prehistoric Hunter-Gatherers: The Emergence of Cultural Complexity*, edited by T. D. Price and J. A. Brown, pp. 201–231. Academic Press, New York.
Buikstra, J. E.
    1977   Biocultural Dimensions of Archeological Study: A Regional Perspective. In *Biocultural Adaptation in Prehistoric America*, edited by R. L. Blakely, pp. 67–84. Southern Anthropological Society Proceedings No. 11. University of Georgia Press, Athens.
Colburn, M. L.
    1985   Faunal Remains from the Hill Creek Site. In *The Hill Creek Homestead and the Late Mississippian Settlement in the Lower Illinois Valley*, edited by M. D. Conner, pp. 171–192. Kampsville Archeological Center Research Series, vol. 1. Center for American Archeology, Kampsville, Illinois.
Cook, D. C.
    1979   Subsistence Base and Health in the Prehistoric Illinois Valley: Evidence

from the Human Skeleton. *Medical Anthropology* 3:109–124.

Cross, P. G.

1983a Faunal Remains from the Mund Phase. In *The Mund Site (11-S-435)*, by A. C. Fortier, F. A. Finney, and R. B. Lacampagne, pp. 318–341. American Bottom Archaeology FAI-270 Site Reports, vol. 5. University of Illinois Press, Urbana.

1983b Vertebrate Faunal Material from the Early Woodland Florence Phase. In *The Florence Street Site (11-S-458)*, by T. E. Emerson, G. R. Milner, and D. Jackson, pp. 146–155. American Bottom Archaeology FAI-270 Site Reports, vol 2. University of Illinois Press, Urbana.

1984 Vertebrate Faunal Remains from the Julien Site. In *The Julien Site (11-S-63)*, by G. R. Milner, pp. 223–243. American Bottom Archaeology FAI-270 Site Reports, vol. 7. University of Illinois Press, Urbana.

Earle, T. K., and A. L. Christenson

1980 *Modeling Change in Prehistoric Subsistence Economies*. Academic Press, New York.

Gilbert, R. I., Jr., and J. H. Mielke (editors)

1985 *The Analysis of Prehistoric Diets*. Academic Press, Orlando.

Grayson, D. K.

1984 *Quantitative Zooarchaeology: Topics in the Analysis of Archaeological Faunas*. Academic Press, New York.

1991 The Small Mammals of Gatecliff Shelter: Did People Make a Difference? In *Beamers, Bobwhites, and Blue-Points: Tributes to the Career of Paul W. Parmalee*, edited by J. R. Purdue, W. E. Klippel, and B. W. Styles, pp. 99–109. Scientific Papers, vol. XXIII. Illinois State Museum, Springfield.

Hajic, E. R.

1990 *Late Pleistocene and Holocene Landscape Evolution, Depositional Subsystems, and Stratigraphy in the Lower Illinois River Valley and Adjacent Central Mississippi River Valley*. Unpublished Ph.D. dissertation, Department of Geology, University of Illinois, Urbana-Champaign.

Hawkes, K., and J. O'Connell

1992 On Optimal Foraging Models and Subsistence Transitions. *Current Anthropology* 33:63–66.

Hewitt, J. S.

1983 *Optimal Foraging Models for the Lower Illinois River Valley*. Ph.D. dissertation, Northwestern University. University Microfilms, Ann Arbor.

Hill, F. C.

1975 *Effects of the Environment on Animal Exploitation by Archaic Inhabitants of the Koster Site, Illinois*. Unpublished Ph.D. dissertation, Department of Biology, University of Louisville, Louisville, Kentucky.

Hoffmeister, D. F.

1989 *Mammals of Illinois*. University of Illinois Press, Urbana.

Hoffmeister, D. F., and C. O. Mohr

1972 *Fieldbook of Illinois Mammals*. Dover Publications, New York.

Jochim, M. A.

1988 Optimal Foraging and the Division of Labor. *American Anthropologist* 90:130–136.

Johannessen, S.

1984 Paleoethnobotany. In *American Bottom Archaeology*, edited by C. J. Bareis and J. W. Porter, pp. 197–214. University of Illinois Press, Urbana.

Keene, A. S.

1981 *Prehistoric Foraging in a Temperate Forest: A Linear Programming Model*.

Academic Press, New York.

1983   Biology, Behavior, and Borrowing: A Critical Examination of Optimal Foraging Theory in Archaeology. In *Archaeological Hammers and Theories,* edited by J. A. Moore and A. S. Keene, pp. 137–155. Academic Press, New York.

1985   Nutrition and Economy: Models for the Study of Prehistoric Diet. In *The Analysis of Prehistoric Diets,* edited by R. I. Gilbert, Jr., and J. H. Mielke, pp. 155–190. Academic Press, Orlando.

Kelly, L. S.

1987   Patrick Phase Faunal Materials. In *The Range Site: Archaic Through Late Woodland Occupations,* by J. E. Kelly, A. C. Fortier, S. J. Ozuk, and J. A. Williams, pp. 350–400. American Bottom Archaeology FAI-270 Site Reports, vol. 16. University of Illinois Press, Urbana.

1990a   Dohack Phase Faunal Analysis. In *The Range Site 2: The Emergent Mississippian Dohack and Range Phase Occupations,* by J. E. Kelly, S. J. Ozuk, and J. A. Williams, pp. 237–265. American Bottom Archaeology FAI-270 Site Reports, vol. 20. University of Illinois Press, Urbana.

1990b   Range Phase Faunal Analysis. In *The Range Site 2: The Emergent Mississippian Dohack and Range Phase Occupations,* by J. E. Kelly, S. J. Ozuk, and J. A. Williams, pp. 487–511. American Bottom Archaeology FAI-270 Site Reports, vol. 20. University of Illinois Press, Urbana.

Kelly, L. S., and P. G. Cross

1984   Zooarchaeology. In *American Bottom Archaeology,* edited by C. J. Bareis and J. W. Porter, pp. 215–232. University of Illinois Press, Urbana.

King, F. B.

1992   Analysis of Plant Remains. In *Late Archaic Components at Modoc Rock Shelter, Randolph County, Illinois,* by S. R. Ahler, M. J. Bade, F. B. King, B. W. Styles, and P. J. Thorson, pp. 81–92. Reports of Investigations No. 48. Illinois State Museum, Springfield.

King, J. E.

1981   Late Quaternary Vegetational History of Illinois. *Ecological Monographs* 51:43–62.

King, J. E., and W. H. Allen, Jr.

1977   A Holocene Vegetation Record for the Mississippi River Valley, Southeastern Missouri. *Quaternary Research* 8:307–323.

Klippel, W. E., and W. B. Turner

1991   Terrestrial Gastropods from Glade Sere and the Hayes Shell Midden in Middle Tennessee. In *Beamers, Bobwhites, and Blue-Points: Tributes to the Career of Paul W. Parmalee,* edited by J. R. Purdue, W. E. Klippel, and B. W. Styles, pp. 177–188. Scientific Papers, vol. XXIII. Illinois State Museum, Springfield.

Lyman, R. L.

1984   Bone Density and Differential Survivorship of Fossil Classes. *Journal of Anthropological Archaeology* 3:259–299.

1991   Taphonomic Problems with Archaeological Analyses of Animal Carcass Utilization and Transport. In *Beamers, Bobwhites, and Blue-Points: Tributes to the Career of Paul W. Parmalee,* edited by J. R. Purdue, W. E. Klippel, and B. W. Styles, pp. 125–138. Scientific Papers, vol. XXIII. Illinois State Museum, Springfield.

McMillan, R. B., and W. E. Klippel

1981   Environmental Changes and Hunter-Gatherer Adaptations in the Southern Prairie Peninsula. *Journal of Archaeological Science* 8(3):215–245.

Milner, G. R.
    1982   *Measuring Prehistoric Levels of Health: A Study of Mississippian Period Skeletal Remains from the American Bottom, Illinois.* Ph.D. dissertation, Northwestern University. University Microfilms, Ann Arbor.
    1984   Bioanthropology. In *American Bottom Archaeology,* edited by C. J. Bareis and J. W. Porter, pp. 233–240. University of Illinois Press, Urbana.
Milner, G. R., and V. G. Smith
    1990   Oneota Human Skeletal Remains. In *Archaeological Investigations at the Morton Village and Norris Farms 36 Cemetery,* edited by S. K. Santure, A. D. Harn, and D. Esarey, pp. 111–148. Reports of Investigations No. 45. Illinois State Museum, Springfield.
Neusius, S. W.
    1982   *Early-Middle Archaic Subsistence Strategies: Changes in Faunal Exploitation at the Koster Site.* Ph.D dissertation, Northwestern University. University Microfilms, Ann Arbor.
Parmalee, P. W., and A. E. Bogan
    1980   Vertebrate Remains from Early European and Historic Indian Occupations at the Waterman Site, Randolph County, Illinois. *Transactions of the Illinois State Academy of Science* 73(3):49–54. Springfield.
Purdue, J. R., and B. W. Styles
    1986   *Dynamics of Mammalian Distribution in the Holocene of Illinois.* Reports of Investigations No. 41. Illinois State Museum, Springfield.
    1987   Changes in the Mammalian Fauna of Illinois and Missouri during the Late Pleistocene and Holocene. In *Late Quaternary Mammalian Biogeography and Environments of the Great Plains and Prairies,* edited by R. W. Graham, H. A. Semken, Jr., and M. A. Graham, pp. 144–174. Scientific Papers, vol. XXII. Illinois State Museum, Springfield.
Reidhead, V. A.
    1976   *Optimization and Food Procurement at the Prehistoric Leonard Haag Site, Southeast Indiana: A Linear Programming Approach.* Ph.D. dissertation, Indiana University. University Microfilms, Ann Arbor.
    1979   Linear Programming Models in Archaeology. *Annual Review of Anthropology* 8:543–578.
    1980   The Economics of Subsistence Change: A Test of an Optimization Model. In *Modeling Change in Prehistoric Subsistence Economies,* edited by T. K. Earle and A. L. Christenson, pp. 141–186. Academic Press, New York.
    1981   A Linear Programming Model of Prehistoric Subsistence Optimization: A Southeastern Indiana Example. *Prehistory Research Series* VI(1):1–277. Indiana Historical Society, Indianapolis.
Smith, B. D.
    1986   The Archaeology of the Southeastern United States: From Dalton to de Soto (10,500–500 B.P.). In *Advances in World Archaeology,* vol. 5, edited by F. Wendorf and A. E. Close, pp. 1–92. Academic Press, New York.
Styles, B. W.
    1981   *Faunal Exploitation and Resource Selection: Early Late Woodland Subsistence in the Lower Illinois Valley.* Scientific Papers No. 3. Northwestern University Archeological Program, Evanston, Illinois.
    1984   Review of Prehistoric Foraging in a Temperate Forest: A Linear Programming Model, by Arthur S. Keene. *American Antiquity* 49:433–435.
    1986   Aquatic Exploitation in the Lower Illinois River Valley: The Role of Paleoecological Change. In *Foraging, Collecting, and Harvesting: Archaic Period*

54 | *B. W. Styles*

Subsistence and Settlement in the Eastern Woodlands, edited by S. W. Neusius, pp. 145–174. Occasional Paper No. 6. Center for Archaeological Investigations, Southern Illinois University, Carbondale.

Styles, B. W., S. R. Ahler, and M. L. Fowler
  1983   Modoc Rock Shelter Revisited. In *Archaic Hunters and Gatherers in the American Midwest*, edited by J. L. Phillips and J. A. Brown, pp. 261–297. Academic Press, New York.

Styles, B. W., and F. B. King
  1990   Faunal and Floral Remains from the Bold Counselor Phase Village. In *Archaeological Investigations at the Morton Village and Norris Farms 36 Cemetery*, edited by S. K. Santure, A. D. Harn, and D. Esarey, pp. 57–65. Reports of Investigations No. 45. Illinois State Museum, Springfield.

Styles, B. W., S. W. Neusius, and J. R. Purdue
  1982   The Evolution of Faunal Exploitation Strategies: A Case Study in the Lower Illinois Valley. Paper Presented at the 47th Annual Meeting of the Society for American Archaeology, Minneapolis.

Styles, B. W., and J. R. Purdue
  1991   Ritual and Secular Use of Fauna by Middle Woodland Peoples in Western Illinois. In *Beamers, Bobwhites, and Blue-Points: Tributes to the Career of Paul W. Parmalee*, edited by J. R. Purdue, W. E. Klippel, and B. W. Styles, pp. 421–436. Scientific Papers, vol. XXIII. Illinois State Museum, Springfield.

Styles, B. W., J. R. Purdue, and M. Colburn
  1985   Faunal Exploitation at the Smiling Dan Site. In *Smiling Dan: Structure and Function at a Middle Woodland Settlement in the Illinois Valley*, edited by B. D. Stafford and M. B. Sant, pp. 402–446. Kampsville Archeological Center Research Series, vol. 2. Center for American Archeology, Kampsville, Illinois.

Styles, B. W., J. R. Purdue, and F. B. King
  1984   An Overview of Aboriginal Subsistence in the Prairie Peninsula. Paper presented at the conference on Environmental and Cultural Change in the Prairie Peninsula, Illinois State Museum, Springfield.

Styles, B. W., and K. White
  1991   Shifts in Archaic Period Faunal Exploitation in the Mississippi River Valley: Modoc Rock Shelter Revisited. Paper presented at the 56th Annual Meeting of the Society for American Archaeology, New Orleans.

Styles, T. R.
  1985   *Holocene and Late Pleistocene Geology of the Napoleon Hollow Site in the Lower Illinois River Valley*. Kampsville Archeological Center Research Series, vol. 5. Center for American Archeology, Kampsville, Illinois.

Thorson, P. J., and B. W. Styles
  1992   Analysis of Faunal Remains. In *Late Archaic Components at Modoc Rock Shelter, Randolph County, Illinois*, by S. R. Ahler, M. J. Bade, F. B. King, B. W. Styles, and P. J. Thorson, pp. 52–80. Reports of Investigations No. 48. Illinois State Museum, Springfield.

Wing, E. S., and A. B. Brown
  1979   *Paleonutrition: Method and Theory in Prehistoric Foodways*. Academic Press, New York.

4. Nutrition, Small Mammals, and Agriculture

Christine R. Szuter

Abstract: The significant role of small mammals in the diet of prehistoric agriculturalists in the Greater Southwest is addressed in this paper. Changes in methodologies have led to greater recovery of small animals, thus allowing for the assessment of their depositional history and a consideration of their role in the diet. The modifications prehistoric inhabitants made to their environment through agriculture and associated activities created an environment particularly favorable to small animals. The hunting of small animals, however, extended far beyond garden hunting and was incorporated into other daily activities. Changes in socioeconomic and demographic factors that accompanied agricultural activities also contributed to the inclusion of small animals in the diet.

Introduction

In our own modern society we have only recently considered the nutritive value of small portions of meat. Formerly a healthy and nutritious diet would have included a substantial proportion of meat—at least four servings per day. In prehistoric societies of the American Southwest, large game may have rarely been an option for most members of society, and small game may have taken on even greater significance in the diet than previously imagined.

In this paper, I argue that changing interpretative methodologies have led to the greater recovery of small animal remains from prehistoric sites.[1] The presence of the small animal remains in large quantities has forced archaeologists to reconsider their role in the prehistoric diet and their contribution to the health and nutritional status of prehistoric peoples. Second, I show that the influx into and importance of small animals in the diet are the results of agricultural activities and associated anthropogenic environmental change.[2] I

Paleonutrition: The Diet and Health of Prehistoric Americans, edited by Kristin D. Sobolik. Center for Archaeological Investigations, Occasional Paper No. 22. © 1994 by the Board of Trustees, Southern Illinois University. All rights reserved. ISBN 0-88104-078-9.

draw from the archaeological literature on the American Southwest, high-lighting research from the Hohokam culture of southcentral Arizona. I define a small animal as one smaller than a cottontail—a category that includes the majority of birds, amphibians, reptiles, insects, and rodents—and I restrict my discussion to rodents.

Methodological Considerations: The Recovery of Small Animal Remains

Archaeological evidence that rodents were part of the prehistoric diet is elusive. Archaeologists have not directed their recovery techniques toward research questions regarding the role of small animals in the diet, and the consumption of rodents is not necessarily an activity that leaves an abundance of direct archaeological evidence. The lack of adequate recovery procedures, coupled with the general lack of archaeological evidence, does not lead to a clear understanding of the role of small animals in the prehistoric diet.

One of the major widespread methodological changes in excavation techniques during the past two decades centers on retrieval strategies employed at sites. Ultimately, research interests structure what is retrieved from excavations, and what is retrieved further reinforces prevailing research interests. If only known and readily accepted economic species (for example, jack rabbits, cottontails, antelope, and deer) are selectively brought back from an excavated site, then interpretations of subsistence practices and paleonutrition focus on those animals. If, however, all bones (particularly small and unidentifiable ones) are retrieved, then discussion of the role of small animals in the diet can be broached.

I conducted a regional analysis of animal use among prehistoric agriculturalists in the Sonoran Desert by examining 136 Late Archaic and Hohokam faunal assemblages (Szuter 1991). Detailed information for each assemblage and site, including excavation strategy and size of mesh screens, was recorded. The results of that regional study demonstrated that changes in excavation and retrieval strategies through time affected the composition of and subsequent interpretations of animal use.

Excavations of Hohokam sites conducted prior to the mid-1970s had faunal assemblages dominated by artiodactyl remains compared to excavations carried out after that time. Based on the composition of those faunal assemblages, archaeologists (i.e., Greene and Mathews 1976) argued that deer was a critical and substantial component of the Hohokam diet. In other words, the significance of large game to the diet was emphasized over the contribution of small animals because that is what had been recovered.

The decisions made during archaeological recovery ultimately determine the relative composition of different animal species to the assemblage. Recovery strategies start with an archaeologist choosing a particular site and what portion of it will be excavated. Once an area is delimited, excavation procedures—covering a vast array of possibilities—are put into effect. Mesh size is one of those choices. A now-overstated maxim among archaeologists is that finer mesh will increase the quantity of smaller-sized remains that are recovered. Since the late 1960s archaeologists have demonstrated that repeatedly (Clason and Prummel 1977; Payne 1972; Struever 1968; Thomas 1969). Soil put through flotation and water-screening devices held a vast array of animal bones as well as charred plant remains that had previously been left undiscovered.

As excavation and retrieval strategies changed during the late 1970s, smaller animals were recovered more frequently and therefore formed larger percentages of faunal assemblages. Specifically, rodents were more abundant. Nonetheless, their presence was often explained as a result of their behavior; that is, they had burrowed and died at the site. Little or no attention was given to the depositional context of rodents and to whether they were indeed intrusive.

What has not been systematically addressed, however, is how variation in screening procedures on a regional scale affect faunal recovery. For example, although use of quarter-inch mesh screen is the orthodox recovery procedure at most Hohokam sites, the manner in which the screening is carried out can deviate substantially from that standard. At some sites all of the feature fill passes through a quarter-inch mesh screen; at others only a portion of it does. Some archaeologists screen overburden while others do not. Other decisions affect what is recovered from the screen. Is everything that does not pass through the screen collected? Or are only items "larger than a quarter" retrieved? While the date of publication, and thus standards prevailing at different times, offers some clues as to the differences in recovery strategy, it does not explain the variability in the quantity of different taxonomic groups found in 136 faunal assemblages examined. The question, then, is whether a portion of that variability is attributable to variation in screening practices.

I initially assumed that quarter-inch mesh screen was standard, with the inclusion of flotation samples at times. Such was not the case. The fill from the sites passed through half-inch, quarter-inch, eighth-inch, flotation, and fine-mesh water screens. Screening was inconsistent not only between sites but within sites as well. Many archaeologists did not discuss the mesh size employed. Moreover, zooarchaeologists rarely reported their finds in relation to recovery techniques.

The presence of a screen at a site merely indicates that some quantity of dirt passed through that screen and that some, but not necessarily all, of the screened material was retrieved. In order to assess the relationship between mesh size and quantity of small animals recovered, information on screening techniques was recorded for each site.

The median percentage of rodent remains recovered from all 136 sites is 5. When half-inch screens were used during excavation, the identified rodent percentage is always less than the median of 5. If the mesh size was decreased to one-quarter inch, but not all feature fill and overburden were screened, then the percentage never exceeds 20.2 for any one site. On the other hand, when all feature fill passed through a quarter-inch mesh screen, the quantity of rodent remains ranges up to 100%, and very frequently exceeds 20%. Greater variability in the percentage of rodent remains in the assemblage was observed among a group of sites where all feature fill passed through quarter-inch screen.

The addition of flotation samples to the quarter-inch screening procedure does not noticeably increase the range of rodent percentages—probably because material from flotation samples account for a small fraction of all faunal remains. A closer examination of the material recovered from flotation samples and fine mesh water screening, however, indicates that an abundance of smaller animals are recovered. While the use of flotation samples leads to the recovery of small animals, the impact of that discovery has not been systematically assessed. Because flotation samples are collected for the ethnobotanist and not the zooarchaeologist, the samples may not be representative of deposited faunal remains. In addition, unless ethnobotanists are knowledgeable about microfaunal remains, they may not collect them for the zooarchaeologist. Finally, faunal remains need to be reported by screening technique in order to fully understand their effect on animals recovered.

An example of the impact of water screening in the southern Southwest is Gillespie's (1989) analysis of the faunal assemblage from AZ AA:16:161, a Hohokam site located in the Avra Valley outside of Tucson. He demonstrates the importance of water-screening techniques on faunal recovery. The soil from a 1 x 1 m grid, 24 cm deep, in a pithouse yielded 36% of the bone from the entire site. Gillespie enumerates five additional consequences of water screening: (1) a greater abundance of smaller vertebrates, (2) a greater number and diversity of rodents and small vertebrates, (3) a higher percentage of unidentified bone, (4) a higher percentage of *Lepus* fragments not identified to species, and (5) a skewing in the relative frequencies of different skeletal elements. In addition, a burned woodrat element was recovered. Water screening has significant implications for understanding prehistoric hunting. Small animal use may have been more pervasive and may have contributed greatly to the diet.

The results of this regional analysis indicate that the percentage of rodent remains recovered from a site is affected not only by mesh size but also by consistency of screening techniques used at a site. Excavation strategies and recovery techniques affect characteristics of the faunal assemblage that then impact our interpretations of prehistoric diet and nutrition.

Relationship Between Rodents, the Environment, and People

Descriptions and data from ethnographic and ecological sources substantiate the existence of a symbiotic relationship between rodents and people that is mediated by the environment. Since small animals are diverse, numerous, and easy to study, considerable ecological research has been conducted on their habitat preference. Numerous changes in small animal populations occur in environments that have been modified by humans.

Generally, rodent populations are attracted to areas of human disturbance. When grazing and cultivation remove vegetation, rodent densities have been shown to decrease (Reynolds 1980) because their food and cover have been eliminated. Cultivated fields, however, that have not been tilled support greater species diversity than conventionally tilled fields (Warburton and Klimstra 1984). Untilled fields have both crop residue and vegetative cover between the rows that increase habitat complexity. Conventional tilling, on the other hand, removes plants and diminishes both cover and food, thus reducing the wildlife carrying capacity (1984:329). An untilled field would be comparable to a prehistoric field where many noncultivated plants remain, thereby leading to an increase in rodent density.

Such human disturbance of the environment leads to the invasion of pioneer plants or disturbance plant communities that are highly attractive to rodents (Pelikan and Nesvadboda 1979:209) because they provide food and shelter. Likewise, "edge" areas that act as connectors, or links, between different habitats create a habitat for a variety of rodents and birds (Wegner and Merriam 1979).

The developmental cycle of an agricultural field—from planting, through harvest, through field abandonment—creates a continuous change of micro-habitats that leads to fluctuations in rodent populations—from the clearing of a field, to the planting of the corn, to the harvest and corn stubble left in the field (Fleharty and Navo 1983:372). As the growing season progresses, rodent densities increase. At the end of the season the corn stubble, while providing good cover, offers little food, and therefore rodent densities decrease. Overall, modern cultivation does not completely destroy all natural habitats; neither would prehistoric agriculture have done so. Those areas located along fence-rows, shelterbelts (areas of undisturbed natural vegetation left along the edges of farmlands), ditches, and waterways support a diversity of small animal populations.

Rodents also benefit farmers by consuming weeds and insects that may harm crops and by burrowing, which increases soil friability—an advantage in clay or caliche soils found in the southern Southwest. Rodents, therefore, thrive alongside cultivated fields with their associated disturbance communities.

High species diversity in rodent communities seems closely related to the presence of food and vegetative cover found in plant communities occupying disturbed areas. Traditional agricultural systems include the intentional encouragement of volunteer plants as well as the minimal plowing of fields. Both are practices that enhance plant and, subsequently, animal populations. The archaeological implications of such practices are that traditional or prehistoric agriculture must have altered the environment in a way that encouraged pioneer plants that attracted small mammals. Those small animals, of course, could then be procured. Such ecological studies indicate that certain stages in the developmental cycle of fields, as well as any type of environmental modification that increases plant diversity, also increase small animal species diversity.

The increase in numbers and in species diversity of animal populations, however, is not sufficient evidence to argue for their use as a prehistoric food source. Both ethnographic and archaeological data need to be used in conjunction with ecological studies to argue that small animals were an integral part of the prehistoric diet.

Ethnographic sources attesting to the use and importance of rodents in the diet are abundant. A variety of indigenous peoples in the Southwest captured small game using a simple technology involving snares and traps (Spier 1928:113), direct capture, or bows and arrows (Castetter and Bell 1942:68; Castetter and Underhill 1935:42; Cushing 1920:599; Lumholtz 1902:248; Underhill 1946:85). Rodents were also killed by hurling rocks by hand or with a slingshot (Bennett and Zingg 1976:115, 117, 119; Champion 1963:340; Malkin 1956:75). Burrows were flooded and nests were burned in order to force out animals (Lumholtz 1912:330; Underhill 1946:85). Probes, in the form of shaped sticks, were poked down burrows to skewer lurking prey (Castetter and Underhill 1935:42; Cushing 1920:599). Direct archaeological evidence of such hunting practices is sparse because most of the known techniques relied upon implements made of perishable materials.

Specialization in the procurement of small game did not merely occur; rather, it was an activity that accompanied other subsistence pursuits such as the gathering of wild plants or the tending of agricultural fields (Underhill 1936:49). Magic, ceremony, and ritual were not associated with hunting small game. Because restrictions on who could hunt small game did not exist, women and small children as well as boys and men could bring home those animals (Underhill 1936:49). And since many of the animals were crop predators, hunting them served the dual purpose of ridding fields of pests while contributing to the diet.

Garden hunting—the capture of animals associated with cultivated fields—is a subsistence strategy used in response to the demands and effects of agriculture (Linares 1976). Linares (1976:332) argues that the "hunting" of those animals fills the niche that domesticated animals occupied in the Old World by substituting "*culturally created* for naturally existing mammalian biomass" (emphasis added). Garden hunting as a subsistence strategy is complementary but not restricted to agriculture. It can be done along with other activities such as field tending, collecting mesquite wood, and harvesting saguaro fruit. The capture of small animals, then, is quite complementary to other subsistence pursuits.

Once caught, small animals required very little preparation. Rodents were easily spitted and roasted with or without skinning and eviscerating (Bennett and Zingg 1976:114, 119; Cushing 1920:599; Lumholtz 1902:262; Pennington 1963:91–92). Animals (their meat, viscera, and bones) were then eaten. Any bones not consumed were disposed of informally—thrown in the garbage or inadvertently dropped into the fire during cooking.

While direct evidence of hunting small animals is minimal, numerous indirect arguments suggest that it was indeed practiced prehistorically. Differential burning and contextual analyses, immunological studies of animal protein, and coprolite studies all point to the inclusion of rodents in the diet.

The Role of Small Animals in the Diet

That archaeologists only recently have discussed rodents as a food source and a contribution to the diet is directly attributable to changing interpretative methodologies (Reinhard et al. 1991; Semé 1984; Simonetti and Cornejo 1991; Sobolik 1993; Stahl 1982; Szuter 1982, 1984, 1991; Yohe et al. 1991).

The determination of intrusive versus cultural rodent remains requires the use of multiple lines of evidence (Szuter 1982, 1984, 1991:159–165), including, but certainly not limited to, an examination of (a) ethnographic accounts that discuss the use of rodents as food, (b) ecological studies on the behavior of rodents, (c) trapping studies of rodents at and around archaeological sites, (d) experimental archaeological studies, and (e) archaeological evidence, such as the context and condition of the bone recovered, coprolite analysis, and more recently immunological studies (Yohe et al. 1991).

One of the more direct lines of evidence indicating that rodents were eaten prehistorically is the inclusion of rodent bones, teeth, and hair in human coprolites. Coprolite specimens from southwestern sites provide strong evidence that prehistoric inhabitants ingested small animals—bones and all. While such a practice might be expected during hunting-and-gathering Archaic times, humans continued to eat small animals even when they began agricultural pursuits (Reinhard et al. 1991).

Unfortunately, human coprolites are more likely to be recovered from dry cave sites and some open air Anasazi sites than from Hohokam sites. Arguments that rodents formed a part of the Hohokam diet, therefore, rely more on the context and condition of the bone, particularly the burning of skeletal elements. In Chile, Simonetti and Cornejo (1991) have also examined burned bones of select species of rodents to argue that rodents were a part of the diet. Although bone can become burned as a result of several activities that are not all associated with food preparation, one method of cooking rodents may result in differential skeletal burning.

The southwestern ethnographic record describes a method of preparing rodents that involves spitting them and roasting them whole over an open fire. Although most rodents were probably eaten whole—bones, viscera, and all—because of their small size, spitting and roasting them over an open fire may have resulted in the burning and loss of some skeletal elements. The bones that were covered with very little flesh would have burned readily as the animals were held over a roasting pit. If the rodents were roasted whole, the differential burning of the skeletal elements might have occurred. Peripheral elements, such as the metapodials, phalanges, carpi, tarsi, and caudal vertebrae, would be more likely to show evidence of burning than those elements covered by greater amounts of flesh.

Although general trash burning may also result in a similar pattern of burned skeletal elements (that is, the peripheral elements would be burned, while the nonperipheral elements that were covered with more flesh would not be), an examination of the depositional context could rule out that possibility. Burned elements that are also associated with nonperipheral unburned bone would suggest that the rodent was caught in a trash fire. If the burned elements are associated with an ashy lens, however, then their deposition may represent a cleaning episode of a hearth or roasting feature.

I examined the burned rodent elements from Hohokam sites including the Las Colinas site and a series of sites located along the Salt-Gila Aqueduct to determine if there was differential burning of rodent skeletal elements. At Las Colinas, 65% of the burned rodent elements were peripheral elements, such as the caudal vertebrae, metapodials, phalanges, and tarsi. At the SGA sites, the figure was 75%. Consequently, the differential burning of rodent bones, along with the ethnographic and ecological studies, supports the hypothesis that rodents were part of the Hohokam diet.

Nonetheless, not all remains at those sites can be attributed to cultural practices. Some of the remains are undoubtedly intrusive. The intrusive rodents presumably either died in their burrows, were dragged into the site by other animals, or were trapped in open features. An examination and comparison of weathering patterns between rodents and lagomorphs also demonstrated different depositional histories for rodents.

Rodent bones enter a site in a variety of ways. All the remains from a site are not necessarily the result of the same depositional processes. Their deposition may be quite complex and not always easy to determine; however, a detailed contextual and attribute analysis of remains from Hohokam sites supports the argument that rodents comprised part of the diet and contributed to the health and nutritional needs of the Hohokam.

Broader Implications of Garden Hunting

The alterations that the Hohokam made in their environment through agriculture and house construction provided an environment that was favorable to rodent populations. The need to rid their fields of rodent pests therefore provided an additional source of protein to their diet. While the procurement of rodents was associated with agricultural fields, it was an activity that went beyond garden hunting. Capturing rodents accompanied other activities: gathering saguaro fruit, collecting firewood, and traveling to other villages. For those reasons, direct archaeological evidence of rodent consumption will always be more elusive than that of larger animals, particularly since most of the bones were probably consumed. Coupled with problems in interpreting the rodent remains recovered from sites, strong arguments documenting the quantity and degree of reliance on them will always be difficult to make. Simulation studies comparing the rodent and lagomorph biomass available from human disturbance of the environment with the agricultural output of cultivated crops could provide information on the contribution of small animals to the diet (John Speth, personal communication 1990). Overall, it is possible to strengthen these arguments through the use of finer recovery techniques as well as through more precise documentation of archaeological context and determination of the modifications of the bone.

Notes

1. William Gillespie and I presented a more extensive paper on this topic at the 2nd Southwest Symposium, Albuquerque, New Mexico, in 1990. That paper will be published in 1994 by the University of New Mexico Press in the symposium volume *The Ancient Southwestern Community: Models and Methods for the Study of Prehistoric Social Organization*, edited by W. W. Wills and Robert D. Leonard.

2. This research is based on my published dissertation, *Hunting by Prehistoric Horticulturalists in the American Southwest* (Garland Press 1991) in the series "Evolution of North American Indians," edited by David Hurst Thomas.

References

Bennett, W. C., and R. M. Zingg
    1976   *The Tarahumara: An Indian Tribe of Northern Mexico*. Reprinted. Rio Grande Press, Glorieta, New Mexico. Originally published 1935, University of Chicago Press, Chicago.
Castetter, E. F., and W. H. Bell
    1942   *Pima and Papago Indian Agriculture*. Inter-Americana Studies No. 1. University of New Mexico Press, Albuquerque.
Castetter, E. F., and R. M. Underhill
    1935   *Ethnobiological Studies in the American Southwest: II The Ethnobiology of the Papago Indians*. University of New Mexico Press, Albuquerque.
Champion, J. R.
    1963   *A Study in Culture Persistence: The Tarahumaras of Northwestern Mexico*. Columbia University Press, New York.
Clason, A. T., and W. Prummel
    1977   Collecting, Sieving, and Archaeozoological Research. *Journal of Archaeological Science* 4:171–176.
Cushing, F. H.
    1920   *Zuni Breadstuff*. Museum of the American Indian Heye Foundation, New York.
Fleharty, E. D., and K. W. Navo
    1983   Irrigated Cornfields as Habitat for Small Mammals in the Sandsage Prairie Region of Western Kansas. *Journal of Mammalogy* 64:367–379.
Gillespie, W.
    1989   Vertebrate Faunal Remains (Hawk's Nest and AZ AA:16:161). In *Hohokam Archaeology along Phase B of the Tucson Aqueduct Central Arizona Project, Volume 4: Small Sites and Specialized Reports*, edited by J. Czaplicki and J. Ravesloot, pp. 85–98. Archaeological Series No. 178. Cultural Resource Management Division, Arizona State Museum, University of Arizona, Tucson.
Greene, J. L., and T. W. Mathews
    1976   Faunal Study of Unworked Mammalian Bones. In *The Hohokam Desert Farmers and Craftsmen*, by E. Haury, pp. 367–373. University of Arizona Press, Tucson.
Linares, O. F.
    1976   Garden Hunting in the American Tropics. *Human Ecology* 4(4):331–349.
Lumholtz, C.
    1902   *Unknown Mexico: A Record of Five Years' Exploration of the Western Sierra*

Jalisco; and among the Tarascos of Michoacan, vol. 1. Charles Scribner's Sons, New York.

1912   *New Trails in Mexico.* Charles Scribner's Sons, New York.

Malkin, B.
    1956   Seri Ethnozoology: A Preliminary Report. *Davidson Journal of Anthropology* 2(1):73–83.

Payne, S.
    1972   Partial Recovery and Sample Bias: The Results of Some Sieving Experiments. In *Papers in Economic Prehistory*, edited by E. S. Higgs, pp. 49–64. Cambridge University Press, London.

Pelikan, J., and J. Nesvadboda
    1979   Small Mammal Communities in Farms and Surrounding Fields. *Folia Zoologica* 28:209–217.

Pennington, C. W.
    1963   *The Tarahumar of Mexico: Their Environment and Material Culture.* University of Utah Press, Salt Lake City.

Reinhard, K. J., C. R. Szuter, and J. R. Ambler
    1991   Small Animal Exploitation as Evidenced in Coprolite Analysis. Ms. in possession of authors.

Reynolds, T. D.
    1980   Effects of Some Different Land Management Practices on Small Mammal Populations. *Journal of Mammalogy* 61:558–561.

Semé, M.
    1984   The Effects of Agricultural Fields on Faunal Assemblage Variation. In *Papers on the Archaeology of Black Mesa, Arizona, Volume II*, edited by S. Plog and S. Powell, pp. 139–157. Southern Illinois University Press, Carbondale .

Simonetti, J. A., and L. E. Cornejo
    1991   Archaeological Evidence of Rodent Consumption in Central Chile. *Latin American Antiquity* 2:92–96.

Sobolik, K. D.
    1993   Direct Evidence for the Importance of Small Animals to Prehistoric Diets: A Review of Coprolite Studies. *North American Archaeologist* 14(3):227–244.

Spier, L.
    1928   *Havasupai Ethnography.* American Museum of Natural History, New York.

Stahl, P. W.
    1982   On Small Mammal Remains in Archaeological Context. *American Antiquity* 47:822–829.

Struever, S.
    1968   Flotation Techniques for the Recovery of Small-scale Archaeological Remains. *American Antiquity* 33:353–362.

Szuter, C. R.
    1982   The Interpretation of Rodents from Hohokam Sites. Paper presented at the 47th Annual Meeting of the Society for American Archaeology, Minneapolis.
    1984   Faunal Exploitation and the Reliance on Small Animals among the Hohokam. In *Hohokam Archaeology along the Salt-Gila Aqueduct Central Arizona Project, Volume VII: Environment and Subsistence*, edited by L. Teague and P. Crown, pp. 139–170. Archaeological Series No. 150. Cultural Resource Management Division, Arizona State Museum, University of Arizona, Tucson.
    1991   *Hunting by Prehistoric Horticulturalists in the American Southwest.* Garland

Publishing, New York.

Thomas, D. H.
1969   Great Basin Hunting Patterns: A Quantitative Method for Treating Faunal Remains. *American Antiquity* 34:392–401.

Underhill, R. M.
1936   *The Autobiography of a Papago Woman.* American Anthropological Association Memoir No. 48. Menasha, Wisconsin.
1946   *Papago Indian Religion.* Columbia University Press, New York.

Warburton, D. B., and W. D. Klimstra
1984   Wildlife Use of No-till and Conventionally Tilled Corn Fields. *Journal of Soil and Water Conservation* 39:327–330.

Wegner, J. F., and G. Merriam
1979   Movement of Birds and Small Mammals Between a Wood and Adjoining Farmland Habitats. *Journal of Applied Ecology* 16:349–357.

Yohe, R. M., II, M. E. Newman, and J. S. Schneider
1991   Immunological Identification of Small-Mammal Proteins on Aboriginal Milling Equipment. *American Antiquity* 56:659–666.

5. The Integration and Quantification of Economic Data from a Late Preclassic Maya Community in Belize

Cathy J. Crane and H. Sorayya Carr

Abstract: Six seasons of excavations at Cerros, a Late Preclassic Maya community (ca. 300–50 B.C.) in northern Belize, resulted in the recovery of large assemblages of floral and faunal remains. In order to ascertain overall trends in the economy of the community, it was necessary to standardize the way in which the archaeobotanical, faunal, and molluscan remains were quantified. Our integrated approach allowed us to obtain a more holistic picture of the Maya subsistence economy, and it demonstrated that significant economic changes coincided with important sociopolitical changes in the community, which occurred around 100 B.C. Those changes are believed to have been the result of elite dietary preferences. Archaeological pollen samples provided additional information about plant utilization and documented the effects of the community's land-use practices upon the tropical environment.

Introduction

For many years, it was assumed that the ancient Maya had relied upon swidden agriculture with maize, beans, and squash forming the core of their diet. However, the discovery that many sites had populations too large to have been supported by swidden agriculture alone led to a number of debates about Maya subsistence. Some archaeologists argued that the Maya must have been dependent upon other resources such as root crops (Bronson 1966), ramon nuts (Puleston 1968), or seafoods (Lange 1971). It was not until 1978, however, that flotation was first used in the Maya Lowlands at the sites of Cuello (Miksicek 1991) and Cerros (Cliff 1982) to recover the actual remains

Paleonutrition: The Diet and Health of Prehistoric Americans, edited by Kristin D. Sobolik. Center for Archaeological Investigations, Occasional Paper No. 22. © 1994 by the Board of Trustees, Southern Illinois University. All rights reserved. ISBN 0-88104-078-9.

66

of the resources utilized by the Maya. Although the systematic use of flotation is slowly becoming more commonplace, it is still not universally used by Mayanists.

The Problem

The subsistence data that have been collected to date indicate that the Maya utilized a wide diversity of plant and animal resources. The combination of those foods in their diet was important nutritionally, and a true understanding of subsistence requires examining the role of all resources, especially since plants and animals, including humans, form interrelated parts of an ecological system. For example, the deforestation resulting from Maya agriculture, construction, and firewood gathering altered the composition of the tropical forest, creating new habitats for successional plants. The altering of those habitats also affected animal populations and potentially influenced the availability of meat sources. The choice of how or whether to exploit a certain resource depends not only upon the availability of that resource but also upon its perceived importance in relation to other economic pursuits. Therefore in order to understand both the nutritional status of the ancient Maya and their overall economy, it is essential to take an integrated approach to the study of botanical and faunal remains and to tie the subsistence data in with the other archaeological data.

In the Maya area, however, it is rare to find the floral and faunal data truly integrated. Typically the various classes of data are analyzed by different specialists at different institutions, and the communication between them is often sporadic. The molluscs are usually analyzed by one person and the vertebrates by another. Bone artifacts and utilized bones (such as stingray spines used in bloodletting rituals) are often sent to another specialist and may never be seen by the faunal analyst. The archaeobotanical remains and pollen are also frequently analyzed by different specialists.

Our research at the site of Cerros was not exempt from such problems, and as a result, an additional joint effort was required to integrate our data. The Cerros vertebrate fauna was analyzed by Carr (1986) and the molluscs by Hamilton (1987). Crane (1989, 1991) analyzed the archaeobotanical remains and pollen. Each of us used the standard methods of our fields to analyze and quantify the remains (e.g., Grayson 1984; Hastorf and Popper 1988).

An initial attempt by Cliff and Crane (1989) to integrate the Cerros subsistence data, however, encountered problems resulting from the different ways the data sets had been partitioned before quantification. In the case of the vertebrate fauna, minimum number of individuals (MNI), fragment counts, and biomass had been calculated separately for each excavation operation, whereas the archaeobotanical remains from all operations had been collapsed into one assemblage and ubiquity percentages calculated for each of the developmental stages. The molluscs from each lot had been identified and counted, but those data could not be used without adding crucial provenience information and making additional calculations.

We decided to standardize the quantification of our data by calculating ubiquity percentages for the vertebrates and molluscs in the same manner as was done for the archaeobotanical remains. Ubiquity, or presence, analysis disregards the absolute quantity of a taxon present, instead considering only the percentage of samples in which it occurs. Although ubiquity is commonly used in archaeobotany, it is seldom used by zooarchaeologists. Some zooarchaeologists have, however, recommended its use as a conservative quantification approach when there is a probable loss of a large (but unknown) portion of the faunal assemblage through taphonomic processes (Wheeler and Jones 1989:152–153). Moreover, our intention was to apply one quantification method to all the faunal and botanical data for the purposes of the integrative study, and interpretive difficulties inherent in the more "precise" zooarchaeological techniques such as MNI are compounded when they are applied to a broader range of materials. We chose to use ubiquity to document general trends in the Cerros faunal data, and it proved to be useful for that purpose. In fact, the trends shown by the ubiquity percentages tended to duplicate the trends shown by the original vertebrate MNI, biomass, and percentage of fragments quantifications.

Cerros

The site of Cerros was founded around 300 B.C. in a low, swampy area along the coast of Corozal Bay in northern Belize (Figure 5-1). It began as a small, egalitarian community, but by the end of the Late Preclassic it had developed into a large civic-ceremonial center surrounded by a 1,200 m-long canal and a dispersed settlement (Cliff 1982; Robertson and Freidel 1986; Scarborough 1991). During the transformation of the site into a major center, the Maya buried the original village under a massive limestone rubble plaza and monumental architecture, which helped to preserve the organic remains in the underlying village deposits. Large assemblages of archaeobotanical remains, vertebrate faunal remains, and molluscs were recovered by both flotation and quarter-inch screening of the subplaza village deposits (Feature 1A). In addition, pollen profiles were obtained from three localities in the subplaza village deposits.

Based on his excavations of Feature 1A, Cliff (1988) established a five-stage developmental sequence for the initial 300 years of occupation at Cerros. During Stages I–III, Cerros is thought to have been an egalitarian community. Significant socioeconomic changes occurred during Stage IV (ca. 100–50 B.C.). Differences in the domestic architecture, burials, and artifacts from that stage suggest the existence of a ranked society, and the first monumental architecture at Cerros was built during that time.

Unfortunately no subsistence data were recovered from Stage I deposits, and only a small number of samples were obtained from Stage V. As a result, our research was restricted to Stages II–IV, which date from approximately 275 to 50 B.C. Although archaeobotanical and faunal remains provide an incomplete record of the foods consumed by a population, it is still possible to

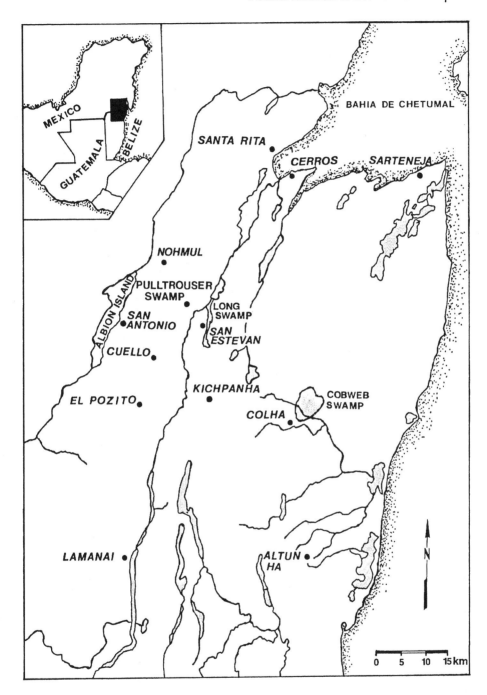

Figure 5-1. *Location of Cerros and other sites.*

draw some conclusions about the Maya diet at Cerros. In particular, we have been able to document changes in the subsistence economy, which occurred around 100 B.C. and coincided with the emergence of an elite class.

Carbonized plant remains were present in 238 flotation samples from the subplaza village deposits. Excluding the wood charcoals, which have not been identified, 20 plant taxa were represented. The ubiquity percentages indicate that maize, which occurred in up to 87% of the samples, was a major staple of the community from the beginning, and the amount of maize consumed did not change significantly over time (Figure 5-2). This indirect evidence for high levels of maize consumption during the Late Preclassic is supported by isotopic and elemental analyses of human skeletal remains from Lamanai, a site located approximately 80 km up the New River from Cerros (White and Schwarcz 1989:463). Squash rind, which occurred in up to 23% of the samples, was less common than maize, but the amount of squash consumed at Cerros also appears to have remained stable over time.

In contrast, the consumption of the tree fruits nance *(Byrsonima crassifolia)* and coyol palm *(Acrocomia mexicana)* increased dramatically. The number of samples containing nance endocarps increased from 32% to 71% in Stage IV, and coyol palm endocarps increased from 10% to 34%. The archaeobotanical and pollen data from Cerros and other sites (e.g., Miksicek 1991) indicate that the Maya consumed a variety of tree crops. However, unlike nance and the coyol palm, which have dense endocarps that preserve well, the other trees are too poorly represented in the Cerros archaeobotanical assemblage for any temporal trends to be discernible. Tree fruits such as nance provided the Maya with seasonal sources of vitamins A and C as well as minerals but were not high-yield staples. Modern Maya eat nance fruits raw or ferment them to make wine. The coconutlike kernels of the coyol palm are high in fat, and ethnohistorically the Maya used them to make a hot drink and as a source of oil (Tozzer 1941:200).

Approximately 10,000 bone fragments representing 50 vertebrate families were recovered from the subplaza village deposits. The Cerros Maya exploited a variety of aquatic resources, including a number of fish species, blue crabs, and an occasional sea turtle (Figure 5-3). Both estuary and reef species were exploited. Fish provided the Maya with protein as well as unsaturated fats, calcium, potassium, phosphorus, iron, vitamins, and several essential trace elements (Hamblin 1985:165). At Cerros aquatic resources were more common during Stages II and III, occurring in up to 91% of the samples. In contrast, only 65% of the samples from Stage IV contained aquatic resources (Figure 5-4).

Terrestrial and amphibious resources exploited by the Maya at Cerros included the domesticated dog, white-tailed deer, brocket deer, collared peccary, paca, opossum, armadillo, rabbit, felid, birds, and several species of turtles (Figure 5-5). Although those animals occurred less frequently than aquatic resources in the samples from Stages II and III, they still contributed significantly to the diet because of their larger biomass.

The percentage of samples containing terrestrial fauna increased from 41 in Stage II to 86 in Stage IV, involving significant increases in the consumption of

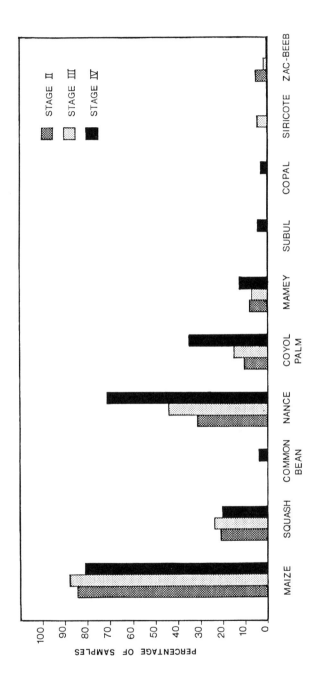

Figure 5-2. *Ubiquity percentages of archaeobotanical remains (not all taxa are shown).*

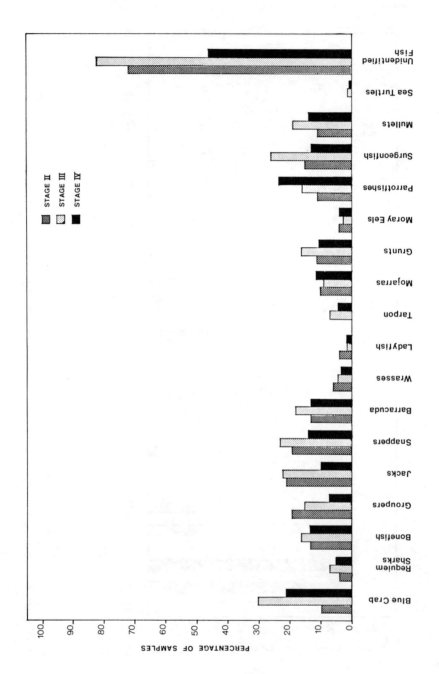

Figure 5-3. *Ubiquity percentages of aquatic vertebrate and crustacean fauna (not all taxa are shown).*

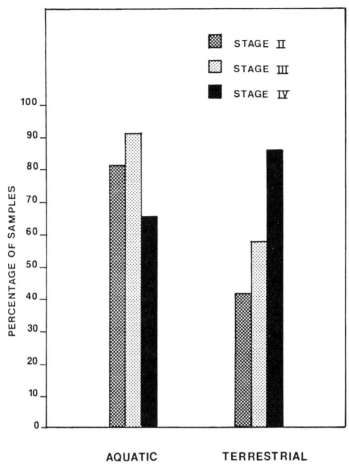

Figure 5-4. *Ubiquity percentages of all aquatic and terrestrial vertebrate and crustacean fauna.*

dog, white-tailed deer, collared peccary, and turtles. Dog raising provided a steady source of meat that could be relied upon when agricultural work requirements or inclement weather interfered with hunting and fishing. The increase in turtle consumption was probably the result of the Maya creating a new habitat for turtles when they constructed the main canal. As a result, turtles were more readily available for exploitation.

The pollen data from the site indicate that by Stage IV the Maya had largely deforested the settlement area. That deforestation created new habitats for animals that prefer secondary growth such as the white-tailed deer and collared peccary. While the exploitation of those animals and others with broad habitat tolerances such as opossum, armadillo, and rabbit increased during Stage IV, there was a decrease in the exploitation of brocket deer, which tends to prefer high bush.

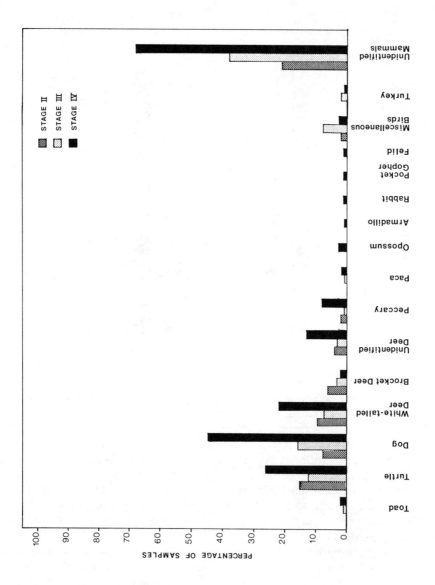

Figure 5-5. *Ubiquity percentages of terrestrial and amphibious vertebrate fauna (not all taxa are shown).*

The exploitation of marine molluscs at Cerros was heavily focused upon the mud conch (*Melongena melongena;* Figure 5-6). Over 3,200 mud conch specimens were present in 274 samples from the subplaza deposits, and the amount of mud conch consumed did not change significantly over time. Mud conch is commonly found today in the muddy bottom of Corozal Bay, but it is only one of a number of edible molluscs in the bay. Mud conch may have been more heavily exploited than the others because it is a predaceous carnivore that can be lured by leaving a bag of rotten meat overnight in shallow water (Abbott 1954:61). The Cerros Maya may have set out bait to lure mud conch. However, it is also likely that the conch was attracted to garbage that the Maya disposed of in the bay, and as a result, it could have been collected in large numbers immediately adjacent to the settlement. Although no nutritional data for mud conch could be found, molluscs in general provide fewer calories and less protein per unit weight than vertebrates, but they are higher in calcium (Wing and Brown 1979:141).

Changes in mollusc exploitation during Stage IV included increased utilization of conch (*Strombus*), venus (*Chione*), marginella (*Prunum*), and apple snail (*Pomacea*) as well as the appearance of several new species. Although conch was a food source, it was also the preferred shell used in artifact manufacturing at Cerros (Hamilton 1987), which could account for its increased exploitation. The occurrence of ark (*Anadara*), whelk (*Busycon*), and tree oyster (*Isognomon*) in Stage IV may also be due to their use in artifact manufacturing.

Although the increase in the consumption of deer, peccary, dog, turtles, and tree fruits during Stage IV may represent a temporal change in subsistence for the community as a whole, it is more likely that it was the result of elite dietary preferences. By Stage IV, the village was almost exclusively occupied by the newly emergent elite class, and consequently, a majority of the subsistence data from that stage came from elite contexts.

Dietary changes are often initiated by a desire for higher social status that is achieved in part by adopting an upper-class diet. Elites tend to desire a diet composed of the rarest items, which are more costly to obtain (Wing and Brown 1979:12). At the coastal site of Cerros seafoods were readily available, and the nonelites consumed large quantities of them. In general, the nonelites were more oriented to the exploitation of marine habitats. Although the elites also consumed seafoods, they were more oriented to the exploitation of terrestrial resources and the freshwater aquatic resources of the canal, aguadas, and the New River. The elites may have had privileged access to the best agricultural lands (including fruit trees) and the game, such as deer, that were attracted to field edges. The elite preference for a diet high in venison has been documented at other Maya sites such as Seibal (Pohl 1985). Both the elites and nonelites at Cerros, however, consumed large quantities of maize.

Although the elites had a slightly more diverse diet, it is impossible without human skeletal remains to determine if their diet was more nutritious than that of the nonelites. An analysis of human skeletal remains from the nearby site of Cuello showed that the Late Preclassic inhabitants had a higher incidence of linear enamel hypoplasia (LEH) than their predecessors at the site. That study concluded that the Late Preclassic Maya had poorer overall

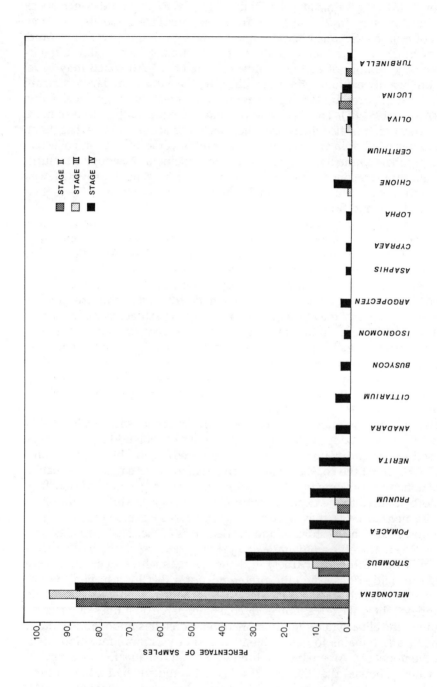

Figure 5-6. *Ubiquity percentages of molluscs (not all taxa are shown).*

nutritional and health conditions since the increase in LEH was caused by systemic disturbances such as malnutrition and various other disease processes occurring during childhood (Saul and Saul 1991:143–144). Unfortunately the study did not examine possible differences between elite and nonelite health and nutritional status. Studies of skeletal remains from Maya sites such as Copán have shown that by the Late Classic the nonelites were less healthy (Whittington 1986).

Conclusion

One limitation of our data in determining diet was differential preservation, which was most noticeable in the archaeobotanical assemblage. Tropical forests are characterized by high species diversity, and ethnographic studies have documented that the Maya utilized a large number of those plants for food and medicinal purposes. However, only a small number were represented by the archaeobotanical remains. Since several economic plants were represented only by the pollen, by combining archaeobotanical and palynological data, we have been able to get a more complete picture of the plants utilized or cultivated by the Maya. Another limitation was the lack of subsistence data from the Stage IV nonelite households, which were located in the dispersed settlement surrounding the village. The limited testing of those structures did not uncover any sealed midden deposits, and consequently, we do not know how their diet compared with that of the village occupants.

One of the most positive aspects of our research for the study of Maya diet is that we have the largest assemblages of botanical and faunal remains collected to date from a Late Preclassic Maya site. The remains were recovered from a series of well-sealed domestic deposits, and the archaeological history of the deposits has been well documented. As a result we have been able to examine changes in the subsistence economy that accompanied the development of complex society—for example, significant increases in the consumption of deer, peccary, dog, turtles, and tree fruits. Finally, our integrated approach allowed us to obtain a more holistic picture of the Maya subsistence economy.

An integrated approach to the study of paleonutrition is essential because humans are broad-spectrum omnivores whose basic nutritional requirements can be met by many combinations of a variety of plant and animal foods (Wing and Brown 1979:2). Floral and faunal remains provide an incomplete record of the foods utilized by a population, but they furnish dietary evidence unobtainable through the studies of human skeletal remains and coprolites. The integration of all available evidence pertaining to the prehistoric diet results in the most complete dietary reconstruction possible.

References

Abbott, R. T.
   1954   *American Seashells.* D. Van Nostrand, Princeton, New Jersey.

Bronson, B.
  1966   Roots and the Subsistence of the Ancient Maya. *American Antiquity* 22:162–64.
Carr, H. S.
  1986   *Faunal Utilization in a Late Preclassic Maya Community at Cerros, Belize.* Unpublished Ph.D. dissertation, Department of Anthropology, Tulane University, New Orleans.
Cliff, M. B.
  1982   *Lowland Maya Nucleation: A Case Study from Northern Belize.* Unpublished Ph.D. dissertation, Department of Anthropology, Southern Methodist University, Dallas.
  1988   Domestic Architecture and Origins of Complex Society at Cerros. In *Household and Community in the Mesoamerican Past*, edited by R. R. Wilk and W. Ashmore, pp. 199–226. University of New Mexico Press, Albuquerque.
Cliff, M. B., and C. J. Crane
  1989   Changing Subsistence Economy at a Late Preclassic Maya Community. In *Prehistoric Maya Economies of Belize*, edited by P. A. McAnany and B. L. Isaac, pp. 295–324. Research in Economic Anthropology Supplement 4. JAI Press, Greenwich.
Crane, C. J.
  1989   The Archaeobotany and Palynology of Cerros, Belize: The Subsistence Economy of a Late Preclassic Community. Paper presented at the 54th Annual Meeting of the Society for American Archaeology, Atlanta.
  1991   Archaeobotanical and Palynological Research at a Late Preclassic Maya Community, Cerros, Belize. Paper presented at the Conference on Ancient Maya Agriculture and Biological Resource Management, University of California, Riverside.
Grayson, D. K.
  1984   *Quantitative Zooarchaeology: Topics in the Analysis of Archaeological Faunas.* Academic Press, Orlando.
Hamblin, N. L.
  1985   The Role of Marine Resources in the Maya Economy: A Case Study from Cozumel, Mexico. In *Prehistoric Lowland Maya Environment and Subsistence Economy*, edited by M. Pohl, pp. 159–173. Papers of the Peabody Museum of Archaeology and Ethnology Vol. 77. Harvard University, Cambridge.
Hamilton, R.
  1987   The Archaeological Mollusca of Cerros, Belize. Paper presented at the 52nd Annual Meeting of the Society for American Archaeology, Toronto.
Hastorf, C. A., and V. S. Popper (editors)
  1988   *Current Paleoethnobotany: Analytical Methods and Cultural Interpretations of Archaeological Plant Remains.* University of Chicago Press, Chicago.
Lange, F. W.
  1971   Marine Resources: A Viable Subsistence Alternative for the Prehistoric Lowland Maya. *American Anthropologist* 73:619–39.
Miksicek, C. H.
  1991   The Natural and Cultural Landscape of Preclassic Cuello. In *Cuello: An Early Maya Community in Belize*, edited by N. Hammond, pp. 70–84. Cambridge University Press, Cambridge.
Pohl, M.
  1985   The Privileges of Maya Elites: Prehistoric Vertebrate Fauna from Seibal. In *Prehistoric Lowland Maya Environment and Subsistence Economy*, edited by M.

Pohl, pp. 133–145. Papers of the Peabody Museum of Archaeology and Ethnology Vol. 77. Harvard University, Cambridge.

Puleston, D. E.
1968   Brosimum alicastrum *as a Subsistence Alternative for the Classic Maya of the Central Southern Lowlands*. Unpublished Master's thesis, Department of Anthropology, University of Pennsylvania, Philadelphia.

Robertson, R. A., and D. A. Freidel (editors)
1986   *Archaeology at Cerros Belize, Central America, Vol. I: An Interim Report*. Southern Methodist University Press, Dallas.

Saul, F. P., and J. M. Saul
1991   The Preclassic Population of Cuello. In *Cuello: An Early Maya Community in Belize*, edited by N. Hammond, pp. 134–158. Cambridge University Press, Cambridge.

Scarborough, V. L.
1991   *Archaeology at Cerros, Belize, Central America, Vol. III: The Settlement System in a Late Preclassic Maya Community*. Southern Methodist University Press, Dallas.

Tozzer, A. M.
1941   *Landa's Relación de las Cosas de Yucatan: A Translation*. Papers of the Peabody Museum of American Archaeology and Ethnology Vol. XVIII. Harvard University, Cambridge.

Wheeler, A., and A. K. G. Jones
1989   *Fishes*. Cambridge University Press, Cambridge.

White, C. D., and H. P. Schwarcz
1989   Ancient Maya Diet: As Inferred from Isotopic and Elemental Analysis of Human Bone. *Journal of Archaeological Science* 16:451–474.

Whittington, S.
1986   Disease Stress in the Lower Classes of Late Classic Copán. Paper presented at the 51st Annual Meeting of the Society for American Archaeology, New Orleans.

Wing, E. S., and A. B. Brown
1979   *Paleonutrition: Method and Theory in Prehistoric Foodways*. Academic Press, New York.

6. Feeding Specialists: The Effect of Specialization on Subsistence Variation

George Gumerman IV

Abstract: Specialization, the production of goods or services that are exchanged for other goods or services, contributes to subsistence variation. The context of specialization, the intensity of production, and the personnel involved in production have the greatest effect on how subsistence resources are procured. Archaeological data from the Chimu at Pacatnamu on the north coast of Peru and the Wanka of the Mantaro Valley of highland Peru are compared to data on the market economy of the Aztecs. The data demonstrate that full-time specialists attached to elite individuals typically consumed ideal staple finance foods such as maize. Part-time and kin-based specialists were more self-sufficient, and their specialization minimally affected subsistence. Markets, especially in the major centers, allow specialists to procure diverse and exotic foods. This analysis illustrates the importance of exploring detailed variation among various groups within a society.

Introduction

Understanding individual behavior within cultures has recently become a trend in archaeology (Brumfiel 1992; Earle 1991; Gero 1991; Hodder 1986). That growing interest, however, has yet to inspire a more detailed understanding of subsistence (cf. Crabtree 1990; Gumerman 1991a, 1991b; Hastorf 1990, 1991). Typically, diet is examined for a society as a whole rather than for different status, generational, and gender groups. Yet we know that within a society different groups, comprised of decision-making individuals, consume diverse resources for a variety of economic, political, and ideological reasons. In this paper I explore the diet of one group of individuals: specialists. Although exceptional research by Brumfiel and Earle (1987), Costin (1986,

Paleonutrition: The Diet and Health of Prehistoric Americans, edited by Kristin D. Sobolik. Center for Archaeological Investigations, Occasional Paper No. 22. © 1994 by the Board of Trustees, Southern Illinois University. All rights reserved. ISBN 0-88104-078-9.

1991a), Clark and Perry (1990), and others has greatly expanded our understanding of specialization and how it is defined archaeologically, we really do not know much about specialists. What types of food specialists ate and why they ate them are simple questions that need answering. I will attempt to answer those questions while examining how specialization caused subsistence variation among the Chimu and Wanka of Peru and the Aztecs of the Valley of Mexico.

Specialization and Subsistence

Specialization, the production of goods or services that are "exchanged" for other goods or services, is often investigated by using several parameters that describe the organization of production. First, the context of specialization defines how production is controlled and includes attached and independent specialization. Independent specialists, as the name implies, are not controlled by the ruling elite and typically produce goods for the general populace that are used on a regular basis. In contrast, attached specialists are bound to an elite patron or institution for whom they provide services and produce wealth or luxury items (Brumfiel and Earle 1987; Costin 1986, 1991a).

The resources consumed by a specialist are clearly affected by the context of specialization. Depending on what is produced and how the product is distributed, independent specialists generally fulfill their subsistence needs through a system of exchange, either through markets or reciprocal exchange (see Brumfiel 1980; Brumfiel and Earle 1987). That is, goods or services are exchanged for other necessities, such as subsistence resources, or for wealth items that can be converted into other goods (D'Altroy and Earle 1985). The diet of independent specialists would therefore contain resources that are storable and transportable—qualities amenable to exchange. Their diet may also be diverse because they are exchanging goods and services for available resources.

Attached specialists are generally supplied sustenance through a system of staple finance because they constitute a part of the political economy and are sustained by the elites they serve (Brumfiel and Earle 1987; D'Altroy and Earle 1985; Earle 1987). Therefore, subsistence goods mobilized by the elites would dominate the diet of attached specialists. Resources that are easily intensified, provide sustainable yields, and are easily mobilized and stored would be important in a system involving staple finance.

A second parameter that is important in causing variation in the diet of attached and independent specialists is the intensity of production. If specialized production is full-time, there is little time for subsistence production, and diet therefore depends on staple finance and exchange. In contrast, if production is part-time, it is possible to produce and collect subsistence resources while not engaged in specialized activities (Hagstrum 1989). Of course, the proceeds of independent specialization may be exchanged for subsistence resources, but generally the specialists are relatively self-sufficient, relying on their own or kin's labor to produce subsistence goods.

The scale and personnel involved in specialized production also affect subsistence. In kin-based systems of specialization there is often a division of labor where some members are not intimately involved in specialized production and are therefore able to procure subsistence resources. At the other extreme, work groups consist of laborers who are all producing specialized goods on a full-time basis and are unable to produce subsistence resources. Their subsistence, therefore, must be obtained through exchange or staple finance.

The following discussion compares three societies that, to varying degrees, incorporated specialized production into their economies. The Chimu employed a variety of specialists, including administrators, craftsmen, and specialized fishermen. In contrast, the Wanka had only limited part-time independent specialists such as potters, weavers, and stone tool manufacturers. Finally, the Aztecs, with their market economies, were especially known for their diverse specialized activities.

Chimu Specialists at Pacatnamu

The Chimu were a large state society on the north coast of Peru during the Late Intermediate period (A.D. 1000–1470; Figure 6-1). My research focuses on the site of Pacatnamu, which was occupied prior to the Imperial Chimu's conquest of Jequetepeque Valley (Donnan and Cock 1986; Gumerman 1991a, 1991b). Excavations at Pacatnamu were oriented toward defining socioeconomic status and variation in diet. A system of dry screening (6.4 to 0.5 mm) was used to recover artifactual and subsistence remains from primary contexts (Gumerman 1991b). Data were standardized by volume, allowing for comparisons between different contexts.

Variation in architecture, beads, copper, and textiles define several socioeconomic groups at Pacatnamu, some of which were specialists. The data indicate that both attached and independent specialists were producing goods. Furthermore, the nobility were considered administrative and ritual specialists who were removed from subsistence production.

The nobility at Pacatnamu were apparently involved in administration and in ritual activities and were provided sustenance by the commoners (Gumerman 1991b). It is assumed, primarily from the monumental and ceremonial nature of the architecture, that they were full-time specialists who were not producing subsistence goods. The nobility were clearly differentiated from the commoners by architectural variation and an abundance of wealth. They resided in the formal, monumental huaca complexes that typically contained a pyramid and a quadrangle (group of rooms in a walled enclosure) constructed with adobe bricks. Associated administrative and ceremonial features included flanker mounds, altars, niched rooms, storage rooms, courtyards, and *concilios*. *Concilios* were U-shaped structures within large, open rooms that probably served as meeting places (Chiswell 1988). The commanding presence of those features and the monumental scale of the architecture suggest that administrative and ritual activities were performed on a full-time basis. The nobility controlled the majority of the wealth, which

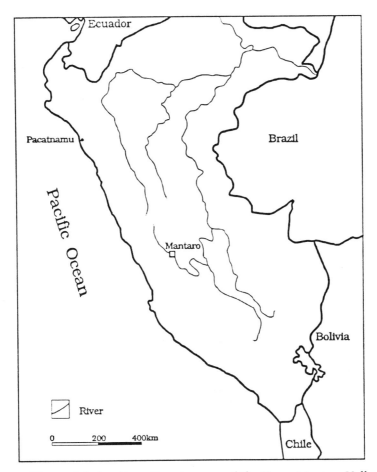

Figure 6-1. *Location of Pacatnamu and the Upper Mantaro Valley Project area in Peru.*

included colored beads and elaborate textiles, often constructed from wool. The commoners lived on the margin of the city in nonmonumental, informal, cane-walled structures and had primarily plain-weave, nondyed, cotton textiles and few beads. The extreme variation between nobility and commoners is indicative of a class-based society where the nobility typically control resources and labor and do not produce subsistence goods.

The nobility therefore consumed higher frequencies of staple finance foods such as maize. Standardized frequencies of maize (per liter of sampled soil) demonstrate that nobility contexts contained over twice as many cobs as commoner contexts and that kernels were also more abundant (Figure 6-2). The storability and transportability of maize made it an ideal staple finance food, and it is also very productive with a high yield, increasing its cost efficiency over other resources and often resulting in a narrower diet (Christenson 1980).

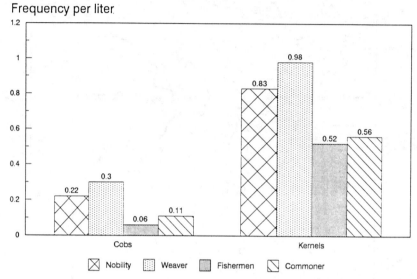

Figure 6-2. *Standardized frequency distribution of* Zea mays *at Pacatnamu.*

Other foods such as camelid (cf. *Lama gama*), chile pepper (*Capsicum* sp.), and coca *(Erythroxylum novogranatense)* were also consumed in higher frequencies, but probably because of the ability of the nobility to afford such costly resources (Figure 6-3). Chile peppers, for instance, although providing important vitamins, were condiments and as such were probably considered a luxury food. Llamas were not native to coastal Peru and were undoubtedly costly to maintain in the extremely arid climate. These resources were also ideologically important, were used in a variety of rituals, and legitimized the nobility's status (Gumerman 1991a).

The most striking finding, however, was the food that the full-time specialists did *not* eat. The nobility rarely consumed opportunistic resources, such as wild plants and shellfish, because they did not have the occasion to gather them (Figure 6-4)[1]. Furthermore, those resources are not typical staple finance foods because shellfish store and transport poorly and the wild plants generally have lower productivity and are less controllable than agricultural products. Commoners, in contrast, utilized an abundance of such resources because they were not specialists and had the opportunity to easily gather wild plants and shellfish. Many of the wild plants—such as amaranth (*Amaranthus* sp.), mallow (*Sida* sp.), vervain (*Verbena* sp.), and husk tomato (*Physalis peruviana*)—are adventives, weeds that grow along canals and within agricultural fields. Ethnographic evidence demonstrates that they are often tended and collected during agricultural activities (Franquemont et al.

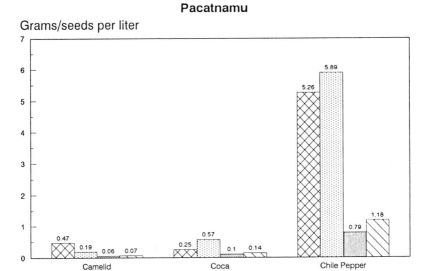

Figure 6-3. *Standardized frequency of camelid (grams per liter), coca, and chile pepper (seeds per liter) at Pacatnamu.*

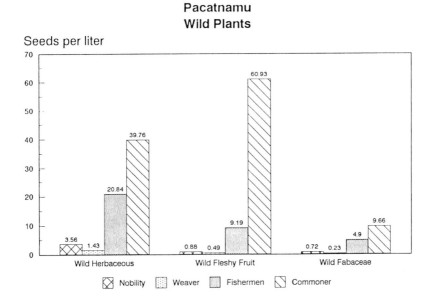

Figure 6-4. *Standardized frequency distribution of wild plants at Pacatnamu.*

1990:20; Gade 1975:80; Weismantel 1988), as was probably the case at Pacatnamu. The shellfish, including clams (*Tivella* sp. and *Donax peruvianus*), mussels (*Mytilus* cf. *edulis*), and several gastropods (*Tegula* spp. and *Thais* spp.), are mostly near-shore, intertidal species that could have been easily collected with minimal technology and experience. Division of labor may also have affected shellfish collecting, with individuals not involved in other activities participating in shellfish gathering.

Another specialist activity identified at Pacatnamu was the weaving of textiles, an activity that was apparently attached to the nobility. High frequencies of spindles, elaborate textiles, wool threads, and a variety of colors suggest that the weaving of high-quality textiles was occurring within two nobility groups. The nature of that production, however, is difficult to define and may only represent intensified household production. Regardless, they were probably part-time specialists, because workshops, per se, were not located, and a variety of domestic activities were apparent. It is also possible that the specialization constituted a division of labor, perhaps based on gender or kinship where certain family members were producing textiles while others were providing subsistence resources (Gumerman 1991b).

The fact that diet does not appear significantly different between the proposed attached specialists and the other nobility groups may relate to the provisioning of both through a system of staple finance. Nevertheless, contexts where specialized weaving occurs contain slightly more maize than those of other nobility groups and over twice as much as those of commoners (Figure 6-2). Interestingly, there are fewer wild plant resources in that context than in those of other groups—nobility, commoners, and fishermen (Figure 6-4). It thus appears that the specialized weavers did not frequent the valley bottom and had little opportunity to collect wild resources. In contrast, some wealth food was more prevalent among the weavers (Gumerman 1991a, 1991b). Coca was over twice as abundant, and chile pepper was slightly more common than among other nobility groups. Camelid remains were less common than in other nobility groups but more abundant than in commoner contexts (Figure 6-3).

It is important to note that the sample size from weaver contexts was small, and a larger sample is needed to confirm the observed patterns. Furthermore, the nature of attached specialization—personnel involved and the intensity of production—at Pacatnamu was not clearly defined. It is, therefore, difficult to arrive at any definitive conclusions about attached specialization and diet at Pacatnamu. It is expected, however, that the attached specialists had little time for subsistence production or for gathering opportunistic resources. They therefore consumed staple finance food that was provided by the nobility.

Compared with attached specialization, the evidence for independent specialization at Pacatnamu was much clearer. One group of commoners was identified as specialized fishermen who lived outside the city walls in commoner architecture (Gumerman 1991b). The evidence consists of up to 10 cm of fish scales and bones that were compacted on the floors of processing areas, while residential rooms were located upwind. The faunal analysis suggests that fish were exchanged because there was an abundance of tail and head elements and few vertebrae. High frequencies of beads and copper suggest that fish were exchanged for wealth. It is possible that subsistence resources were also exchanged for fish; however, that activity was probably minimal. If the specialists exchanged either fish or wealth for food, resources, such as maize, would be abundant because they have characteristics important for exchange. That, however, was not the case. Maize was uncommon (Figure 6-2), and even wealth food, such as llama, was rare. However, the high ratio of kernels to cobs suggests that the fishermen obtained processed maize. The high frequency of beads and copper and the fact that the fishermen were "producing" food (fish) suggest that they primarily exchanged food for wealth.

A most likely scenario, and one that ethnohistoric evidence supports, is that fishermen worked part-time while also farming (e.g., Cock 1985; cf. Netherly 1977; Ramirez-Horton 1982; Rostworowski 1981; Sandweiss 1988). Fishermen at Pacatnamu utilized an abundance of wild plants, suggesting that they were only part-time fishermen who performed activities in the valley bottom (probably farming) where those adventives and ruderals grow. Another possibility is that there was division of labor in which nonfishermen (including kin) performed agricultural labor and had the opportunity to collect the plants.

Part-time Specialization of the Highland Wanka

The Wanka of the Mantaro Valley, Peru, are ideal for comparative purposes because specialization was limited and because of the excellent, comprehensive data collected by Earle and colleagues (Costin and Earle 1989; D'Altroy 1992; Earle et al. 1987; Hastorf 1988, 1990, 1993; Lennstrom 1992; Sandefur 1988). Research focused on understanding cultural change from the end of the Late Intermediate period (Wanka II; A.D. 1350–1460) to the Late horizon (Wanka III; A.D. 1460–1533). During Wanka III the Inca subjugated the local Wanka population, which clearly affected production, consumption, and exchange. Hastorf (e.g., 1983, 1988, 1990, 1993) and Sandefur (1988) were particularly concerned with the effect that those changes had on subsistence.

Importantly, specialization among the Wanka was limited to the part-time manufacture of ceramics, textiles, and blades. Apparently, the production involved community-based independent specialization that occurred during periods of nonagricultural activity (Costin 1986, 1991b; Hagstrum 1989; Russell 1988). The primary activity of all Wanka households was agricultural production. Even Wanka elites, unlike Chimu elites, were agriculturalists and not solely administrative specialists. Indeed, within the Wanka II centers there was little evidence of administrative specialization. During Wanka III it is probable that administrative specialists resided at Hatun Xauxa, the Inca administrative center (D'Altroy 1981:83); however, the site was not included in the excavated sample. Specialization, thus, had little effect on subsistence because the majority of individuals were agricultural laborers—not specialists—and because specialization was only part-time and was organized when agricultural tasks were minimal.

Subsistence data exhibit considerable variation among all Wanka sites (Table 6-1). Importantly, the disparities resulted from altitudinal variation as well as from changes in the demand for maize during Wanka III. Sites located in the higher elevations, such as Tunanmarca, were oriented more toward crops suitable for high elevations, whereas sites such as Umpamalca and Hatunmarca were lower in elevation close to areas of maize cultivation. Sites that show evidence of independent, part-time specialized production, such as Umpamalca and Marca, contained respectively high and low frequencies of botanical remains and moderate amounts of faunal remains (Hastorf 1983, 1990; Sandefur 1988). The importance of agricultural production at Umpamalca probably resulted in a high frequency of agricultural products, while at Marca, another agricultural town, the low frequencies may result from depositional factors, since the ubiquity of botanical remains is similar to other sites. The varied patterns demonstrate the importance of agricultural activities that overshadowed independent, part-time, community-based specialization. Diet was therefore minimally affected by specialized activities.

Although there were some exceptions, elites from both time periods had greater quantities of subsistence remains. Hastorf (1988, 1990, 1993) effectively argued that the macrobotanical remains reflect greater social interactions within elite households, including activities relating to feasting. Feasting, an important Andean tradition, is often a form of reciprocity by which elites "repay" their work force. The presence of feasting is also maintained in the stable isotope data. The analysis of human remains indicates that diet between elites and commoners was similar even though macrobotanical remains differed. It is argued that commoners were often fed by elites during feasts—thus causing similarities in their diets (DeNiro and Hastorf 1985; Hastorf 1990). More serving and storage vessels in elite contexts provide supporting evidence for feasting (Costin and Earle 1989).

The stable isotope data also indicate that males consumed more maize than females during Wanka III, the period of Inca subjugation. That finding suggests that some males participated in state work parties and were fed maize or maize beer called *chicha* (Hastorf 1990, 1991; Hastorf and Johannessen 1993). Such a form of production and food exchange is documented ethnohistorically for the Inca, who institutionalized a labor tax called *mit'a* (Murra 1980; Rowe 1946). In the case of the subjugated Wanka, males were probably providing services to the state in the form of construction, military, and agricultural labor. That production was probably fulfilled on a part-time basis, but because the male specialists were attached to the Inca state and they required feeding, they were fed the ideal staple finance food: maize.

Maize consumption was moderate during the earlier Wanka II, possibly associated with the general lack of specialists requiring staple finance. Furthermore, sites were usually located in higher elevations suitable for tuber cultivation, but not for maize. Elite contexts contained more maize, probably because of their ability to gain access to distant resources (Earle et al. 1987; Hastorf 1990). During Wanka III the production of maize increased, with sites located closer to zones suitable for maize agriculture. Although the frequency of maize was similar between Wanka II and III, stable isotope data and a large

Table 6-1. *Standardized Botanical (per 6 kg) and Faunal (per m³)
Remains from Sites in the Mantaro Valley*

Site	Zea mays Kernels	Zea mays Cobs	Solanum *spp.*	Chenopodium	*Legumes*	*Faunal*
Wanka II						
Tunanmarca	1.5	0.3	5.6	32.5	1.0	292.3
Umpamalca	36.4	0.6	7.1	342.2	1.3	193.4
Hatunmarca	3.3	2.7	0.7	16.7	0.6	1292.5
Wanka III						
Hatunmarca	30.0	4.1	2.0	19.0	0.1	640.1
Marca	4.7	2.6	0.4	2.2	0.2	501.0

Sources: Hastorf (1990); Sandefur (1988, personal communication 1992).

increase in maize ubiquity demonstrate that maize production expanded. The increased production coincided with an overall decrease in other botanical remains such as tubers, chenopods, and legumes. A clear factor in the increased production of maize was the establishment of the Inca political economy that contained numerous specialists (e.g., administrators, craftsmen, soldiers) in need of financing (Hastorf 1990). The Inca economy contrasts with the local Wanka population that only participated in limited specialized activities and whose diet therefore was minimally affected by specialization. As indicated in the stable isotope data, however, some of the increased maize production was apparently used in feeding work groups that consisted of male specialists.

Other factors besides specialization, such as socioeconomic status, affected subsistence. Costly resources, such as chile pepper, coca, and maize (during Wanka II) that were not produced locally, were often more abundant among the elite. Overall, however, the Wanka data demonstrate that diet was generally similar across socioeconomic groups because part-time specialization allows for self-sufficiency and subsistence production. Agricultural production was primary to all other activities, and both elites and commoners were agriculturalists. Variation, however, was apparent between females and some males who presumably served the state and received maize for their services.

The Market and Tribute Economy of the Aztecs

Compared with the Wanka and Chimu, subsistence research among the Aztecs of the Valley of Mexico is limited, and archaeological data at the household level are unavailable. However, ethnohistoric data, in combination with the limited archaeological data, provide a means to examine the diet of specialists.

The Aztecs were a large state society that occupied the Valley of Mexico at the time of the Spanish conquest. The Aztec economy depended on markets and a system of tribute to finance the majority of elites within the large cities. A system of tribute was the primary means of financing political activities and of supplying the elites with goods that were produced on their land or land that was subjugated. Items of wealth and subsistence goods were both integrated into the system (e.g., Berdan 1975; Brumfiel 1987; Hicks 1986). Generally, rulers were supported by tribute from commoners, but some elites worked their own land. Commoners were usually agriculturalists and/or craft specialists, living in rural hamlets (e.g., Berdan 1975; Brumfiel 1980; Carrasco 1971; Gibson 1971; Hicks 1986).

Specialization within the Aztec empire was diverse and included, for example, administrators, lapidaries, feather workers, warriors, priests, and long-distance traders. Some specialists were part-time, and others produced goods or provided services on a full-time basis. Specialists occasionally received agricultural land for their work, sometimes hiring agricultural laborers to work their fields (Brumfiel 1987:106). Other specialists, especially craftsmen attached to the elites, produced luxury goods and were supplied through a system of staple finance (Hicks 1987). Specialists who produced goods rather than services either brought their goods to the market or were attached to and paid tribute to elite patrons (Brumfiel 1987).

The market system served the general population and, importantly, a variety of specialists. The market's function, however, was highly variable depending on its location. For instance, the Tlatelolco market at the capital of Tenochtitlan was immense and occurred daily, whereas markets in the hinterland were more specialized and peripheral (see Berdan 1975). Goods were often sold in the market for wealth items (cloth and cacao) and then exchanged for subsistence goods (see Berdan 1975; Brumfiel 1987; Calnek 1978). The use of markets probably caused patrons to consume a greater diversity of food because the system of distribution incorporated foods from various regions of Mesoamerica. Recalling the Tlatelolco market, the chronicler Diaz del Castillo notes the variety of food: "Let us go on and speak of those who sold beans and sage and other vegetables and herbs . . . and [of] those who sold fowls, cocks with wattles, rabbits, hares, deer, mallards, young dogs . . . the fruiterers, and the women who sold cooked food, dough and tripe in their own part of the market" (1928:299). The effect of such a market on subsistence would have been especially great at the larger urban markets where wealthy patrons could afford exotic resources (e.g., Calnek 1978).

Many Aztec specialists, such as skilled warriors, were highly ranked. Undoubtedly, their diet was similar to that of the nobility, since they could afford costly resources and were provided some resources through staple finance. Warriors probably consumed an abundance of maize because it is a perfect staple finance food for such activities—it is storable and easily transportable. Indeed, once regions became subjects of the Aztec empire, maize production for staple finance increased dramatically (Brumfiel 1987:109). Other resources, such as beans, chia, and amaranth, were also stored (e.g., Sahagun 1950–1982:8:37) and may have been used for staple finance.

Feasting was probably also an important activity of warriors and other high-ranking specialists, significantly affecting the types of food they consumed. Besides many of the staples, such as maize tamales, feasting involved the consumption of meat, including dog and various fowls, which were probably highly valued foods (Sahagun 1950–1982:4:123, 8:37, 9:48). Part of the feasting also involved the consumption of humans (see Conrad and Demarest 1984; Price 1978). War captives were often sacrificed and taken to the captor's home where strips of the flesh were made into a ritual stew. The flesh was served only to the captor's relatives; the captor did not eat the flesh of his prisoner because of the bond between captor and prisoner. The captor, however, did eat the flesh of a relative's captive (see Berdan and Anawalt 1992). The emperor Motecuhzoma also consumed human flesh, since he was awarded the thigh of captives (Sahagun 1950–1982) and perhaps the flesh of young boys.

Rulers also appear to have eaten a variety of goods, many of which were exotic. Most meals contained hundreds of dishes prepared from wild fowl, venison, boar, rabbit, fish, fruits, and vegetables. After the meal, the emperor drank chocolate made from the highly valued cacao bean. Many other wealthy specialists, such as the nobility and some merchants, consumed chocolate, but the emperor always drank the highest quality (Berdan and Anawalt 1992).

Other specialists within the large centers, such as full-time craft producers and construction workers, were probably lower ranked and were provided subsistence from the elites they served. Their diet likely contained an abundance of resources, such as maize, that have characteristics suitable for staple finance. Costly and exotic foods, such as chocolate, were probably much less common in the diet of the lower-ranking specialists.

In the Aztec hinterland, subsistence patterns were presumably similar to what was observed among the Wanka of Peru. In general, most elites and commoners apparently consumed similar types and amounts of resources because production was oriented toward agriculture (Hicks 1986). Specialization within the hinterland was typically part-time (Brumfiel 1987)—occurring during periods of nonagricultural activity—and therefore probably had a minimal effect on diet. Hinterland markets served the specialists; were "periodic," or "peripheral"; and were probably quite specialized. Such markets usually served to distribute specialized goods, while also acting as buffers in times of hardship (see Berdan 1975; Hicks 1986).

Overall, the extreme diversity of specialized production among the Aztecs probably had an extensive effect on diet. In some instances, such as full-time specialists within Tenochtitlan, diet presumably consisted of food supplied through staple finance, supplemented by a variety of market-exchanged resources. As the ethnohistoric data document, a variety of foods, including a diversity of animals, fruits, nuts, and staples, were available in the urban markets to individuals such as specialists who were unable to produce their own subsistence resources. Thus, the urban markets caused specialists to consume a diverse array of resources. Other specialists were part-time, and their nonfood production had little effect on subsistence. Specialization, however, provided them with the opportunity to exchange goods to supplement their needs—especially true for hinterland specialists who used markets with less diverse produce.

Conclusions and Future Directions

Archaeological and ethnohistorical data from the Aztecs, Chimu, and Wanka demonstrate that specialized production of goods and services caused variation in diet. The Chimu and Aztec societies differed from the Wanka society because the degree and intensity of specialization varied. Full-time specialization—such as administrative and ritual specialists—as well as part-time specialization—such as the fishermen at Pacatnamu—was important to the Chimu and Aztec economies. The procurement strategy for full-time specialists was typically tribute and taxation. They, therefore, consumed foods suitable for staple finance, such as maize, that were easily stored and transported and that produced high yields. Importantly, opportunistic resources were uncommon among full-time specialists because they lacked the occasion or need to collect them. Among the Aztecs, the market system created opportunities for specialists to procure an assortment of food, and thus their diet was diverse. The diversity was probably especially significant for the elites who were able to afford exotic and costly resources.

Evidence of full-time specialization was rare in the excavated sample of Wanka households. Part-time specialization was evident, but agricultural production took precedence over all other activities (see Costin 1986; Hagstrum 1989). Part-time specialists were relatively self-sufficient and probably procured many of their own resources. Exceptions were possible male *mit'a* laborers whose labor was removed from the household and who therefore consumed more staple finance food such as maize. Administrative specialization was also rare; however, it is possible that the Inca administrative center of Hatun Xauxa housed full-time administrators. The lack of intense specialization among the Wanka resulted in relatively similar diets between socioeconomic groups.

Depending on the context of specialization, specialists also received staple finance. For instance, attached specialized weavers at Pacatnamu were likely provided staples from the elites they served, and some Wanka males were apparently attached specialized laborers who consumed more staple finance maize than the females. In contrast, independent specialists fulfilled their subsistence needs through a variety of sources, depending on the intensity and scale of specialization. Some, like the fishermen at Pacatnamu, probably procured many of their own resources, especially since their specialization involved food. Exchange and markets were probably important to the procurement of food by many independent specialists, such as Aztec craftsmen.

The scale and personnel involved in specialized production also influenced the procurement of resources. Family members not involved in specialized production often contributed to fulfilling subsistence needs. In contrast, many full-time production activities were located away from the household, and those specialists were usually unable to rely on kin to provide subsistence. Their diet, therefore, consisted of food obtained through staple finance or exchange.

In sum, future research should focus on collecting subsistence data at the household level. We need to go beyond the level of analysis where we generalize the diet of an entire society. The Aztecs did not eat just maize, beans, and squash; rather, different groups of individuals—such as specialists, elites, and commoners—ate differently because of economic, political, and ideological variation within the society. In terms of specialization, it is essential to clearly define the nature of specialization and its effect on diet. As archaeologists studying diet we need to add the spice necessary to understand specific dietary variation. It is only by digesting the details of that variation that we can begin to explain diet in general.

Acknowledgments

I especially thank Patricia Anawalt, Christopher Donnan, and Timothy Earle for their helpful advice. Comments from Elizabeth Brumfiel, Cathy Costin, Frederick Hicks, Virginia Popper, and Kristin Sobolik on early drafts of this paper are greatly appreciated. Christine Hastorf and Elsie Sandefur generously allowed the use of their UMARP data. I also thank the National Science Foundation (Grant BNS-8706295), the UCLA Friends of Archaeology, and the UCLA Department of Anthropology for their financial support of the research reported here. Support for the overall Pacatnamu Project was provided by the National Geographic Society, the National Endowment for the Humanities, and several generous private supporters.

Note

1. The rare nature of these resources in nobility contexts is further evidence of full-time specialization. Subsistence resources, however, were not used to define classes; rather, status was examined independently of diet to avoid circular arguments.

References

Berdan, F. M. F.
    1975   *Trade, Tribute, and Market in the Aztec Empire*. Ph.D. dissertation, University of Texas at Austin. University Microfilms, Ann Arbor.
Berdan, F. M. F., and P. R. Anawalt
    1992   *Codex Mendoza*. University of California Press, Berkeley.
Brumfiel, E. M.
    1980   Specialization, Market Exchange, and the Aztec State: A View from Huexotla. *Current Anthropology* 21:459–478.
    1987   Elite and Utilitarian Crafts in the Aztec State. In *Specialization, Exchange, and Complex Societies*, edited by E. M. Brumfiel and T. K. Earle, pp. 102–118. Cambridge University Press, Cambridge.

1992   Distinguished Lecture in Archeology: Breaking and Entering the Eco-system—Gender, Class, and Faction Steal the Show. *American Anthropologist* 94:551–567.

Brumfiel, E. M., and T. K. Earle
1987   Specialization, Exchange, and Complex Societies: An Introduction. In *Specialization, Exchange, and Complex Societies,* edited by E. M. Brumfiel and T. K. Earle, pp. 1–9. Cambridge University Press, Cambridge.

Calnek, E. E.
1978   El Sistema de Mercado de Tenochtitlan. In *Economía Política e Ideología en el México Prehispanico,* edited by P. Carrasco and J. Broda, pp. 97–114. Editorial Nueva Imagten, Mexico City.

Carrasco, P.
1971   Social Organization of Ancient Mexico. In *Archaeology,* edited by G. F. Ekholm and I. Bernal, pp. 349–375. Handbook of Middle American Indians, vol. 10, R. Wauchope, general editor. University of Texas Press, Austin.

Chiswell, C. E.
1988   The Discovery of a Class of Special Function Rooms at Pacatnamu. Paper presented at the 28th Annual Meeting of the Institute of Andean Studies, Berkeley.

Christenson, A. L.
1980   Change in Human Niche in Response to Population Growth. In *Modeling Change in Prehistoric Subsistence Economies,* edited by T. K. Earle and A. L. Christenson, pp. 31–72. Academic Press, New York.

Clark, J. E., and W. J. Parry
1990   Craft Specialization and Cultural Complexity. *Research in Economic Anthropology* 12:289–346.

Cock, G. A.
1985   *From the Powerful to the Powerless: The Jequetepeque Valley Lords in the 16th Century, Peru.* Unpublished Master's thesis, Archaeology Program, University of California, Los Angeles.

Conrad, G. W., and A. A. Demarest
1984   *Religion and Empire: The Dynamics of Aztec and Inca Expansionism.* Cambridge University Press, Cambridge.

Costin, C. L.
1986   *From Chiefdom to Empire State: Ceramic Economy among the Prehispanic Wanka of Highland Peru.* Unpublished Ph.D. dissertation, Department of Anthropology, University of California, Los Angeles.

1991a   Craft Specialization: Issues in Defining, Documenting, and Explaining the Organization of Production. In *Archaeological Method and Theory,* vol. 3, edited by M. B. Schiffer, pp. 1–56. University of Arizona Press, Tucson.

1991b   Textiles, Women, and Political Economy in Late Prehispanic Peru. Paper presented at 90th Annual Meeting of the American Anthropological Association, Chicago.

Costin, C. L., and T. Earle
1989   Status Distinction and Legitimation of Power as Reflected in Changing Patterns of Consumption in Late Prehispanic Peru. *American Antiquity* 54:691–714.

Crabtree, P. J.
1990   Zooarchaeology and Complex Societies: Some Uses of Faunal Analysis for the Study of Trade, Social Status, and Ethnicity. In *Archaeological Method and Theory,* vol. 2, edited by M. B. Schiffer, pp. 155–206. University of Arizona Press, Tucson.

D'Altroy, T. N.
   1981   *Empire Growth and Consolidation: The Xauxa Region of Peru under the Incas.* Unpublished Ph.D. dissertation, Department of Anthropology, University of California, Los Angeles.
   1992   *Provincial Power in the Inka Empire.* Smithsonian Institution Press, Washington, D.C.
D'Altroy, T. N., and T. K. Earle
   1985   Staple Finance, Wealth Finance, and Storage in the Inka Political Economy. *Current Anthropology* 26:187–206.
DeNiro, M. J., and C. A. Hastorf
   1985   Alteration of $^{15}N/^{14}N$ and $^{13}C/^{12}C$ Ratios of Plant Matter During the Initial Stages of Diagenesis: Studies Utilizing Archaeological Specimens from Peru. *Geochimica et Cosmochimica Acta* 49:97–115.
Diaz del Castillo, B.
   1928   *The Discovery and Conquest of Mexico.* Mexico Press, Mexico City.
Donnan, C. B., and G. A. Cock
   1986   *The Pacatnamu Papers, Vol. 1.* Museum of Cultural History, University of California, Los Angeles.
Earle, T. K.
   1987   Specialization and the Production of Wealth: Hawaiian Chiefdoms and the Inka Empire. In *Specialization, Exchange, and Complex Societies*, edited by E. M. Brumfiel and T. K. Earle, pp. 64–75. Cambridge University Press, Cambridge.
   1991   Toward a Behavioral Archaeology. In *Processual and Postprocessual Archaeologies: Multiple Ways of Knowing the Past*, edited by R. W. Preucel, pp. 83–94. Occasional Paper No. 10. Center for Archaeological Investigations, Southern Illinois University, Carbondale.
Earle, T. K., T. D'Altroy, C. Hastorf, C. Scott, C. Costin, G. Russell, and E. Sandefur
   1987   *Archaeological Field Research in the Upper Mantaro, Peru, 1982–1983: Investigations of Inka Expansion and Exchange.* Monograph 28. Institute of Archaeology, University of California, Los Angeles.
Franquemont, C., T. Plowman, E. Franquemont, S. R. King, C. Niezgoda, W. Davis, C. R. Sperling
   1990   *The Ethnobotany of Chinchero, an Andean Community in Southern Peru.* Fieldiana, Botany, New Series No. 24. Field Museum of Natural History, Chicago.
Gade, D. W.
   1975   *Plants, Man, and the Land in the Vilcanota Valley of Peru.* W. Junk Publishers, The Hague.
Gero, J. M.
   1991   Who Experienced What in Prehistory? A Narrative Explanation from Queyash, Peru. In *Processual and Postprocessual Archaeologies: Multiple Ways of Knowing the Past*, edited by R. W. Preucel, pp. 126–139. Occasional Paper No. 10. Center for Archaeological Investigations, Southern Illinois University, Carbondale.
Gibson, C.
   1971   Structure of the Aztec Empire. In *Archaeology*, edited by G. F. Ekholm and I. Bernal, pp. 376–394. Handbook of Middle American Indians, vol. 10, R. Wauchope, general editor. University of Texas Press, Austin.
Gumerman, G., IV
   1991a Dietary Differences Between Socio-Economic Groups: A Peruvian Compar-

ison. Paper presented at the 90th Annual Meeting of the American Anthropological Association, Chicago.

1991b   *Subsistence and Complex Societies: Diet Between Diverse Socio-Economic Groups at Pacatnamu, Peru.* Ph.D. dissertation, University of California, Los Angeles. University Microfilms, Ann Arbor.

Hagstrum, M. B.
1989   *Technological Continuity and Change: Ceramic Ethnoarchaeology in the Peruvian Andes.* Unpublished Ph.D. dissertation, Department of Anthropology, University of California, Los Angeles.

Hastorf, C. A.
1983   *Prehistoric Agricultural Intensification and Political Development in the Jauja Region of Central Peru.* Unpublished Ph.D. dissertation, Department of Anthropology, University of California, Los Angeles.
1988   The Use of Paleoethnobotanical Data in Prehistoric Studies of Crop Production, Processing, and Consumption. In *Current Paleoethnobotany: Analytical Methods and Cultural Interpretations of Archaeological Plant Remains,* edited by C. A. Hastorf and V. S. Popper, pp. 119–144. University of Chicago Press, Chicago.
1990   The Effect of the Inka State on Sausa Agricultural Production and Crop Consumption. *American Antiquity* 55:262–290.
1991   Gender, Space, and Food in Prehistory. In *Engendering Archaeology: Women and Prehistory,* edited by J. M. Gero and M. W. Conkey, pp. 132–159. Basil Blackwell, Cambridge.
1993   *Agriculture and the Onset of Political Inequality Before the Inka.* Cambridge University Press, Cambridge.

Hastorf, C. A., and S. Johannessen
1993   Pre-Hispanic Political Change and the Role of Maize in the Central Andes of Peru. *American Anthropologist* 95:115–138.

Hicks, F.
1986   Prehispanic Background of Colonial Political and Economic Organization in Central Mexico. In *Ethnohistory,* edited by R. Spores, pp. 35–54. Supplement to the Handbook of Middle American Indians, vol. 4, V. R. Bricker, general editor. University of Texas Press, Austin.
1987   First Steps Toward a Market-Integrated Economy in Aztec Mexico. In *Early State Dynamics,* edited by H. J. M. Claessen and P. van de Velde, pp. 91–107. E. J. Brill, Leiden.

Hodder, I.
1986   *Reading the Past: Current Approaches to Interpretation in Archaeology.* Cambridge University Press, Cambridge.

Lennstrom, H. A.
1992   *Intrasite Spatial Variability and Resource Utilization in the Prehistoric Peruvian Highlands: An Exploration of Method and Theory in Paleoethnobotany.* Unpublished Ph.D. dissertation, Department of Anthropology, University of Minnesota, Minneapolis.

Murra, J. V.
1980   *The Economic Organization of the Inca State.* Supplement No. 1 to Research in Economic Anthropology. JAI Press, Greenwich.

Netherly, P. J.
1977   *Local Level Lords on the North Coast of Peru.* Ph.D. dissertation, Cornell University. University Microfilms, Ann Arbor.

Price, B. J.
    1978   Demystification, Enriddlement, and Aztec Cannibalism: A Materialist Rejoinder to Harner. *American Ethnologist* 5(1):98–115.
Ramirez-Horton, S.
    1982   Retainers of the Lord or Merchants: A Case of Mistaken Identity? In *El Hombre y su Ambiente en los Andes Centrales*, edited by L. Millones and H. Tomoeda, pp. 123–136. Senri Ethnological Studies No. 10. National Museum of Ethnology, Osaka.
Rostworowski de Diez Canseco, M.
    1981   *Recursos Naturales Renovables y Pesca, Siglos XVI y XVII*. Instituto de Estudios Peruanos, Lima.
Rowe, J. H.
    1946   Inca Culture at the Time of the Spanish Conquest. In *The Andean Civilizations*, edited by J. H. Steward, pp. 183–330. Handbook of South American Indians. Bureau of American Ethnology Bulletin 143. Smithsonian Institution, Washington, D.C.
Russell, G. S.
    1988   *The Impact of Inka Policy on the Domestic Economy of the Wanka, Peru: Stone Tool Production and Use*. Unpublished Ph.D. dissertation, Department of Anthropology, University of California, Los Angeles.
Sahagun, B. de
    1950–1982   *Florentine Codex*. Translated and edited by C. E. Dibble and A. J. O. Anderson. Monographs of the School of American Research and the Museum of New Mexico No. 14. School of American Research and the University of Utah.
Sandefur, E. C.
    1988   *Andean Zooarchaeology: Animal Use and the Inka Conquest of the Upper Mantaro Valley*. Unpublished Ph.D. dissertation, Archaeology Program, University of California, Los Angeles.
Sandweiss, D. H.
    1988   The Fishermen of Chincha: Occupational Specialization on the Late Prehispanic Andean Coast. In *Economic Prehistory of the Central Andes*, edited by E. S. Wing and J. C. Wheeler, pp. 99–118, BAR International Series 427. British Archaeological Reports, Oxford.
Weismantel, M. J.
    1988   *Food, Gender, and Poverty in the Ecuadorian Andes*. University of Pennsylvania Press, Philadelphia.

7. Indirect Evidence in Paleonutrition Studies

Mark Q. Sutton

Abstract: Indirect data form the primary component in the study of ancient diet and nutrition, and archaeologists make a variety of assumptions, often with good cause, about the role of resources whose remains are discovered in archaeological sites. Several specific issues, including differential recovery, comparability of data, and analytical difficulties, complicate that approach. This essay reviews the various issues and techniques associated with both the collection and analysis of indirect dietary data and concludes that such research suffers from coarse recovery techniques, a myopia regarding "big ticket" resources, and a bias regarding health and nutrition.

Introduction

There has always been an archaeological interest in the dietary remains of prehistoric peoples. An increasing effort is being made toward the identification and analysis of dietary remains, as witnessed by the contributions, among others, of Wing and Brown (1979), Gilbert and Mielke (1985), Miksicek (1987), Hastorf and Popper (1988), and the authors of this book. We are moving in the right direction.

Data relating to prehistoric diet and nutrition are present in the archaeological record in two major forms: direct and indirect. Direct evidence of diet and nutrition consists of coprolites (actually direct evidence of consumption, though not necessarily as food), pathologies on human skeletal remains, and isotopic studies of human bone. All other categories of data (burned bone of known game animals, carbonized seeds of known economic plants, and so forth) actually comprise indirect data since their presence in the archaeological record only implies, however strongly, their consumption by people. It is the purpose of this paper to examine—incorporating the presentations of each of the authors from the *Indirect Studies* section (Chapters 2 through 6)—the

Paleonutrition: The Diet and Health of Prehistoric Americans, edited by Kristin D. Sobolik. Center for Archaeological Investigations, Occasional Paper No. 22. © 1994 by the Board of Trustees, Southern Illinois University. All rights reserved. ISBN 0-88104-078-9.

variety of data that forms indirect evidence of diet, to discuss their recovery, and to review the assumptions under which they are interpreted.

The Database

Indirect dietary data consist of a variety of remains that falls into three basic categories: identifiable through visible means (macrofloral, pollen, phytoliths, macrofaunal), identifiable through nonvisible means (e.g., residues and proteins), and technological (tools presumably used for procurement and processing and features for collection or storage). The remains of each of the components can be quantified, but their link to diet is often assumed. Of import is the recognition that, due to preservation, processing, and recovery techniques, the ecofactual materials recovered from a site, by whatever means, do not represent the entire range of materials used by prehistoric peoples.

Visible Remains

Visible remains are those that can be identified visually, either through macro- or microscopic means. Most are collected by rather gross methods, from screens (or sieves) in the field or through some specialized laboratory processing such as flotation (also usually with screens). Both pollen and phytoliths (microscopic) are subject to different collection and processing techniques.

Floral

The visible remains of plants are present in the archaeological record in several forms: as macroremains of seeds, charcoal, and fibers, and as microremains of pollen and phytoliths. Although many archaeobotanical studies heretofore have dealt primarily with macroremains, it is now becoming customary for botanical analyses to include micro- as well as macrostudies.

Charred seeds are typically viewed as cultural in origin (Miksicek 1987:234–235; Minnis 1981:147), often associated with dietary activities. However, they may enter site soil by a variety of means, including rodents and ants (e.g., Lawlor 1992). Many such remains are often viewed as having entered the record accidentally (e.g., seeds that fell onto the edge of a fire and were charred while prehistoric peoples were processing them). While that may be how some seeds enter the record, it is not the only way. Seeds, even of a known economic plant, may also be incorporated into a site as the result of the use of the plant itself rather than its seeds (Minnis 1981:145), or perhaps in fuel (Miller and Smart 1984). For example, if the superstructure of a house was constructed of plant materials that contained seeds (e.g., juniper) and the house burned, charred seeds could enter the record in large numbers. Clearly the seeds would not be of dietary significance. Such an issue might be resolved if the context of the seeds was considered (see Pearsall 1988) and if additional floral analysis was conducted on the remains of the structure (thus linking the seeds and charcoal as the same species). Such a technique could be applied to hearths as well, attempting to tie in seeds with firewood. Thus, while charcoal is generally not considered a dietary constituent, its identification and interpretation could be helpful in determining whether certain other materials were actually dietary remains (also see Smart and Hoffman 1988).

Pollen is usually associated with paleoenvironment studies rather than as an indicator of prehistoric diet. However, pollen can be used in dietary studies in a number of instances, including in the identification of stored materials and processed foods (e.g., a pollen wash from a metate) and in the delineation of potential resources within a region (and how that may have changed over time). In addition, pollen may be identified directly as a dietary constituent in coprolites (Bryant 1975; Wilke 1978:70). The same basic principles apply to phytoliths (see Piperno 1988, 1991).

Fritz (Chapter 2) reviews the value of archaeological plant remains, concentrating on macrobotanical data. She discusses first the weaknesses of the data sets in their ability to reconstruct prehistoric diets (essentially taphonomic and interpretational), concluding that the archaeobotanical record is "incomplete, indirect, and skewed." Next, Fritz considers the strengths of the record, including the lack of other such lines of evidence, time depth, and regional variation. She argues for the use of paleobotanical data in conjunction with other techniques, including stable isotope ratio data, measures of ubiquity, and the integration of coprolite data with macrofloral data. Fritz notes that "more than anything else [we] need to recover, analyze, and integrate as many types of subsistence information as possible" and that if used judiciously, paleoethnobotanical data can be very useful.

Faunal

Faunal remains include a variety of materials: primarily bone, but also shell, soft tissues, chitin, and even impressions in a matrix. Archaeologists tend to focus on bone and shell and often do not look for or recover other materials, except in unusual circumstances. Like floral remains, not all faunal remains in the archaeological record represent cultural activity, as many noncultural faunal remains may be present in archaeological sites. Of the cultural remains, not all are the result of dietary activities. Various animal products (or the live animals themselves) were used for nonfood purposes and so enter the record along with the dietary remains. It is sometimes difficult to distinguish the two—a major interpretive problem.

Styles (Chapter 3) recognizes that the recovered faunal data from a site do not represent a "complete inventory of animal foods" for a variety of reasons (taphonomic processes, recovery, and analysis) but argues that studies can document broad-based changes in subsistence patterns over time and space. Much of her discussion centers around the nutritional content of certain animal resources and their role in prehistoric diet. Several linear programming models are reviewed with respect to their utility for predicting diet in the prehistoric record of two river valleys. This is, in effect, an optimal foraging approach using a currency other than calories. While this approach can be quite fruitful and interesting, there are several cautions to note. First, a correct ranking of resources (in whatever currency) requires that the resource universe be fully known, a criterion clearly not met in most optimal foraging studies. Second, people make dietary decisions for a variety of reasons, some unrelated to nutrition and many not individually "optimal" in an evolutionary ecological sense. While such conditions admittedly are difficult to model, they cannot be ignored. In effect, such studies are of human ecology rather than of cultural ecology.

We also tend to focus on the remains of large animals, often ignoring small ones. That tendency results in the utilization of techniques designed to recover large animal remains, an analytical self-fulfilling prophesy. However, the processing of large animals may result in their remains being highly fragmented. Even if the focus of some prehistoric economy was on large animals, we may miss the evidence if we are not looking for small bone. As we refine our techniques in the recovery of bone (primarily by using finer-mesh screen), we are beginning to recognize the importance of small animals in the diet. That recognition will likely result in the reevaluation of long-held theories regarding the subsistence focus of many archaeological cultures (e.g., the Paleoindian of North America).

Nevertheless, in spite of the advances in method and theory, the remains of some fauna are often ignored. Rodent remains are often attributed to natural processes, despite some good evidence to the contrary (as mentioned previously). Insects are almost always ignored, both at recovery and during analysis (there are exceptions; Madsen and Kirkman 1988). The omission is due, in part, to preservation problems, techniques that focus on other fauna, and ethnocentrism regarding insect consumption. The point is emphasized by Szuter (Chapter 4), who contends that rodents were an important component in aboriginal diet, both to hunter-gatherers and to agriculturalists (the Hohokam in her examples). This message must be clearly understood. Small animals in general may account for a much larger proportion of the diet than is currently recognized. The consumption of insects was (and is) very widespread, as is the consumption of rodents. The use of birds and reptiles is also likely underrated. We archaeologists suffer from a bias toward large animals in our thinking and considerations of ethnographic and prehistoric cultures. Clearly, our thinking must change if we are to understand and document the full range of cultural adaptation both present and past.

Nonvisible Remains

Nonvisible remains are those that must be identified through chemical analyses, even if the material itself is visible. Such remains fall into two basic categories: visible but unidentified organic residues and nonvisible chemical constituents. The first category has received considerable attention from the physical sciences, and the identification of materials through gas chromatography, mass spectrometry, and infrared spectroscopy is becoming increasingly sophisticated (e.g., Biers and McGovern 1990; Heron et al. 1991). The second category includes stable isotope studies and immunological techniques. Stable isotope studies may be a direct measure of general diet and are not discussed further (but see Sillen et al. [1989] for a cautionary note). Techniques on the horizon include DNA analysis and more sensitive immunological techniques.

A relatively new technique, also included in the second category, is the recovery and analysis of protein residues from archaeological samples. The immunological technique is often erroneously called "blood residue analysis," but it identifies all protein residues, not just those from blood, and it can be used for both plants and animals. Very small quantities of proteins do preserve on stone tools, in coprolites, and in soils, and those proteins can be recovered and identified, sometimes to the genus level (e.g., Newman 1990; Newman et al. 1993; Yohe et al. 1991). The technique is very promising but is limited by several factors: the relatively few antisera available, the limit of sensitivity, and the continued laboratory processing of materials that could destroy the residues. Archaeologists should be warned *not* to wash the artifacts in the laboratory, or they may wash away the data.

Application of the technique has very important analytical implications. It is now possible to identify proteins on specific tools, thus aiding in their functional interpretation. For example, millingstones (metates) are usually thought of as seed-processing tools. However, Yohe and colleagues (1991) identified the presence of various animal proteins, indicating that the animals were processed on the milling equipment. Not only did the identification provide evidence of resource use and associated technology, it also shed light on the processing of the bones from the animals, whose visibility in the conventional faunal record was much reduced.

Another important application of the technique is in expanding the breadth of resources identified at a site, resources that may not be present in the traditional dietary record. The following example illustrates the value of the technique. The macrofaunal analysis of the materials from a 3,000-year-old site (CA-SBR-6580) in southern California resulted in the identification of turtle *(Clemmys marmorata)* and "large mammal" (Sutton et al. 1993). However, pronghorn *(Antilocapra americana),* deer *(Odocoileus* sp.), waterfowl, fish, rodent (rat), lagomorph, and either porcupine or squirrel were identified in the immunological analysis of both flaked and ground stone artifacts (Newman 1993). The lack of visible faunal remains from similarly aged sites in the region has led researchers to suggest a reliance (specialization) on plant resources (see Moratto 1984:153). However, the identification of a wider range of utilized animal resources suggests that the subsistence adaptation of that archaeological culture should be reevaluated.

The Technological Component

Another aspect of indirect dietary studies (noted only briefly here) is the technology of food production, procurement, processing, transport, storage, and consumption. A considerable portion of the technological inventory of people is dedicated to diet in some manner. The understanding of an agricultural system (fields, irrigation systems, roads, and so forth) could provide significant insight into the diet and nutrition of a particular population.

In addition, the delineation of the function of features (e.g., storage or processing) and of tools provides considerable data regarding diet. For example, we assume that we know the function of certain tools and so infer dietary components based on those assumptions. In the case of the millingstones noted above (Yohe et al. 1991), such assumptions were shown to be at least partly in error, forcing some revision in the presumed structure of the aboriginal diet.

Issues of Recovery

The recovery of any archaeological data is dependent on a variety of factors, including, but not limited to, (1) preservation and taphonomy (including postrecovery damage), (2) techniques used in the field and laboratory, and (3) specimen recognition in the field and laboratory (a topic not discussed in this paper). After "recovery," materials must be properly classified and interpreted (see Lyman [1987] for a more complete discussion of faunal materials). Because of these and other factors (e.g., seasonality), it is recognized that the ecofactual assemblage from a site likely does not represent the total inventory of resources used (Styles, Chapter 3). However, as recovery and analytical techniques improve, the disparity between the actual and recovered assemblages should decrease.

Preservation and Taphonomy

Organic remains generally decompose and/or are subject to a variety of destructive processes after deposition and are not commonly recovered from archaeological sites. To be preserved, organics usually must be waterlogged, frozen, desiccated, or charred (the majority of recovered plant remains). Different materials preserve differently; plants that have a dense inedible part (corncobs) or less dense but normally ingested whole (small seeds) are more likely to be preserved in a site than roots or tubers (Minnis 1981:149; Munson et al. 1971:422). Bone and shell are much more likely to be preserved than soft tissues. The alteration of resources during processing is also an important issue in preservation.

The processes noted above combine to remove evidence of many plant and animal resources from sites and so result in the archaeological records being "incomplete." However, in spite of preservation and taphonomic problems, many data do survive in the archaeological record, and it is reasonably clear that the harder we look, the more we find. Thus, the perceived incompleteness of the record may be at least partly an illusion; perhaps we just do not look hard enough.

Field Techniques

A majority of archaeological sites are excavated using field screening, dry and/or wet. The use of quarter-inch mesh screen to process site soils is commonplace but is a rather crude method for the recovery of subsistence-related data (and even for some artifacts). The use of that screen size results in the loss of many of the very faunal data that we seek. The loss increases in percentage as the type of animal gets smaller (Grayson 1984:168–172). In fact, some species (e.g., small mammals [Shaffer 1992] and small fish [Gobalet 1989]) may be missed entirely, resulting in a miscalculation of relative importance and the development of a spurious subsistence model. As the analytical aspects of dietary models become more sophisticated, it is astonishing to see the continued (and customary) use of quarter-inch screen in the field.

The use of witness samples of site soil may identify the microconstituents within a midden while promoting the economical processing of site soils. A column sample (i.e., 10 cm^3) can be taken and micro-screened, thus identifying any materials that may have escaped the primary screening. Such a technique should be employed across a site, rather than in one locality, to establish control and to determine differential distribution, if any, of microremains.

Two other points worth considering are contamination of samples and the problem of specimen recognition in the field. In any sampling of features or soils, especially for pollen or phytoliths, one must exercise great caution to avoid contamination. Special training in how to take such samples is necessary. The recognition of materials is another concern. Charred seeds, bone, and other ecofacts may be retained in the screen, but if the screener does not collect them, they are discarded and thus not "recovered." As with collection of soil samples, training is the key.

Laboratory Techniques

Once materials are collected in the field and returned to the laboratory, recognition, recovery, identification, and analysis must still be done. Macroremains enter the laboratory either as soil samples to be processed or as recognized ecofacts (seeds, charcoal, and the like) segregated in the field.

Soil samples (other than those for pollen or phytoliths) are frequently subject to flotation techniques designed to recover macrobotanical remains but not other classes of data (but see Bodner and Rowlett 1980; Toll 1988). If other information is recovered, so much the better, but many data (e.g., faunal remains and debitage) are often lost. However, examination of the entire sample, and not just the float fraction, would likely result in the recovery of a greater quantity and diversity of data and provide a baseline for understanding the types of remains lost in the normal screening process.

Materials recovered in the screens and from soil samples must then be identified and catalogued, a process requiring special expertise and comparative collections. It may be that these remains are sent to specialists, often nonarchaeologists, for identification.

Other, special, samples are processed in different ways. The extraction of proteins from archaeological specimens, for example, requires selection of presumably uncontaminated samples, the entire process of which could bias the results. In some sense, the extraction of proteins from tools is an issue of preservation and recovery, since the proteins were "collected" in the field (e.g., existing on a stone tool).

General Issues of Interpretation

Three major themes are threaded throughout the various chapters (2 through 6) in *Indirect Studies:* (1) the need to use independent data sets in the study of paleonutrition, (2) the noncomparability of many studies, and (3) the problem of the incompleteness of the record. The first point is not really an issue; everyone agrees that it is the correct approach. It is the implementation of new techniques and the gathering of the appropriate data that remain to be accomplished. The same is generally true of the second point, and there is an increasing effort (e.g., this book) to standardize approaches and/or to make the results comparable.

The third issue is multidimensional. It is true that the database is limited, but it is not clear why. One possibility is that the archaeological record itself is incomplete. Taphonomy is a central issue in discussing the archaeological record, and there is little question that materials entering the archaeological record (defined here as what is present in the landscape rather than just what has been discovered) are altered to some degree prior to their recovery by an archaeologist. Generally, dietary data (seeds, bones, leaves, and so forth) must be recognizable to be recovered. Efforts to increase the threshold of recognition continue, and smaller and smaller materials are being identified. The continuing development of pollen and phytolith studies is a leap in the right direction.

Resources

A major objective in dietary studies is the delineation of which resources were and were not used, how, when, and why (an analysis of return rates would be helpful). Many investigators list potential resources as a starting point for their analyses. Such a list is often based on the modern distributions of plants and animals, ethnographic information, and related data. However, the mere presence of something within an area does not necessarily indicate its use by the resident population, and it is use, not presence, that defines a resource to a particular culture (see Szuter, Chapter 4). For example, to most Native American groups, insects formed an important part of the diet (e.g., Sutton 1988). However, to the Euramerican populations that replaced the Indians, insects were pests, not resources. If a potential resource is not used by a particular group, there may be an interesting circumstance worthy of research, even if it is difficult to identify.

This difficulty in identification is of importance. Since we recognize only positive data, it is necessary to demonstrate the use of an item to determine that is was a resource. Because of a variety of factors, such as preservation and processing, evidence of use may be lacking. The development of more sophisticated recovery techniques will help, but the problem will remain. We must be aware of it (see Chapter 4).

Positive and Negative Data

Most studies of floral and faunal data deal with positive evidence, the presence of specific species. Ordinarily, little attempt is made to explain or account for negative information, the absence of species (assuming that a species was actually absent and that poor recovery was not the issue). However, if deer were absent from the faunal assemblage at a particular site where they were expected (listed as a likely resource), there would be a discussion of why deer were absent (e.g., site function, schlepping, religion). But such interpretations seem to be conducted only with "big ticket" species. If insect remains were not identified, no explanation would be made; the absence would be ignored.

This is not necessarily to advocate that each absent species be explained, although significant inferences could result from such discussions. For example, in a diet-breadth optimal foraging model, the use of resources is predicted and tested against the record and the absence of a predicted resource is subject to interpretation. We should at least recognize the importance of small, less archaeologically visible, species to prehistoric diet and make a more serious attempt to deal with those species, whether present or absent.

Integration of Results

Given the recovery of data relating to diet and nutrition from a site, the archaeologist must still integrate the various lines of data (including direct data) into a coherent picture of prehistoric subsistence. Although such integration sounds logical, it is rarely done. Crane and Carr (Chapter 5) attempt integration in their dietary reconstruction of a Late Preclassic Maya site but find several limitations, primarily the collection and processing of the data and the lack of communication between the faunal and floral specialists. That there is so little communication between specialists, that recovery techniques are so crude, and that flotation was not undertaken at Maya sites until the late 1970s is quite remarkable. Archaeologists have apparently emphasized architecture and art rather than trying to figure out what people were actually doing.

We can hope that the above example is not typical, since a number of good integrative studies have been conducted (e.g., Thomas 1983). Other projects integrating disparate lines of data include that of Holden (1991) in Peru, who used midden sample, mummy gut content, and coprolite data in dietary reconstruction, and of Sutton (1993) in southern California, who employed traditional floral and faunal data, coupled with a cluster analysis of the coprolite data, to infer dietary preference and seasonality.

Even nonconcordant data are useful, as they can point to different ideas and solutions to problems. Gumerman (Chapter 6) demonstrates that point in noting that the isotopic and macrobotanical data implied different production between elite and commoners among the Wanka of highland Peru. The argument of feasting to account for that difference points to the use of those data in a much broader context than mere nutrition.

A Focus on the Elaborate

Many archaeological studies focus on conspicuous sites and high-status individuals, with little work being conducted on unobtrusive sites (e.g., those representing commoners). That approach can result in a skewed database and erroneous interpretations. A case in point is the settlement-subsistence patterns of the ancient Maya. While most archaeologists were studying the elaborate high-profile sites, a majority of the Maya sites (being quite unpretentious and representing most of the population) were ignored. The subsequent recognition of that element of the record has fundamentally altered our view of the Maya. The same argument has been made for the American Southwest (Upham 1988).

That same perspective seems to permeate archaeology as a discipline. Low-visibility archaeology (lacking permanent architecture and elaborate material culture), primarily of hunter-gatherer cultures, attracts fewer researchers, is awarded less grant money, and receives fewer positions in academic departments and less respect than the archaeology of "complex" societies. What seems lost is the realization that hunter-gatherer archaeology is also quite complex, represents the majority of human existence, and can address many interesting questions of paleonutrition and adaptation.

Gumerman (Chapter 6) compares the diets of various levels of specialists (elite, attached, independent, full- and part-time) with that of commoners (there being some overlap) of the Wanka. His thesis is that the diets of those diverse groups were different and distinguishable in the archaeological record. He notes that archaeologists tend to "lump" subsistence-related data and then "reconstruct" the diets of entire cultures without regard to internal variability. He is correct that that is commonly done and most likely results in a misunderstanding of the complexity of the culture under study. While Gumerman deals with the diet of specialists, he properly recognizes that nonspecialist diets may also vary, based either on age, gender, generation, season, or other criteria. Such research may be quite difficult using ordinary archaeological data but may be possible with other data sets (e.g., coprolites; Sutton 1993).

Gumerman's argument of differential diets is based on several hypotheses about the nature of economic activities of the various levels of specialists, plus the premise that specialists had an economic advantage over nonspecialists. While the hypotheses appear well-supported by other data (e.g., ethnographic analogy), they must continue to be the topic of research and cannot become unconsciously accepted assumptions. One of the complicating factors in the argument is the relative paucity of data regarding commoner diet and economy (as Gumerman and others have noted), which could skew the results of the analysis.

Added to the discovery of foods and food combinations that were eaten by the various groups is the identification of food sources that were not exploited. Gumerman argues that full-time specialists did not utilize "opportunistic" food resources (e.g., nondomesticates obtained by farmers) but were limited to a more narrow diet (in the sense of a diet-breadth model) "imposed" by the elite and the economic system (staple finance foods that were storable). If a nutritional analysis was made of the various food components of the differing diets, it may be that nutritional stress was placed on the upper-class people as a result of the more narrow diet. Evidence of such stress likely is present in the archaeological record (demography, skeletal pathologies, and so forth) if we become clever enough to find it.

Paleonutrition?

Strictly speaking, most studies of paleonutrition are not studies of paleo*nutrition*. Rather, many such studies concentrate on delineating the gross components of diet (species lists and frequency). Very little is known about the actual nutritional content of many faunal and floral resources, and such analyses are not conducted as often as needed. Some (poor) reasons for that failure are a myopic focus on calories (particularly in optimal foraging studies), an inadequate understanding of human nutritional needs (the current understanding is based on data from Western cultures), and a lack of critical evaluation of dietary components.

Much of our understanding of human nutritional requirements is based on estimates from U.S. government studies of modern Americans, and those estimates are often used by anthropologists in their assessments of the nutritional needs of other groups. Human populations are both geographically and temporally diverse, and they adapt to different environments by both biological and cultural means. It would be remarkable if, given that evolution, all populations shared the same nutritional requirements. The situation is beginning to change as the literature on the variability (cultural, biological, and geographic) of human nutritional needs (e.g., Johnson 1987) continues to grow.

This same bias is true in discussions of health. We assume that prehistoric health is measurable in terms of modern Western standards, that complete health is "normal" and any deviation is "abnormal." It would be easy to imagine that a population could be unhealthy (by our standards) but still biologically successful. It is necessary to broaden our view of health and biological and cultural success.

There are few specific studies on the nature of nutritional stress in prehistory (but see Minnis 1985), how such stress may have affected adaptation (perhaps even beneficially), or what means were employed to solve the problem (if any). What we do is list some resources used; we know little of why they were used.

Conclusion

It is apparent that archaeologists are moving toward a more comprehensive view of dietary reconstruction, using both direct and indirect data (including chemical analyses). However, problems still remain. We continue to have a biased view of the resource base, and recovery and analytical techniques hinder interpretation. We must broaden our views of health, nutrition, and variation and increase our efforts at data recovery and analysis. Further, we must begin to look at diet as being more than a list of foods and nutrients. We should be attempting to discover cuisine—the cultural aspects of food preference, combinations, methods of preparation, and so forth—and its anthropological implications in antiquity. The situation is improving; this volume is evidence of that.

Acknowledgments

I appreciate the comments of Donna Butler, Robert E. Parr, Kristin Sobolik, Robert M. Yohe II, and several anonymous reviewers on a draft of this paper.

References

Biers, W. R., and P. E. McGovern
  1990   *Organic Contents of Ancient Vessels: Materials Analysis and Archaeological Investigation.* Research Papers in Science and Archaeology No. 7. Museum Applied Science Center for Archaeology, University of Pennsylvania, Philadelphia.
Bodner, C. C., and R. M. Rowlett
  1980   Separation of Bone, Charcoal, and Seeds by Chemical Flotation. *American Antiquity* 45:110–116.
Bryant, V. M., Jr.
  1975   Pollen as an Indicator of Prehistoric Diets in Coahuila, Mexico. *Bulletin of the Texas Archeological Society* 46:87–106.
Gilbert, R., and J. Mielke (editors)
  1985   *The Analysis of Prehistoric Diets.* Academic Press, Orlando.
Gobalet, K. W.
  1989   Remains of Tiny Fish from a Late Prehistoric Pomo Site near Clear Lake, California. *Journal of California and Great Basin Anthropology* 11:231–239.
Grayson, D. K.
  1984   *Quantitative Zooarchaeology.* Academic Press, New York.
Hastorf, C. A., and V. S. Popper (editors)
  1988   *Current Paleoethnobotany: Analytical Methods and Cultural Interpretations of Archaeological Plant Remains.* University of Chicago Press, Chicago.
Heron, C., R. P. Evershed, L. J. Goad, and V. Denham
  1991   New Approaches to the Analysis of Organic Residues from Archaeological Remains. In *Archaeological Sciences 1989,* edited by P. Budd, B. Chapman, C. Jackson, R. Janaway, and B. Ottaway, pp. 332–339. Oxbow Monograph 9. Oxford.
Holden, T. G.
  1991   Evidence of Prehistoric Diet from Northern Chile: Coprolites, Gut Contents, and Flotation Samples from the Tulán Quebrada. *World Archaeology* 22:320–331.
Johnson, F. E. (editor)
  1987   *Nutritional Anthropology.* Alan R. Liss, New York.

Lawlor, E. J.
  1992   Effects of Mojave Desert Rodents and Harvester Ants on Carbonized Seeds:
          Preliminary Results. Paper presented at the Great Basin Anthropological
          Conference, Boise.
Lyman, R. L.
  1987   Zooarchaeology and Taphonomy: A General Consideration. *Journal of
          Ethnobiology* 7:93–117.
Madsen, D. B., and J. E. Kirkman
  1988   Hunting Hoppers. *American Antiquity* 53:593–604.
Miksicek, C. H.
  1987   Formation Processes of the Archaeobotanical Record. In *Advances in Archae-
          ological Method and Theory*, vol. 10, edited by M. B. Schiffer, pp. 211–247.
          Academic Press, New York.
Miller, N. F., and T. L. Smart
  1984   Intentional Burning of Dung as Fuel: A Mechanism for the Incorporation of
          Charred Seeds into the Archaeological Record. *Journal of Ethnobiology* 4:15–28.
Minnis, P. E.
  1981   Seeds in Archaeological Sites: Sources and Some Interpretive Problems.
          American Antiquity 46:143–152.
  1985   *Social Adaptation to Food Stress: A Prehistoric Southwestern Example*. Univer-
          sity of Chicago Press, Chicago.
Moratto, M. J.
  1984   *California Archaeology*. Academic Press, New York.
Munson, P. J., P. W. Parmalee, and R. A. Yarnell
  1971   Subsistence Ecology of Scovill, A Terminal Middle Woodland Village.
          American Antiquity 36:410–431.
Newman, M. E.
  1990   *The Hidden Evidence from Hidden Cave, Nevada*. Ph.D. dissertation, Depart-
          ment of Anthropology, University of Toronto.
  1993   Immunological Residue Analysis of Samples from CA-SBR-6580. Appendix
          3. In The Siphon Site (CA-SBR-6580): A Millingstone Horizon Site in Summit
          Valley, California, by M. Q. Sutton, J. S. Schneider, and R. M. Yohe II, pp. 79–83.
          San Bernardino County Museum Association Quarterly 40(3).
Newman, M. E., R. M. Yohe II, H. Ceri, and M. Q. Sutton
  1993   Immunological Protein Residue Analysis of Non-lithic Archaeological
          Materials. *Journal of Archaeological Science*, 20:93–100.
Pearsall, D. M.
  1988   Interpreting the Meaning of Macroremain Abundance: The Impact of
          Source and Context. In *Current Paleoethnobotany: Analytical Methods and Cultural
          Interpretations of Archaeological Plant Remains*, edited by C. A. Hastorf and V. S.
          Popper, pp. 97–118. University of Chicago Press, Chicago.
Piperno, D. R.
  1988   *Phytolith Analysis: An Archaeological and Geological Perspective*. Academic
          Press, San Diego.
  1991   The Status of Phytolith Analysis in the American Tropics. *Journal of World
          Prehistory* 5:155–191.
Shaffer, B. S.
  1992   Quarter-Inch Screening: Understanding Biases in Recovery of Vertebrate
          Faunal Remains. *American Antiquity* 57:129–136.

Sillen, A., J. C. Sealy, and N. J. van der Merwe
  1989   Chemistry and Paleodietary Research: No More Easy Answers. *American Antiquity* 54:504–512.
Smart, T. L., and E. S. Hoffman
  1988   Environmental Interpretation of Archaeological Charcoal. In *Current Paleoethnobotany: Analytical Methods and Cultural Interpretations of Archaeological Plant Remains*, edited by C. A. Hastorf and V. S. Popper, pp. 167–205. University of Chicago Press, Chicago.
Sutton, M. Q.
  1988   *Insects as Food: Aboriginal Entomophagy in the Great Basin*. Anthropological Papers No. 33. Ballena Press, Menlo Park, California.
  1993   Midden and Coprolite Derived Subsistence Evidence: An Analysis of Data from the La Quinta Site, Salton Basin, California. *Journal of Ethnobiology* 13:1–15.
Sutton, M. Q., J. S. Schneider, and R. M. Yohe II
  1993   The Siphon Site (CA-SBR-6580): A Millingstone Horizon Site in Summit Valley, California. *San Bernardino County Museum Association Quarterly* 40(3).
Thomas, D. H.
  1983   *The Archaeology of Monitor Valley: 2. Gatecliff Shelter*. Anthropological Papers Vol. 59, Pt. 1. American Museum of Natural History, New York.
Toll, M. S.
  1988   Flotation Sampling: Problems and Some Solutions, with Examples from the American Southwest. In *Current Paleoethnobotany*, edited by C. A. Hastorf and V. S. Popper, pp. 36–52. University of Chicago Press, Chicago.
Upham, S.
  1988   Archaeological Visibility and the Underclass of Southwestern Prehistory. *American Antiquity* 53:245–261.
Wilke, P. J.
  1978   *Late Prehistoric Human Ecology at Lake Cahuilla, Coachella Valley, California*. Contributions of the University of California Archaeological Research Facility No. 38. Berkeley.
Wing, E. S., and A. B. Brown
  1979   *Paleonutrition: Method and Theory in Prehistoric Foodways*. Academic Press, New York.
Yohe, R. M., II, M. E. Newman, and J. S. Schneider
  1991   Immunological Identification of Small-Mammal Proteins on Aboriginal Milling. *American Antiquity* 56:659–666.

II.   Coprolite Studies

8.
Corn Preparation among the Basketmaker Anasazi: A Scanning Electron Microscope Study of *Zea Mays* Remains from Coprolites

Kate Aasen Rylander

Abstract: What does the coprolite record tell us about the diet of the earliest Anasazi of the American Southwest, the "Basketmakers"? Recent study of over 80 human fecal specimens from four Basketmaker-component archaeological sites clarified the importance of corn in Basketmaker diet and yet illustrated that the consumption of "wild," or uncultivated, foods played a major role in their subsistence as well. Of critical concern is how the plant and animal food items found within the coprolites were prepared prior to ingestion, and how this preparation affected the nutrients' absorption by the human body. This paper addresses the preparation of one of the Basketmaker Anasazi's principal food items—corn. The scanning electron microscope is used to observe the external microstructure of modern experimentally ground *Zea mays* pericarp. Corn remains recovered from archaeological coprolites are compared to the variously prepared experimental specimens.

Introduction

One of the most direct means of analyzing prehistoric diet is to study the undigested portions of meals preserved in ancient feces. Since first recognizing the importance of studying coprolites over a century ago, archaeologists have sought to define diet, subsistence practices, and the nutrition of prehistoric populations from around the world. A fertile area of research is the Four Corners region of the American Southwest where the Anasazi culture once flourished (approximately A.D. 1–1300). The advent of prehistoric agriculture among the Anasazi, as it is reflected in the coprolite record, has inspired numerous ideas, theories, and controversies. Coprolite analyses of

Paleonutrition: The Diet and Health of Prehistoric Americans, edited by Kristin D. Sobolik. Center for Archaeological Investigations, Occasional Paper No. 22. © 1994 by the Board of Trustees, Southern Illinois University. All rights reserved. ISBN 0-88104-078-9.

the Basketmaker Anasazi, a culture that predated the Puebloan Anasazi and was found below the Puebloan horizon in many sites, are especially interesting. This paper seeks to answer three questions: (1) What does the coprolite record tell us about the diet of those earliest Anasazi (specifically, Basketmaker II)? (2) What insights does scanning electron microscope (SEM) analysis give us about the preparation of Basketmaker foods? and (3) What is the impact of those preparation techniques on the nutrient content of the food consumed?

Basketmaker Anasazi Diet

What is known about Basketmaker diet? Briefly, early researchers believed the Basketmaker Anasazi subsisted primarily on corn *(Zea mays)*, as had their Puebloan descendants, but hunted various game when available or necessary (e.g., Kidder and Guernsey 1919). Another (Hough 1930) estimated that the diet of the Basketmaker was derived primarily (85%) from cereal (corn), although various wild plants and animals were collected or hunted.

So what has changed in the analysis of Basketmaker Anasazi subsistence in the last 100 years? The basic list of identified food remains and the corn-dominated composition of Basketmaker diet have not changed even though the list of "wild" plant items consumed has grown. The analysis of Basketmaker diet is complicated by the fact that few Basketmaker feces were collected for analysis during the late nineteenth- and early twentieth-century excavations. Even fewer were analyzed for their pollen and macrofossil content. Approximately 250 Anasazi coprolites have been studied to date—and most of those fecal remains are associated with the later Puebloan periods (see Minnis 1989).

Recent macrofossil and pollen analyses of over 80 coprolites from four Basketmaker II Anasazi sites have partially remedied that situation. That research clarifies the importance of corn in Basketmaker diet and illustrates the adaptability of the Anasazi to their local environment. Sixty-five coprolites from Turkey Pen Ruin (Grand Gulch, Cedar Mesa, Utah), one coprolite from Woodchuck Cave (Shonto Plateau), five feces from Three Fir Shelter on Black Mesa (Arizona), and nine scats from Dust Devil Cave (southern Utah) have now been analyzed. Detailed descriptions of the coprolite analyses exist elsewhere (Aasen 1984, 1986; Reinhard 1994). All four sites offered the opportunity to study Basketmaker II feces and to compare the relative reliance on corn agriculture.

Corn Macrofossils and the Basketmaker Coprolite Record

Dust Devil Cave, situated between Navajo Mountain and the San Juan River in southern Utah, presented researchers with both Archaic and Basketmaker coprolites. Nine fecal samples from Level VI, a stratum dated to Basketmaker II, were analyzed for their pollen and macrofossil content. Dust

Devil Cave Basketmaker Anasazi enjoyed corn, various wild plant foods such as Indian ricegrass *(Oryzopsis hymenoides)*, and meat (as evidenced by singed bone) in the same meal. Corn pericarp (the exterior surface of the corn kernel) appeared in four samples and was abundant in two of the feces. No kernel peduncles (kernel attachment structure) were recovered from the coprolites. The most abundant remain in at least half of the coprolites was a powdery sand-fiber-tissue mixture. That mixture may be indicative of the grinding of food items.

Woodchuck Cave, a large deep recess located on the Shonto Plateau in Arizona, contained a single coprolite associated with a burial radiocarbon dated to 2050 ± 100 (University of Arizona). Macrofossils from the sample were again dominated by a powdery fiber and sand mixture, although only a few pieces of cf. *Zea mays* pericarp were recovered. Unburned bone was the single most abundant item in the macrofossil inventory, which also included Indian ricegrass, charcoal, and a few insects.

The excavation of Three Fir Shelter, located on a tributary of Coal Mine Wash near the eastern escarpment of Black Mesa, provided a well-dated (2150–2590 B.P.; Francis Smiley, personal communication 1986) Basketmaker site with an abundance of well-preserved perishable materials. The importance of corn to the Three Fir Shelter inhabitants is partially addressed through coprolite analysis in that three of the four human coprolites contained corn macrofossils, two of them dominated by *Zea* pericarp. Coprolites were characterized by combinations of corn and burned Indian ricegrass seed, a mixture of sand and fibers, an abundance of caramelized and possibly parched pinenut *(Pinus* sp.) shell, or crushed juniper *(Juniperus* sp.) seed fragments. The collection of plants from the local environment was an important feature of Basketmaker diet at Three Fir Shelter.

The analysis of 65 coprolites from Turkey Pen Ruin and a preliminary visual observation of an additional 250 coprolite fragments from the site provide the most extensive research available on Basketmaker II Anasazi fecal remains. Turkey Pen Ruin is situated on a particularly spectacular canyon known as Grand Gulch in southeastern Utah. Like Three Fir Shelter, the site offered the opportunity to study well-preserved organic remains, and the abundance of coprolites found there was legendary. A macrofossil and pollen study of the first 30 coprolites (Aasen 1984) and a subsequent study of an additional 11 samples (Aasen 1986) indicated that Basketmaker II Anasazi at the site often ate both domesticated and wild plant foods in a single meal (or at least within a period of a few meals). The macrofossil content of the analyzed fecal specimens showed an overwhelming abundance of corn.

Although corn dominated the macrofossil inventory, wild plant food items were represented in the coprolite record by numerous pinenut shell fragments, ground Indian ricegrass seed, and whole Rocky Mountain beeweed *(Cleome serrulata)* seeds—often contained in the same corn-dominated sample. Many of the coprolites containing corn also contained numerous Chenopodiaceae (goosefoot family) leaves. The presence of the leaves could indicate the addition of chenopod leaves to cornmeal or the use of the leaves as a green in a corn-rich meal.

Visual inspection by the author of 250 more coprolite fragments from the screened and unscreened strata at Turkey Pen Ruin using 10X on a stereomicroscope indicated that all specimens contained *Zea mays*. Corn pericarp was visible in both interior and exterior views of the coprolites and was usually the dominant macrofossil.

In summary, corn obviously played a significant role in the diet of the Basketmaker II Anasazi. All four Basketmaker sites held coprolites that contained corn or were dominated by corn macrofossils. Basketmaker individuals collected plant items from their local environment, either to supplement their corn diet (as at Turkey Pen Ruin; and for at least two coprolites from both Dust Devil Cave and Three Fir Shelter) or to provide the basis for an entire meal. In addition to corn macrofossils, a sand and fiber mixture was the most abundant item in many Basketmaker samples. That mixture may reflect the grinding of various plant items with stone implements.

Archaeological Corn Remains: Some Research Questions

Visual inspection of the corn remains in Basketmaker coprolites seemed to show that corn had been variously prepared. I had first observed such differences in the condition of the corn macrofossils at Turkey Pen Ruin. Specifically, corn remains from the ruin's coprolites exhibited a range of different sizes and a degree of uniformity within each sample. Several coprolites, in addition to the abundant corn pericarp, contained cupule fragments or kernel peduncles that one might attribute to the eating of corn off the cob. Other samples contained small, uniform pieces of pericarp that I thought represented the grinding of corn.

I wanted to know (1) if corn preparation and processing methods could be described further and (2) if corn preparation had changed through time or varied from site to site.

Experimental Methods

Since I wanted to learn more about how to recognize whether corn had been ground prior to its consumption and incorporation into the archaeological coprolite samples, I decided to grind corn kernels and cook them in various ways in order to obtain modern correlates to which the archaeological samples could be compared. I expected that if the corn had been ground, it would exhibit some unique characteristics including (1) striations or scrapes on the pericarp surface, (2) uniformity of overall pericarp size throughout the sample, and (3) lack of striations on the pericarp surfaces. If striations were absent, then perhaps the pericarp fragments would exhibit some other feature characteristic of grinding such as overall abrasion, or wear.

Research on corn preparation among the various Indian groups of the Southwest provided a plethora of different corn preparation techniques.

Probably well over 150 such recipes exist among the Hopi, Zuni, Tewa, other Pueblo Indian groups, Navajos, and practicing corn agriculturalists of the region. As Whiting in his ethnobotany of the Hopi observed "there are almost innumerable ways of preparing it [corn]" (1939:15).

Historic Zuni, for example, prepared mature corn differently from green or stored corn. Mature corn was roasted while still on the cob, or the kernels were removed and parched (Cushing 1920:265). The swollen and browned kernels were then cracked, retoasted, and ground into a "fine flour" (1920:266). Ripened corn was also baked on the ear, shelled, and then boiled in water (1920:292). Ground cornmeal was prepared in a number of ways and varied in size: just cracked open, coarse meal, and finer flour (1920:293–294). Ashes or finely ground lime were sometimes added to produce a fermented mush (1920:294–295). Often two sizes of cornmeal (coarsely ground and fine) were mixed with warm water to produce a fermented mixture that formed a yeast when lime and salt were added (1920:294). Cornmeal was also used to make mushes, dumplings of all varieties, griddle cakes, and various breads (1920:297–305).

As one can see, the ethnographic record is very informative, but the variety entailed by those methods and their permutations produces an overwhelming number of experimental variables. To simplify, I chose to grind, boil, and parch dried kernels of flint/flour corn for the preliminary experiments.

Dried corn kernels were obtained from Native Seed/SEARCH (Tucson). Experimentation proceeded using a red variety of Santo Domingo Pueblo flint/flour kernel. The kernels were variously ground: some were lightly ground with the grain of the kernel, some were ground against the kernel grain, and others were completely ground to flour and pericarp fragments. The orientation of the kernel to the grinding surface could not be tracked in this case. All kernels were ground with moderate-to-light pressure using a sandstone metate and mano. Sandstone was chosen for the grinding implements because all archaeological groundstone recovered at Turkey Pen Ruin was sandstone (Powers 1984). Finally, several kernels were parched over an open wood fire (away from the direct flame) or boiled in an open pot for 15 minutes (no salt or other additives). Because the results of these experiments are extensive, I will focus on the preliminary results of the grinding experiments.

Use of the Scanning Electron Microscope

Differences in the microstructure of corn pericarp within the Turkey Pen Ruin coprolites were not readily visible with a .8X-to-75X stereomicroscope. The use of the scanning electron microscope (SEM) offered another avenue of research.

The use of the SEM in the study of plant tissue is not without precedent. Applications in the field of microbiology and plant physiology/anatomy have been variously reviewed (see Greenhaugh and Evans 1971; Oatley et al. 1965; Pomeranz 1976). One interesting study that has some bearing on my research includes a published report by Watson and colleagues (1975) in which long-grained rice was ground nine different ways. The surface lipids and ash, as well as the protein contents, were quantified, and the milled material was examined using the SEM. Results indicated that there was variation in the amounts of pericarp and aleurone removed from the rice grains by the various milling techniques as well as variation in the amount of external surface material removed by milling from different areas on the same rice grain using a single milling procedure. Likewise, I expected some variation in the alteration of corn pericarp within the same sample.

SEM Methods

Archaeological specimens of corn pericarp retrieved from the Turkey Pen Ruin coprolites and modern pieces of corn kernels that were variously prepared were observed using an International Scientific Instruments SEM Model DS 130 located on the University of Arizona campus (Tucson). That model uses secondary electron emission and operates between 10 and 20KV. All specimens were coated with approximately 30 nanometers of gold by a Hummer 1 Modified sputtercoater prior to viewing.

Hundreds to thousands of corn macrofossils were identified in each of the Turkey Pen Ruin coprolites. Examination of all the fragments was not feasible because of cost and the preliminary nature of the study. Instead, 10 pieces of pericarp were chosen for further analysis from each of the first 28 human fecal specimens. Pericarp fragments from 10 of the coprolites were examined with the SEM during the preliminary phase. Results of the SEM examination of corn pericarp fragments from two of the 10 coprolites are highlighted in this paper because the results set parameters for further study and are characteristic of the 10 samples studied. First, however, it was necessary to study and describe modern kernels that had been dried but had not been ground.

Morphologically, a corn kernel consists of the bran, the endosperm, and the germ, or embryo. The bran is the outermost layer of the grain forming a protective fibrous covering. The bran is further divided into the pericarp (more properly the epi-, mesi- and endocarp), the testa, and the "tip cap," which covers the top of the grain (Food and Agricultural Organization of the United Nations [FAO] 1953:6–7). Endosperm forms the bulk of the corn kernel, making up 80 to 84% of the grain. The exterior of the endosperm is termed the aleurone layer, a layer rich in fat and protein. Translucent hard/flinty and floury endosperm are underlain by a starchy interior. The embryo or germ is located along the end of the grain, which attaches to the cupule of the corncob.

Results

Photos (Figure 8-1) of the exterior pericarp of a modern mature flint/flour Santo Domingo Pueblo corn kernel taken with the SEM show a longitudinal cell structure. Under 40X to 75X, these cells are seen as close-knit striae when in fact they are actually elongated cells that are either rounded at their tips or angled. The bran's lenticular cell structure runs perpendicular to the kernel's point of attachment to the cob. At the interface between cells, crosswise tendrils appear, creating a fibrous interwoven network.

Examination of experimentally ground corn provided some interesting comparisons. Dried Santo Domingo flint/flour kernels were placed on a metate, and a sandstone mano was used to begin grinding. A few (no more than five) motions back and forth on the metate produced a residue consisting of entirely broken and fragmented kernels, the flour or starch of those kernels, abundant pericarp fragments, and several kernel fragments that were not completely broken apart. One of the kernel fragments (Figure 8-2) exhibits numerous cuts and scrapes (note the cross-hatch scratches). The epicarp shows striations both across the grain and with the grain. Exfoliation of the outermost pericarp (the epicarp) is apparent.

Several pericarp fragments that had resulted from the grinding process were also examined. SEM photos (Figure 8-3) show the uneven removal of the outermost layers of pericarp from the surface of the grain. The fibrous nature of the external pericarp is revealed. The grinding affected the fragment, for example, in only one area. The underlying tendrils, or filaments, are not torn, even though the outer layers of pericarp were removed. Some fragments of pericarp found within the ground residue, however, exhibit no grinding scratches at all (Figure 8-4). The torn margins do not appear different from pieces of pericarp torn with tweezers and also examined with the SEM. A limitation to observing grinding on corn pericarp is apparent: not all fragments will be diagnostic of grinding; some fragments may appear unaltered.

Closer examination of the scratches and grooves produced on the metate-ground kernel samples using a higher magnification indicated that grinding of the kernel with the grain (along the longitudinal cell structure) versus grinding against the grain produced somewhat different results.

Scraping of the dried kernels of Santo Domingo flint/flour red in one direction with the grain using light-to-moderate pressure produced the alteration of the kernel shown in Figure 8-5. Some scratches were produced on the kernel surface, although in more altered areas of the surface, exfoliation of the epicarp down to the aleurone level is clearly shown (note the basketweave structure). The gradual bevel of all layers of the bran is also apparent—layers are shorn off in jagged succession. Preliminary study indicated that the angle of that bevel and the examination of the torn margins of the corn fragments could become important to the identification of grinding. Other photographs of the same fragment show deep lacerations along its margins that were also diagnostic of grinding.

Interestingly, grinding with the grain seemed to aid in exfoliation of the epicarp away from the grain—that is, the epicarp flaked away along the lenticular cells. Grinding against the grain produced much more tearing and uneven pieces of epicarp (evident from the more visible nature of the scratches viewed in Figure 8-2). Again, corn kernels were scraped across a sandstone surface (this time against the corn grain) no more than fives times. Closer examination of the ground fragments showed the various ragged grooves and scratches produced on the corn pericarp by grinding against the grain (Figure 8-6). The sandstone grinding surface used in this case produced grooves of varying depth and distance apart. Rough edges were produced, and pieces or chunks of pericarp exfoliated or were pulled up during the grinding process. Many small fragments with rolled edges of varying thickness were produced. It also became apparent from viewing the photographs that a coarser grain of sandstone would produce deeper striations than a finer sandstone or a more worn (through use), oiled, or otherwise prepared implement.

Completely ground cornmeal (blue flour) from Santa Ana Pueblo was examined with the SEM. Photographs of the corn pericarp show extreme degradation (Figure 8-7), not surprising since a hammer mill was used to grind the meal (Santa Ana Pueblo, personal communication 1992). No surface is left without some indentation, nick, or scratch. Other characteristics of this type of grinding included the smallness of pericarp left within the meal and the beveling and extreme wear along the margins of the pericarp fragments. Examination of another sample of a blue flour corn handground by a Hopi did not exhibit features diagnostic of pummeling during processing in a hammer mill. Instead, an overall abrasion of the pericarp surface was noted on several fragments (Figure 8-8).

Archaeological corn remains from 10 Turkey Pen Ruin coprolite samples were examined using the SEM. Several of the samples were characterized by small, mostly uniform pieces of corn pericarp thought to represent grinding. The results from SEM examination of two of the samples (13–1 and 20–26) are characteristic of the 10 samples examined and generally represent the preliminary study.

Examination of the two samples revealed a range of pericarp degradation. Sample 13-1 (Level A6) exhibited pieces of pericarp with abrasions that were at right angles to each other (Figure 8-9). The abrasions were of various depths and ran both with and against the grain, as one might expect if the kernel tumbled over and over in the process of being ground. Pericarp fragments (mostly along fragment margins) also showed abrasion and degradation of the upper epicarp surface down to and exposing the fibrous microstructure (Figure 8-10)—a feature similar to that exhibited by the modern experimentally ground material. Other fragments showed sharp cuts across the grain of the kernel, which sheared only the upper epicarp layers.

Coprolite 20-26 (Level D1) produced corn fragments (Figure 8-11) that appeared shorn in a fashion similar to those in sample 13-1. Note the abrasion on the edge of the fragment. It is worn down to the microstructure underneath, but the individual fibers are not torn away. One fragment presented a groove (Figure 8-12) that ran against the grain of the kernel, similar to what had been seen on the ground modern reference materials. That "groove," when studied at higher magnification, appeared to be the result of an object's moving in a single direction into the pericarp surface, thereby creating a gouge of uneven depth and "torn" margins. One might expect the indentations produced by a set of teeth during chewing to be more regular and to show a somewhat curved depression into the pericarp surface (reflecting the

Figure 8-1. *Surface of modern, dried Santo Domingo flint/flour corn kernel. Note the lenticular cell structure.*

Figure 8-2. *Surface of partially ground kernel. Note cross-hatched network of scratches.*

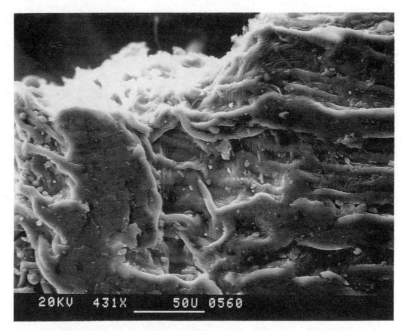

Figure 8-3. *Experimentally ground pericarp fragment showing surface degradation. Underlying structure remained intact.*

Figure 8-4. *Experimentally ground pericarp fragment displaying no evidence of grinding.*

Figure 8-5. *Experimentally ground pericarp fragment showing degradation after grinding with the kernel grain.*

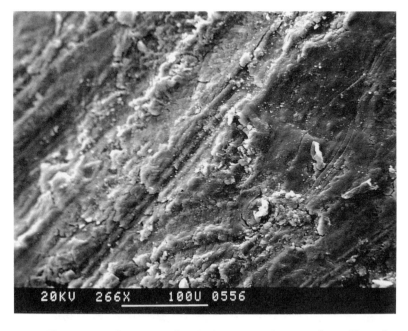

Figure 8-6. *Grooves and striations on pericarp surface of kernel ground against the kernel grain.*

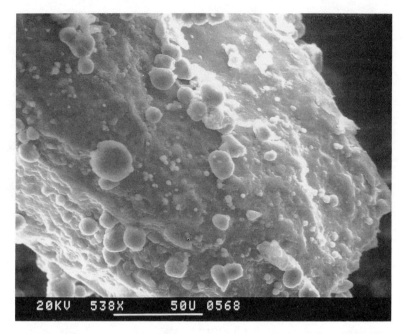

Figure 8-7. *Corn pericarp fragment of hammer-milled blue flour corn (Santa Ana Pueblo).*

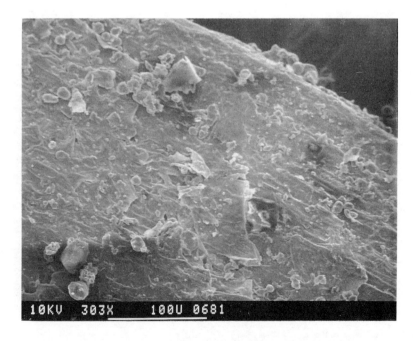

Figure 8-8. *Corn pericarp fragment of hand-milled Hopi blue flour corn.*

Figure 8-9. *Coprolite pericarp specimen 13-1 (Level A6).*

Figure 8-10. *Coprolite pericarp specimen 13-1 (Level A6). Note wear along margin of pericarp fragment.*

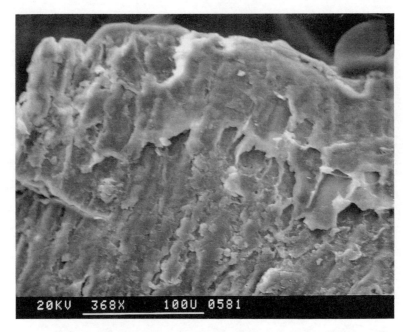

Figure 8-11. *Coprolite pericarp specimen 20-26 (Level D1). Degradation of pericarp surface apparent along margin.*

Figure 8-12. *Coprolite pericarp specimen 20-26 (Level D1). Grooves on pericarp surface produced by possible grinding.*

shape of the tooth). Further work would identify the differences between grinding grooves produced by sandstone surfaces and teeth indentations produced by persistent chewing.

Summary and Conclusions

Analyses of 80 Basketmaker II coprolites from four southwestern archaeological sites provided a database in which corn preparation and processing could be studied. At Turkey Pen Ruin, corn occurred in all coprolites analyzed ($N = 65$) or visually observed ($N = 250$). Variation in the appearance of the corn pericarp within those coprolites led me to believe that corn may have been processed in a number of different ways.

The use of the SEM, while not new to the study of plants or plant remains, offered an avenue of research that could provide answers as to how corn had been prepared prior to ingestion. Preliminary study of corn pericarp from 10 Turkey Pen Ruin coprolites and accompanying experimentation with modern corn grinding suggested that the corn found in some of the coprolites was probably prepared by a method such as grinding. Pericarp margins on several archaeological fragments appeared abraded and worn to the point where the underlying microstructure of the pericarp was exposed; that feature was also noted on several experimentally ground corn pericarp pieces. On their exteriors a few archaeological specimens displayed either grooves or cuts (across the grain) that compared to modern correlates of grinding against the grain.

However, preliminary SEM study also indicated that both modern and archaeological pericarp fragments sometimes carried no distinguishing characteristics as to grinding. Therefore, a complete analysis of corn remains should combine SEM analysis with a general description of pericarp size and overall uniformity of size within the sample. Any unique characteristics, such as the presence of starch or indication of roasting, should be noted because those features may be distinctive to a particular processing method. Currently, corn pericarp fragments from the Turkey Pen Ruin coprolites are being measured so that overall size may be compared.

There is variance among the samples that is not accounted for by the grinding. That variance may be the result of cooking methods, comsumptive behavior, or digestive processes as yet undescribed. Since the analysis of the variety of cooking methods and the resultant alteration to the kernel pericarp are not complete, it is possible that some features thought to represent grinding may actually represent some other cooking or processing method. For example, I am curious to see how boiled or roasted pericarp tears along the margins when chewed. Experimentation with different corn recipes and SEM photography of the physical manifestations continue.

Nutritional implications of the different grinding techniques and cooking methods are numerous because each part of the corn kernel presents a unique chemical and nutrient composition (FAO 1953:10–14). The overall nutritive composition of a corn repast is therefore affected by which parts of the kernel are consumed and how they have been prepared. Table 8-1 shows examples of

Table 8-1. *Some Navajo Corn Recipes and Their Nutritive Values*

Name	Preparation	Typical Serving (g)	Moisture	KCAL / PRO	CHO / FIB	FAT / ASH	Na / K	Ca / Mg	P / Fe	Zn / Cu
Plain hominy corn	Dried raw corn, boiled	285	65.9	393 / 10.3	75.0 / 4.8	5.7 / 1.4	86 / 416	63 / 137	16.5 / 2.28	3.7 / tr[a]
Hominy corn with ash	Dried raw corn, boiled in ash-water, rinsed	191	61.0	290 / 8.4	55 / 5.7	3.8 / 1.1	73 / 225	65 / 132	34 / 2.3	2.9 / 0.2
Roast corn, dried	Fresh corn, roasted, dried	100	1.0	383 / 9.9	73.3 / 8.2	5.6 / 2.0	104 / 593	13 / 121	29 / 2.2	2.6 / 0.4

different Navajo corn recipes and their respective nutritive values. Both the availability of different nutrients and the overall caloric value of the individual corn meal vary with the preparation it has received.

If shucked corn kernels are soaked in lime water or lye prior to drying or storage, the calcium content of the whole corn is affected as is the niacin availability (FAO 1953:17). Niacin in the corn kernel occurs not only in the "free" state but also in other arrangements as both a coenzyme and/or in a "precursor" combined with some proteinlike substance (1953:42). When niacin is part of a precursor, it is apparently not in a form that can be absorbed by the human body. The soaking of the grain in a weak alkali or strong acid thus promotes the availability of niacin during the digestion process (1953:42). Certain research indicates that this particular preparation of corn with lime may help to explain why there is little pellagra (a niacin-deficiency-produced disease) among human groups preparing their maize in such a manner (1953:42).

Ultimately, the grinding of corn plays a major role in the overall digestibility and bodily utilization of the corn crop. If the whole grain is crushed during the grinding process, more nutrients are available to the population consuming the meal. However, the removal of pericarp (bran) and other parts of the grain decreases the nutritive value of the meal. Valuable minerals and a certain amount of fiber are lost if the pericarp is completely winnowed from the grain. Even more nutrients would be lost if the aleurone (a protein- and niacin-rich layer) has been removed along with the bran (FAO 1953:19). Most niacin (overall percentage of total), for example, is located in the aleurone layer. If the whole grain is consumed, the niacin is readily available. In contrast, if the kernels are ground and the aleurone and accompanying pericarp winnowed out, problems may occur with niacin deficiency. Indeed, a type of grinding or milling (e.g., machine milling) that removes the aleurone layer may increase the chance of a population's acquiring pellagra (FAO 1953:42).

Yet another example of different grinding techniques affecting the nutritive value of the cornmeal available to the consuming population concerns other vitamins such as thiamine. Most vitamins in the corn kernel—for example, thiamine—are located primarily within the embryo and in the outermost layer of the endosperm (which includes the aleurone). The differential location of the vitamins within the kernel will impact the nutritive value of the corn depending on whether the kernel is milled or eaten whole (FAO 1953:13).

Although the use of coprolites in studying diet or paleonutrition is somewhat limited, archaeological fecal specimens provide a very direct means of studying what food items an ancient population consumed. Further, coprolites contain remains that can be identified and quantified. It is acknowledged that they present only the preserved and undigested food residue from a meal(s) eaten by a single individual, but that information provides a base upon which other dietary studies can be built.

When the identification of remains is complete, new insights can be gleaned from the study of a food item's preparation. The overall nutritive values of the food consumed could be better approximated if the cooking and grinding methods exhibited by the archaeological materials could be identified. Caloric and nutrient values could then be narrowed and the new values used to further model the nutrition of a prehistoric population.

Acknowledgments

Many individuals have contributed to both the coprolite analyses discussed in this paper and the subsequent SEM study of corn remains found therein. I would like to thank W. D. Lipe (Washington State University, Pullman) and R. G. Matson (University of British Columbia, Vancouver) for their retrieval of the botanical remains from Turkey Pen Ruin, Cedar Mesa, Utah. Dr. Lipe first suggested the analysis of coprolites from this shelter as part of my Master's thesis and then allowed further subsistence research on those remains. I thank him for that opportunity. Additional thanks go to Kim Smiley (University of Northern Arizona, Flagstaff) for sending me coprolites from Three Fir Shelter (at Black Mesa) for study and for suggesting numerous avenues of research into Basketmaker prehistory. I thank Richard Ambler for his generosity in opening his extensive collection of coprolites to me, especially those from Dust Devil Cave. David Bentley of the SEM Facility (Biological Sciences) at the University of Arizona, Tucson, was instrumental in the SEM analysis, and the time he devoted to the project's outcome is greatly appreciated. Dan Rylander provided insightful editorial comment. Finally, thanks to Kristin Sobolik (University of Maine) for her encouragement in presenting this research and her continued patience with my ever-recurring delays.

References

Aasen, D. K.
   1984   *Pollen, Macrofossil, and Charcoal Analyses of Basketmaker Coprolites from Turkey Pen Ruin, Cedar Mesa, Utah.* Unpublished Master's thesis, Department of Anthropology, Washington State University, Pullman.
   1986   Southwestern Archaic and Basketmaker Subsistence—the Coprolite Record. Paper presented at the 51st Annual Meeting of the Society for American Archaeology, New Orleans.
Cushing, F. H.
   1920   *Zuni Breadstuff.* Indian Notes and Monographs Vol. VIII. Museum for the American Indian (Heye Foundation), New York.
Food and Agriculture Organization of the United Nations (FAO)
   1953   *Maize and Maize Diets: A Nutritional Survey.* Rome, Italy.
Greenhaugh, G. N., and L. V. Evans
   1971   Electron Microscopy. *Methods in Microbiology* 4:517–565.
Hough, W.
   1930   Ancient Pueblo Subsistence. *Proceedings of the 23rd International Congress of Americanists*:67–69. New York.

Kidder, A. V., and S. J. Guernsey
  1919   *Archaeological Explorations in Northeastern Arizona.* Bureau of American Ethnology Bulletin No. 65. U.S. Government Printing Office, Washington, D.C.
Minnis, P.
  1989   Prehistoric Diet in the Northern Southwest: Macroplant Remains from Four Corners Feces. *American Antiquity* 36:410–431.
Oatley, C. W., W. C. Nixon, and R. F. W. Pease
  1965   Scanning Electron Microscopy. *Advances in Electronics and Electron Physics* 21:181.
Pomeranz, Y.
  1976   Scanning Electron Microscopy in Food Science and Technology. *Advances in Food Research* 22:206–308.
Powers, M.
  1984   *The Salvage of Archaeological Data from Turkey Pen Ruin, Grand Gulch Primitive Area, San Juan County, Utah.* Contributions to Anthropology Series No. 808. Division of Conservation Archaeology, San Juan County Museum Association, Farmington, New Mexico.
Reinhard, K.
  1994   Diet and Disease at Turkey Pen Cave, An Anasazi Basketmaker II Habitation. In *Health and Disease in the Prehistoric Southwest II*, edited by S. Rhine and R. T. Steinbock. Maxwell Museum Press, University of New Mexico, Albuquerque, in press.
Watson, C. A., E. Dikeman, and R. A. Stermer
  1975   A Note on Surface Lipid Content and Scanning Electron Microscopy of Milled Rice as Related to Degree of Milling. *Cereal Chemist* 52:742–747.
Weber, C.
  n.d.   Nutritive Value of Traditional Navajo Foods. Ms. on file, Agricultural Extension Office, University of Arizona, Tucson.
Whiting, A. E.
  1939   *Ethnobotany of the Hopi.* Bulletin 15. Museum of Northern Arizona, Flagstaff.

9. Anasazi Diet: Variety in the Hoy House and Lion House Coprolite Record and Nutritional Analysis

Linda Scott Cummings

Abstract: Coprolites from a Pueblo III occupation of Hoy House and Lion House in Johnson Canyon, Colorado, immediately south of Mesa Verde, have been examined for both pollen and macrofloral remains. Common and occasional elements of the diet are identified. Diets, as represented by those databases, are examined for nutritional completeness. Probable nutritional deficiencies and strengths of the diet are noted and discussed. Deficiency-related diseases that might have affected those populations, based on interpretation of the nutritional adequacy of the diet, are also noted. A descriptive report of the pollen contents of the coprolites has been published previously (Scott 1979). Stiger (1977) describes the macrofloral contents of the same coprolites. This paper concentrates on a nutritional evaluation of the diet, which is represented by pollen and macrofloral remains recovered from the coprolites. It addresses the nutritional consequences of that diet on the local population.

Introduction

Coprolites collected during archaeological investigations at Hoy House and Lion House in the summer of 1974 have been examined for pollen (Scott 1979), macrofloral, faunal, and parasite (Stiger 1977) data. Material recovered from coprolites is considered direct evidence of diet.[1] Hoy House, a large Pueblo III cliff dwelling with at least 60 rooms and 4 kivas, and Lion House, a slightly smaller Pueblo III cliff dwelling with 46 rooms and 6 kivas, are both located in tributaries of Johnson Canyon, immediately south of Mesa Verde National Park on the Ute Mountain Indian Reservation. Two periods of construction activity were noted at each of the cliff dwellings: between A.D. 1130 and 1150 and during the early 1200s (Nickens 1977:74). Coprolites

Paleonutrition: The Diet and Health of Prehistoric Americans, edited by Kristin D. Sobolik. Center for Archaeological Investigations, Occasional Paper No. 22. © 1994 by the Board of Trustees, Southern Illinois University. All rights reserved. ISBN 0-88104-078-9.

examined in this study were not dated other than through association with the occupation of Hoy House and Lion House. Johnson Canyon is peripheral to Mesa Verde in terms of precipitation and would have been more severely affected by climatic deteriorations or droughts. Environmental stress and drought, resulting in a strain on all levels of the trophic structure, including human and nonhuman food chains, had been postulated for Johnson Canyon. If that postulate is true, evidence of disease and malnutrition should be more prevalent in the Johnson Canyon materials than in coprolite records from elsewhere in the Mesa Verde area. There is evidence of possible crop failure for Hoy House in the pollen record from the midden.

Fifty-nine coprolites were examined from Hoy House and Lion House, indicating that the diet was composed primarily of the cultigens *Zea mays*, *Cucurbita*, and *Phaseolus*, with heavy reliance on the possibly encouraged *Cleome* and other manipulated or wild plants such as Cheno-ams, *Oryzopsis*, *Physalis*, and the Umbelliferae. Animals for which the most evidence was recovered are dog/coyote, deer, jackrabbit, birds, and small rodents.

The pollen data from a stratigraphic column in the trash midden at Hoy House (Scott 1976) indicate that a nearly climaxed forest probably existed on top of the mesas near Johnson Canyon at the time of the initial occupation of Hoy House during the mid-1100s and that extensive clearing of arable land on nearby mesa tops began shortly after establishment of the community. That activity appears to have continued with greater efficiency during the second occupation of Hoy House in the early 1200s. The final and rapid rise in arboreal pollen, particularly *Pinus* (pine), following abandonment is typical of pollen records from the Mesa Verde district. In fact Martin and Byers state that "the rise in tree pollen is so clear cut that we have come to expect a similar rise in any late prehistoric profile from Mesa Verde which extends through the thirteenth century" (1965:125). The rise in arboreal pollen frequency is linked to natural reforestation of the area following abandonment rather than to any climatic change.

Pollen samples from the midden at Hoy House provide the only temporal data on the relationship between possible use and discard of plants at that cliff dwelling during its occupation. The pollen record from the trash midden at Hoy House (Scott 1976) notes a very large percentage of *Cleome* (beeweed) throughout the second period of occupation. *Zea* (corn) pollen is initially moderately high in the lowest sample of that midden, but it declines and does not rise again in frequency until shortly before the final abandonment of the site. *Cleome* pollen, on the other hand, is very abundant (> 50%). From this evidence it appears that corn was not as plentiful at the site as might be expected and that people were relying more heavily on encouraged plants such as *Cleome*, Cheno-ams (which might have been encouraged), and gathered plants. Several workers, myself included, have inferred a population too large for the carrying capacity of the land, possible overuse and exhaustion of agricultural lands, reduction in available calories, and subsequent partial abandonment followed by full abandonment of Hoy House.

Stratigraphic pollen samples from both Hoy House and Mud House exhibit considerable increases in the quantity of *Cleome* pollen deposited in trash middens during Pueblo III occupations, suggesting that a change in diet was widespread among the cliff dwellers. While *Cleome* is noted in trash middens outside the Mesa Verde area, it is only occasionally noted in extremely large frequencies at a time coinciding with a decline in *Zea mays* pollen.

Discussion

The most common elements of the diet for occupants of Hoy House and Lion House, based on coprolite analysis, are *Zea mays* (maize, corn), Cheno-ams (goosefoot, amaranth or pigweed), *Cleome* (beeweed), *Cucurbita* (squash—includes both *C. pepo* and *C. moschata*), *Oryzopsis* (Indian ricegrass), Umbelliferae (carrot/parsley family), *Portulaca* (purslane), *Physalis* (ground-cherry), *Opuntia* (prickly pear), *Lepidium* (pepperweed), *Phaseolus* (common beans), *Typha* (cattail), *Pinus edulis* (pinyon pine nuts), deer, jackrabbit, bird/turkey, small rodents, and probably dog/coyote (Table 9-1). Remnants of those plants, in the form of macrofloral remains or pollen, and animals, noted from the presence of hair, feathers, and/or bone, are interpreted as regular components of the diet because of their ubiquity.

Ubiquity of corn, beeweed, and Cheno-am remains in the coprolites points to these plants as constant components of the diet. Beeweed greens were cooked for use as both pottery paint and food. Dried cooked greens were also available on a year-round basis and were reconstituted, for use as both pottery paint and food, according to historic records. Evidence for beans comes from Mark Stiger's study (1977) of the macrofloral remains, as well as from recovery of a limited quantity of *Phaseolus* pollen. Meat included in the diet cannot be recognized either microscopically or macroscopically. Rather, meat consumption is represented indirectly by recovery of bone, feathers, hair, and so forth, which tend to be underrepresented. Therefore, it is likely that recovery of hair, feathers, and/or bone grossly underestimates meat consumption. Examination of dietary components for nutritional values will focus on these plants and animals as being the most likely regular components of the diet.

Minor components of the diet for which pollen and/or macrofloral evidence exists are *Artemisia* (sagebrush), Compositae (sunflower family), *Eriogonum* (wild buckwheat), *Coryphantha* (ball cactus), *Plantago* (plantain), *Prunus* (chokecherry), *Ribes* (currant), and *Shepherdia* (buffalo berry). The pollen record also indicates the presence of several plants that might have been used medicinally: *Ephedra* (Mormon tea); Labiatae (mint family)—specifically *Poliomintha* or *Salvia*; and *Sphaeralcea* (globe mallow). Animal remains recorded infrequently are mouse, squirrel, and cicada.

Although we cannot reconstruct quantities of food consumed, we can examine diet on the basis of nutritional completeness, assuming an adequate supply of all food. Recommended dietary allowances, as established by the Committee on Dietary Allowances, are used as guidelines to identify quantities of nutrients required for health.

In the plant portion of the diet, seeds usually provide the highest quantities

Table 9-1. *Ubiquity of Pollen and Macrofloral Remains from Hoy House Coprolites*

Pollen Type	Pollen (%)	Macrofloral (%)	1st Dominant Pollen Type (%)	2d Dominant Pollen Type (%)
Juniperus	59	3		5
Picea	2			
Pinus	90	12	3	10
Populus	2			
Quercus	56			
Ambrosia	44			
Artemisia	81	6	5	10
Compositae (Asteraceae)	63	2		
Cercocarpus	56			
Cheno-ams	100	32	24	27
Cleome	95	5	39	15
Cucurbita pepo	24	20		
Cucurbita moschata-type	37		7	
Ephedra nevadensis-type	20			
Ephedra torreyana-type	2			
Eriogonum	5	2		
Erodium	2			
Gramineae (Poaceae)	10			
Labiatae (Lamiaceae)	2			2
Lepidium	19			
Coryphantha vivipara	9			
Opuntia	14	23		
Oryzopsis	54	3	5	2
Phaseolus	7	17		
Phlox	2			
Physalis		28		
Plantago	2			
Portulaca	27	18	2	
Prunus		3		
Ribes	2			
Sarcobatus	17			
Scirpus	3			
Shepherdia	2	5		
Sphaeralcea	7			
Typha	17		3	
Umbelliferae (Apiaceae)	46		7	10
Zea mays	95	95	5	7

of protein. Cheno-am seeds (both *Chenopodium* and *Amaranthus*) are excellent sources of protein (Tables 9-2 through 9-4). *Opuntia* seeds are also a good source of protein, if they are ground so that the body can make use of the nutrients, as are *Portulaca* and *Eriogonum* seeds. *Zea mays* flour and *Phaseolus* contribute smaller quantities of protein to the diet per 100 g serving. Meat, of course, contributes larger quantities of and more complete proteins (Tables 9-5 through 9-7).

Dark green leafy vegetables and orange fruits and vegetables contribute the largest quantities of vitamin A to the diet per 100 g serving. At least on a seasonal basis, widely available greens, such as Cheno-ams, *Cleome*, *Portulaca*, and to a lesser extent *Lepidium*, are good sources of vitamin A. *Zea mays* flour is also an excellent source of vitamin A, making it the most reliable source on a year-round basis.

Relatively few foods have been tested for vitamin D and E content. Therefore, it is not possible to address probable quantities consumed in the diet. However, since vitamin D is synthesized in the body, it is likely that people living in temperate climates spent enough time in the sun for their bodies to function adequately in synthesizing it. Vitamins B-6, B-12, and folacin were also not regularly reported for most of the wild plants examined, so no interpretation of availability is attempted. We should note, however, that beans and sunflower seeds are rich sources of the B vitamins.

Vitamin C is present in relatively large quantities in many foods consumed by the Anasazi, including *Phaseolus*, *Artemisia* leaves, *Amaranthus* and *Chenopodium* greens, *Cucurbita*, *Opuntia*, *Ribes*, and *Zea mays*. Of the storable foods, *Cucurbita* and *Opuntia* fruits are good sources of vitamin C. *Opuntia* stems were available for harvest year-round and are also good sources of vitamin C. Vitamin C appears to have been readily available on a seasonal basis. Since vitamin C deteriorates in stored foods and is often at least partially destroyed by cooking, it is likely that seasonal deficiencies of vitamin C were common. Bean sprouts would have been an excellent source of vitamin C if they were available for consumption during the winter when other fresh vegetables and greens were not.

The best plant sources of calcium in the diet are *Chenopodium*, *Amaranthus*, and *Cleome* greens; *Opuntia* tunas; and *Amaranthus* and *Chenopodium* seeds. Animal bones that are cracked and boiled often increase the calcium value of soup or stew. If fresh greens were not available, it is possible that calcium deficiency was common on a seasonal basis.

The best sources of potassium in the diet are seeds of *Chenopodium*, *Helianthus* (sunflower), *Lepidium*, *Pinus edulis*, and *Typha* (cattail). *Amaranthus* and *Lepidium* greens are also good sources of potassium.

Iron is most abundant in meats and in *Chenopodium* and *Cleome* seeds, sunflower seeds, *Amaranthus* seeds, *Opuntia* seeds, and *Artemisia* greens. Corn has a relatively low iron bioavailability (1%–7%), while meat has a higher absorption rate (12%–20%) (Bothwell and Charlton 1981:11). Corn is certainly not the most important source of iron in the Anasazi diet; indeed, ground *Chenopodium* seeds are much more important.

On the basis of coprolite evidence from Hoy House and Lion House,

Table 9-2. *Nutritional Contents of Plant Food Remains Identified in Coprolites*

Food Category	Scientific Name	Common Name	Cooking Method	Energy (kcal)	Carbo. (g)	Fiber (g)	Protein (g)	Fat (g)
Legumes	*Phaseolus vulgaris*	Common bean	Boiled	78.00	9.56	1.92	4.47	0.57
Leaf and stalk vege-tables	*Artemisia*	Sagebrush	Dried/ground	295.00	50.22	2.41	22.76	7.24
	Amaranthus	Amaranth	Boiled	21.00	4.11	1.31	2.11	0.18
	Chenopodium	Lamb's 1/4s		32.00	5.00	1.80	3.20	5.00
	Cleome	Beeweed	Raw	62.00	6.30	2.00	8.10	5.00
	Lepidium	Pepperweed	Raw	32.00	5.50	1.10	3.40	1.05
	Plantago	Plantain	Raw leaf	61.00	14.60		2.50	3.00
	Portulaca	Purslane greens	Raw	21.00	3.80	0.90	1.70	0.40
			Boil/drain	15.00	2.80	0.80	1.20	0.30
	Umbelliferae	Parsley/carrot family						
Vine and ground fruits	*Cucurbita pepo*	Squash fruit		—	—	3.50	4.04	0.90
	Cucurbita moschata-type	Squash (mesocarp)	Raw	45.00	11.69	1.40	1.00	1.00
Condi-ments/ medicines	Labiatae	Mint family	Leaf, dried	—	60.73	18.05	10.62	12.74
			Seed	472.00	47.87	25.30	16.62	26.25
Nuts	*Pinus*	Pine nuts	Dried	568.00	19.30	4.71	11.57	60.98
Berries/ fruits	*Juniperus*	Juniper						
	Opuntia	Prickly pear cactus	Fruit, sk.	41.00	9.57	1.81	7.30	5.10
			Seed	—	—	49.60	16.60	17.20
			Bud	5.40	5.62	4.24	5.23	5.62
			Stem	37.00	8.80	2.17*	1.26*	0.37*
	Physalis	Ground-cherry	Raw	148.57	11.10	2.63	1.87	3.20
	Prunus	Chokecherry						
	Ribes	Currant	Raw	44.00	10.18	1.90	8.80	5.80
	Shepherdia	Buffalo berry	Raw				2.30	3.00
Flowers	*Cucurbita*	Squash	Raw	72.00		6.30	3.39	0.95
Seeds	*Artemisia*	Sagebrush		—	—	—	31.30	38.10
	Amaranthus	Amaranth	Raw	138.82	63.90	6.08	15.02	6.57
	Chenopodium	Pigweed	Raw	372.60	42.40	15.60	16.80	5.23
	Cleome	Beeweed	Raw	427.39	15.64	16.77	23.17	30.24
	Eriogonum	Wild buck-wheat		—			63.80	8.60
	Helianthus	Sunflower	Seed, dried	570.00	19.26	4.06	23.90	48.44
			Flour	383.33	35.90	1.20	37.00	10.60
	Lepidium	Pepperweed	Raw	32.00	5.50	1.10	2.60	7.00
	Oryzopsis	Indian rice-grass		—	—		11.90	2.20
	Plantago	Plantain	Raw	45.94		13.68	17.03	7.62
	Portulaca	Purselane	Raw	—	—	19.57	20.82	16.64
	Typha	Cattail	Rhizome		83.81	13.00	6.60	3.24
			Shoot		—	6.20	2.08	0.60
Zea	*Zea mays*	Maize, corn	Flour	376.07	73.60	1.47	9.90	5.60
			Boiled	108.00	25.11	0.60	3.32	1.28

Sources: Laferriere (1988); Watt and Merrill (1963); previously published in Cummings (1994a, 1994b).
Notes: Dashes were copied from Laferriere where pattern of use suggests they indicate the specific vitamin or mineral was not tested for. Asterisks indicate several sources (references) were averaged.

Table 9-3. Vitamin Contents of Plant Foods Represented in Coprolites

Scientific Name of Food	Fat-Soluble Vitamins				B-6 (mg)	Vit. C (mg)	Water-Soluble Vitamins						
	Vit. A (IU)	Caro-tene	Vit. E (mg)	Vit. K (mcg)			Thiamin (mg)	Ribo. (mg)	Niacin (mg)	B-12 (mcg)	Folacin (mcg)	Biotin (mcg)	B-5 (mg)
Phaseolus	0.25RE				—	11.7	0.224	0.147	0.10		—		—
Artemisia	420.00					80.00	0.08	0.16	1.40				0.218
Amaranth	277RE					41.00	0.02	0.13	0.56	8.95	—		
Chenop.	2910.0RE					37.00	0.10	0.26	0.90				
Cleome	5972.7RE					2.20							
Lepidium	900RE / 700a-t	2.19	0.700										
Plantago					0.278	64.00	0.115	0.225	1.38				
Port. R	2500.00					25.00	0.03	0.10	0.50				
B	2100.00					12.00	0.02	0.06	0.40				
Umbell.													
Cucurbita pepo	—					16.25	0.0375	0.0345	0.428				
Cucurbita moschata-type	780RE				0.154	21.00	0.10	0.20	1.20		0.02567		0.40
Labiatae L	590.00RE					32.38	0.754	0.336	5.72				
S	3.60RE						0.869	0.166	5.82				
Pinus	2.90					2.00	1.24	0.223	4.37				
Juniperus													
Opuntia F	5.10					14.00	0.014	0.060	0.46				
S	—					—	—		—				
B	1.48*		12.04				0.66	2.84	21.90				
Stem	50.0RE				—	19.00	0.04	0.04	0.20				
Physalis	139.0RE					8.50	0.10	1.40	2.60				
Prunus						8.10	0.03	0.07	0.75				
Ribes					0.50	27.70	0.04	0.03	0.30		0.003		0.18
Shepherdia	29.00RE				0.08								0.286

Table 9-3.—Continued

Scientific Name of Food	Fat-Soluble Vitamins				Water-Soluble Vitamins								
	Vit. A (IU)	Caro-tene	Vit. E (mg)	Vit. K (mcg)	B-6 (mg)	Vit. C (mg)	Thiamin (mg)	Ribo. (mg)	Niacin (mg)	B-12 (mcg)	Folacin (mcg)	Biotin (mcg)	B-5 (mg)
Cucurbita	194.70RE	2.27				27.79	0.096	0.193	0.825				
Artemisia													
Amaranthus	—					3.43	0.16	0.23	1.18				
Chenop.	—					1.21	0.35	0.43	1.08				
Cleome	—					—							
Eriogonum													
Helian. S	50.00						2.29	0.250	4.50				
Helian. F	—	5.58				—	2.55	0.470	29.25				
Lepidium	—					69.00	0.08	0.260	1.00				
Oryzopsis													
Plantago													
Portulaca S													
Typha													
Zea mays	510.– 300.00* 21.70				60.00 60.00	6.20 0.00	0.44 0.215	0.13 0.072	1.93 1.61		10.10 46.40	6.60	550.00 878.00

Sources: Laferriere (1988); Watt and Merrill (1963); previously published in Cummings (1994a, 1994b).

Notes: Dashes were copied from Laferriere where pattern of use suggests they indicate the specific vitamin or mineral was not tested for. Asterisks indicate several sources (references) were averaged. R = Raw; B = Boiled; F = Fruit; L = Leaf; S = Seed; RE = Retinol (1 I.U. of vitamin A = .3 mg retinol [Wing and Brown 1979:20]); a-t = alpha-tocopherols.

Table 9-4. *Minerals, Electrolytes, and Trace Elements in Plant Foods Represented in Coprolites*

Scientific Name of Food	Minerals		Electrolytes			Trace Elements				
	Calcium (mg)	Phosphor. (mg)	Magnes. (mg)	Sodium (mg)	Potassium (mg)	Iron (mg)	Cop. (mg)	Mang. (mg)	Zinc (mg)	Selen. (mcg)
Phaseolus	15.50	66.50	64.50	51.00	207.50	1.3	—	—	0.17	
Artemisia	1.14	313.00	347.00	62.00	3.02	32.30			3.90	
Amaranthus	209.00	72.00	55.00	21.00	641.00		2.26	—	—	
Chenop.	258.00	45.00	—	—	—	0.70	—	—	—	
Cleome	209.00	13.00	32.00	27.00	130.00	2.10	0.40	—	1.00	
Lepidium	148.00	57.00		9.50	578.00		2.10			
Plantago										
Portulaca R	103.00	39.00		—	—	3.50				
Portulaca B	86.00	29.00		—	—	1.20				
Umbell.										
Cucurbita pepo	18.45	23.80	—	—	—	0.59				
Cucurbita moschata-type	48.00	33.00	34.00	4.00	352.00	0.70	0.072		0.15	
Labiatae L	1.65	91.00	428.00	11.00	1.07	28.12			4.70	
Labiatae S	529.00	604.00				10.00	1.66		5.32	
Pinus	8.00	35.00	234.00	72.00	628.00	3.06	4.28	1.04	4.28	
Juniperus										
Opuntia F	56.00	24.00	85.00	5.00	220.00	0.30				
Opuntia S	—	152.00	74.80	67.60	163.00	9.45	0.32		1.45	
Opuntia B	2.65	1.15	6.73	0.426	12.32	—	—			
Stem	110.00	20.00	—	—	—	0.50				
Physalis	9.50	3.70				0.95				
Prunus	4.50	11.00	7.00	0.00	184.50	0.11	0.06	0.05	0.12	
Ribes	25.00	198.00	10.00	1.00	—	0.310	70.00	144.00	120.00	
Shepherdia	20.00									
Cucurbita	99.69	49.00	24.00	5.00	173.00	11.40	—	—		
Artemisia										
Amaranthus	200.85	535.79	255.79	102.87	355.70	9.72	9.30	3.18	3.47	
Chenopodium	590.35	375.00	444.00	9.00	1690.00	37.40	1.65	5.30	—	
Cleome	1.86	464.41	119.63	32.97	438.03	67.80	0.414	1.37	2.12	
Eriogonum	—	—								
Helian. S	118.00	771.00	354.00	16.50	805.00	6.94	1.75	2.02	5.06	
Helian. F	354.00	898.00			890.00	13.20				
Lepidium	81.00	76.00		14.00	606.00	1.30				
Oryzopsis						—				
Plantago										
Portulaca	—									
Typha S	174.04	32.06	34.35	64.12	606.85	2.75	0.847	9.43	0.687	34.35
Zea mays F	18.00	29.00	121.00	104.00	593.00	2.40			2.60	
Zea mays B	2.00	103.00	32.00	17.00	249.00	610.00	53.00	194.00	480.00	

Sources: Laferriere (1988); Watt and Merrill (1963); previously published in Cummings (1994a, 1994b).
Notes: Dashes were copied from Laferriere where pattern of use suggests they indicate the specific vitamin or mineral was not tested for. Asterisks indicate several sources (references) were averaged. R = Raw; B = Boiled; F = Fruit; L = Leaf; S = Seed.

Table 9-5. *Nutritional Contents of Animal Food Remains Identified in Coprolites*

Meat Category	Scientific Name	Common Name	Cooking Method	Energy (kcal)	Carbo. (g)	Fiber (g)	Protein (g)	Fat (g)
Insect	*Platypedia putrami*	Cicada			2.9			
Mammal	*Odocoileus hemionus*	Deer	Flesh—raw	126.0	0	0	21.0	4.0
Mammal	*Canis* sp.	Dog/coyote						
Insect	*Melanoplus femurrubrus*	Red-legged grasshopper						
Rodent	*Peromyscus* sp.	Mouse						
Rodent	*Lepus* sp.	Rabbit	Flesh—raw	162.0	0	0	21.0	8.0
			Flesh—ck	216.0	0	0	29.3	10.1
Rodent		Squirrel						
Bird	*Meleagris gallopavo*	Turkey	Flesh—raw	62.0	0	0	24.0	6.6
			Flesh—ck	90.0	0	0	31.5	6.1
			Liver—raw	38.0	2.9	0	21.2	4.0
			Liver—ck	74.0	3.1	0	27.9	4.8

Sources: Laferriere (1988); Watt and Merrill (1963); previously published in Cummings (1994a, 1994b).

animals represented in the Anasazi diet are bird, squirrel, small rodents, sheep, cicada, deer, dog/coyote, gopher, jackrabbit, mouse, and turkey. Bones and other remains in coprolites indicate that meat was probably a common component of the diet. Liver is the most concentrated form of animal iron and was likely consumed by prehistoric peoples, including the Anasazi. Meat likely contributed the majority of the iron to the diet, supplemented by small quantities from plant sources.

Many of the animals represented in the Anasazi diet such as deer and rodents, which tend to frequent agricultural fields, were common pests around villages. They could have been hunted readily in or near gardens, providing additional meat for the diet and a reduction of pests to the agricultural crops. Turkeys appear to have been kept in increasingly large numbers through time. The utilization of mule deer and jackrabbits appears to have increased, while that of bighorn sheep and cottontail rabbits decreased (Emslie 1977; Stiger 1977:54). Bighorn sheep and cottontail rabbits are commonly found in forested areas, whereas jackrabbits prefer grasses and open shrubby habitats and fields. Deer may be found in both habitats (Shelford 1963:285–289; Stiger 1977:57). Decreases in bighorn sheep and cottontail rabbit consumption, accompanied by an increase in jackrabbit consumption, suggest a decline in forested areas and an increase in cleared areas probably used as agricultural fields.

Burials from the Dolores Archaeological Program provide the nearest data for examination of physical remains for anomalies. Evidence of cribra orbitalia

Table 9-6. *Vitamin Contents of Animal Foods Represented in Coprolites*

Food	Fat-Soluble Vitamins			Water-Soluble Vitamins								
	Vit. A (IU)	Carotene	Vit. E (mg)	B-6 (mg)	Vit. C (mg)	Thiamin (mg)	Ribo. (mg)	Niacin (mg)	B-12 (mcg)	Folacin (mcg)	Biotin (mcg)	B-5 (mg)
Cicada												
Deer												
Flesh—raw	—				—	.23	.48	6.3				
Dog/coyote												
Grasshopper												
Mouse												
Rabbit												
Flesh—raw	—				—	0.05	0.07	11.3				
Flesh—ck	—				—	0.08	0.06	12.8				
Squirrel												
Turkey												
Flesh—raw	—					—	0.08	0.14	8.0			
Flesh—ck	—			0.46	—	0.05	0.18	7.7	37.0	7.0		0.94
Liver—raw	17,700				—	0.18	1.93	13.2				
Liver—ck	17,500			0.52	—	0.16	2.09	14.3	47.5	666.0		5.96

Sources: Laferriere (1988); Watt and Merrill (1963); previously published in Cummings (1994a, 1994b).
Note: Dashes were copied from Laferriere where pattern of use suggests they indicate the specific vitamin or mineral was not tested for.

Table 9-7. *Minerals, Electrolytes, and Trace Elements in Animal Foods Represented in Coprolites*

Food	Minerals			Electrolytes		Iron (mg)	Trace Elements				
	Calcium (mg)	Phosphor. (mg)	Magnes. (mg)	Sodium (mg)	Potassium (mg)		Cop. (mg)	Mang. (mg)	Zinc (mg)	Selen. (mcg)	Chrom. (mcg)
Cicada	20.0	259.0	26.0	130.0	385.0	1.8	0.96	0.25	3.10		
Deer											
Flesh—raw	10.0	249.0		—	—	—					
Dog/coyote											
Grasshopper											
Mouse											
Rabbit											
Flesh—raw	20.0	352.0		43.0	385.0	1.3					
Flesh—ck	21.0	259.0		41.0	368.0	1.5					
Squirrel											
Turkey											
Flesh—raw	8.0	212.0		66.0	315.0	1.5					
Flesh—ck	8.0	251.0	26.0	130.0	367.0	1.8	0.09	0.21	3.10		
Liver—raw	—	—		63.0	60.0	—					
Liver—ck	11.0	272.0	15.0	55.0	141.0	7.8	0.56	0.25	3.09		

Sources: Laferriere (1988); Watt and Merrill (1963); previously published in Cummings (1994a, 1994b).
Note: Dashes were copied from Laferriere where pattern of use suggests they indicate the specific vitamin or mineral was not tested for.

and porotic hyperostosis are the only indicators of nutritional deficiency in bodies from the area, although there is evidence for growth arrest (Stodder 1987). Since cribra orbitalia may result from a deficiency in iron or possible general nutritional deficiency associated with an insufficient food supply, a large portion of the population appears to have suffered some degree of iron-deficiency anemia. Sandford (1984) notes that cribra orbitalia may result from a combination of magnesium and iron deficiencies, age-related stresses such as weaning diarrhea, growth requirements, and possibly inadequate dietary intake. The most precarious time of life nutritionally is the "period of transition from breast feeding to a diet of semi-solid and solid foods" (Pearson 1980:3).

Since cribra orbitalia is often associated with iron deficiency, specific examination of factors that contribute to iron deficiency is important. Those factors include insufficient iron intake, malabsorption, and iron losses. Synergistic relationships between deficiencies of vitamins C, B-6, B-12, and folacin and iron absorption may contribute to malabsorption or inefficient use of iron (Cummings 1989). Other factors influencing iron absorption include its bioavailability, which is higher in meat sources and lower in vegetable sources; presence or absence of phytates, tannins, and fiber; and pathological blood loss resulting from such conditions as wounds, gastrointestinal bleeding, nosebleeds, and menorrhagia, as well as parasitism (Carlson et al. 1984; Cummings 1989; Hummert 1983; Sandford 1984; Sandford et al. 1983; Van Gerven et al. 1981).

Evidence of pinworm infestation was recovered from 7% of the Hoy House coprolites. Modern recovery of evidence of pinworm infestation through direct fecal examination is not effective. In fact, a positive result of 5% recovery during fecal examination is expected when 100% of the modern population is known to be infested. Therefore, nearly all Hoy House inhabitants were probably infested with pinworms (Stiger 1977:44), signaling the probability that blood loss from parasite infestation contributed to iron deficiency.

"Iron deficiency is the most prevalent nutritional problem in the world today" (Scrimshaw 1991:46). Iron deficiency is often unrecognized in modern societies and also might have been in prehistoric societies, since symptoms, including listlessness and fatigue, are often subtle. Iron deficiency can result in diminished work capacity and productivity, and it increases the possibility of acquiring and dying from infections because the deficiency impairs the immune system. Iron deficiency is noted most often where diets are predominantly vegetarian. When meats are consumed with vegetables, a larger portion of the iron in the vegetable is absorbed. Vitamin C also enhances the absorption of iron, while tannins, fibers, and phytates inhibit absorption. Iron absorption also increases if the individual is deficient and in need of iron.

Summary and Conclusions

Examination of the prehistoric Anasazi diet for nutritional components indicates that the most likely sources of deficiencies are the water-soluble vitamins, which do not store well if the plant is dried and do not readily survive cooking, and iron. Sufficient intake of iron was probably tied directly to quantity of meat available in the diet, although certainly some of the vegetable foods contributed significant quantities of iron as well.

Chenopodium and *Amaranthus* seeds were a nutritionally important and significant part of the Anasazi diet. *Chenopodium* seeds are much better sources of iron than are *Amaranthus* seeds. Approximately 100 g of ground *Chenopodium* seeds contain two to three times the amount of iron necessary per day for a healthy male or female adult. However, since iron is not readily bioavailable from plant sources, it is likely that several hundred to a thousand grams or possibly more of ground *Chenopodium* seeds would need to be eaten to actually provide the necessary daily amount. Ground *Chenopodium* seeds are also high in calcium, containing approximately three times the quantity of calcium in *Amaranthus* seeds. Either seed, however, made a valuable contribution to the calcium intake in the diet. *Opuntia* fruits are also excellent sources of calcium. *Chenopodium* seeds contain a large quantity of potassium, approximately five times that contained by *Amaranthus* seeds, although both appear to have been good sources of potassium.

Fresh *Chenopodium* and *Amaranthus* greens are good sources of vitamin C, as are other greens, but the seeds are relatively poor sources; they contain approximately one-tenth or less the quantity of vitamin C per unit weight of the greens. The best sources of riboflavin are *Opuntia* buds and *Physalis* fruits. Niacin is high in sunflower seeds and *Opuntia* buds. Figures on quantities of folate, or folacin, are not available for many native plants, so none have been identified as good sources of that nutrient. Vitamin C and iron, then, are the most likely candidates for seasonal deficiencies.

Specific symptoms associated with deficiencies of these vitamins and minerals are reviewed below. Modern studies suggest that the recommended daily allowance of vitamins and minerals is not, in fact, optimal for good health but rather functions to keep the body from suffering deficiency symptoms. Therefore, we may suppose that the Anasazi also needed more than the minimum quantities of nutrients assumed in this reconstruction to remain healthy and to thrive. However, all interpretations and suppositions concerning nutrition are based on the recommended daily allowance.

Scurvy is the disease resulting from an inadequate supply of vitamin C. Primary symptoms are bleeding gums and loose teeth. Vitamin C also stimulates the immune system; thus, a deficiency in vitamin C undoubtedly would have left the Anasazi population more vulnerable to disease. Vitamin C appears to be important in the body's ability to fight colds, flu, other diseases, and allergies. Vitamin C also appears to be important in maintaining energy. An increase in consumption of vitamin C results in an increased ability to store glycogen in muscles and the liver, which is crucial since glycogen is an energy-storage material (Gottlieb and Keough 1984). Therefore, deficiency in vitamin C is likely to be associated with fatigue and diminished work output. Vitamin C also helps lower cholesterol and helps prevent blood cells from clotting. Scurvy may manifest itself in the skeletal population as tooth loss.

Iron-deficiency anemia often manifests itself in lethargy, apathy, brittle nails, depression, dizziness, fainting spells, fatigue, hair loss, headaches, heartburn, irritability, itching, pale lips and skin, poor appetite, rapid pulse, sore tongue, and weak legs. Specifically, iron-deficiency anemia reduces the ability of red blood cells to carry oxygen by decreasing production of hemoglobin. Modern studies on work capacity indicate that increased quantities of consumed iron improve a person's ability to work, even over the work ability of people showing no signs of iron-deficiency anemia. Iron-deficiency anemia manifests itself on the bones in the form of cribra orbitalia.

Insufficient quantities of food (and hence calories), seasonal deficiencies of fresh greens, and periodic hunting failures probably caused the majority of the nutritional problems associated with the Anasazi diet. Seasonal availability of greens high in vitamin C and destruction of that vitamin during storage were probably important contributing factors, not only in conditions occurring directly from vitamin C deficiency (such as scurvy) but also in iron-deficiency anemia, since vitamin C is important in facilitating iron absorption. Perhaps these seasonal fluctuations are responsible for the modern Pueblo Indian practice of sprouting beans in kivas. Bean sprouts are an excellent source of vitamin C at a time of year when the diet is deficient in that nutrient. Coprolite studies demonstrate that the Anasazi diet included many more plants than the often-referenced triad of corn-beans-squash. The assemblage of plant and animal foods recovered from the coprolites at Hoy House and Lion House is very similar to that noted in coprolites from other Anasazi sites. The total complement of foods available to and used by the Anasazi had the potential to provide a good nutritional base for healthy living with some seasonal deficiencies.

Note

1. The subject matter in this paper has been previously published in different forms in two regional volumes (see Cummings [1994a, 1994b] in the *References* section).

References

Bothwell, T. H., and R. W. Charlton
  1981   Iron Deficiency Anemia Producing Evidence of Marrow Hyperplasia in the Calvarium. *Pediatrics* 25:621–628.
Carlson, D. S., G. J. Armelagos, and D. P. Van Gerven
  1984   Factors Influencing the Etiology of Cribra Orbitalia in Prehistoric Nubia. *Journal of Human Evolution* 3:405–410.
Cummings, L. Scott
  1989   *Coprolites from Medieval Christian Nubia: An Interpretation of Diet and Nutritional Stress.* Unpublished Ph.D. dissertation, Department of Anthropology, University of Colorado, Boulder.
  1994a Agriculture and the Mesa Verde Area Anasazi Diet: Description and Nutritional Analysis. In *Soil, Water, Biology, and Belief in Prehistoric and Traditional*

Southwestern Agriculture, edited by H. W. Toll. Special Publication No. 2. New Mexico Archaeological Council, Santa Fe.

    1994b Anasazi Diet: Variety and Nutritional Analysis. In *1991 Anasazi Symposium*, edited by J. E. Smith and A. Hutchinson, pp. 303–318. Mesa Verde Museum Association, Mesa Verde, Colorado.

Emslie, S. D.

    1977 *Interpretation of Faunal Remains from Archaeological Sites in Mancos Canyon, Southwestern Colorado*. Unpublished Master's thesis, Department of Anthropology, University of Colorado, Boulder.

Gottlieb, W., and C. Keough (editors)

    1984 *Understanding Vitamins and Minerals*. Rodale Press, Emmaus, Pennsylvania.

Hummert, J. R.

    1983 *Childhood Growth and Morbidity in a Medieval Population from Kulubnarti in the* Batn el Hajar *of Sudanese Nubia*. Unpublished Ph.D. dissertation, Department of Anthropology, University of Colorado, Boulder.

Laferriere, J. E.

    1988 *Nutricomp*. Computer software.

Martin, P. S., and W. Byers

    1965 Pollen and Archaeology at Wetherill Mesa. In *Contributions of the Wetherill Mesa Archeological Project*, assembled by D. Osborne, pp. 122–135. Society for American Archaeology Memoir No. 19. Salt Lake City.

Nickens, P. R.

    1977 *Environment and Adaptation in Johnson Canyon, Southwestern Colorado: Pueblo III Communities in Transition*. Unpublished Ph.D. dissertation, Department of Anthropology, University of Colorado, Boulder.

Pearson, P. B.

    1980 World Nutrition: An Overview. In *Nutrition, Food, and Man: An Interdisciplinary Perspective*, edited by P. B. Pearson and R. Greenwell, pp. 1–37. University of Arizona Press, Tucson.

Sandford, M. K.

    1984 *Diet, Disease, and Nutritional Stress: An Elemental Analysis of Human Hair from Kulubnarti, A Medieval Sudanese Nubian Population*. Unpublished Ph.D. dissertation, Department of Anthropology, University of Colorado, Boulder.

Sandford, M. K., D. P. Van Gerven, and R. R. Meglen

    1983 Elemental Hair Analysis: New Evidence on the Etiology of Cribra Orbitalia in Sudanese Nubia. *Human Biology* 55:831–844.

Scott, L. J.

    1976 Hoy House—A Palynological Study. In *The Johnson-Lion Canyon Project, Report of Investigation III*, assembled by P. R. Nickens, pp. 8–49. Bureau of Indian Affairs, Albuquerque.

    1979 Dietary Inferences from Hoy House Coprolites: A Palynological Interpretation. *The Kiva* 44:257–279.

Scrimshaw, N. S.

    1991 Iron Deficiency. *Scientific American* 265(4):46–52.

Shelford, V. E.

    1963 *The Ecology of North America*. University of Illinois Press, Chicago.

Stiger, M. A.

    1977 *Anasazi Diet: The Coprolite Evidence*. Unpublished Master's thesis, Department of Anthropology, University of Colorado, Boulder.

Stodder, A. W.

    1987 The Physical Anthropology and Mortuary Practice of the Dolores

Anasazi: An Early Pueblo Population in Local and Regional Context. In *Dolores Archaeological Program: Supporting Studies: Settlement and Environment.*, compiled by K. L. Petersen and J. D. Orcutt, pp. 339–506. United States Department of the Interior, Bureau of Reclamation, Engineering and Research Center, Denver.

Van Gerven, D. P., M. K. Sandford, and J. R. Hummert
  1981   Mortality and Culture Change in Nubia's *Batn el Hajar*. *Journal of Human Evolution* 10:395–408.

Watt, B. K., and A. L. Merrill
  1963   *Composition of Foods*. Agriculture Handbook No. 8. United States Department of Agriculture, Washington.

Wing, E. S., and A. B. Brown
  1979   *Paleonutrition: Method and Theory in Prehistoric Foodways*. Academic Press, New York.

10. | Callen's Legacy

Vaughn M. Bryant, Jr.

The study of human coprolites, as a recognized science, is barely 30 years old. Its founder, Dr. Eric O. Callen, has been dead for more than 20 years. As a tribute to him, it is fitting to look back at how the discipline began, how it has progressed during the last 30 years, and where it will be as we enter the next century.

Dr. Callen ushered in the modern age of human coprolite analysis in the early 1960s (Callen and Cameron 1960). From then until his untimely death a decade later, he worked with missionary zeal to convince archaeologists, botanists, zooarchaeologists, and anyone else who would listen of the importance of prehistoric human fecal research. Although his initial success was limited, he would feel vindicated today by the growing importance given to the discipline of coprolite studies. He would have been especially gladdened by symposia and books, such as this one, devoted in part to studies of coprolite analyses.

Eric Callen was an unlikely person to become the "father" of coprolite analysis. He spent his professional career as a professor of plant pathology at McGill University in Montreal after receiving a doctorate in botany from the University of Edinburgh. Callen's first exposure to coprolites occurred during the early 1950s after a conversation with Thomas Cameron, a member of the McGill University parasitology faculty.

The story begins with archaeologist Junius Bird. In the late 1940s Bird excavated the site of Huaca Prieta de Chicama in the coastal region of Peru. During his excavation he collected what he believed to be dried samples of human feces (coprolites). He also collected a few samples from the preserved intestines of a human mummy. During a visit to McGill University in 1951, Bird gave the Peruvian samples to Cameron and asked him to examine them for evidence of human parasites. Meanwhile Callen, who was searching for records of ancient fungal pathogens that infect maize, learned of the Peruvian coprolite specimens and asked Cameron for a few samples to study.

It is ironic that the first detailed coprolite study was begun by two scientists: one looking for ancient human parasites and the other searching for traces of

Paleonutrition: The Diet and Health of Prehistoric Americans, edited by Kristin D. Sobolik. Center for Archaeological Investigations, Occasional Paper No. 22. © 1994 by the Board of Trustees, Southern Illinois University. All rights reserved. ISBN 0-88104-078-9.

ancient maize pathogens. Neither had any formal training in paleoethno-botany or in anthropology.

The Peruvian coprolites revealed little data on human parasites and contained no evidence of early maize pathogens, but the specimens did contain a wide array of dietary items. That discovery convinced both scientists that coprolites, more than any other type of prehistoric material, were the key to understanding ancient dietary and nutritional patterns (Callen and Cameron 1955).

After his initial Peruvian study, Callen devoted the next decade to examining human coprolites from other important sites. Next he studied coprolite specimens from the Ocampo caves in Mexico; then he turned to other sites near Tehuacan, also in Mexico (Callen 1965, 1967a). Next came a study of the Neanderthal site of Lazaret in France, where he examined six coprolites that were purported to be 90,000 years old (Callen 1969), and finally, he examined 10 coprolite samples from the Glen Canyon region of the American Southwest (Callen and Martin 1969). At the time of his death in 1970, he had begun a study of prehistoric coprolites from the site of Pikimachay near the city of Ayacucho in the Andean region of Peru.

Unfortunately, during the decade that Callen worked on coprolites, he never taught a course on coprolite analysis; he never supervised a graduate student's work on human coprolites; and he often endured the ridicule of colleagues in botany, and some in archaeology, who believed coprolite studies were a waste of time. Although never openly bitter about his situation, Callen often confided that he wished someone would publicly praise his work, or at least give recognition to the importance of human coprolite studies.

In 1970, just three months before his death, I visited Callen at MacDonald College of McGill University. During that visit he was upbeat about his upcoming trip to Peru to begin work on coprolites, which he hoped would reveal the earliest records of cultigen use in South America. However, he remained pessimistic about the acceptance of coprolite studies and about the minor impact such studies seemed to be having on other fields of science, such as botany and archaeology. He lamented that since 1960 less than a dozen other researchers had collected or examined human coprolites. And, as he noted, of that dozen only a few had continued to pursue other coprolite studies after completing their first study.

A few months later, during the summer of 1970, Callen died of a heart attack while working in Ayacucho, Peru. The next summer I was invited to Peru to continue the Ayacucho coprolite studies that Callen had begun. Callen's laboratory in Peru was locked the day after his death. Nearly a year later, I was the first person to enter his laboratory. Boxes on the floor and faded paper bags contained coprolites with labels in Spanish. On the table was an array of items, including dozens of widemouthed jam jars with their contents long since dried into thin, dark bands of hardened, varnishlike material. Index cards, microscope slides, plastic bags of dried plant materials, forceps and probes scattered like pick-up-sticks, and opened notebooks lay around the room on chairs and tables. A pencil sketch of a chili pepper seed was only half finished, as if Callen had planned to complete it the next day.

I sat on what was once Callen's chair, blew the dust off one of his notebooks, and began reading pages filled with cryptic notes about the many coprolite samples—citations that at first made little sense to me. But then, who among us leaves complete notes at the end of each day thinking that someone else might have to complete an experiment we had just begun? In the margin of various pages were tragic reminders to himself of how many nitroglycerine tablets he had taken, when he had chest pains, and even one short underlined message saying, "I must leave soon."

I closed the notebook, looked at the table filled with half-processed coprolite specimens, and wondered why Callen had refused to leave his work even when the threat of a fatal heart attack seemed imminent. I glanced at the table full of half-processed specimens and wondered if they were really worth a man's life.

For the rest of that first day I sifted through his notes, poked at trays full of macroremains, and looked at his prepared microscope slides, searching for answers. Each day for the rest of my stay in Ayacucho, I lived in awe of Callen's work and pondered what legacy he had left for the rest of us who had to continue in his footsteps.

When Callen began his studies of coprolites, the greatest problem he faced was finding a way to rehydrate dried coprolites without injuring their most delicate plant and animal contents. Until Callen's time, previously used coprolite analysis methods had proven unsatisfactory. They included using pliers and hammers to break open dried coprolites, grinding dried specimens through coarse screens, or pulling samples apart with one's fingers. Callen's first contribution was solving the rehydration problem (Callen and Cameron 1960). He discovered that soaking dried coprolites in a weak solution of trisodium phosphate, a technique he had learned from several zoologists (van Cleave and Ross 1947), rehydrated fecal material yet caused no harm to even the most delicate plant or animal tissues. He also discovered that the rehydration procedure restored the original foul fecal odor.

During the next decade Callen developed a technique to concentrate insect remains in coprolites by using benzene (Callen 1965). Today, that technique is no longer used because of the dangerous carcinogenic effects of benzene. He also searched for ways to determine when meat protein had been eaten, even if no physical evidence was identifiable (Callen 1967a). He believed, for example, that during the rehydration stage of coprolite analysis the appearance of a crust, or "chemical skin," as he called it, on the surface of the trisodium phosphate solution signaled the presence of consumed meat protein. After his death that technique would also be discarded by later coprolite analysts because additional tests showed no positive correlation between the eating of meat and the later development of a chemical skin (Reinhard and Bryant 1992).

Callen believed the ubiquity, or presence-absence, method of reporting coprolite data was sufficient, and he never tried to develop other techniques of quantifying coprolite contents (Callen 1965). Callen was also the first to recognize the potential value of phytoliths in identifying plant foods that were once eaten. In his report of coprolites from the Tehuacan Valley, Callen used the presence of phytolith crystals to confirm that the original inhabitants had eaten two different types of cacti (*Opuntia* and *Lemaireocereus*), and he noted that when maguey *(Agave)* leaves were roasted before being eaten, their raphide crystals shattered in a manner that could be recognized in coprolite remains (Callen 1967a). However, aside from his work at Tehuacan, Callen did not pursue the use of coprolite phytolith analysis in any of the other coprolite projects he completed before his death.

After Callen, other coprolite analysts made limited use of phytolith data. In the late 1960s I examined the phytoliths found in 43 prehistoric human coprolites from Conejo Shelter in southwest Texas (Bryant 1969, 1974a). Later, in the mid-1980s, John Jones identified squash phytoliths in ancient Peruvian coprolites recovered from lowland sites near the Pacific Ocean (Jones 1988). Most recently, Linda Scott Cummings found and identified phytoliths in coprolite specimens she examined from Nubian sites in Africa and from Anasazi sites in the American Southwest (Cummings 1990). In spite of the limited success reported in each of the above-mentioned studies, the full potential of phytolith analyses in human coprolites is yet to be realized.

Callen reported that seeds in coprolites could offer clues about milling and grinding techniques and that other types of macrofossils could detail methods of food preparation and cooking (Callen 1967b). Even so, he would have been amazed at the level of sophistication that is now possible through the use of scanning electron microscopy. In a recent study of Basketmaker-period prehistoric coprolites from the American Southwest, Kate Aasen Rylander (this volume) used SEM analyses to examine tiny chewed and ground fragments of maize kernels. From those data she was able to reconstruct probable food preparation techniques and the potential nutritional value of the specific maize types that were consumed.

Although aware of their presence and potential importance, Callen never extracted, or examined, pollen grains trapped in coprolites. The same was true of parasites. Although he and Cameron were the first to search for endoparasites in human coprolites (Callen and Cameron 1955), it was researchers such as Gary Fry who became a pioneer in the search for endoparasites in human coprolites (Fry and Moore 1969).

During the twenty years since the death of Eric Callen, the field of coprolite analysis has advanced—slowly at first, and then more rapidly (Reinhard and Bryant 1992). One of the initial questions that plagued Callen, and the other early analysts of his day, was how to *prove* a coprolite was of human origin. He relied on color and smell during the rehydration process as clues to validation (Callen 1963). In one report, Callen (1968) even stated that he was able to confirm whether individuals living in Mexico more than 2,000 years ago had been drinking maguey beer just from the smell emitted during a coprolite's rehydrated phase.

As a test of Callen's method of identifying human coprolites, Fry examined the fecal remains produced by a number of animals housed at the Salt Lake City zoo. His purpose was to see which animals, if any, might produce feces that mimic the color and smell of human coprolites (Fry 1970). He found that the feces of one animal, the coatimundi, mimicked the color, but not the smell, produced by a human coprolite. Nearly a decade later Glenna Dean discovered that human coprolites sometimes do not produce the dark color or the distinctive smell during the rehydration process unless they are air-dried for at least three days after being deposited (Williams-Dean 1978).

Other attempts to identify the certainty of human coprolites include experiments during the early 1970s by researchers such as Jones and Fry, who were the first to experiment with immunological techniques (e.g., the double agar diffusion test) to see if they could be used to verify the certainty of human coprolites (John Jones, personal communication 1977). Jones and Fry found their tests were reliable but abandoned the technique because it was too expensive for use on a routine basis. More recently, Robert Yohe and Margaret Newman have been using immunological techniques like the cross-over electrophoresis test to search for proteinaceous traces that can identify the genus of the animal producing a coprolite specimen (Newman et al. 1993). An added benefit of Yohe and Newman's study is the discovery that coprolites also contain traces of other proteins that can be linked to specific genera of animals used as meat, even when no visual macrofossil traces of meat remain.

Another problem that confronted early coprolite analysts was how to quantify coprolite contents. In addition to Callen's ubiquity system, other researchers perfected new ways to quantify coprolite contents. Richard Yarnell, for example, introduced the now-popular percentage-estimate method of quantification (Yarnell 1969). Others, such as Lewis Napton and Fry, were among the first to quantify coprolite contents by weight (Fry 1969; Napton 1969). Later, researchers such as Jones used unit volume as a quantification technique (Jones 1988).

From the earliest period of coprolite research, specialists have debated the amount of material that one should examine from a single coprolite. Callen believed the whole coprolite should be examined, especially when conducting ubiquity studies (Callen 1967a). Others have argued against processing whole coprolites, saying that it is essential to save a portion for future studies (Bryant 1974b). Even today, analysts are not in agreement as to exactly how much of a single coprolite should be examined. Some still believe that it is sufficient to extract a small subsample, such as a cubic centimeter or a few grams; others claim one should cut each coprolite in half along the longest axis and examine only half, reserving the other portion for future studies (Sobolik 1991b).

Callen and many of the coprolite analysts who have followed him believe that realistic dietary records can be reconstructed only when large numbers of individual specimens are examined from a single site or from a single time period. That, they claim, is the only way to develop a reliable reconstruction of dietary and nutritional data from the coprolite record left behind by a given culture. In a recent study, however, Karl Reinhard (1988) argues that such a policy may not be necessary. His research on Anasazi-age coprolites in the American Southwest suggests that only 18 to 20 coprolites need to be examined from each time period at a given site. Beyond that number, Reinhard argues, the researcher will gain little information (Reinhard 1988). On the other hand, as Jones mentions in his study of Peruvian coprolites (Jones 1988), examining as few as 18 to 20 coprolites per level from his site would not have provided an adequate reconstruction of ancient diets.

Callen made no attempt to recover pollen from the coprolites he examined, even though he recognized the importance of pollen data from coprolites. Palynologists like Paul Martin were among the first to search for pollen in coprolites. In the mid-1960s Martin and Floyd Sharrock (1964) were the first to publish the results of a pollen study of human coprolites. And, although Martin and others showed how useful coprolite pollen data could be, a wider potential use of pollen studies was not realized until Gerald Kelso (Kelso 1976) and Dean (Williams-Dean 1978) conducted their studies of how pollen grains move through the human digestive tract. In separate studies they discovered that pollen grains with different shapes and sizes move through the digestive system at different speeds. Expanding on that idea, later analysts, such as Rylander (Aasen 1984) and Kristin Sobolik (1988), used pollen concentration values found in prehistoric coprolites not only to reconstruct specific dietary elements but also to ascertain when certain foods were eaten and which foods might have been eaten together.

Determining what is in a coprolite may not always be a simple task. When Callen began his work, he relied on the signs he could see with the naked eye and through a dissecting microscope. Later, coprolite analyses became more sophisticated. By the early 1970s I began using the increased resolution potentials of scanning electron microscopy in coprolite analyses (Bryant and Williams-Dean 1975). More recently, others such as Rylander (this volume) have been using SEM studies to increase the potential information that can be gleaned from coprolite data.

Chemical analyses of coprolites is another area that Callen knew nothing about. However, today all sorts of new chemical techniques are being applied to coprolite analyses. Although most of the techniques are still in the experimental stage, many believe they may soon become routine. In the mid-1970s, John Moore used gas chromatography techniques to identify plant taxa in coprolites even though no macrofossil traces of the plants remained (Moore et al. 1984). Others, such as Jeff Huebner of the University of Texas at Austin, are experimenting with stable isotope studies of coprolite components in the hope of finding a better way to reconstruct the ratio of plant to animal material in prehistoric diets and the ratio of C^3 to C^4 plants that were used as food.

Early studies by Don Lin and his colleagues (1978) were among the first to focus on a search for steroids in human coprolites. In their initial study they proved that meaningful data could be derived from traces of residual steroids. Even so, like other types of chemical applications, the potential of steroid research in coprolite studies is yet to be fully tested.

What is the future of coprolite studies? What problems still remain to be solved? What is being done to encourage researchers to enter the field of coprolite analysis? Those are critical topics that need to be addressed.

One of the biggest problems that has plagued the discipline from its inception is lack of professional recognition for those who conduct coprolite studies. That, I believe, is one of the primary reasons why many researchers have conducted at least one coprolite study during the past three decades but why very few have continued with a second or third. Lack of professional recognition is also why no coprolite analyst has been able to gain an academic appointment specifically because of that skill. Coprolite analysts who are currently part of the academic system admit that they were not hired for their expertise in analyzing coprolites but for skills in teaching or another research field.

A corollary problem for coprolite analysts is academic identity. To gain the skills needed for coprolite studies, students should train at the master's level in either botany or anthropology, then earn a doctorate in the other field. Once trained in that manner, however, they find that colleagues in biology often will not accept them as "real" botanists. Likewise, many in anthropology often think of them as "botanists" posing as anthropologists. To someone in academia who is already tenured, such an identity crisis is bothersome but is no longer critical. For doctoral students, and those with recent degrees, being a coprolite specialist is not something to note too prominently in a résumé.

Other equally important problems in coprolite research still need to be resolved. Topping the list is the need to establish a unified method for reporting coprolite data. Currently, coprolite analysts summarize their data in many different forms (i.e., ubiquity, volume, weight, percentage). Such lack of agreement on how data should be presented often makes regional comparisons or larger geographical correlations of published coprolite data difficult to summarize (Sobolik 1991a).

Another unsolved problem is determining exactly what, and how much of a given food source, was eaten. For example, what does a single seed, or even a dozen seeds, from a fruit type represent? What does a single animal hair, a few reptile scales, or a large number of tiny fish bones reveal about how much meat may have been eaten? Although we are making some progress in the area of quantification through the use of new techniques such as chemical analyses, there are still many dietary gaps that we have yet to understand. A similar problem centers on using coprolite data to reconstruct which foods were eaten together as part of a single meal. Resolving questions such as those will give us important new clues about the habits of past cultures. Those and other quantitative questions will be the challenges for us in the future.

Although determining the sex and origin of those who produce a coprolite is becoming more sophisticated, finding a quick and inexpensive method to resolve those questions should be another one of our goals for the future. Likewise, gaining precise information about the nutritional value of prehistoric diets is an area of increasing importance. Cummings has tried to address that issue (this volume), as have others (e.g., Sobolik 1991a) who have used nutrition as the centerpiece for dietary studies of ancient cultures.

Other areas of future research should include searching for traces of viruses and bacteria in coprolites. Although some attempts in both those areas have been tried (Williams-Dean 1978), past tests have not proven productive. More effective techniques of endoparasite extraction and identification are needed. Once they are perfected, they will help us learn more about the spread of ancient diseases and the health of prehistoric cultures (Reinhard and Bryant 1992).

Today, as in 1970 when Callen died, the field of coprolite research is still young. Perhaps the discipline has expanded enough to move it from the realm of infancy to that of adolescence. Regardless, the discipline of coprolite studies is not yet a mature science, nor is it flooded with too many analysts.

Callen would be gladdened to know that the discipline he began has gained greater acceptance and recognition today than it did during his lifetime. However, if Callen were still alive, he would probably echo what most of us believe—that we still have a long way to go.

References

Aasen, D. K.
  1984   *Pollen, Macrofossil, and Charcoal Analyses of Basketmaker Coprolites from Turkey Pen Ruin, Cedar Mesa, Utah.* Unpublished Master's thesis, Department of Anthropology, Washington State University, Pullman.
Bryant, V. M., Jr.
  1969   *Late Full-Glacial and Postglacial Pollen Analysis of Texas Sediments.* Unpublished Ph.D. dissertation, Department of Botany, University of Texas, Austin.
  1974a   Prehistoric Diet in Southwest Texas: The Coprolite Evidence. *American Antiquity* 39:407–420.
  1974b   The Role of Coprolite Analysis in Archaeology. *Texas Archeological Society Bulletin* 45:1–28.
Bryant, V. M., Jr., and G. Williams-Dean
  1975   The Coprolites of Man. *Scientific American* 232(1):100–109.
Callen, E. O.
  1963   Diet as Revealed by Coprolites. In *Science in Archeology*, edited by D. Brothwell and E. Higgs, pp. 186–194. Basic Books, London.
  1965   Food Habits of Some Pre-Columbian Indians. *Economic Botany* 19:335–343.
  1967a   Analysis of the Tehuacan Coprolites. In *The Prehistory of the Tehuacan Valley: Environment and Subsistence*, vol. 1, edited by D. Byers, pp. 261–289. University of Texas Press, Austin.
  1967b   The First New World Cereal. *American Antiquity* 32:535–538.
  1968   Plants, Diet, and Early Agriculture of Some Cave Dwelling Pre-Columbian Mexican Indians. *Actas y Memorias del XXXVII Congreso Internacional de Americanistas* 2:641–656.
  1969   Les coprolithes de la cabane acheuleenne du Lazaret: Analyse et diagnostic. *Mémoires de la Société Préhistorique Française* 7:123–124.
Callen, E. O., and T. W. M. Cameron
  1955   The Diet and Parasites of Prehistoric Huaca Prieta Indians as Determined by Dried Coprolites. *Proceedings of the Royal Society of Canada* 1955:51.
  1960   A Prehistoric Diet Revealed in Coprolites. *The New Scientist* 90:35–40.
Callen, E. O., and P. S. Martin
  1969   Plant Remains in Some Coprolites from Utah. *American Antiquity* 34:329–331.
Cummings, L. Scott
  1990   *Coprolites from Medieval Christian Nubia: An Interpretation of Diet and Nutritional Stress.* Unpublished Ph.D. dissertation, Department of Anthropology, University of Colorado, Golden.

Fry, G. F.
  1969   *Prehistoric Diet at Danger Cave, Utah, as Determined by the Analysis of Coprolites*. Unpublished Masters thesis, Department of Anthropology, University of Utah, Salt Lake City.
  1970   *Prehistoric Human Ecology in Utah: Based on the Analysis of Coprolites*. Unpublished Ph.D. dissertation, Department of Anthropology, University of Utah, Salt Lake City.
Fry, G. F., and J. G. Moore
  1969   *Enterobius vermicularis*: 10,000 Year Old Human Infection. *Science* 166:1620.
Jones, J. G.
  1988   *Middle to Late Preceramic (6000–3000 B.P.) Subsistence Patterns on the Central Coast of Peru: The Coprolite Evidence*. Unpublished Masters thesis, Department of Anthropology, Texas A&M University, College Station.
Kelso, G.
  1976   *Absolute Pollen Frequencies Applied to the Interpretation of Human Activities in Northern Arizona*. Unpublished Ph.D. dissertation, Department of Anthropology, University of Arizona, Tucson.
Lin, D. S., W. E. Connor, L. K. Napton, and R. E. Heizer
  1978   The Steroids of 2000-Year-Old Human Coprolites. *Journal of Lipid Research* 19:215–221.
Martin, P. S., and F. W. Sharrock
  1964   Pollen Analysis of Prehistoric Human Feces: A New Approach to Ethnobotany. *American Antiquity* 30:168–180.
Moore, J. G., A. W. Grundman, H. J. Hall, and G. F. Fry
  1984   Fecal Odorgrams: A Method for Partial Reconstruction of Ancient and Modern Diets. *Digestive Diseases and Sciences* 29:907–911.
Napton, L. K.
  1969   The Lacustrine Subsistence Pattern in the Desert West. In *Archeological and Paleobiological Investigations in Lovelock Cave, Nevada*, edited by R. Heizer and L. Napton, pp. 28–97. Kroeber Anthropological Society Special Publication No. 2. University of California, Berkeley.
Newman, M. E., R. M. Yohe II, H. Ceri, and M. Q. Sutton
  1993   Immunological Protein Residue Analysis of Non-Lithic Archaeological Materials. *Journal of Archaeological Science* 20:93–100.
Reinhard, K. J.
  1988   *Diet, Parasitism, and Anemia in the Prehistoric Southwest*. Unpublished Ph.D. dissertation, Department of Anthropology, Texas A&M University, College Station.
Reinhard, K. J., and V. M. Bryant, Jr.
  1992   Coprolite Analysis: A Biological Perspective on Archaeology. In *Archaeological Method and Theory*, vol. 4, edited by M. B. Shiffer, pp. 245–288. University of Arizona Press, Tucson.
Sobolik, K. D.
  1988   The Importance of Pollen Concentration Values from Coprolites: An Analysis of Southwest Texas Samples. *Palynology* 12:201–214.
  1991a   *Paleonutrition of the Lower Pecos Region of the Chihuahuan Desert*. Unpublished Ph.D. dissertation, Department of Anthropology, Texas A&M University, College Station.
  1991b   *The Prehistoric Diet and Subsistence of the Lower Pecos Region, as Reflected in Coprolites from Baker Cave, Val Verde County, Texas*. Studies in Archeology No. 7. Texas Archeological Research Laboratory, University of Texas, Austin.

van Cleave, H., and J. Ross
   1947   A Method of Reclaiming Dried Zoological Specimens. *Science* 105:319.
Williams-Dean, G.
   1978   *Ethnobotany, and Cultural Ecology of Prehistoric Man in Southwest Texas.*
           Unpublished Ph.D. dissertation, Department of Anthropology, Texas A&M
           University, College Station.
Yarnell, R. A.
   1969   Contents of Human Paleofeces. In *The Prehistory of Salts Cave, Kentucky,*
           edited by P. Watson, pp. 1–56. Illinois State Museum, Springfield.

III. Bioarchaeology

11. Cartesian Reductionism and Vulgar Adaptationism: Issues in the Interpretation of Nutritional Status in Prehistory

Alan H. Goodman

Abstract: Paleonutrition studies can provide insights into the dynamics of life in past societies. Those insights, however, are at risk because of an increasing focus on short-term adaptations. In this paper I review three short-term focused interpretations of indicators of nutritional status. I argue that those interpretations share a reductionistic and decontextualized approach to human biology, while failing to consider the long-range and systemic consequences of compromised nutritional status.

Introduction

The ultimate value of homeostatic reactions cannot be judged, therefore, until all of the consequences of such changes have been recognized.
—Dubos 1978:79

The only biological adjustment we can make to deleterious environmental factors is not true adaptation but a form of tolerance achieved at the cost of impaired functioning.
—Dubos 1978:78

In order to provide a basis for discussion of the effects of undernutrition on prehistoric groups, this paper was originally meant to review the functional consequences of undernutrition in contemporary peasants. Although this "ethnobioarchaeological" approach to undernutrition is still an implied focus, the overriding theme has changed.

At the 1991 American Anthropological Association meeting I presented a paper in a symposium on the possible intersections between medical ecology and political economy. Hans Baer, who had coorganized the symposium and who spoke before me, made the point that medical ecologists had focused on

Paleonutrition: The Diet and Health of Prehistoric Americans, edited by Kristin D. Sobolik. Center for Archaeological Investigations, Occasional Paper No. 22. © 1994 by the Board of Trustees, Southern Illinois University. All rights reserved. ISBN 0-88104-078-9.

finding adaptations, and perhaps in the process had missed quite a bit, including great human cost and suffering and the systemic links between affliction and political-economic processes.[1] In response, I challenged that that characterization was not true for prehistoric medical ecology (including paleonutrition and paleoepidemiology). Recent publications suggest that I may have spoken too soon.

The purpose of this paper is to assess a recent trend in international nutrition and paleonutrition in which signs of compromised nutritional status are viewed as evidence for adaptation. I suggest that those reinterpretations, rather than providing new insights, reify an old Cartesian and mechanistic view of human physiology. Relying on the hope that the human body can homeostatically adapt to insults and deprivations, the theoretical model suggests a disease process in which an insult invades the body and the body homeostatically adjusts. All other systems are disconnected in Cartesian terms from the readjusting subsystem. In the most extreme form, that thinking suggests a vulgarization of the concept of adaptation: signs of stress are seen as adaptations for no other reason than that they exist in stressed but surviving organisms.

The practical implication of that view is serious. In pursuit of adaptations, the functional costs to the individual and to larger social units are ignored. There is no attention to the consequences of not being able to adapt. Furthermore, whereas the interaction between insult and host is usually assumed to lead to adaptive readjustment, there is little need to comprehend, much less change, underlying conditions.

In this paper I summarize new interpretations of the meaning of three nutritional status indicators. First, I review Neiburger's (1990) assessment that linear enamel hypoplasias indicate poor dietary status. Neiburger's comments are used only as a brief example of an extremely mechanistic view of the relationship between dietary intake and physiological perturbation. Stuart-Macadam's (1992) self-titled "new perspective" on porotic hyperostosis and iron deficiency is then discussed. Her view of physiology is seemingly that it is accommodating without costs.[2] Lastly, I review Seckler's (1982) thesis that the mild-to-moderately malnourished, as evidenced by short stature, are actually "small but healthy." Rather than as a sign of stress, Seckler reinterprets small body size to be a sign of healthy, homeostatic adjustment. This older example, played out in the very real world of international nutrition, comes complete with well-honed politics of support for the status quo and provides a third example of excess adaptationism.

Signs of Stress or of Adaptation: Contested Interpretations

Linear Enamel Hypoplasia and Mechanistic Thinking

Extrapolations as to nutritional or social stress based on the incidence of enamel hypoplasias occurring in extinct populations are assumptions

based on little scientific fact and should . . . be discouraged.
—Neiburger 1988:253

In a comment on a study of linear enamel hypoplasias (LEH) in Neander-thals, Neiburger states general objections to paleonutritional inference from LEH frequencies. He believes that Ogilvie and her coworkers' (1989) study of LEH in Neanderthals is "an error prone interpretation" and more generally that enamel hypoplasia is "a poor indicator of dietary stress" (1990:231). Neiburger proposes that there is a sort of mass amnesia amongst anthro-pologists regarding the etiology of enamel hypoplasias. Apparently because of their lack of training in the rigors of hard sciences such as dentistry (Neiburger's field), anthropologists are especially subject to uncritically following the latest trends, which in this case relates LEH to nutritional status. Paleopathologists, in his view, uncritically consider enamel hypoplasia to be a sort of perfect assay of dietary adequacy. In particular, Ogilvie and colleagues (1989) are wrong to infer nutritional problems in Neanderthals from high LEH prevalences. Inferences, Neiburger exhorts, cannot be based on an imperfect indicator.

The specifics of Neiburger's comments are easily refuted. LEHs are usually considered to be indicators of nutritional status during development, not dietary status (Goodman 1991; Goodman and Rose 1991). The difference between the two concepts is critical. By diet, Neiburger seems to mean what is eaten. However, nutritional status is defined as "the state resulting from the balance between the supply of nutrients on the one hand and the expenditure of the organism on the other" (McLaren 1976:3). It is the end result of numer-ous factors affecting access to and utilization of nutrients. Nutritional status is a more complex concept than dietary intake. LEH does not directly reflect diet; however, hypoplasias do provide a window into the past physiological activity of ameloblasts, the enamel-forming cells, which are affected by diet and other conditions that contribute to the nutritional status of the organism.

What is more serious and disturbing about Neiburger's evaluation is the suggestion that a one-to-one relationship between insult and physiological response is likely. He is seemingly looking for an easily interpreted, invari-able, and unchanging relationship between cause and effect, between pathogenic organism and disease. However, disease processes are complex; one rarely finds a one-to-one relationship between exposure to an insult and disease. Host and pathogen dialectically interact (Levins and Lewontin 1985). The disease process is not linear and not invariant. Neiburger eventually implies that further studies using LEH should cease, given the imperfect relationship. Of course, that logic would stop nearly all medical research.

In summary, Neiburger's critique of inferences made on the basis of LEH correctly points to the need for paleopathologists to pay attention to studies of LEH among living individuals and not to be overly specific about etiology. However, stripped of his misinterpretation of the concept of nutritional status, Neiburger's view of disease etiology remains simplistically mechanistic. He implies that human physiologies should have invariant responses. In the following sections I will try to show that his mechanistic view sets the table for considering stress indicators as adaptations.

Anemia, Porotic Hyperostosis, and Vulgar Adaptationism

> The acceptance of the two concepts, that diet is of little importance to the
> development of iron deficiency anemia, and that iron deficiency is an
> adaptive response to stress, has a profound effect on the interpretation of
> porotic hyperostosis.
>
> —Stuart-Macadam 1992:44

Recent reinterpretations of the cause and adaptive significance of porotic hyperostosis in prehistoric skeletons, as embraced in the preceding quote, extend a mechanistic view of physiology to the problematic of considering pathology as a sign of adaptation (see also Kent et al. 1991). In a paper titled "Porotic Hyperostosis: A New Perspective," Stuart-Macadam (1992) proposes that paleopathologists have improperly interpreted porotic hyperostosis to be secondary to a dietary deficiency, most likely iron. In her view, there has been little concern for nondietary factors. Stuart-Macadam proposes that "within the context of this new perspective porotic hyperostosis is seen not as a nutritional stress indicator, but as an indication that a population is attempting to adapt to the pathogen load in its environment" (1992:39). What is actually new about this new perspective, and more importantly, what is correct and useful?

What is not new is the interpretation that diet is not always the key to the etiology of anemia. Most researchers would agree that diet and nondietary factors are of potential importance. In some cases parasitism (and parasite load) is certainly the main determinant of iron loss and anemia. That case is likely when parasitism leads to gastrointestinal bleeding (Solomons and Keusch 1981). However, dietary iron intake is frequently the key to iron status. For examples, Dallman and colleagues (1984) have shown that low iron intake is the main cause of anemia in infants, children, and women in the United States, and Calvo and Gnazzo (1990) similarly show that diet is the main determinant of anemia in urban Argentinean children. Just as focusing exclusively on diet is simplistic, focusing exclusively on parasitism is equally simplistic. That point of view has been well taken in the paleopathology literature, at least since the review by Mensforth and coworkers (1978; see also Mensforth 1991).

Up to this point the Stuart-Macadam critique of the literature on porotic hyperostosis parallels Neiburger's critique of the LEH literature. Both suggest that diet is overemphasized, and both misinterpret the concept of nutritional status. Both are excessively Cartesian in their conception of physiological processes. Stuart-Macadam's work differs in illustrating an excessive adaptationism.

Following the lead of Weinberg (1984) on iron withholding, Stuart-Macadam (1992) interprets iron deficiency as *an adaptive response to stress* (emphasis added). What is problematic about her interpretation is that it is a narrow view of adaptation. Weinberg (1984) makes the point that iron supplementation can lead to pathogen growth. He logically proposes that humans have evolved a physiological defense to some pathogens that includes iron-withholding mechanisms. However, in Dubos's terms (1978), iron withhold-ing should be seen as an adjustment rather than an adaptation. There is no clear evidence that hypoferremia increases the long-term adaptation of the organism, and there is not a clear relationship between iron withholding, chronic iron status, and porotic hyperostosis. Cartesian reductionism creeps in. It is as if iron can be sequestered from microorganisms without affecting the need for iron in the host.

Iron deficiency—sometimes even at levels where hemoglobin and hemato-crits are normal, that is iron deficiency without anemia—leads to a suite of functional costs. A variety of organs and systems show structural changes with borderline iron deficiency. Vyas and Chandra advise that the wide spread costs of iron deficiency are not surprising because iron is "an essential cofactor of several enzyme systems that play an important role in metabolic processes and cell proliferation" (1984:45). Those enzymes are aconitase, cata-lase, cytochrome C, cytochrome C reductase, cytochrome oxidase, formimino-transferase, monoamine oxidase, myelperoxidase, peroxidase, ribonucleotidyl reductase, succinic dehydrogenase, tyrosine hydroxylase, tryptophan pyro-lase, and xanine oxidase (Vyas and Chandra 1984). Many of them are involved in vital functions such as DNA synthesis, mitochondrial electron transport, catecholamine metabolism, and neurotransmitter detoxification.

The consequences of iron deficiency on an organismal level can be divided into three areas: (1) resistance to disease, (2) work capacity/activity, and (3) cognition and behavior. Iron deficiency has a variety of effects on immuno-competence and infection. Especially noteworthy is its effect on cell-mediated immunity (Dallman 1987). Experimentally induced iron deficiency results in a reduction in lymphocyte proliferation, the production of rosette-forming T cells, and the microbicidal capacity of neutrophils (Dallman 1987; Sherman 1992; Vyas and Chandra 1984). In humans, iron supplements have lead to a decreased prevalence of diarrhea and upper- and lower-respiratory infections. After reviewing and finding flawed studies of the supposedly protective effects of iron deficiency against infection, Vyas and Chandra conclude that "it can be stated with confidence that iron supplementation within physiological needs to prevent anemia or in doses necessary to correct anemia may reduce, but certainly not increase, the risk of infection" (1984:49).

Although the relationship between iron deficiency and cognition is harder to specify (partly because iron deficiency is often confounded with other nutrient deficiencies), Pollitt has shown that mild iron deficiency, without low hemoglobin, is associated with learning deficiencies (1987). Of particular note are changes in attention and memory control processes. Those results suggest that iron is a critical element for the normal functioning of the nervous system and that cognitive functions can be disrupted by relatively mild iron deficiency.

The effects of iron deficiency and anemia on work capacity are profound (Scrimshaw 1991). Work capacity has frequently been shown to be propor-tional to hemoglobin concentration. Anemic subjects cannot maintain the work times of normal subjects and reach a lower mean maximal workload. Anemic Guatemalan laborers performed much more poorly on the Harvard

Step Test than did their nonanemic peers, and the work output and pay of Indonesian rubber tappers correlate almost perfectly with their hemoglobin levels (Scrimshaw 1991). If decreased oxygen affinity and increased cardiac output are the "adaptive" responses to anemia, then those adaptations can cover for deficiency only when the organism is sedentary or at rest. That is, it is an adaptation that does not work well in the real world, perhaps unless one is very wealthy.

In a review of nutrition and host defense, Keusch proposes in response to Weinberg (1977) that the "longterm benefits of hypoferremia are entirely unknown. What is known is the cost—anemia" (1979:287). In light of that evaluation, it would be extremely problematic science, not to mention onerous public policy, to suggest that contemporary individuals with anemia are either adapting or have adapted. Is porotic hyperostosis a sign of adaptation or a sign of nutritional deficiency? I suggest that it is quite clearly a sign of nutritional deficiency from a variety of systemic consequences can be inferred.

Small but Healthy?

> The homeostatic theory postulates a *threshold* relationship. Smallness may *not* be associated with functional impairments. . . . the mild to moderately malnourished people in the deprivation theory are simply "small but healthy" people in the homeostatic theory (emphasis in original).
>
> —Seckler 1982:129

> Regulation of the rate of growth is likely an important defense mechanism against functional impairments due to malnutrition which would otherwise accompany poverty.
>
> —Seckler 1982:133

Although the previous sections of this paper have focused on nutrition in the past, the debate over the interpretation of small body size has been waged in the arena of contemporary politics and sciences. That debate is reviewed here because it suggests a number of lessons for the study of nutritional status in the past, and it has the potential to spill over into the study of prehistoric nutrition.

Except for a limited number of ethnic groups, there is surprisingly little variation in group mean height attributable to *group-level* genetic differences (Dietz 1983; Graitcer and Gentry 1981; Habicht et al. 1974). Therefore, because of the universality of the growth pattern at the group level, it is possible to estimate prevalences of stunting in groups and to target groups at risk. With anthropometric data, nutritionists and international health researchers have a powerful tool for targeting groups at risk.

Malnutrition has traditionally been defined by degree of severity. Severe malnutrition is obvious from clinical signs. However, at the mild and moderate levels, growth (size) may be the only measurable sign of malnutrition. Heights and weights are frequently collected in international health programs, not only because they are easy measures to take but because they are sensitive ones. They have the potential to identify malnutrition before it becomes severe and life threatening.

In 1980 the economist David Seckler challenged fundamental assumptions about the meaning and consequences of short stature. As quoted above, Seckler proposed that short individuals in developing countries are short because they have adapted to chronically marginal food availability; the body adjusts to low nutrient availability by reducing growth (1980, 1982). He further suggests that that homeostatic adjustment occurs without adaptive cost. The individuals are essentially "small but healthy" (1980:225). In fact, Seckler asserts that small individuals may be better adapted than larger individuals to an environment in which food scarcity is a chronic problem. His argument should sound vaguely reminiscent.

The implications of considering the formerly marginally malnourished to be small but healthy are profound. In India alone, where Seckler focused his analysis, his rethinking could "clear the books" of hundreds of millions of malnourished peasants. With a simple rethinking, the problem has seemingly gone away. Of course the problem of marginal malnutrition only appears to have been solved. The contested area directly concerns whether the small individuals are, indeed, healthy. If Seckler is correct, then it follows that there are few functional inferences that can be made on the basis of anthropometric data. The small are not marginally malnourished. They are healthy, homeostatically adjusted and adapted.

In a review of the literature on the interrelationship of diet, growth, and infectious disease, Martorell (1980) found that poor growth status is almost invariably associated with both marginal diets and increased disease. The synergetic relationship between diet and disease is often so strong that it is difficult to ascertain the precise cause of poor growth status (Martorell 1989; also see Tompkins 1988). Growth status seems to be a sign of the cumulative stress experienced by an individual, of which poor diet and disease are likely to be of main importance, and, parenthetically, is why growth is a measure of nutritional, not dietary, status. The primary proximate causes of short stature are impoverished diets and disease. To then affirm that short stature is adaptive implies a sanctioning of the presence of the conditions leading to short stature (Martorell 1989), which might ultimately be traced back to poverty and inequality in access to resources (McKeown 1988).

In addition to increased morbidity, poor growth status is associated with a number of other functional consequences. Chavez and Martinez (1982) have systematically addressed the functional cost of marginal diets and small body size in their nutrition-supplementation study. In the late 1960s pregnant mothers and their infants from Tezonteopan, Mexico, were divided into two groups: one received daily nutritional supplementation, and the other group did not. Chavez and Martinez found that the better-nourished/taller children had fewer disease episodes and especially had shorter durations of disease. As well, the better-nourished children displayed more exploratory behaviors, cried less, and talked at an earlier age. Functional cost in terms of decreased activity and learning may be signaled by growth stunting.

A wealth of studies have shown that poor growth is related to an increased risk of mortality, the ultimate indicator of adaptive failure (see Alam et al. 1989; Chen et al. 1980; Lerberghe, 1988; Smedman et al. 1987). Alam and co-workers (1989) show that children in Bangladesh with small arm circumferences are 12 times more likely to die than children with more adequate arm circumferences. Lerberghe sums up his recent review of the relationship between childhood stunting and mortality by stating: "If both stunting and mortality are different outcomes . . . of a succession of stresses on children's health, then the measure of the height of children in a community is an even more valuable tool for evaluation" (1988:259). He continues: "The measurement of the prevalence of stunted children then becomes an operationally fairly feasible, be it indirect, measurement of poverty related disease frequency. . . . The prevalence of stunted children in a community appears to be a good overall indicator of the health status of a community of children" (1988:259).

Martorell persuasively summarizes the interacting scientific and political difficulties of the small-but-healthy hypothesis by asserting the following four points. First, children and adults in developing countries are short as a result of chronically poor diets and frequent infection during development. To consider stunting to be adaptive is to intimate that its causes—impoverished diets and increased exposure to disease—are desirable. Second, growth retardation, "rather than an innocuous response to environmental stimuli, is a warning signal of increased risk of morbidity and mortality" (1989:15). Third, the conditions that cause stunting also affect other functions such as cognition and work capacity. Finally, stunted girls who grow up short are at increased risk of delivering growth-retarded infants with a greater chance of dying (1989:15).

In thinking about how Seckler could have made such a nearsighted interpretation of the adaptive consequences of stunting, Pelto and Pelto (1989) suggest that he fell victim to the "quitting early" problem (also see Harris 1988). They propose that many scientists are guilty of quitting before they have evaluated the long-term causes and consequences of apparent adaptations.

The implication that can be derived from the "small but healthy" debate is that many paleonutritionists also quit too soon. We quit before systemically analyzing the implications of disease patterns on the individual and society. In a contemporary context, Chavez and Martinez (1982) have shown that moderately malnourished children may be sick as much as half their childhoods. It is difficult to comprehend the burden that such a level of illness must place on a mother in a developing community (Leatherman 1987), and there is no reason to suggest that the burden of illness was any less in most past societies. Just as LEH is imperfectly related to nutrition and health status, linear growth is also an imperfect measure. Nonetheless, they are both useful.

Just as anemia is not a cost-free homeostatic adaptation, small body size does not come without costs to other functional systems.

Conclusions: Paleonutrition and Vulgar Adaptationism

Don't look for the meaning, look for the use.
—Wittgenstein's Aphorism

Don't look for the use, look for the abuse.
—Callahan's Corollary of Wittgenstein

The study of the diets of prehistoric peoples is a relatively benign undertaking. One need not worry that faulty theories or methods might lead directly to human suffering. The work of reconstructing prehistoric diets does not have much to do with how to choose a president or even with current infant mortality rates. A mistake, unlike the improper administration of anesthesia, will not lead to coma. On the other hand, there are links between the human condition now and in the past. Convictions about the past interact with convictions about the present. They reinforce each other. The purpose of this paper has been not only to explore connections between ideas about past and present nutritional status but also to consider implications of commonly held interpretations.

Recent interpretations of the meaning of nutritional-status indicators have in common an underlying assumption that physiological processes are mechanistic and homeostatic. Thus, dietary inadequacy and all that might follow from it can be adjusted to with little or no cost. Neiburger (1990) is befuddled by the lack of a clear and consistent relationship between dietary deficiency and the formation of enamel defects. Stuart-Macadam (1992) suggests that the cause of porotic hyperostosis is complex but misinterprets the organism's ability to withhold iron (and by extension porotic hyperostosis) as an adaptation to parasitism. These new explanations could be viewed as benign reinterpretations of what are commonly referred to as "stress indicators," reflecting a worldview in which physiology is seen as no more complex than house plumbing. However, I suggest that they are not totally benign, rather that they lead to an excess of emphasis on the organism's ability to adjust (after all it is still alive!) and an attribution of adaptation before all the costs have been accounted for.

Does it make a difference whether nutritional-status indicators such as LEH, porotic hyperostosis, and anthropometry are considered signs of stress or of adaptation? On one level, the difference might not be so great if both perspectives considered the costs of adjustment and the cause of the need to adjust, that is, if the biological process were considered in full social and political-economic context. However, such uses, or one should say misuses, of adaptation tend to cast a narrow beam of light, whereas a focus on stress casts a broader beam. A focus on stress redresses an imbalance of excess adaptationism by concentrating on the costs and limits of adaptation (Goodman et al.

1988). Lastly, to paraphrase Martorell (1989), it is ludicrous to focus on adaptation when the conditions are of sociopolitical exploitation and impoverishment. Clearly, the only adaptation is to change the system, not to adjust to it.

Fortunately, it is possible to test whether these signs of undernutrition are adaptive. Data can resolve the differences in perspective. For permanent and deciduous enamel developmental defects, Goodman and Armelagos (1988) and Blakey and Armelagos (1985), respectively, have found that defects at Dickson Mounds are associated with decreased survival. What is significant about their work is the effort to see if the indicator is associated with a change in other measures of morbidity and mortality. In the Dickson context, it would be problematic to see enamel developmental defects as signs of adaptation, unless one were to say that death is an adaptation. Conversely, Harris lines are infrequently associated with increased morbidity (Goodman et al. 1984). For those reasons one might question their use as a stress indicator. Clearly, more research should be done on the potential morbidity and mortality consequences associated with LEH, anemia, and growth faltering in prehistoric populations.

Returning to ethnobioarchaeology and the original theme of this paper, I find that one of the exciting things about the three indicators discussed is that they all have parallels in contemporary nutrition work. Growth and LEH can be studied in both prehistoric and contemporary individuals, and one can make inferences between blood measures of iron status and skeletal markers of iron deficiency. Thus, by studying the context and meaning of nutritional-status indicators in contemporary settings, it may be possible to make surer inferences about their meaning in prehistory.

A brief ethnobioarchaeological example involves work on enamel defects among Nahuatl children in highland Mexico (Goodman et al. 1991). Our research was conducted with the same children who had been involved in the previously discussed dietary supplementation study of Chavez and Martinez (1982). We found that nonsupplemented children had approximately twice the LEH frequency of the supplemented children. Differences were especially great during the first and fourth years (Figure 11-1). The data suggest that change in nutritional intake can greatly decrease the frequency of LEH. Interestingly, LEH rates around ages two and three in the supplemented group were quite high, possibly due to endemic parasitism.

The prevalence of defects in the nonsupplemented children is similar to rates often observed in prehistoric groups. In Tezonteopan, that prevalence of LEH is associated with high respiratory and diarrheal morbidity between the ages of one and three years, growth stunting, and effects on childhood activity and learning. From those data we can begin to pose the question of whether similar rates in prehistoric populations might infer comparable functional consequences.

Stressful environmental conditions, which are frequently linked to political and economic processes, can lead to an increase in recoverable signs of stress. Those signs are significant to interpreting adaptation because they suggest a concurrent lowering of resistance to disease, decreased work and productive

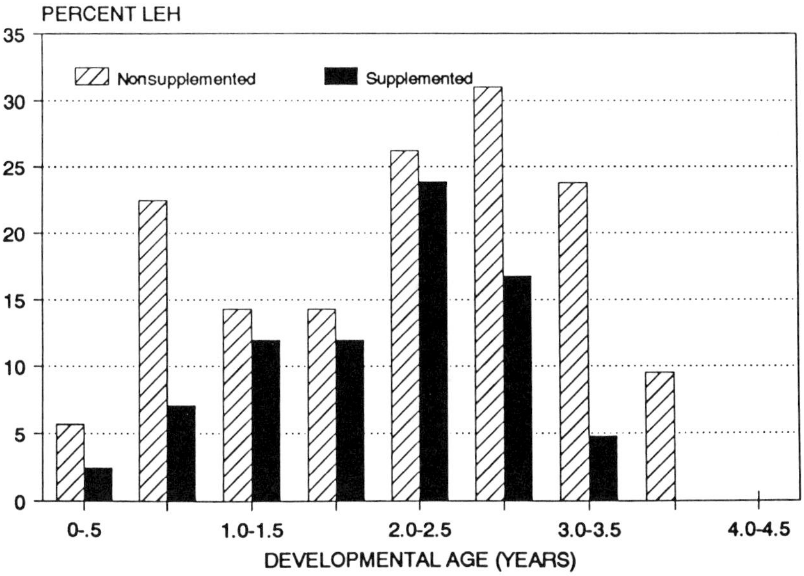

PERCENT LEH

Figure 11-1. *Frequency of linear enamel hypoplasias on permanent maxillary central incisors by half-year developmental periods, nonsupplemented vs. nutritionally supplemented children, Tezonteopan, Mexico (Goodman et al. 1991).*

capacity, less interest in and ability to engage in social and discretionary activities, and decreasing fertility and fecundity (Allen 1984; Buzina et al. 1989). If anything, however, they suggest maladaptation instead of adaptation. But, it is not the organism that is maladapted; rather, the sign of disrupted development more accurately suggests that the social system has failed to buffer against stress.

Paleonutrition studies can provide unique insights into the dynamics of past societies and the evolution of the human condition. Unfortunately, however, those insights are at risk because of a narrow focus on presumed short-term adaptations. Paleonutritionists need to focus on the full process, including the conditions—which often involve political-economic inequalities—that lead to the need to adapt and the long-term consequences of adjustments.

Acknowledgments

In addition to anonymous reviewers, I wish to thank Kristin Sobolik (University of Maine), Merrill Singer (Hispanic Health Council, Hartford), Pertti Pelto (University of Connecticut), and Robert Mensforth (Cleveland State University) for their useful comments on an earlier version of this manuscript. I especially wish to thank Dr. Patty Stuart-Macadam (University of Toronto) for her comments, which helped to clarify points of agreement and disagreement. She has brought new insights to the study of porotic hyperostosis. The Tezonteopan study was support by a grant from the National Institutes of Health (R03 DE08607).

Notes

1. I interpret Baer to mean by "adaptation" a response that increases tolerance or adjustment to a given environment. That response may have survival value. I prefer to call such responses "adjustments" or "coping strategies" rather than adaptations, unless the long-term consequences are known to be "adaptive."

2. In private correspondence Stuart-Macadam has made clear that she agrees with the costs of anemia. However, that is less clear from published material.

References

Alam, N., B. Wojtyniak, and M. Rahaman
    1989   Anthropometric Indicators and Risk of Death. *American Journal of Clinical Nutrition* 49:884–888.

Allen, L.
    1984   Functional Indicators of Nutritional Status of the Whole Individual or the Community. *Clinical Nutrition* 35:169–175.

Blakey, M., and G. J. Armelagos
    1985   Deciduous Enamel Defects in Prehistoric Americans from Dickson Mounds: Prenatal and Postnatal Stress. *American Journal of Physical Anthropology* 66:371–380.

Buzina, R., C. Bates, J. van der Beek, G. Brubacher, R. Chandra, L. Hallberg, J. Heseker, W. Mertz, L. Pietrzik, E. Pollitt, A. Pradilla, K. Suboticanec, H. Sandstead, W. Schalach, G. Spurr, and J. Westenhofer
    1989   Workshop in Functional Significance of Mild-to-Moderate Malnutrition. *American Journal of Clinical Nutrition* 50:172–176.

Calvo, E. B., and N. Gnazzo
    1990   Prevalence of Iron Deficiency in Children Aged 9–24 mo from a Large Urban Area of Argentina. *American Journal of Clinical Nutrition* 52:534–540.

Chavez, A., and C. Martinez
    1982   Growing Up in a Developing Community. Instituto Nacional de la Nutrición, Mexico City.

Chen, L, A. Chowdhurry, and S. Hoffman
    1980   Anthropometric Assessment of Energy-Protein Malnutrition and Subsequent Risk of Mortality among Preschool Aged Children. *American Journal of Clinical Nutrition* 33:1836–1845.

Dallman, P.
    1987   Iron Deficiency and the Immune Response. *American Journal of Clinical Nutrition* 46:329–334.

Dallman, P., R. Yip, and C. Johnson
    1984   Prevalence and Cause of Anemia in the United States, 1976 to 1980. *American Journal of Clinical Nutrition* 39:437–445.

Dietz, W.
1983   One for All? Thoughts on Reference Standards for Growth in Short Populations. *Nutrition Research* 3:129–131.
Dubos, R.
1978   Health and Creative Adaptation. *Human Nature* (January) 74–82.
Goodman, A. H.
1991   Paleopathological Inference and Neanderthal Dental Enamel Hypoplasias:
A Reply to Neiburger. *American Journal of Physical Anthropology* 85:461–462.
Goodman, A., and G. J. Armelagos
1988   Childhood Stress and Decreased Longevity in a Prehistoric Population.
American Anthropologist 90:938–944.
Goodman, A., D. Martin, G. Armelagos, and G. Clark
1984   Indications of Stress from Bones and Teeth. In *Paleopathology at the Origins
of Agriculture*, edited by M. N. Cohen and G. J. Armelagos, pp. 13–49. Academic
Press, Orlando.
Goodman, A., C. Martinez, and A. Chavez
1991   Nutritional Supplementation and the Development of Linear Enamel
Hypoplasias in Children from Tezonteopan, Mexico. *American Journal of Clinical
Nutrition* 53:773–781.
Goodman, A, and J. C. Rose
1991   Dental Enamel Hypoplasias as Indicators of Nutritional Status. In *Advances
in Dental Anthropology*, edited by M. Kelley and C. Larsen, pp. 279–293. Wiley-
Liss, New York.
Goodman, A., R. B. Thomas, A. C. Swedlund, and G. J. Armelagos
1988   Biocultural Perspectives on Stress in Prehistoric, Historical, and Contem-
porary Population Research. *Yearbook of Physical Anthropology* 31:169–202.
Graitcer, P., and E. Gentry
1981   Measuring Children: One Reference for All. *Lancet* 2:297–299.
Habicht, J.-P., R. Martorell, C. Yarbrough, R. Malina, and R. Klein
1974   Height and Weight Standards for Preschool Children: How Relevant Are
Ethnic Differences in Growth Potential? *Lancet* 1:611–615.
Harris, M.
1988   Cultural Materialism: Alarums and Excursions. In *Waymarks: The Notre
Dame Inaugural Lectures in Anthropology*, edited by K. Moore, pp. 107–126.
University of Notre Dame Press, Notre Dame.
Kent, S., E. D. Weinberg, P. Stuart-Macadam
1991   Dietary and Prophylactic Iron Supplements: Helpful or Harmful? *Human
Nature* 1:53–79.
Keusch, G. T.
1979   Nutrition as a Determinant of Host Response to Infection and the Metabolic
Sequelae of Infectious Diseases. In *Seminars in Infectious Disease*, vol. II, edited by
L. Weinstein and B. N. Fields, pp. 265–303. Stratton Intercontinental Medical
Book Corp., New York.
Leatherman, T.
1987   *Illness, Work, and Social Relations in the Southern Peruvian Highlands.*
Unpublished Ph.D. dissertation, Department of Anthropology, University of
Massachusetts, Amherst.
Lerberghe, W.
1988   Linear Growth Retardation and Mortality. In *Linear Growth Retardation in
Less Developed Countries*, edited by J. C. Waterlow, pp. 245–264. Raven Press,
New York.

Levins, R., and R. Lewontin
  1885   *The Dialectical Biologist*. Harvard University Press, Cambridge.
McKeown, T.
  1988   The Origins of Human Disease. Basil Blackwell, New York.
McLaren, D.
  1976   Concepts and Context of Nutrition. In *Nutrition in the Community*, edited by
          D. McLaren, pp. 3–12. John Wiley and Sons, London.
Martorell, R.
  1980   Interrelationship Between Diet, Infectious Disease, and Nutritional Status.
          In *Social and Biological Predictors of Nutritional Status, Physical Growth, and
          Neurological Development*, edited by L. Greene and F. Johnston, pp. 81–106.
          Academic Press, New York.
  1989   Body Size, Adaptation, and Function. *Human Organization* 48:15–20.
Mensforth, R. P.
  1991   Paleoepidemiology of Porotic Hyperostosis in the Libben and Bt-5 Skeletal
          Populations. *Kirtlandia* 46:1–47.
Mensforth, R. P., C. O. Lovejoy, J. W. Lallo, and G. J. Armelagos
  1978   The Role of Constitutional Factors, Diet, and Infectious Disease in the
          Etiology of Porotic Hyperostosis and Periosteal Reactions in Prehistoric Infants
          and Children. *Medical Anthropology* 1:1–59.
Neiburger, E.
  1988   Enamel Hypoplasia—A Poor Indicator of Nutritional Stress. (Abstract).
          American Journal of Physical Anthropology 75:253.
  1990   Enamel Hypoplasias: Poor Indicators of Dietary Stress. *American Journal of
          Physical Anthropology* 82:231–232.
Ogilvie, M., B. K. Curran, and E. Trinkaus
  1989   Incidence and Patterning of Dental Enamel Hypoplasia among the
          Neanderthals. *American Journal of Physical Anthropology* 79:25–41.
Pelto, G., and P. Pelto
  1989   Small but Healthy? An Anthropological Perspective. *Human Organization*
          48:11–15.
Pollitt, E.
  1987   Effects of Iron Deficiency on Mental Development: Methodological
          Considerations and Substantive Findings. In *Nutritional Anthropology*, edited by
          F. Johnston, pp. 225–254. Alan R. Liss, New York.
Scrimshaw, N.
  1991   Iron Deficiency. *Scientific American* (October) 46–52.
Seckler, D.
  1980   Malnutrition: An Intellectual Odyssey. *Western Journal of Agricultural
          Economics* 5:219–227.
  1982   Small but Healthy? Some Basic Problems in the Concept of Malnutrition. In
          Newer Concepts in Nutrition and Their Implications for Policy, edited by P. V.
          Sukhatme, pp. 139–148. Maharashtra Association for the Cultivation of Science,
          Pune, India.
Sherman, A. R.
  1992   Zinc, Copper, and Iron Nutriture and Immunity. *Journal of Nutrition*
          122:604–609.
Smedman, L., G. Sterky, L. Mellander, and S. Wall
  1987   Anthropometry and Subsequent Mortality in Groups of Children Aged 6–
          59 Months in Guinea-Bissau. *American Journal of Clinical Nutrition* 46:369–373.

Solomons, N., and G. T. Keusch
  1981   Nutritional Implications of Parasitism. *Nutrition Reviews* 39(4):149–160.
Stuart-Macadam, P.
  1992 Porotic Hyperostosis: A New Perspective. *American Journal of Physical Anthropology* 87:39–47.
Tompkins, A.
  1988   The Risk of Morbidity in the Stunted Child. In *Linear Growth Retardation in Less Developed Countries,* edited by J. C. Waterlow, pp. 185–199. Raven Press, New York.
Vyas, D., and R. K. Chandra
  1984   Functional Implications of Iron Deficiency. In *Iron Nutrition in Infancy and Childhood,* edited by A. Stekel, pp. 45–59. Raven Press, New York.
Weinberg, E.
  1977   Infection and Iron Metabolism. *American Journal of Clinical Nutrition* 30:1485–1490.
  1984   Iron Withholding: A Defence Against Infection and Neoplasia. *Physiological Reviews* 64:65–102.

12. Diet and Health of Paleoindians: An Examination of Early Holocene Human Dental Remains

Joseph F. Powell and D. Gentry Steele

Abstract: The traditional, or "received," view of Paleoindian diet and subsistence is one in which late Pleistocene and early Holocene populations were focused on the procurement and consumption of large game. In contrast, a "revised" view posits that most human populations from the Pleistocene on practiced generalized, broad-spectrum hunting and gathering, with extensive use of floral resources. That contrast between the received and revised views provided a framework for the examination of North American early Holocene Paleoindian dental remains. Results indicate that Paleoindians were similar to later Archaic populations in levels of dental caries, abscessing, and enamel hypoplasia. Paleoindian dental wear is also similar to that of Archaic groups, although the pattern of anterior-posterior dental attrition is more like Upper Paleolithic groups than Archaic populations. Scanning electron microscopy of Paleoindian upper first molars supports the above results and indicates that the individuals examined exhibit microwear defects nearly identical to those noted for early and middle Archaic populations. Although tentative, results do suggest that the revised view of Paleoindian adaptations merits serious consideration.

Introduction

Archaeologists have devoted much time and effort to understanding the dietary habits of Paleoindians. As a result, the archaeological literature is filled with Paleoindian subsistence models derived from cultural ecology (Cleland 1976; Stoltman and Baerreis 1983), economics (Christenson 1980), and culture history (Dragoo 1976; Sayles and Antevs 1941). Until recently, however, the skeletal remains of Paleoindians were virtually ignored as a source of

Paleonutrition: The Diet and Health of Prehistoric Americans, edited by Kristin D. Sobolik. Center for Archaeological Investigations, Occasional Paper No. 22. © 1994 by the Board of Trustees, Southern Illinois University. All rights reserved. ISBN 0-88104-078-9.

information about the diet and health of early New World populations (Steele and Powell 1992; Turner 1992). In this paper we explore evidence of diet and subsistence during the late Pleistocene and early Holocene, using the earliest known human skeletal remains (8500–10,000 B.P.) from North America.

One of the problems in examining osteological remains for evidence of Paleoindian diets is determining which skeletal remains qualify as "Paleo-indian" (Young 1986, 1988). Because of the limited number and fragmentary nature of Paleoindian skeletal specimens, we elected to use the term in the broadest sense, to indicate populations living between 8500 and 11,000 B.P., following Steele and Powell (1992), Young (1986, 1988), and Young and colleagues (1987). The date of 8500 B.P. coincides with the last of the Great Plains fluted point traditions and their immediate derivatives and slightly overlaps the Early Archaic period in other regions of North America (Jennings 1983). However, in calling late Pleistocene and early Holocene populations Paleoindians, we imply nothing about the mode of subsistence or lifeway of those groups.

Models of Early Holocene Subsistence

Current models of Pleistocene-Holocene subsistence can be divided into two groups following Dent's (1985) terminology: the traditional "received view" and a less traditional "revised view." In the received view, faunal exploitation is seen as the focal point of early Paleoindian adaptations (Funk 1978; Kelly and Todd 1988; Stoltman 1978), although incidental use of floral resources is not out of the question (Kelly and Todd 1988:233). The "great and persistent" climatic changes occurring between 14,000 B.P. and 9000 B.P. (Davis and Jacobson 1985:366) provided an impetus for "focally adapted" (following Cleland's [1976] use of the term) Paleoindians to make a subsistence transition to smaller vertebrates, plants, and invertebrates (Funk 1978; Stoltman 1978; Stoltman and Baerreis 1983). That process was gradual, with true broad-spectrum adaptations appearing during the Middle Archaic (Caldwell 1958).

More recently, alternative models have been presented as a response to the received view (Dent 1981, 1985; Dincauze 1981; Kornfeld 1988; Meltzer and Smith 1986; Olsen 1990; Smith 1986). The revised view argues that "the assumption that *all* Paleoindian and Early Archaic groups were specialists is questionable, as the evidence for a focal adaptation is weak" (Meltzer and Smith 1986:4; emphasis ours). Proponents of these models see the ecological changes between the Pleistocene and Holocene as having minimal impact on human subsistence strategies, primarily because there were many diverse, species-rich ecosystems during the Pleistocene and early Holocene (Dent 1981, 1985; Meltzer and Smith 1986). However, they recognize that some Paleo-indian groups did focus on larger game, such as caribou (Spiess et al. 1985) or bison (Frison 1978), given certain ecological conditions (Meltzer and Smith 1986).

The contrast between the received and revised views provided us with a framework in which data from early Holocene populations were examined. If the received view is correct, Paleoindian remains should be somehow different from Archaic individuals, reflecting the difference between big-game hunting and generalized Archaic subsistence. If the revised model is correct, Paleoindians and Archaic populations should be similar in diet and health as a result of a more consistent subsistence strategy through time.

While these differing viewpoints and their expected effects on human dentition offer a framework in which to examine Paleoindian diets, the limited sample size of early Holocene human skeletal material prevents a thorough test of any hypothesis. We can, however, present preliminary evidence to suggest serious consideration of alternative views or substantiation of current views of Paleoindian diets by asking four basic questions:

1. Does the health of Paleoindians (as determined by dental infection, growth disruption, and other dental disorders) differ in any significant way from that of later Archaic populations employing a "diffusive" subsistence strategy?
2. Do the rates and patterns of dental attrition in Paleoindians differ from those observed in Archaic populations?
3. Is dental microwear uniform among geographically and temporally isolated Paleoindian individuals, reflecting similar subsistence or behavioral patterns in those individuals?
4. What, if any, evidence is there for extensive plant consumption in Paleoindians, and what evidence is there for the antiquity of plant consumption?

Materials and Methods

For our study we examined the skeletal remains of 10 individuals from eight archaeological localities that date to the early Holocene. Those specimens are listed in Table 12-1. In addition to the 10 individuals, there are at least 12 other specimens that are, or may prove to be, of great antiquity but were unavailable for study. Because the only skeleton that unequivocally predates 10,000 years B.P. (Buhl, Idaho) was unavailable to us and was recently reburied (Wisner 1992), we were unable to make assessments of the health and diet of Clovis, Folsom, or other early Paleoindian groups. We instead concentrated on those individuals who fall within the early Holocene and are typically thought to represent the transition from focal to diffusive subsistence patterns.

Given the limits of the available collections, we chose to pool all early Holocene remains in a composite Paleoindian sample, realizing that the individuals are scattered across a wide geographic area during 1,400 years of prehistory. However, by pooling individuals, we were able to make general comparisons between Paleoindian specimens and Archaic samples. As stated above, the limited sample size prevents us from testing competing hypotheses but does offer a chance to explore early Holocene dental health in comparison with later Archaic populations.

Table 12-1. *Probable and Affirmed Paleoindian Specimens from North America*

Locality	N Preservation	Sex	Age at Death	Dates (B.P.)	Mean Age
Browns Valley, MN[a]	1 skeleton	Male	20–30	8700 ± 110	8,700
Pelican Rapids, MN[b]	1 skeleton	Female	15–20	8500–10,000	8,750
Sauk Valley, MN[c]	1 skeleton	Male	25–40	8500–10,000	8,750
Shifting Sands, TX[d]	1 teeth	Indeterminate	15–20	8500–10,000	8,750
Whitewater Draw, AZ[e]	1 skeleton	Female	30–50	8390–10,420	9,405
	1 skeleton	Female	35–50	8390–10,420	9,405
Wilson-Leonard, TX[f]	1 skeleton	Female	20–35	9470 ± 170	9,470
Horn Shelter, TX[g]	1 skeleton	Male	35–45	9470–9650	9,560
	1 skeleton	Indeterminate	11–13	9470–9650	9,560
Gordon Creek, CO[h]	1 skeleton	Female	25–30	9700 ± 250	9,700

Sources: [a]Jenks (1937); [b]Jenks (1936); [c]Jenks and Wilford (1938); [d]Owsley (personal communication 1991); [e]Waters (1986); [f]Steele (1989); Weir (1985); [g]Young (1985, 1986, 1988); [h]Breternitz et al. (1971).

Analysis of Paleoindian dental remains was conducted following standard osteological procedures for estimating age and sex (Steele and Bramblett 1988). The Paleoindian sample is composed of three males, five females, and two individuals of indeterminate sex ranging in age from adolescent (12 years) to older adult (35–50+ years). The age ranges listed in Table 12-1 are rather broad because of the poor preservation of age-indicative skeletal structures in most of the individuals.

All 10 individuals in Table 12-1 were represented by dental remains, and all data presented here are based on permanent teeth. Data on dental attrition were recorded using methods presented in Smith (1983) and Scott (1979). Anterior-to-posterior wear gradients were calculated from the Smith scores. Mean Scott scores for maxillary molars were generated for Paleoindians and other populations and were compared graphically. Linear enamel hypoplasias were recorded for each tooth using the scoring procedure of Rose and associates (1991). The data were used to estimate the age of occurrence for each hypoplastic defect following Goodman and colleagues (1980). Dental caries, alveolar resorption, and abscessing were scored following Rose and associates (1991). Finally, high-resolution casts of the occlusal surfaces of maxillary and mandibular molars were created for three individuals (Wilson-Leonard, Gordon Creek, and Whitewater Draw II) following modified cleaning and casting procedures of Rose (1983). Casts of left maxillary molars were sputtered with 200 Å of gold palladium and examined using a JEOL scanning electron microscope (SEM) at 15kev and a 30° beam angle. The protocones of each first molar were photographed at 100X, 500X, and 1,500X magnifications and compared qualitatively and quantitatively following Marks and colleagues (1988) and Teaford (1991).

Results

Developmental Disturbances

Four of seven Paleoindians (57%) had at least one tooth with evidence of enamel hypoplasia. Eight of 150 observable Paleoindian teeth (5.3%) presented hypoplastic defects, a figure somewhat lower than the percentage of affected teeth in Early and Middle Archaic groups (Cassidy 1972; Marks et al. 1988). The proportion of hypoplastic defects per tooth was 0.06 for Paleoindians and ranged from 0.87 to 1 in Early, Middle, and Late Archaic samples (Cassidy 1972; Marks et al. 1988). Figure 12-1 presents the frequency of Paleoindian enamel hypoplasias per half-year enamel unit. All hypoplastic defects occurred between the ages of 2.5 and 5 years, with the greatest frequency at 3.5 years. The age-of-occurrence data are comparable to Archaic populations and are especially similar to the frequencies observed at the Archaic Bug Hill site in Oklahoma (Rose et al. 1983).

Dental Disease

Only one of the Paleoindian teeth observed was affected by dental caries. A circular occlusal-surface carious lesion was located on the lower right

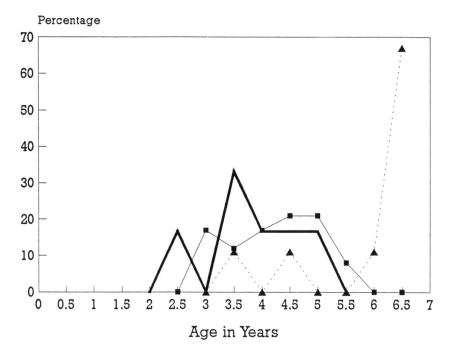

Figure 12-1. *Frequency of linear enamel hypoplasia in early and middle Holocene hunter-gatherers by half-year enamel units. Data were recorded following Rose et al. (1991) and Goodman et al. (1980). Comparative data are from Marks et al. (1988).*

third molar of the Wilson-Leonard individual. The caries rate per person and per tooth in the Paleoindian sample is lower than in other hunting-and-gathering populations, including the Ipiutak Eskimo (Table 12-2). Dental abscessing is higher in Paleoindians than in other groups on a per-tooth basis (0.725) but comparable to Middle Archaic hunter-gatherers at Indian Knoll when presented as the number of abscesses per person (1.25; Table 12-2). Many of the Paleoindian teeth exhibit some degree of alveolar resorption (74.5% of 122 teeth), with an average of 11.2 affected teeth per person.

Macroscopic Dental Wear

Dental wear among individuals in the Paleoindian sample is primarily flat, a pattern typical of hunter-gatherers (Smith 1983). One exception is the Gordon Creek specimen, who exhibits partial "cupped" wear (dentin is removed more rapidly than enamel edges) on the lower right first molar. Using Smith's (1983) scoring procedure, we compared the rate of anterior to

Table 12-2. *Proportions of Dental Disorders per Tooth and per Person in Paleoindians and Selected New World Populations*

Populations	Carious Lesions (per tooth)		(per person)		Abscesses (per tooth)		(per person)	
Paleoindians	0.004	(203)	0.10	(10)	0.725	(122)	1.25	(10)
South American Archaic[a]	0.082	(207)	0.19	(37)				
Seminole Sink Archaic[b]	0.280	(64)	1.80	(10)				
Indian Knoll[c]	0.040	(1958)	0.50	(145)	0.267	(1952)	1.77	(295)
Fourche Maline[d]	0.070	(928)	0.84	(45)				
Ipiutak Eskimo[e]	0.144	(922)	2.89	(46)	0.250	(922)	0.50	(46)

Note: Values in parentheses indicate sample size.
Sources: [a]Data from Turner (1992); [b]data from Marks et al. (1988); [c]Cassidy (1972), abscess values calculated as an average of male and female rates; [d]data from Powell (1985), southeastern U.S. hunter-gatherers; [e]data from Costa (1980), probable caribou hunting economy.

posterior wear for upper teeth (Figure 12-2). Populations in the upper portion of the figure are those whose anterior teeth are more worn than their posterior teeth. The wear gradient of the Paleoindian sample was closer to European Upper Paleolithic samples than to North American Eskimo or Archaic populations. Among the small sample of Upper Paleolithic and Paleoindian remains, anterior teeth appear to be worn as rapidly as, or more rapidly than, distal teeth.

Scott wear scores for upper and lower molars were compared by age, sex, geographic location, and antiquity. We found that Paleoindian molar wear did not change over time, by geographic location, or by sex. As expected, we found that younger individuals had lower mean wear scores than older individuals. The mean Scott scores for upper first molars was 28 in Paleoindians, slightly higher than mean in Archaic hunter-gatherers at Indian Knoll (mean = 21.4), and considerably higher than wear in horticulturalists/agriculturalists from the Hardin Village (mean = 15.4) and Campbell (mean = 19.3) sites (Scott 1979).

Dental Microwear Studies

Dental microwear analysis of the Wilson-Leonard, Whitewater Draw II, and Gordon Creek specimens provides some information about the texture and content of items consumed or orally processed by Paleoindians. Qualitatively, the three individuals differ in their pattern of wear. The Whitewater Draw specimen has frequent pits and fine striations (Figures 12-3 and 12-4), while the Gordon Creek specimen has larger, more frequent striations and gouges (Figure 12-5). The Wilson-Leonard individual appears to have frequent pits and some evidence of moderate-to-large striations (Figure

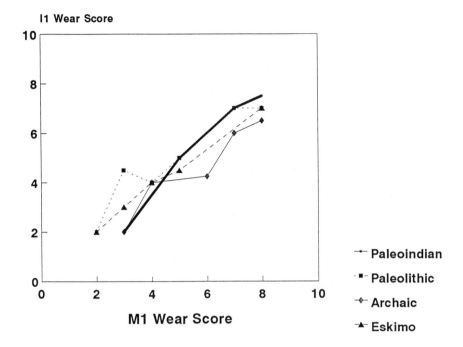

Figure 12-2. *Anterior-posterior tooth wear gradients for upper teeth of Old and New World hunter-gatherers. Comparative data are from Smith (1983).*

12-6). Higher-magnification photomicrographs for all three individuals document that the margins of enamel defects are smoothed and rounded, with some areas of polished enamel observed in each individual. Unfortunately, we were unable to use the Wilson-Leonard specimen for high-magnification quantitative comparisons because of the presence of enamel etching that obliterated many features on the occlusal surface of the tooth (Figure 12-6).

Quantitative comparisons of pit diameter, striation width, striation frequency, and pit frequency support the qualitative analysis. Figure 12-7 documents the frequency of pits and striations. Gordon Creek and the Whitewater Draw specimens differ from one another, especially in the frequency of pits. The Whitewater Draw individual is more similar to the Archaic populations in the frequency of pits and striations than is Gordon Creek.

Discussion

It is difficult to make very many, if any, generalizations about Paleoindian health and diet without assuming that the individuals in the sample are representative of all populations living between 8500 and 10,000

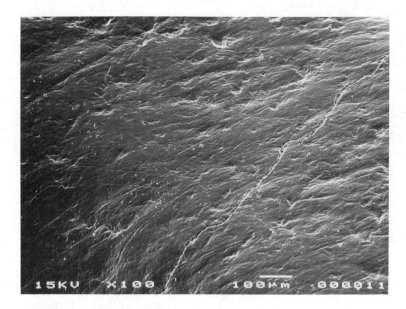

Figure 12-3. *SEM photomicrograph of dental attrition in the Whitewater Draw II upper left first molar (100X). Note the numerous pits and striations.*

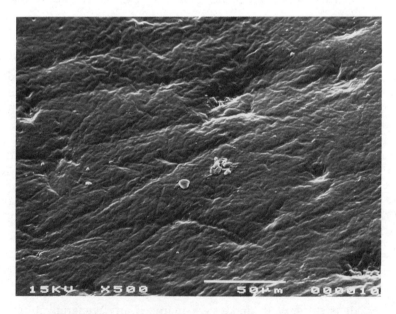

Figure 12-4. *High-magnification photomicrograph of enamel surface of the Whitewater Draw II upper left first molar (500X). Note that pits and striations are smoothed along their margins.*

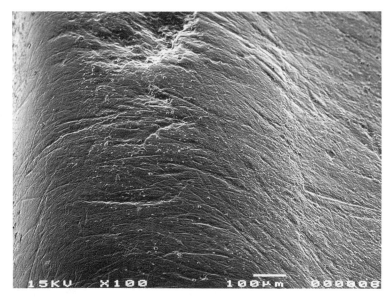

Figure 12-5. *SEM photomicrograph of dental attrition in the Gordon Creek upper left first molar (100X). The enamel surface contains large gouges and numerous striations but relatively few pits.*

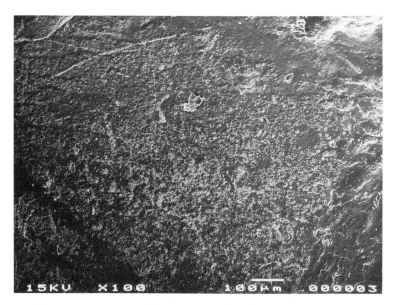

Figure 12-6. *SEM photomicrograph of dental attrition in the Wilson-Leonard upper left first molar (100X). The enamel surface is covered with pits, with some large striations (upper left corner). The textured appearance is due to acid etching and exposure of enamel prisms.*

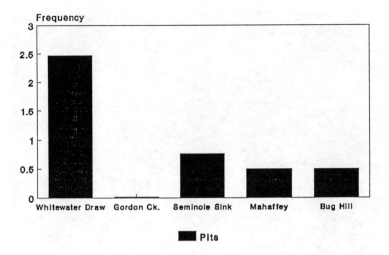

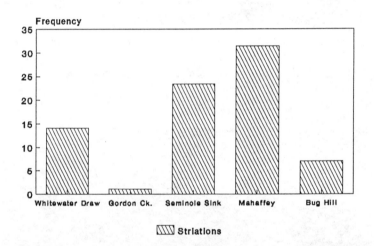

Figure 12-7. *Quantitative SEM microwear: Frequency of pits and striations in Paleoindians compared with Early and Middle Archaic populations from Texas and Oklahoma. Comparative data are from Marks et al. (1988).*

B.P. We can state with certainty that at least some Paleoindians living during that time suffered from periodic growth disruption, dental disease, and dental caries. We can also say that in some individuals dental wear was present, either as flat wear or cupping. What we cannot know with certainty is the proportion of individuals in the population affected by those conditions. Presuming that the sample is representative, the level of health in Paleoindians is typical of that found in other New and Old World hunter-gatherers.

There was evidence that Paleoindians, like other hunter-gatherers, experienced episodes of growth disruption. The age of occurrence of linear enamel hypoplasia is similar to that of Archaic groups, but the number of hypoplastic defects per tooth and the proportion of teeth with hypoplasia were considerably lower than in Archaic groups. These data suggest that Paleoindians may have experienced fewer periodic disruptions in health and/or diet than did later Holocene populations.

Dental attrition in the Paleoindian sample follows a hunter-gatherer pattern and is more like Upper Paleolithic hunter-gatherers in Europe than Eskimo or Archaic populations. This may be a result of small sample size, but it may also reflect "even more use of the anterior dentition than that found in Eskimo peoples well known for use of anterior teeth as tools" (Smith 1983:126). Cupped wear was present in the remains of one individual from the Gordon Creek site. Smith states that cupped wear "could indicate either the use of ground grain or nuts, etc., or the presence of fine grit particles (sand or opaline phytoliths from plant foods)" (1983:257). This may provide circumstantial evidence for plant consumption as early as 9700 B.P.

Dental microwear analyses provide the best data on the diet of early Holocene human populations in the New World. Three types of microscopic enamel damage have been noted in the Paleoindian sample: pitting, striations, and polish. Pitting, or "compression fracturing," of enamel occurs when hard materials are processed in the mouth. Striations are associated with grit introduced either through a coarse diet, accidental food contamination, or the use of stone grinding implements (Marks et al. 1988; Walker et al. 1978), where the widths of striations indicate the relative size of particles consumed. Enamel polishing, and the smoothing of margins in striations and pits, is associated with the consumption of dietary fiber (Marks et al. 1988; Walker et al. 1978).

Enamel pitting in the Whitewater Draw (Figures 12-3 and 12-4) and Wilson-Leonard (Figure 12-6) specimens is similar to compression fracturing observed in the Early Archaic Seminole Sink population (Marks et al. 1988) and in individuals from the Early-to-Middle Archaic Bering Sinkhole (Bement 1991). It also resembles the type of damage noted in Archaic individuals at the Bug Hill and Mahaffey sites in eastern Oklahoma (Marks et al. 1988). Marks and associates (1988), Hartnady and Rose (1991), and Harmon and Rose (1988) have suggested that enamel fracturing patterns in the Archaic groups resulted from consumption of nut hull fragments accidentally or intentionally included in the diet. The presence of compression fracturing in some Paleoindians suggests the consumption of hard foods such as nut hulls or hard seeds, although without corroborating macrobotanical evidence we cannot rule out ingestion of other hard materials such as bone. Gross enamel chipping, especially of the anterior teeth, has been observed in maritime-adapted Eskimo populations by Turner and Cadien (1969). Enamel chipping in Eskimos was attributed to the oral processing and ingestion of bone, as when consuming fish or other small vertebrates whole. None of the Paleoindian teeth exhibited that form of gross enamel damage. Furthermore, the polish and smoothing of defects (Figure 12-4) in all three Paleoindians is consistent with either oral processing or consumption of plant materials, especially fibrous plants (Walker et al. 1978).

The frequency of pits and striations differs between the two Paleoindian specimens for whom quantitative data were recorded (Figure 12-7). Differences cannot be attributed to differential wear by sex or age, since both of the individuals are the same sex and approximately the same biological age. We suggest that these individuals, if not the populations they represent, were processing different kinds or quantities of material in their mouths, which resulted in the wear differences observed.

Conclusions

On the basis of the level of osseous and dental health, and on the analysis of dental macro- and microwear, we cannot distinguish Paleoindians from their later Holocene descendants. Furthermore, the SEM data suggest that some plant foods were a part of the diet of three geographically and temporally separated individuals. There is also evidence that individuals in the Paleoindian sample were consuming different amounts of grit and hard materials in their diets. However, we are unable to conclude that this evidence represents differences between groups of Paleoindians in diet, food choice, food availability, food preparation, nondietary oral processing of material, and other cultural and environmental factors. Given the polish and striations noted, and the similarities both qualitatively and quantitatively to Archaic populations, we suggest that Paleoindian diets contained coarse materials, moderate amounts of dietary grit, and a considerable amount of vegetable fiber.

Although the results of our study are preliminary, they do suggest that the revised view of Paleoindian adaptations merits serious consideration. The data presented here lend tentative support to the concept that there was little noticeable change in human diet and subsistence between the late Pleistocene and early Holocene in North America. If a transition from a primarily hunting-based subsistence to a wider range of resources did occur, it was not as dramatic as once presumed and appears to have predated 9700 B.P. Investigations of North and South American human skeletal remains *older* than 10,000 B.P.—including paleopathologic, isotopic, and trace element studies coupled with examinations of macrobotanical and faunal assemblages at Paleoindian sites—should provide a more substantial basis for evaluating Paleoindian diets and the nature of dietary change in the earliest period of North American prehistory.

Acknowledgments

Our research on Paleoindians would not have been possible without the assistance of several institutions that provided access to Paleoindian skeletal remains. Our thanks to the University of Colorado; Hamlin University; the Peabody Museum, Harvard University; the Strecker Museum, Bayler University; and the National Museum of Natural History, Smithsonian

Institution. We also thank the following individuals for their hospitality and assistance during our research: Calvin Smith; David Hunt; Doug Owsley; Doug Ubelaker; Genevieve Fisher; Barbara O'Connel; and Fred Lang. Doug Owsley and Al Redder kindly allowed us to examine Paleoindian remains in their care. Our thanks also go to David Carlson for use of computing facilities, to Donny Hamilton, Charles Hermesch, Shannon Mills, and Robert J. Gillen for providing dental casting materials, and to Diane Holliday for allowing us access to illustrations of the Horn Shelter remains. Special thanks to Michael Pendleton for his assistance in mounting, coating, examining, and photographing dental microwear specimens, and to the Palynology Laboratory, Texas A&M University, for providing funds used in the SEM analysis. The comments of Della Cook, Clark Spencer Larsen, Kris Sobolik, and the anonymous reviewers helped us improve earlier versions of this paper.

References

Bement, L. C.
1991 *Hunter-Gatherer Mortuary Practices During the Archaic in Central Texas.* Unpublished Ph.D. dissertation, Department of Anthropology, University of Texas, Austin.

Breternitz, D. A., A. C. Swedlund, and D. C. Anderson
1971 An Early Burial from Gordon Creek, Colorado. *American Antiquity* 36:170–182.

Caldwell, J. R.
1958 *Trend and Tradition in the Prehistory of the Eastern United States.* American Anthropological Association Memoir 88. Washington, D.C.

Cassidy, C. M.
1972 *A Comparison of Nutrition and Health in Pre-agricultural and Agricultural Amerindian Skeletal Populations.* Ph.D. dissertation, University of Wisconsin. University Microfilms, Ann Arbor.

Christenson, A. L.
1980 Change in the Human Food Niche in Response to Population Growth. In *Modeling Change in Prehistoric Subsistence Economies*, edited by T. K. Earle and A. L. Christenson, pp. 31–72. Academic Press, New York.

Cleland, C. E.
1976 The Focal-Diffuse Model: An Evolutionary Perspective on the Prehistoric Cultural Adaptations of the Eastern United States. *Midcontinental Journal of Archaeology* 1:59–76.

Costa, R. L.
1980 Incidence of Caries and Abscesses in Archaeological Eskimo Skeletal Samples from Point Hope and Kodiak Island, Alaska. *American Journal of Physical Anthropology* 52:501–514.

Davis, R. B., and G. L. Jacobson
1985 Late Glacial and Early Holocene Landscapes in Northern New England and Adjacent Areas of Canada. *Quaternary Research* 23:341–368.

Dent, R. J.
1981 Amerind Society and the Environment: Evidence from the Upper Delaware Valley. In *Anthropological Careers: Essays Presented to the Anthropological Society of*

Washington During Its Centennial Year, 1979, pp. 74–85. Anthropological Society of Washington, Washington, D.C.

1985   Amerinds and the Environment: Myth, Reality, and the Upper Delaware Valley. In *Shawnee Minisink: A Stratified Paleoindian-Archaic Site in the Upper Delaware Valley of Pennsylvania*, edited by C. W. McNett, Jr., pp. 123–163. Academic Press, New York.

Dincauze, D.
1981   Paleoenvironmental Reconstruction in the Northeast: The Art of Multi-disciplinary Science. In *Foundations of Northeast Archaeology*, edited by D. Snow, pp. 51–96. Academic Press, New York.

Dragoo, D. W.
1976   Some Aspects of Eastern North America: Testing a New Climatic-Environmental Hypothesis. *Ohio Journal of Science* 68:257–272.

Frison, G. C.
1978   *Prehistoric Hunters on the High Plains*. Academic Press, New York.

Funk, R. E.
1978   Post-Pleistocene Adaptations. In *Northeast*, edited by B. G. Trigger, pp. 16–27. Handbook of North American Indians, vol. 15, W. Sturtevant, general editor. Smithsonian Institution, Washington, D.C.

Goodman, A. H., G. J. Armelagos, and J. C. Rose
1980   Enamel Hypoplasias as Indicators of Stress in Three Prehistoric Populations from Illinois. *Human Biology* 52:515–528.

Harmon, A. M., and J. C. Rose
1988   The Role of Dental Microwear Analysis in the Reconstruction of Prehistoric Diet. In *Diet and Subsistence: Current Archaeological Perspectives*, edited by B. V. Kennedy and G. M. LeMoine, pp. 267–272. Proceedings of the 19th Annual Chacmool Conference, Archaeological Association of the University of Calgary, Calgary, Alberta.

Hartnady, P., and J. C. Rose
1991   Abnormal Tooth-loss Patterns among Archaic-Period Inhabitants of the Lower Pecos Region, Texas. In *Advances in Dental Anthropology*, edited by M. A. Kelly and C. S. Larsen, pp. 267–278. Wiley-Liss, New York.

Jenks, A. E.
1936   *Pleistocene Man in Minnesota: A Fossil* Homo sapiens. University of Minnesota Press, Minneapolis.

1937   *Minnesota's Browns Valley Man and Associated Burial Artifacts*. Memoirs of the American Anthropological Association No. 49. American Anthropological Association, Menasha, Wisconsin.

Jenks, A. E., and L. A. Wilford
1938   Sauk Valley Skeleton. *Bulletin of the Texas Archaeological and Paleontological Society* 10:162–163.

Jennings, J. D.
1983   Origins. In *Ancient North Americans*, edited by J. D. Jennings, pp. 1–41. W. H. Freeman, San Francisco.

Kelly, R., and L. C. Todd
1988   Coming into the Country: Early Paleoindian Hunting and Mobility. *American Antiquity* 53:231–244.

Kornfeld, M.
1988   The Rocky Folsom Site: A Small Folsom Assemblage from the Northwestern Plains. *North American Archaeologist* 9:197–222.

Marks, M. K., J. C. Rose, and E. L. Buie
  1988 Bioarchaeology of Seminole Sink. In *Seminole Sink: Excavation of a Vertical Shaft Tomb, Val Verde County, Texas*, compiled by S. A. Turpin, pp. 75–118. Plains Anthropologist Memoir No. 22. Plains Anthropological Society, Lincoln.
Meltzer, D. J., and B. D. Smith
  1986 Paleoindian and Early Archaic Subsistence Strategies in Eastern North America. In *Foraging, Collecting, and Harvesting: Archaic Period Subsistence and Settlement in the Eastern Woodlands*, edited by S. Neusius, pp. 3–31. Occasional Paper No. 6. Center for Archaeological Investigations, Southern Illinois University, Carbondale.
Olsen, S.
  1990 Was Early Man in North America a Big Game Hunter? In *Hunters of the Recent Past*, edited by L. B. Davis and B. O. K. Reeves, pp. 103–110. Unwin Hyman, Winchester, Massachusetts.
Powell, M. L.
  1985 The Analysis of Dental Wear and Caries for Dietary Reconstruction. In *The Analysis of Prehistoric Diets*, edited by R. I. Gilbert, Jr., and J. H. Mielke, pp. 307–338. Academic Press, Orlando.
Rose, J. C., S. A. Anton, A. C. Aufderheide, J. E. Buikstra, L. Eisenberg, J. B. Gregg, E. E. Hunt, E. J. Neiberger, and B. Rothschild
  1991 *Paleopathology Association Skeletal Database Committee Recommendations*. Paleopathology Association, Detroit, Michigan.
Rose, J. C., M. K. Marks, and E. B. Riddick
  1983 Bioarchaeology of the Bug Hill Site. In *Bug Hill: Excavation of a Multicomponent Midden Mound in the Jackfork Valley, Southeast Oklahoma*, edited by J. C. Rose, M. K. Marks, and E. B. Riddick, pp. 241–278. New World Research Report of Investigations No. 81–1. Pollock, Louisiana.
Rose, J. J.
  1983 A Replication Technique for Scanning Electron Microscopy: Applications for Anthropologists. *American Journal of Physical Anthropology* 62:255–261.
Sayles, E. B., and E. Antevs
  1941 *The Cochise Culture*. Medallion Papers 29. Gila Pueblo, Globe, Arizona.
Scott, E. C.
  1979 Dental Wear Scoring Technique. *American Journal of Physical Anthropology* 51:213–217.
Smith, B. D.
  1986 The Archaeology of the Southeastern United States: From Dalton to de Soto (10,500–500 B.P.). In *Advances in World Archaeology*, vol. 5, edited by F. Wendorf and A. E. Close, pp. 1 – 92. Academic Press, New York.
Smith, B. H.
  1983 *Dental Attrition in Hunter-Gatherers and Agriculturalists*. Ph.D. dissertation, University of Michigan. University Microfilms, Ann Arbor.
Spiess, A. E., M. L. Curran, and J. R. Grimes
  1985 Caribou (*Rangifer tarandus* L.) Bones from New England Paleoindian Sites. *North American Archaeologist* 6(2):145.
Steele, D. G.
  1989 Recently Recovered Paleoindian Skeletal Remains from Texas and the Southwest (Abstract). *American Journal of Physical Anthropology* 78:307.
Steele, D. G., and C. A. Bramblett
  1988 *Anatomy and Biology of the Human Skeleton*. Texas A&M University Press, College Station.

Steele, D. G., and J. F. Powell
    1992   Peopling of the Americas: Paleobiological Evidence. *Human Biology* 64:303–336.
Stoltman, J. B.
    1978   Temporal Models in Prehistory: An Example from Eastern North America. *Current Anthropology* 19:703–746.
Stoltman, J. B., and D. Baerreis
    1983   The Evolution of Human Ecosystems in the Eastern United States. In *Late-Quaternary Environments of the United States Vol. 2, The Holocene,* edited by H. Wright, pp. 252–268. University of Minnesota Press, Minneapolis.
Teaford, M. F.
    1991   Dental Microwear: What Can It Tell Us about Diet and Dental Function? In *Advances in Dental Anthropology,* edited by M. A. Kelly and C. S. Larsen, pp. 341–356. Wiley-Liss, New York.
Turner, C. G., II
    1992   New World Origins: New Research from the Americas and Soviet Union. In *Ice Age Hunters of the Rockies,* edited by D. J. Stanford and J. S. Day, pp. 7–50. Denver Museum of Natural Sciences and University of Colorado Press, Niwot, Colorado.
Turner, C. G., II, and J. D. Cadien
    1969   Dental Chipping in Aleuts, Eskimos, and Indians. *American Journal of Physical Anthropology* 31:303–310.
Walker, A., H. M. Hoeck, and L. Perez
    1978   Microwear on Mammalian Teeth as a Diet Indicator. *Science* 201:908–910.
Waters, M. R.
    1986   Sulphur Springs Woman: An Early Human Skeleton from South-Eastern Arizona. *American Antiquity* 51:361–365.
Weir, F. A.
    1985   An Early Holocene Burial at the Wilson-Leonard Site in Central Texas. *Mammoth Trumpet* 2(1):1–3.
Wisner, G.
    1992   Idaho Burial Suggests Life of Hardships. *Mammoth Trumpet* 7(2):1–2.
Young, D. E.
    1985   The Paleoindian Skeletal Material from Horn Rock Shelter in Central Texas. *Current Research in the Pleistocene* 2:39–40.
    1986   *The Paleoindian Skeletal Material from Horn Shelter, Number 2 in Central Texas: An Analysis and Perspective.* Unpublished Master's thesis, Department of Anthropology, Texas A&M University, College Station.
    1988   The Double Burial at Horn Shelter: An Osteological Analysis. *Central Texas Archaeologist* 11:11–115.
Young, D. E., S. Patrick, and D.G. Steele
    1987   An Analysis of the Paleoindian Double Burial from Horn Shelter No. 2, in Central Texas. *Plains Anthropologist* 32:275–299.

13. | Dietary Reconstruction from Human Bone Isotopes for Five Coastal New England Populations

Bruce J. Bourque and Harold W. Krueger

Abstract: This paper presents dietary reconstructions for five coastal New England populations based on the following stable isotopic ratios in human bone: $^{13}C/^{15}C$ (collagen), $^{15}N/^{14}N$ (collagen), and ^{13}C(apatite)/^{13}C(collagen). The reconstructions are compared with conventional reconstructions that are based largely on faunal remains and historical accounts. The populations range from Blue Hill Bay, Maine, to Seabrook, New Hampshire. Comparisons are made with a small population from coastal southern New England, the Boucher population from Lake Champlain, Vermont, and white-tailed deer from North Haven Island, Penobscot Bay, Maine. The main goals of the paper are to estimate the importance of marine protein in the diets of those groups and to assess the relative effectiveness of the isotopic and conventional approaches.

Introduction

In this paper we examine dietary data from four prehistoric populations and one early contact period skeletal population in the Gulf of Maine region (Figure 13-1). Our main goal is to compare conventional methodologies used for dietary reconstruction with newer ones that are based on human bone isotopes. Such a comparison allows us to revise models of prehistoric diet in the region and to make observations about the relative merits of the two approaches.

Conventional dietary reconstructions in the region usually rely on archaeological fauna from coastal shell middens and, for the early historic period, on historic documents. Our isotopic reconstructions are based on all available individuals from the five human skeletal populations associated with our faunal and historical data sets. Also included are samples from the Boucher

Paleonutrition: The Diet and Health of Prehistoric Americans, edited by Kristin D. Sobolik. Center for Archaeological Investigations, Occasional Paper No. 22. © 1994 by the Board of Trustees, Southern Illinois University. All rights reserved. ISBN 0-88104-078-9.

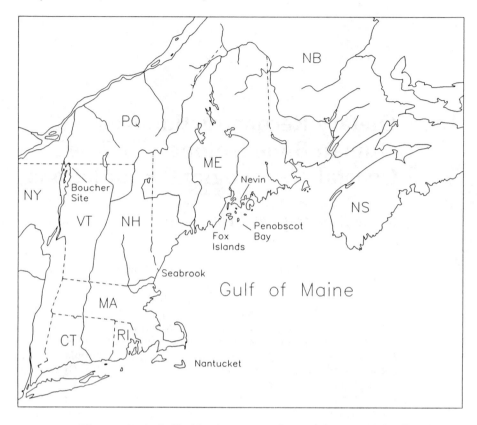

Figure 13-1. *Gulf of Maine region showing locations of archaeological sites and places mentioned in the text.*

site on Lake Champlain in Vermont (Figure 13-2B); three late prehistoric individuals from Nantucket Island, Massachusetts (Figure 13-2Nt); and four white-tailed deer from North Haven Island, Maine (Figure 13-2NHD).[1]

Marine Exploitation in the Gulf of Maine

The large and numerous shell middens of the Gulf of Maine attracted some of the first scientific archaeologists in North America, beginning in the 1880s with Jeffries Wyman and Edwin S. Morse. Interest in the region, however, dropped dramatically after about 1920, as American archaeologists began to look to more exotic research universes. The musings of early investigators left the nature of prehistoric maritime exploitation open to question.

Archaeological interest in the region revived in the late 1960s, when several workers there began to revisit the issue of prehistoric maritime exploitation (e.g., Bourque 1975, 1976, 1992; Sanger 1973, 1975; Snow 1972, 1974; Tuck 1971).

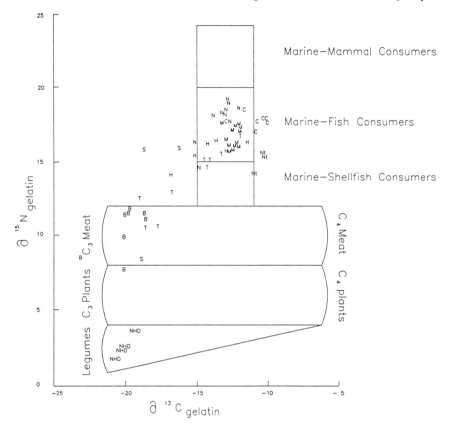

Figure 13-2. *Individual analyses of $\partial^{15}N_{gelatin}$ vs. $\partial^{13}C_{gelatin}$ for coastal Maine populations. Model framework after Krueger (1985). Protein source diagram.*

Moorehead Phase (4500–3800 B.P.)

Most research focused on the Archaic period, especially the late Archaic (ca. 6000–3000 B.P.) when large, elaborate "red paint cemeteries" were deposited between the Kennebec and St. John rivers. Those cemeteries comprised numerous (but generally boneless) "graves" furnished with a wide variety of lithic artifacts, including elaborate stone artifacts ranging from the utilitarian to the symbolic.

In 1971, using extant collections from coastal sites, Bourque (1992:14–26) argued that human maritime exploitation in Penobscot Bay (Figure 13-2) might have begun as early as the Middle Archaic period (ca. 7500–6000 B.P.). Bourque (1992:34–43) also defined the Late Archaic Moorehead phase (ca. 4500–3800 B.P.) as a cultural context for the red paint cemeteries. Moorehead phase people used swordfish *(Xiphias gladius)* rostra as a raw material, suggesting a specialized maritime hunting orientation.

On the basis of excavations of a Moorehead phase habitation component at the Turner Farm site (29.9) on North Haven Island, one of the Fox Islands in Penobscot Bay, Bourque (1975, 1976) later suggested that its economy was focused on deep-water marine fish, particularly swordfish and cod (*Gadus morhua*). About the same time, Sanger (1975) argued for a later onset of maritime exploitation, after about 4000 B.P., when he estimated that the Gulf of Maine became a significant source of marine protein. Despite differing opinions regarding the onset of maritime exploitation, both Sanger (1975:60–72) and Bourque (1975:43, 1976:29) agreed that the Moorehead phase ended abruptly by about 3800 B.P. and that that change was accompanied by the cessation of deep-water marine exploitation.

During the 1980s, Ritchie's (1969:281ff) Small Stemmed Point tradition (ca. 5000–4500 B.P.; Bourque 1983:63) emerged as a likely cultural ancestor of the Moorehead phase. That technology is in evidence at several coastal sites on the western and central Maine coast (Bourque 1994a; Robinson 1985:22–48). Scant faunal evidence for Small Stemmed Point diet has come from the earliest component at the Turner Farm site, which dates between about 5200 and 4500 B.P. and from the Seabrook Marsh site in Seabrook, New Hampshire, which dates about 4500 B.P. (Bourque 1983, 1994a; Robinson 1985; Spiess and Lewis 1994). Both components include swordfish and cod bone, confirming the early origin of maritime exploitation in the Gulf of Maine.

Susquehanna Tradition (3800–3500 B.P.)

A sharp archaeological discontinuity separates the Moorehead phase from the later Susquehanna tradition about 3800 B.P. Apparently sudden and complete, it has been widely regarded as the result of a population replacement, possibly as far east as the St. John River, by people from southern New England and New York (Bourque 1975:43–44, 1994a; Sanger 1973:131–132).

Faunal data from Susquehanna tradition strata at the Turner Farm site indicate a marked decline in marine exploitation (Spiess and Lewis 1994). Shell refuse was abundant, but no swordfish and very few seals or cod; indeed, few fish of any kind were recovered. In short, Susquehanna tradition occupants of the Turner Farm site were apparently its least marine oriented.

Ceramic Period (2700–500 B.P.)

Archaeological evidence for the Susquehanna tradition disappears from the study area by 3500 B.P., long before its demise in southern New England or New York. The nature of human occupation in Maine during the next several centuries remains unclear as a result of a paucity of archaeological evidence.

Data from several Maine sites indicate that by about 2700 B.P. marine resources had once again become important (see, e.g., Sanger 1982, 1987; Spiess and Lewis 1994). Penobscot Bay faunal samples indicate a dramatic increase in shoal-water species, particularly flounder (mainly *Psuedo-*

pleuronectes americanus) and sturgeon (mainly *Acipenser sturio*). Seal hunting (*Phoca vitulina* and *Halichoerus grypus*) also increased manyfold. At the Moshier Island site in Casco Bay, faunal samples resemble those from Penobscot Bay, except that cunner *(Tautogolabrus adspersus)* is abundant instead of flounder (Nathan Hamilton, personal communication 1992).

Early Postcontact Period (post-500 B.P.)

Except for brief voyages of exploration, Europeans did not penetrate the Gulf of Maine until after 1600. Yet early seventeenth-century historic accounts frequently mention copper and brass body ornaments and European vessels navigated by Indians (Bourque and Whitehead 1985). Moreover, there is considerable evidence for extensive internecine warfare throughout the region (Bourque 1989). Data thus indicate that significant European-induced cultural change was underway even before Europeans arrived en masse.

Much of that change was driven by the fur trade. Indians from Nova Scotia and New Brunswick sailed the region's coasts, exchanging European manufactured goods for furs and moose hides in Maine and transporting them to European traders in the Gulf of St. Lawrence where they were exchanged for manufactured goods. The pattern seems to have been well developed by 1600 (Bourque and Whitehead 1985). Beaver and moose were economically important species prehistorically, but the fur trade and the European weapons it provided must have greatly increased hunting pressure.

Archaeological Significance of Shellfish

Three of our five skeletal populations came from graves dug through shell midden, and a fourth came from graves covered by shell midden soon after burial. Soft-shell clam *(Mya arenaria)* is the predominant mollusc. The middens generally have a pH of about 8, which yields excellent bone preservation. Unfortunately, the chitinous shells of crustaceans, almost certainly a significant dietary element, do not survive.

Snow (1972) suggested that shellfish became a staple about 2000 B.P. when humans learned how to exploit marine resources. Sanger suggested that shellfish collection began earlier, about 3800 B.P., as a result of the above-mentioned population replacement. Bourque (1975:41) noted that the Turner Farm site produced abundant shell refuse dating to approximately 4500 B.P. and that the earlier portion of the coastal archaeological record has been truncated by coastal erosion, probably removing traces of earlier shellfish exploitation.

Isotopic Data from Human Bone

Methodology

Our isotope-based reconstructions use carbon and nitrogen isotopes in gelatin (collagen) and carbon isotopes in bioapatite. Analyses were by

standard method as described in Krueger and Sullivan (1984) and were interpreted on models for ^{13}C in bioapatite versus ^{13}C in gelatin (Krueger and
Sullivan 1984; Figure 13-3) and on a "protein-source" diagram from Krueger
(1985; Figure 13-4). The models are based on the expected isotopic composition of bioapatite and of gelatin formed from various possible diets.[2] They
define sole-source diets and can also be used to describe mixing lines produced by multisource diets. The ellipses on Figures 13-3 and 13-5 represent
coefficients of variation instead of standard deviations because the latter are
affected by the magnitude of the means (Schoeninger [1989:59] after Blalock
[1972:88]).

Skeletal Populations (Figure 13-2)

1. Three individuals were recovered from the Seabrook Marsh site.
2. Ten individuals excavated during the 1930s from the Nevin site at Blue
Hill, Maine (40-1), represent the Moorehead phase (5000–4500 B.P.;
Bourque 1992:124–125; Byers 1979; Hamilton et al. 1993; Shaw 1988). The
cemetery is unique among Moorehead phase cemeteries in that, as in the
Turner Farm cemetery, bone was preserved by overlying shell midden.
Many burial furnishings are virtually identical to artifacts recovered
from the Turner Farm Moorehead phase midden (about 4500–4300 B.P.;
Bourque 1983).
3. Well-preserved bones from nine individuals were recovered from a
large Susquehanna tradition cemetery at the Turner Farm site. Ten charcoal dates from Susquehanna tradition deposits there range from 4020 ±
80 [SI-2393] to 3480 ± 75 B.P. [SI-4248] and average 3696 B.P. (Bourque
1994a).
4. Fourteen individuals came from a partially eroded multiple burial
intruded into shell midden on Great Moshier Island, Casco Bay
(Hamilton 1979; Yesner 1987). Despite a date of 970 ± 145 B.P. (GX-7061-
G) on human rib collagen, we regard the series as probably midsixteenth
century because smelted (European) tubular copper beads were found in
association.[3] Recent analysis has demonstrated that the burial pit actually included two separate groups. That discovery may ultimately provide a key to reconcile the radiocarbon date with the presence of
European copper.
5. Six individuals were recovered from a multiple burial intrusive into
late ceramic period (ca. 800–500 B.P.) shell midden at the Crocker Site
(29.81), North Haven Island. Collagen from one individual dated to 1165
± 125 B.P. (GX-14542). An additional individual of comparable date from
the nearby Parsons site (29.47) on Vinalhaven Island has been included
in that population.
6. Seven individuals from late sixteenth-century burials came from four
different upper Penobscot Bay sites, all within 20 mi of each other. They
have been dated to about the late sixteenth century on the basis of
numerous associated metal artifacts (James Bradley, personal communication 1990).
7. For comparative purposes, we have also included 12 individuals from
the early ceramic period Boucher site (ca. 2300–2600 B.P.; Heckenberger

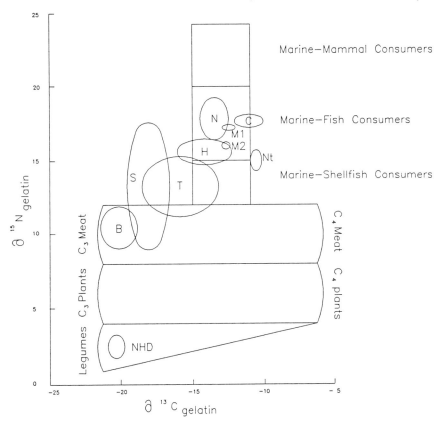

Figure 13-3. *Ranges of $\partial^{15}N_{gelatin}$ vs. $\partial^{13}C_{gelatin}$ for coastal Maine populations. Model framework after Krueger (1985). Protein source diagram.*

et al. 1990:112–113; Krigbaum 1989), three late prehistoric individuals from Nantucket Island, Massachusetts (Medaglia et al. 1990), and four prehistoric white-tailed deer from North Haven faunal collections. The Boucher individuals represent inland hunter-gatherers with little regular access to marine protein. The Nantucket individuals had access to marine resources in a moderately productive mid-Atlantic coastal environment. The North Haven deer illustrate the isotopic values of a primary terrestrial herbivore protein source on the Maine coast. Two were from Moorehead phase levels at the Turner Farm (ca. 4500–4300 B.P.), and two were from late ceramic period midden at the Crocker site. Their $\partial^{15}N$ values are considerably lower than those of most northeastern deer, falling comfortably within the legume-consumer range (Figure 13-3). We suspect that those deer, like modern coastal herds, fed heavily upon beach peas (*Lathyrus japonicus*), a legume that grows abundantly along the Maine coast. That legume effect should have carried over to their human consumers.

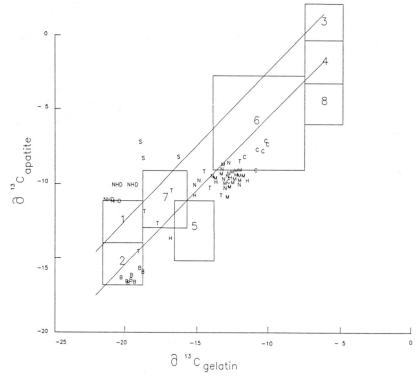

Figure 13-4. *Individual analysis of $\partial^{13}C_{apatite}$ vs. $\partial^{13}C_{gelatin}$ for coastal Maine populations. Framework and numbered dietary fields after Krueger and Sullivan (1984).*

Archaic Maritime Adaptations in the Gulf of Maine

Seabrook Marsh

The coastal Seabrook Marsh site produced cod bone and swordfish rostra, which led Robinson (1985) to infer that the population was marine oriented. At first glance, the Seabrook Marsh isotopic values appear at odds with that inference: two $\partial^{15}N$ values are low, approximating those of marine shellfish consumers; one $\partial^{15}N$ is even lower, falling near the lower limit for carnivores, and its $\partial^{13}C$ values are also low, overlapping those of the interior Boucher population.

That impression may not be entirely warranted. Since deer were probably the primary terrestrial protein source, and since they may have had legume-rich diets as did the deer from North Haven, the Seabrook $\partial^{15}N$ values may underrepresent fish consumption. Moreover, the low $\partial^{13}C$ values probably reflect the slight curtailment of preparation protocols necessitated by poor preservation, which may have left residual humates in the samples. On the

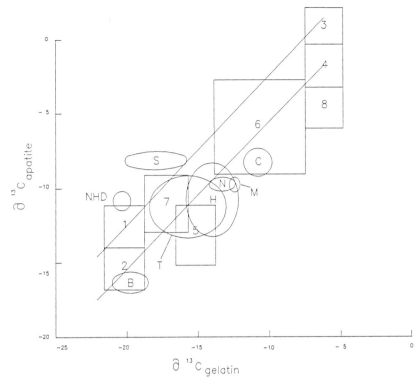

Figure 13-5. *Ranges of $\partial^{13}C_{apatite}$ vs. $\partial^{13}C_{gelatin}$ for coastal Maine populations. Framework and numbered dietary fields after Krueger and Sullivan (1984).*

other hand, the Seabrook Marsh artifact sample is the earliest from a coastal situation to show clear evidence of maritime activity, and thus the isotopic data may accurately reflect an early phase of maritime adaptation.

Nevin

Faunal and artifactual data from Moorehead phase midden at the Turner Farm and Nevin sites and from the Nevin grave furnishings all indicate a strong marine component in the protein diet. The Nevin isotope values confirm the data, falling near the center of the fish-consumer range. Note that for two individuals both $\partial^{13}C$ and $\partial^{15}N$ values fall well below the rest, which we regard as an indication of relatively low marine-protein intake, possibly reflecting dietary preference or their origin in a less marine environment. Nevin values for $\partial^{13}C$ in apatite, like most populations included in this study, suggest a generally protein-rich diet. However, the two aberrant individuals fall close to the herbivore locus.

Interpretation of the data is aided by reference to $\partial^{13}C$ (gelatin) and $\partial^{15}N$

values for our North Haven deer (Figure 13-3). Human consumption of such legume-eating deer may have lowered $\partial^{15}N$ values of the Nevin sample, masking, to some extent, the $\partial^{15}N$ elevation caused by heavy consumption of swordfish, a fish predator whose $\partial^{15}N$ values should approximate those of fish-eating marine mammals. The two aberrant individuals in the population lie on a mixing line between the rest of the population and the North Haven deer values. Plausible explanations include their entry into the population as immigrants, or simply their preference for terrestrial protein.

Turner Farm

Isotopic data from the Turner Farm population is unusual in three respects. First, its $\partial^{13}C$ (apatite and especially gelatin) and $\partial^{15}N$ values are generally low. Second, its coefficient of variation is large. For comparison, a recent study of California populations ranging from the coast to the interior demonstrated no more $\partial^{15}N$ variability than that observed in the single Turner Farm population (Walker and DeNiro 1986). Third, its $\partial^{13}C$ gelatin/apatite values appear more vegetarian than other populations, except for the Seabrook sample.

On the whole, the data support faunally based estimates of low intake of marine protein (Bourque 1994a). The data also suggest relatively great dietary diversity and herbivorousness. We suggest two explanations for that outcome. As with the Nevin population, individual choice of, or access to, diverse foods may have played a role. On the other hand, given the generally anomalous nature of the Susquehanna tradition archaeological record on the Maine coast, the data may well reflect diverse origins of the cemetery population, including regions where marine-protein resources were less abundant. Individual isotopic values may have been in flux after the population arrived on the Maine coast, or some individuals may have retained youthful preferences for terrestrial resources.

Ceramic Period and Protohistoric Maritime Exploitation

Faunal samples from Great Moshier Island (Nathan Hamilton, personal communication 1992), the Crocker site, and several other Fox Islands sites indicate a strong reliance on marine resources, particularly shoal-water fish and seals. Nitrogen isotope values from the Crocker and Great Moshier Island populations reflect that marine focus; $\partial^{15}N$ values are comparable to the Nevin population and well above those of the Turner Farm population. Both also have high $\partial^{13}C$ values, particularly from the gelatin fraction, falling beyond the "marine only" field toward "maize agriculturalists" in Figure 13-4.

What might explain the high $\partial^{13}C$ values? One possibility is that both populations did, in fact, consume maize. Domesticates have yet to be identified archaeologically in the area, but Great Moshier Island lies just to the east of a village at Saco where Samuel de Champlain saw cornfields in 1607

(Biggar 1922–1926:I:395–396). Moreover, Indians farther east, on the Kennebec River told Champlain that they too had recently grown corn (Biggar 1922–1926:I:320–321). Thus the early protohistoric Moshier Island diet might have included maize. The Crocker site lies close enough to the Kennebec that corn might conceivably have been grown there as well at about 1100 B.P. (Smith 1989).

Other isotopic evidence, however, suggests that both populations derived their ∂^{13}C from marine sources. First, both appear to be carnivorous (Figure 13-3). Moreover, recent data published by Medaglia and colleagues (1990) suggest that shoal-water fish, particularly flounder, have elevated bone ∂^{13}C values as a result of their feeding among the detritus of Spartina meadows, probably explaining the high ∂^{13}C values found in their Nantucket series.

Flounder show a marked relative increase in late ceramic period Penobscot Bay sites, and other small shoal-water species were abundant at Great Moshier Island. Thus fish, and not maize, were probably responsible for the high ∂^{13}C values.

A final dimension to be considered in evaluating the Crocker and Moshier Island populations is the abundance of seal in late prehistoric faunal samples from Penobscot Bay and, to a lesser extent, Moshier Island. Although ∂^{15}N values are high, neither population reaches the marine-mammal consumer field in Figure 13-2. As in the case of the Nevin population, however, the consumption of legume-fed deer may be masking a relatively high level of seal consumption. In sum, the Crocker and Moshier Island diets probably fall along a mixing line that extends from somewhere to the right of the marine-mammal consumer field and reflects high levels of seal and shoal-water fish consumption to the North Haven deer sample that reflects the consumption of legume-fed deer.

Sixteenth-Century Burials from Penobscot Bay

Temporal and geographic proximity suggests that the diets of sixteenth-century Penobscot Bay individuals would have been similar to those of the Crocker site sample. Instead, they show a significant shift in all three isotopic values. Both the ∂^{13}C/∂^{15}N and gelatin/apatite ∂^{13}C ratios shift along a mixing line from a high-marine (Crocker: seal and flounder) toward a terrestrial-protein diet (Boucher: cervids).

Just such a shift can be accounted for by the early postcontact changes in native lifestyle summarized above. Rescheduling subsistence activities away from marine exploitation would have been a likely outcome, as would an increase in terrestrial-meat consumption, for meat was not an important trade commodity in the Northeast at that time.

Summary

Fauna-based reconstructions of samples closely associated with our five skeletal populations suggested significant variability in the relative contribution of marine protein to the diet between about 4500 and 500 B.P. Our isotope-based reconstructions agree but indicate a higher relative contribution of marine protein. Temporal shifts in relative terrestrial-marine dietary contributions, in both directions, are also of larger magnitude than can easily be accommodated by prevailing perceptions of temperate hunter-gatherers that focus on ecological adaptation and economic conservatism (Bourque 1994b).

The Role of Bone Isotopic Data in Maritime Dietary Reconstructions

Having compared isotope-based dietary reconstructions to those using conventional data, we now consider what contribution the former can make in advancing our general understanding of prehistoric subsistence, particularly where maritime resources may have been significant:

1. Vegetal dietary remains are rarely recovered in the study area. Clearly, the scarcity of such remains means that carbon isotopes in bone will be helpful in assessing the vegetable contribution to the diet.

2. Fauna-based reconstructions assume that archaeological fauna reflect, with some bias, the diets of those who consumed them; each reconstruction attempts to account for those sources of bias. A series of biases peculiar to coastal sites seems to be the differential recovery of marine versus terrestrial animal remains. Faunal samples associated with the Turner Farm and Crocker populations are dominated by cervid bone, while isotopic-based reconstructions reveal both to have been primarily marine consumers.

The terrestrial bias may arise from differential processing of marine versus terrestrial prey. Marine prey, especially fish, were probably extensively processed at sea; terrestrial game, on the other hand, with their pelts, feathers, bones, and other useful parts, were probably brought in nearly whole. Isotopic data, then, can serve as a check on the overrepresentation of terrestrial species in archaeological faunal collections.

3. Faunal analysts often suspect that samples from coastal sites are biased by the underrepresentation of resources obtained in the interior. However, our analysis actually suggests that most or all terrestrial resources were captured on the coast. Even the relatively low marine-protein intake reflected in the Turner Farm series does not suggest a missing interior resource component. Isotopic data can thus serve as a check on the extent to which coastal faunal samples represent annual dietary range.

4. Fauna-based reconstructions generally describe group diet, while isotope-based reconstructions address individual dietary history and can thus look directly into dietary differences within a population. The Nevin, Turner Farm, and possibly the Seabrook Marsh samples, for example, included individuals who apparently grew to adulthood on a significantly more terrestrial-protein diet than did the rest of their group.

5. Collective dietary variability, as indicated by coefficients of variation,

seems a more sensitive indicator of dietary diversity than does faunal analysis. If used in combination with an empirically based frame of reference, such as Krueger's dietary field models, variability can also signal possible diagenesis, as in the case of our Seabrook sample.

Human bone chemistry holds significant promise for paleodietary reconstruction. However, our results indicate that, in the context of northeastern coastal studies at least, fauna-based reconstructions remain very useful and are generally congruent with isotope-based reconstructions. Their main weakness—their inability to calibrate the relative dietary contributions of marine and terrestrial protein—is precisely where bone chemistry can provide valuable assistance. A combination of both types of reconstruction appears to be the optimal approach.

Notes

1. The following abbreviations are used in Figures 13-2 through 13-5:

Key to Figures 13-2 through 13-5

B	Boucher humans
C	Crocker humans
H	Sixteenth-century Penobscot Bay humans
M	Moshier Island humans (Groups 1 & 2)
M1	Moshier Island human group 1
M2	Moshier Island human group 2
N	Nevin humans
Nt	Nantucket humans
NHD	North Haven deer
S	Seabrook humans
T	Turner Farm humans

Key to Fields in Figures 13-4 and 13-5

1. C_3 plants
2. C_3 plants & C_3 meat
3. C_4 plants
4. C_4 plants & C_4 meat
5. Marine only
6. Mixed (mainly maize)
7. C_3 plants & marine
8. E. African pastoralist (C_3 plants & C_4 meat)

2. Copies of Krueger's poster paper (1985) may be obtained from him at Krueger Enterprises, 711 Concord Avenue, Cambridge, MA 02138.

3. This identification is based on Mass Spectrographic Analysis conducted at Kennecot Copper Corporation's Ledgemont Laboratory on 14 September 1978.

References

Biggar, H. P. (editor)
  1922–1926 *The Works of Samuel de Champlain*. 6 vols. Champlain Society, Toronto.
Blalock, H. M., Jr.
  1972 *Social Statistics*. McGraw Hill, New York.
Bourque, B. J.
  1975 Comments on the Late Archaic Populations of Central Maine: The View from the Turner Farm. *Arctic Anthropology* 12(2):35–45.
  1976 The Turner Farm Site: A Preliminary Report. *Man in the Northeast* 11:21–30.

1983   The Turner Farm Archaeological Project. *National Geographic Society Research Reports* 15:59–65.

1989   Ethnicity on the Maritime Peninsula. *Ethnohistory* 36(3):257–284.

1992   *Prehistory of the Central Maine Coast.* Garland Publications, New York.

1994a   *Diversity and Complexity in Prehistoric Maritime Societies: A Gulf of Main Perspective.* Plenum Press, in press.

1994b   Prehistoric Exchange on the Maritime Peninsula. In *Prehistoric Exchange in North America,* edited by J. E. Ericson and T. Baugh. Plenum Press, in press.

Bourque, B. J., and R. H. Whitehead
1985   Tarrentines and the Introduction of European Trade Goods in the Gulf of Maine. *Ethnohistory* 32(4):327–341.

Byers, D. S.
1979   *The Nevin Shellheap: Burials and Observations.* Papers of the Robert S. Peabody Foundation for Archaeology No. 9. Andover, Massachusetts.

Hamilton, N. D.
1979   Excavation on Great Moshier Island Site. Ms. on file, Maine State Museum, Augusta.

Hamilton, N. D., D. Krader, and S. Mosher
1993   The Nevin Site Fauna. Ms. on file, Maine State Museum, Augusta.

Heckenberger, M. J., J. B. Petersen, L. A. Basa, E. R. Cowie, A. E. Spiess, and R. E. Stuckenrath
1990   Early Woodland Period Mortuary Ceremonialism in the Far Northeast: A View from the Boucher Site. *Archaeology of Eastern North America* 18:109–144.

Krigbaum, J. S.
1989   Subsistence and Health in an Early Woodland Skeletal Population from Vermont. Paper presented at the 54th Annual Meeting of the Society for American Archaeology, Atlanta.

Krueger, H. W.
1985   Sr Isotopes and Sr/Ca in Bone. Poster paper presented at the Biomineralization Conference, Airlie House, Warrentown, Virginia.

Krueger, H. W., and C. H. Sullivan
1984   *Models for Carbon Isotope Fractionation Between Diet and Bone.* ACS Symposium Series No. 258. Stable Isotopes in Nutrition. American Chemical Society, Washington, D.C.

Medaglia, C. C., E. A. Little, and M. J. Shoeninger
1990   *Late Woodland Diet on Nantucket Island: A Study Using Stable Isotope Ratios.* Bulletin of the Massachusetts Archaeological Society 51(2):49–60.

Ritchie, W. A.
1969   *The Archaeology of Martha's Vineyard.* Natural History Press, Garden City, New York.

Robinson, B. S.
1985   *The Nelson Island and Seabrook Marsh Sites: Late Archaic, Marine Oriented People on the Central New England Coast.* Occasional Publications in Northeastern Anthropology No. 9. Rindge, New Hampshire.

Sanger, D.
1973   *Cow Point: An Archaic Cemetery in New Brunswick.* Mercury Series Paper No. 12. Archaeological Survey of Canada, Ottawa.

1975   Culture Change as an Adaptive Process in the Maine-Maritimes Region. *Arctic Anthropology* 12(2):60–75.

1982   Changing Views of Aboriginal Seasonality and Settlement in the Gulf of Maine. *Canadian Journal of Anthropology* 2:195–203.

1987   *The Carson Site and the Late Ceramic Period in Passamaquoddy Bay, New Brunswick.* Mercury Series Paper No. 135. Archaeological Survey of Canada, Ottawa.

Schoeninger, M. J.
1989   Reconstructing Prehistoric Human Diet. In *The Chemistry of Prehistoric Bone,* edited by T. D. Price, pp. 38–67. Cambridge University Press, New York.

Shaw, L. C.
1988   A Biocultural Evaluation of the Skeletal Population from the Nevin Site, Blue Hill, Maine. *Archaeology of Eastern North America* 16:55–77.

Smith, B. D.
1989   The Origins of Agriculture in Eastern North America. *Science* 246:355–357.

Snow, D. R.
1972   Rising Sea Level and Prehistoric Cultural Ecology in Northern New England. *American Antiquity* 37:211–221.
1974   Reply to Newman. *American Antiquity* 39:136–137.

Spiess, A., and R. A. Lewis
1994   Features and Activity Areas: The Spatial Analysis of Faunal Remains. In *Diversity and Complexity in Prehistoric Maritime Socieites: A Gulf of Maine Perspective,* by B. J. Bourque. Plenum Press, in press.

Tuck, J.
1971   An Archaic Cemetery at Port au Choix, Newfoundland. *American Antiquity* 36:343–358.

Walker, P. L., and M. J. DeNiro
1986   Stable Nitrogen and Carbon Isotope Ratios in Bone Collagen as Indices of Prehistoric Dietary Dependence on Marine and Terrestrial Resources in Southern California. *American Journal of Physical Anthropology* 71:51–61.

Yesner, D.
1987   Subsistence and Diet in North-Temperate Coastal Hunter-Gatherers: Evidence from the Moshier Island Site, Southwestern Maine. In *Diet and Subsistence: Current Archaeological Perspectives,* edited by B. V. Kennedy and G. M LeMoine, pp. 207–226. Proceedings of the 19th Annual Chacmool Conference, Archaeological Association of the University of Calgary, Calgary, Alberta.

14.

Ancient Maya Diet at Copán, Honduras, as Determined Through the Analysis of Stable Carbon and Nitrogen Isotopes

David M. Reed

Abstract: Sixty-one stable carbon and nitrogen isotope ratios have been obtained from human and animal bones recovered during the past decade of excavations in the Copán Valley by The Pennsylvania State University's Copán Archaeological Project. Diet, as defined by isotopic measurements, is correlated with differences in social status, sex, and age during the Coner ceramic phase (A.D. 700–1250). It is shown that maize was the dominant staple. A juvenile has a $\delta^{15}N_{AIR}$ value 2.8‰ greater than the adults, a result that suggests children were still nursing before their death. The average $\delta^{13}C_{PDB}$ between males and females is 0.5‰. Individuals buried at elite sites range in $\delta^{13}C_{PDB}$ values 2.1 times greater than persons buried at lower-status sites, a result indicating that the elites had a more varied diet than did the commoners.

Introduction

Paleodietary analysis through the measurement of the stable isotopes of carbon and nitrogen in bone collagen complements ongoing research at The Pennsylvania State University on the long–term adaptability of humans to tropical environments. In particular, the isotopic analysis of a sample from the more than 600 individuals from archaeological excavations in the Copán Valley has yielded insights into the ancient diet of the Late Classic, or Coner phase, Maya.

Ancient Copán was an agrarian Maya polity located in the Copán Valley in western Honduras. Settlement and population were sparse until around A.D. 400. Population density increased rapidly and peaked in size at about 27,500 between A.D. 750 and 900 (Webster et al. 1992:185). A political collapse of

Paleonutrition: The Diet and Health of Prehistoric Americans, edited by Kristin D. Sobolik. Center for Archaeological Investigations, Occasional Paper No. 22. © 1994 by the Board of Trustees, Southern Illinois University. All rights reserved. ISBN 0-88104-078-9.

Copán kingship occurred circa A.D. 820 (Fash 1991:174; Schele and Freidel 1990:32, 342), although population grew for nearly another 100 years, and the valley was populated as late as A.D. 1250 (Webster et al. 1992:194). The Coner ceramic phase spans from A.D. 700 to 1250 (Freter 1992:119), encompassing the rapid demographic rise, peak, and gradual decline of the polity, and includes the centralization and collapse of elite control (Sanders 1986; Webster and Freter 1990a, 1990b).

Recent advances in the application of stable isotope analysis to archaeological remains have given researchers new ways of understanding paleodiet. The interpretation of diet from stable isotopes is predicated on several well-established observations briefly described next and extensively reviewed by DeNiro (1987), Keegan (1989), Schoeninger and Moore (1992), Schwarcz and Schoeninger (1991), and van der Merwe (1982).

Carbon and nitrogen stable isotope ratios in bone collagen reflect the diet of the consumer[1] (DeNiro and Epstein 1978, 1981). The isotopic ratios can be related to either terrestrial plant or marine sources (DeNiro 1987). Terrestrial plants can be divided into three photosynthetic types, either Calvin (C_3), Hatch–Slack (C_4), or Crassulacean Acid Metabolism (CAM). Typically, C_3 plants have a $\delta^{13}C_{PDB}$ value of -27‰; C_4 plants show a mean $\delta^{13}C_{PDB}$ value of -12.5‰; and CAM plants have $\delta^{13}C_{PDB}$ values between -10‰ and -28‰ (Coleman and Fry 1991). Nitrogen isotopes can be used to distinguish between marine animals ($\delta^{15}N_{AIR} > 12‰$) and terrestrial plant sources ($\delta^{15}N_{AIR} < 10‰$). They have also been used to separate between legumes, $\delta^{15}N_{AIR} = 1‰$—all of which are C_3-based—and nonlegumes, $\delta^{15}N_{AIR} = 9‰$ (DeNiro 1987). These isotopic signatures, along with paleobotanical, paleopathological, and social interpretations of the archaeological record, provide a direct method for assessing diet.

Social statuses were assigned to burials by their associated site type, rather than by grave goods. Architecture and energy expenditure for construction have proven better at distinguishing status than other measures. The Copán settlement typology is based on an architectural hierarchy. Site ranking ranges from the highest status at the Main Group and royal residences to the few, but impressive, Type 4 residences of the subroyal elites; through the less impressive Type 3 elite sites; and down to the more numerous Type 1, Type 2, and smaller sites of commoners (Fash 1991; Webster and Freter 1990b; Webster and Gonlin 1988).

The assignment of social status to the skeletal remains was, in part, problematic. While individuals buried at the lower-ranked sites, Types 1 and 2, were undoubtedly low in social status, only a portion of those interred at higher-ranked sites, Types 3 and 4, were likely to have been royal and subroyal people. The burials at higher-ranked sites probably also included lower-ranked individuals (e.g., retainers). If individuals spent only a small portion of their later life in service of the elite or had alternative access to food sources, then any dietary group differences could be confounded. The factors of length of service and age at death are important since the isotopic values from human bone represent about the last 20 years of diet because of the turnover of bone tissue (Chisholm 1989:20–21).

Investigation of floral, faunal, human skeletal, and material remains indirectly indicates the diet of the ancient Copán Maya. For instance, the paleobotanical remains (Lentz 1991) have yielded evidence for the C_4 plant maize *(Zea mays)* and the C_3 plants of bean *(Phaseolus vulgaris)*, squash *(Cucurbita moschata)*, nance *(Byrsonima crassifolia)*, and wild grape *(Vitis* sp.). Other plant remains identified were chayote *(Sechium edule);* bottle gourd *(Lagenaria* sp.); palm, or coyol *(Acrocomia mexicana);* ciruela *(Spondias* sp.); avocado *(Persea americana);* zapote *(Pouteria* sp.); hackberry *(Celtis* sp.); and frijolillo *(Cassia occidentalis)*. The latter plants were likely supplemental or famine foods (Marcus 1982:250).

No paleobotanical remains of the cultivars yam *(Dioscorea trifida);* manioc *(Manihot esculenta);* malanga *(Xanthosoma* sp.); sweet potato *(Ipomoea batatas);* breadnut, or ramon *(Brosimum alicastrum);* chili peppers *(Capsicum annuum);* or cacao *(Theobroma cacao)* have been identified (Lentz 1991). In addition, tools for processing maize (manos and metates) are found in abundance throughout the Copán Valley in Coner phase contexts (Spink 1983). The lack of evidence for processing tools and paleobotanical remains for root crops or ramon lends support to the identification of maize as the major staple food (Lentz 1991). Pollen profiles (Rue 1987) indicate not only the presence of maize but also the intensive clearing of the valley floor and foothills for building materials and swidden agriculture during the later part of the Coner phase.

Faunal remains represent deer *(Mazama americana* or *Odocoileus virginianus);* peccary *(Tayassu* sp.); dog (Canidae); puma, or cougar *(Felis concolor);* jaguar *(Felis onca);* paca *(Agouti paca);* and rabbit *(Sylvilagus brasiliensis)*. Jaguar and cougar were typically found in ritual contexts, while deer and other animals were possibly eaten on occasion.

Stephen Whittington (1989:370) found that the lower-status population at Copán was highly stressed and unhealthy, particularly during the Coner phase. He found that subadults suffered extended chronic illnesses and experienced episodes of acute stress as indicated by enamel hypoplasia and porotic hyperostosis (1989:244, 302, 371). Based on an association between high frequencies of enamel hypoplasia and high mortality, Whittington (1989:256, 371) suggests the age of weaning occurred between 3.5 and 4.5 years of age. Nutritionally related stress was found to be similar between urban and rural residents and between the sexes (Whittington 1989:374). At the other end of the social spectrum, Rebecca Storey (1992) found indications of physiological stress and high mortality, either from malnutrition or disease, among a subadult skeletal sample of the elite-status population from the urban Type 4 site 9N–8.

Materials

Skeletal remains were uncovered during the Proyecto Arqueologico Copán, Segunda Fase. Materials for isotopic analysis were chosen from the collection in Honduras to represent the entire social, political, and demographic spectra and to assess expected dietary variability. Bone specimens were preferentially taken from ribs when available, otherwise several grams of miscellaneous bone fragments were removed from the burial collections.[2] In all, remains of 58 humans and three deer were analyzed.

Methods

A collagen-preparation protocol for isotopic and preservation analyses was developed based on the widely used 1 N HCl and 0.125 N NaOH procedure (Ambrose 1990; DeNiro and Weiner 1988; Schoeninger and DeNiro 1984). Approximately 1 g of bone from each specimen was crushed to pass through a No. 24 mesh screen and washed to remove acid- and base-soluble contaminates. An extract was produced from the demineralized bone by solubilizing collagen at 90° C for 15 hours. The filtered extract was then lyophilized for up to 48 hours to yield collagen for analysis.

For infrared spectral analysis, 1 mg of extract was prepared (DeNiro and Weiner 1988). Well–preserved collagen shows an infrared spectrum similar to modern collagen and well–preserved specimens have a dry weight of collagen greater than 2% (Ambrose 1990; DeNiro and Weiner 1988). Only well–preserved specimens were used for isotopic analysis.

In an evacuated quartz tube, approximately 8 mg of well–preserved collagen, 1 g of black-wire cupric oxide, 1 g of granular copper, and 50 mg of silver were combusted at 900° C for three hours to yield a mixture of carbon dioxide and dinitrogen gases. The gas mixture was cryogenically separated for mass spectrometric analysis. The analytical reproducibility for the isotopic measurements, based on 13 samples of a collagen standard, is $\delta^{13}C_{PDB} = \pm 0.04\%o$ and $\delta^{15}N_{AIR} = \pm 0.12\%o$.

Results and Discussion

Age and sex determinations were made by Rebecca Storey (personal communication, 1991) and Stephen Whittington (1989). Age categories (Table 14-1 and Figure 14-1) were defined in years of age at death. Juveniles were divided into two groups: young or potentially nursing children of ages 2 to 5 and older children of ages 6 to 14. The other divisions were adolescents aged 15 to 19, young adults aged 20 to 34, middle adults aged 35 to 50, and old adults over 50. Infants under the age of 2 were not included in this study.

Figure 14-2 shows the relationship between the Copán human and deer specimens. The three deer have an average $\delta^{13}C_{PDB} = -19.97\%o$ and $\delta^{15}N_{AIR} = 4.07\%o$. They were clearly feeding on C_3 plants and legumes. If deer were a major food source, then the isotopic values for humans would be much closer to the C_3 deer. No material evidence suggests the extensive exploitation of deer. The isotopic evidence is best explained as showing a diet rich in maize with some small supplement from other sources, an inference consistent with the paleopathological and paleobotanical evidence.

Table 14-1. *Mean, Standard Deviation, Range, Minimum, Maximum, and Number of Specimens for the Isotope Ratios in ‰ by Age*

Element	Age Group	Mean	SD	Range	Min	Max	N
Carbon	Young Juvenile	-9.70	—	—	—	—	1
	Older Juvenile	-10.04	.76	1.51	-10.79	-9.28	3
	Adolescent	-8.60	.02	.03	-8.61	-8.58	2
	Young Adult	-9.04	.74	2.11	-10.27	-8.16	13
	Middle Adult	-9.26	.80	2.73	-10.96	-8.23	21
	Old Adult	-9.50	.47	1.53	-10.32	-8.79	11
Nitrogen	Young Juvenile	10.39	—	—	—	—	1
	Older Juvenile	7.89	.82	1.60	7.20	8.80	3
	Adolescent	6.91	.83	1.18	6.32	7.50	2
	Young Adult	7.70	.37	1.18	7.13	8.31	13
	Middle Adult[a]	7.58	.51	1.91	6.39	8.30	19
	Old Adult	7.34	.53	1.99	6.57	8.56	11

[a]Two nitrogen samples were lost during measurement.

Figure 14-1 and Table 14-1 show the relationships between individuals of known age. The mean values for the carbon isotope measurements (see Table 14-1) become more negative, or lighter, with increasing age, suggesting a dietary shift away from maize from adolescent to old adult. Small sample size may be influencing the trend, and clustering by age is imperceptible in Figure 14-1. From Table 14-1 and Figure 14-1, a distinct nitrogen isotope difference between the young juvenile and adults can be discerned. The younger juvenile shows a distinctly different nitrogen isotope value relative to the older juveniles and adults. The difference corresponds to the observed trophic-level effect found between mothers and their nursing children (Carnegie Institute of Washington 1988). The juvenile nitrogen difference also concords with the weaning stress discovered in the paleopathological data for Copán (Storey 1992; Whittington 1989:256, 371).

Figure 14-3 and Table 14-2 exhibit the isotope data when grouped by sex for the adults only. The crosses mark the mean isotope value for males and females plus or minus one standard deviation. The black cross and filled circles distinguish the female data from the gray cross and unfilled circles of the male data. It appears that males and females had slightly different diets on average, and the data cluster into two distinct groups. The difference between the sexes is statistically significant (ANOVA: $F = 6.58$, $p = .01$, $df = 1$).

Figure 14-4 exhibits the isotope data by social status. Individuals from burials at Type 1 sites were ranked lowest, Type 2 were ranked low, Type 3 were ranked high, and Type 4 were ranked highest in social status. Unfilled and filled symbols distinguish between the elite and commoner portions of

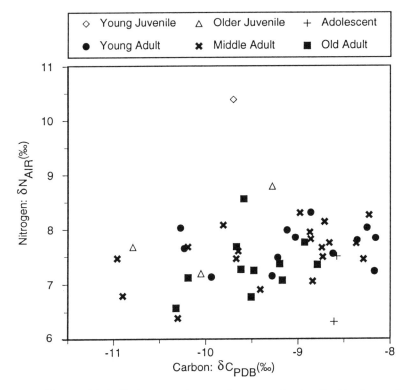

Figure 14-1. *Carbon vs. nitrogen isotope ratios for the Copán specimens by age group.*

the social strata, respectively. The descriptive statistics are listed in Table 14-3 for the four social strata and for the elite and commoner divisions.

Figure 14-4 clearly illustrates a wider carbon isotope distribution for higher social statuses relative to the lower ones. This result indicates that the diets of individuals from elite contexts were more varied than the diets of individuals from the commoner contexts. Paleobotanical remains show that the highest social status had access to a greater variety of plants than did the lower statuses (Lentz 1991), a result that parallels the isotope data.

Conclusions

All evidence indicates that the Copán Maya were obtaining the vast majority of their diet from C_4 plants. For 46 adults the mean $\delta^{13}C_{PDB}$ is $-9.26 \pm 0.72\%$ and the mean $\delta^{15}N_{AIR}$ is $7.56 \pm 0.48\%$. The most probable source for the C_4 dietary signature was maize.

The carbon isotope results suggest that age was a factor in diet. Age either has some physiological effect on carbon isotope fractionation by the human

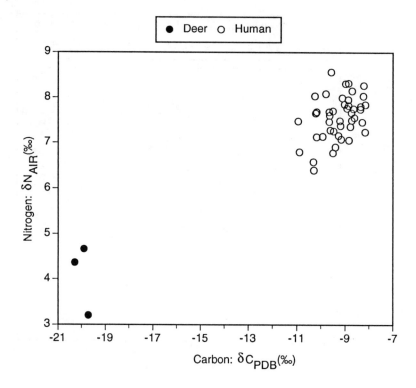

Figure 14-2. *Carbon vs. nitrogen isotope ratios for the deer and adult human specimens.*

body or maize consumption was reduced as age increased. The nitrogen isotope data indicate that the trophic-level fractionation effect between a mother's diet and her child's diet can be observed in archaeologically derived data sets. The $\delta^{15}N_{AIR}$ difference between the juvenile younger than five years old and adults is 2.8‰.

Higher social status appears to have been accompanied by a more varied diet. There exists a difference in the range of the carbon isotope values, although the means are nearly the same. The carbon isotope measurements for specimens from elite contexts span a range 2.1 times greater than those from commoner contexts.

A statistically significant carbon isotope ratio difference of 0.5‰ between males and females suggests that sex was a social factor in diet. This result parallels the observation of higher frequencies of anemia, infection, and a statistically significant higher rate of caries in females than in males (Whittington 1989:287, 313–315, 347, 375).

The isotope data provide another possible line of evidence in support of the hypothesis that the Maya collapse was related to the negative effects of agricultural intensification. Increased reliance upon a single staple crop and a

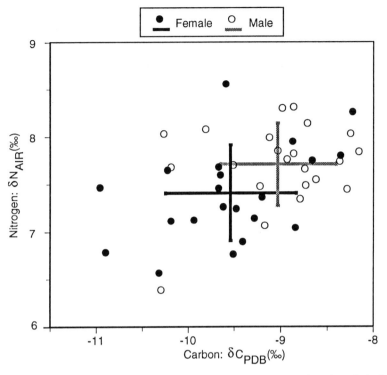

Figure 14-3. *Carbon vs. nitrogen isotope ratios for the adult human specimens grouped by sex.*

Table 14-2. *Mean, Standard Deviation, Range, Minimum, Maximum, and Number of Specimens for the Isotope Ratios in ‰ by Sex*

Element	Sex	Mean	SD	Range	Min	Max	N
Carbon	Male	-9.03	.62	2.14	-10.30	-8.16	23
	Female	-9.54	.71	2.73	-10.96	-8.23	22
Nitrogen	Male[a]	7.71	.43	1.92	6.39	8.31	22
	Female[a]	7.41	.50	1.99	6.57	8.56	21

[a]Two nitrogen samples were lost during measurement.

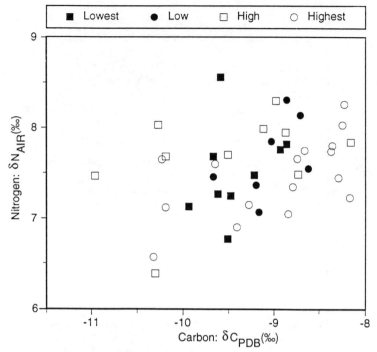

Figure 14-4. *Carbon vs. nitrogen isotope ratios for the adult human specimens grouped by social status.*

corresponding degradation of the local ecosystem from overexploitation and agricultural intensification are often suggested as factors influencing the collapse of complex societies of the Maya (Culbert 1973; Tainter 1988:169–178).

In future research, it may be possible to test cultural evolutionary hypotheses by comparing isotopic data from different time periods and grouped by several social factors with other independent indicators of social change through time. Measurement of additional specimens will allow for the analysis of multiple factors and data patterns, such as age by sex or sex by social status, instead of the single-factor analyses presented here. For instance, the observed difference between the average diet of males and females may, in part, be influenced by social status or age. A larger data set would be valuable in verifying observed patterns, particularly with the underrepresentation of subadults and commoners.

Acknowledgments

The research was performed in the Department of Geosciences Mass Spectroscopy of Minerals Laboratory at The Pennsylvania State University, University Park Campus, under the supervision of Peter Deines

Table 14-3. *Mean, Standard Deviation, Range, Minimum, Maximum, and Number of Specimens for the Isotope Ratios in ‰ by Site Type (Social Status)*

Element	Site Type	Mean	SD	Range	Min	Max	N
Carbon	Lowest	-9.42	.35	1.08	-9.94	-8.86	9
	Low	-9.04	.36	1.05	-9.67	-8.62	7
	High	-9.51	.88	2.80	-10.96	-8.16	10
	Highest	-9.00	.72	2.15	-10.32	-8.17	18
	Commoner	-9.26	.40	1.32	-9.94	-8.62	16
	Elite	-9.18	.81	2.80	-10.96	-8.16	28
Nitrogen	Lowest	7.52	.51	1.79	6.77	8.56	9
	Low	7.68	.44	1.24	7.07	8.31	7
	High	7.68	.52	1.91	6.39	8.30	10
	Highest[a]	7.46	.44	1.69	6.57	8.26	16
	Commoner	7.59	.47	1.79	6.77	8.56	16
	Elite	7.54	.48	1.91	6.39	8.30	26

[a]Two nitrogen samples were lost during measurement.

(Department of Geosciences) and with the guidance of George Milner, David Webster, Henry Harpending, William Sanders (Department of Anthropology), and Rebecca Storey (Department of Anthropology, University of Houston). Bone specimens were taken for analysis and the results of these analyses presented with the kind permission of the Instituto Hondureño de Antropologia e Historia. Research funds were provided to David M. Reed by the National Institutes of Health through a Biomedical Research Support Grant, by the Hill Fellowship Fund through the Department of Anthropology, and from grants by the College of Liberal Arts, The Pennsylvania State University. Additional funds for equipment were provided to Peter Deines by the National Science Foundation (EAR 85-11549).

Notes

1. Measurement of the isotopic composition of a material is expressed in units per mil (‰) as deviations of the isotope ratio in the sample from a reference. The carbon reference is the rostrum from the Cretaceous Pee Dee belemnite formation (PDB); while the nitrogen reference is ambient air (AIR). The notation is expressed as follows: for carbon, $\delta^{13}C_{PDB} = [(^{13}C/^{12}C)_{SAMPLE}/(^{13}C/^{12}C)_{PDB} - 1]\,1000‰$, and for nitrogen, $\delta^{15}N_{AIR} = [(^{15}N/^{14}N)_{SAMPLE}/(^{15}N/^{14}N)_{AIR} - 1]\,1000‰$.

2. Differences in the isotopic composition of collagen extracted from different skeletal elements is insignificant (DeNiro and Schoeniger 1983).

References

Ambrose, S. H.
1990   Preparation and Characterization of Bone and Tooth Collagen for Isotopic Analysis. *Journal of Archaeological Science* 17:431–451.
Carnegie Institute of Washington
1988   Nitrogen Isotope Tracers. *Carnegie Institute of Washington, Yearbook* 88: 133–134.
Chisholm, B. S.
1989   Variation in Diet Reconstructions Based on Stable Carbon Isotopic Evidence. In *The Chemistry of Prehistoric Human Bone,* edited by T. D. Price, pp. 10–37. Cambridge University Press, Cambridge.
Coleman, D. C., and B. Fry (editors)
1991   *Carbon Isotope Techniques.* Series: Isotopic Techniques in Plant, Soil, and Aquatic Biology Series. Academic Press, San Diego.
Culbert, T. P. (editor)
1973   *The Classic Maya Collapse.* University of New Mexico Press, Albuquerque.
DeNiro, M. J.
1987   Stable Isotopy and Archaeology. *American Scientist* 75:182–191.
DeNiro, M. J., and S. Epstein
1978   Influence of Diet on the Distribution of Carbon Isotopes in Animals. *Geochimica et Cosmochimica Acta* 42:495–506.
1981   Influence of Diet on the Distribution of Nitrogen Isotopes in Animals. *Geochimica et Cosmochimica Acta* 45:341–351.
DeNiro, M. J., and M. J. Schoeniger [sic]
1983   Stable Carbon and Nitrogen Isotope Ratios of Bone Collagen: Variations Within Individuals, Between Sexes, and Within Populations Raised on Monotonous Diets. *Journal of Archaeological Science* 10:199–203.
DeNiro, M. J., and S. Weiner
1988   Chemical, Enzymatic and Spectroscopic Characterization of Collagen and Other Organic Fractions from Prehistoric Bones. *Geochimica et Cosmochimica Acta* 52:2197–2206.
Fash, W. L.
1991   *Scribes, Warriors, and Kings: The City of Copán and the Ancient Maya.* Series: New Aspects of Antiquity. Thames and Hudson, London.
Freter, A. C.
1992   Chronological Research at Copán: Methods and Implications. *Ancient Mesoamerica* 3:117–133.
Keegan, W. F.
1989   Stable Isotope Analysis of Prehistoric Diet. In *Reconstruction of Life from the Skeleton,* edited by M. Y. Işcan and K. A. R. Kennedy, pp. 223–236. Alan R. Liss, New York.
Lentz, D. L.
1991   Maya Diets of the Rich and Poor: Paleoethnobotanical Evidence from Copán. *Latin American Antiquity* 2:269–287.

Marcus, J.
  1982   The Plant World of the Sixteenth- and Seventeenth-Century Lowland Maya. In *Maya Subsistence: Studies in Memory of Dennis E. Puleston*, edited by K. V. Flannery, pp. 239–273. Academic Press, New York.

Rue, D.
  1987   Early Agriculture and Early Postclassic Maya Occupation in Western Honduras. *Nature* 326:285–286.

Sanders, W. T.
  1986   *Excavaciones en el Area Urbana de Copán, Tomo 1*. Secretaria de Cultura y Turismo, Instituto Hondureño de Antropologia e Historia, Tegucigalpa.

Schele, L., and D. Freidel
  1990   *A Forest of Kings: The Untold Story of the Ancient Maya*. William Morrow, New York.

Schoeninger, M. J., and M. J. DeNiro
  1984   Nitrogen and Carbon Isotopic Composition of Bone Collagen from Marine and Terrestrial Animals. *Geochimica et Cosmochimica Acta* 48:625–639.

Schoeninger, M. J., and K. Moore
  1992   Bone Stable Isotope Studies in Archaeology. *Journal of World Prehistory* 6:247–296.

Schwarcz, H. P., and M. J. Schoeninger
  1991   Stable Isotope Analyses in Human Nutritional Ecology. *Yearbook of Physical Anthropology* 34:283–321.

Spink, M. L.
  1983   *Metates as Socioeconomic Indicators During the Classic Period at Copán, Honduras*. Unpublished Ph. D. dissertation, Department of Anthropology, The Pennsylvania State University, University Park.

Storey, R.
  1992   The Children of Copán: Issues in Paleopathology and Paleodemography. *Ancient Mesoamerica* 3:161–167.

Tainter, J. A.
  1988   *The Collapse of Complex Societies*. Series: New Studies in Archaeology. Cambridge University Press, Cambridge.

van der Merwe, N. J.
  1982   Carbon Isotopes, Photosynthesis, and Archaeology. *American Scientist* 70:596–606.

Webster, D., and A. C. Freter
  1990a The Demography of Late Classic Copán. In *Precolumbian Population History in the Maya Lowlands*, edited by T. P. Culbert and D. S. Rice, pp. 37–61. University of New Mexico Press, Albuquerque.
  1990b Settlement History and the Classic Collapse at Copán: A Redefined Chronological Perspective. *Latin American Antiquity* 1:66–85.

Webster, D., and N. Gonlin
  1988   Household Remains of the Humblest Maya. *Journal of Field Archaeology* 15:169–190.

Webster, D., W. T. Sanders, and P. van Rossum
  1992   A Simulation of Copán Population History and Its Implications. *Ancient Mesoamerica* 3:185–197.

Whittington, S. L.
  1989   *Characteristics of Demography and Disease in Low–Status Maya from Classic Period Copán, Honduras*. Ph. D. dissertation, The Pennsylvania State University. University Microfilms, Ann Arbor.

15. Health in Transition: Disease and Nutrition in the Georgia Bight

Clark Spencer Larsen and Dawn E. Harn

Abstract: During the last millennium there were two major events with profound implications for the health status of Native Americans on the southeastern Atlantic coast: (1) the adoption of a subsistence economy based at least in part on maize agriculture and (2) the arrival of Europeans and the establishment of Catholic missions. This paper discusses changes in health status via the documentation and interpretation of skeletal indicators of nonspecific stress in a series of human remains from three temporal periods in coastal Georgia and Florida: precontact preagricultural (pre-A.D. 1150), precontact agricultural (A.D. 1150–1550), and contact (post-A.D. 1550). The paper focuses on periostitis, an inflammatory response to either infection or trauma, in order to understand changing patterns of health status during later prehistory and the contact period. Study of those remains revealed an increase in the prevalence of bone pathology, which is likely due to the effects of increasing sedentism and population crowding, and the synergistic interaction of poor nutrition and disease.

Introduction

Working with archaeological human remains, biological anthropologists utilize a range of stress indicators in reconstructing patterns of community health, nutritional status, and well-being in earlier human populations (Larsen 1987). In this regard, various workers have examined skeletal markers of infectious disease vis-à-vis the study of hard-tissue pathology, which we refer to in this paper as periostitis and osteomyelitis. The former condition involves the presence of elevated, irregular surfaces of bones. The latter condition, a far rarer occurrence in human skeletal samples, is a more extensive involvement of the skeletal tissues, including the entire bone cortex such that the medullary cavity takes on a constricted appearance. Only in

Paleonutrition: The Diet and Health of Prehistoric Americans, edited by Kristin D. Sobolik. Center for Archaeological Investigations, Occasional Paper No. 22. © 1994 by the Board of Trustees, Southern Illinois University. All rights reserved. ISBN 0-88104-078-9.

222

infrequent circumstances is it possible to identify specific diseases from these lesions alone. Despite the intractable nature of diagnosing disease from dry bones, the documentation of these osseous pathologies has provided an important measure of generalized, nonspecific stress in a wide variety of archaeological populations.

The Biocultural Setting

In this paper, we examine diachronic and synchronic community health patterns in a series of prehistoric and historic populations from the Georgia Bight, a large embayment on the southeastern Atlantic coast extending from North Carolina to northern Florida that is dominated by a series of marsh and barrier islands. Those islands and the adjacent mainland were occupied by human populations for at least 4,000 years prior to contact by Europeans in the sixteenth century (Thomas et al. 1978). For most of the time prior to the arrival of Europeans, native inhabitants were nonsedentary foragers who derived most of their diet from a combination of hunting, gathering, and fishing. Archaeological documentation of subsistence economy indicates that marine resources from rich estuarine and marine contexts provided most of the protein component of native diets (Reitz 1988). Hunting of deer, smaller mammals, birds, and other animals in combination with the collection of wild plants yielded supplemental foods.

During the twelfth century A.D., cultigens—especially maize—rapidly took on an increasingly important role in the subsistence economy (Larsen 1982). For this region of the Southeast, a rather sparse botanical record has provided little insight into the role of maize in the prehistoric diets of those populations (Larsen 1982; Ruhl 1990). However, recent study of stable carbon and nitrogen isotope ratios in human bone collagen demonstrates a simultaneous decrease in use of marine foods and an increase in reliance on maize during the last several hundred years of prehistory (Larsen, Schoeninger et al. 1992). As in other Mississippian period societies, those dietary changes were accompanied by increases in sedentism, population size, and social complexity.

Archaeological and bioarchaeological evidence from the period following the arrival of Europeans and the establishment of Spanish Catholic missions in the late sixteenth century indicates a reorientation of native diets. Old World cultigens such as wheat and grapes were introduced to the region (Ruhl 1990). It is doubtful, however, that those plants represented a significant component in native foodways (Reitz and Scarry 1985). Studies of stable carbon and nitrogen isotope ratios from the period indicate that maize achieved greater importance in native diets and that marine resources were relied upon even less than in the late prehistoric populations (Larsen, Schoeninger et al. 1992). The high prevalence of dental caries, a disease linked to carbohydrate consumption, in late mission period dentitions is fully consistent with this dietary reconstruction (Larsen et al. 1991). These archaeological and isotopic data argue for an increasingly narrow subsistence base and declining nutritional quality during the late prehistoric and contact periods.

In addition to alteration in the subsistence economy, the arrival of Europeans in the Georgia Bight and in other areas of Spanish Florida occasioned profound social, cultural, and biological changes for native populations. In this regard, the *reducción* strategy employed by Spanish authorities involved the resettlement and concentration of native populations in the vicinity of missions in order to facilitate their religious conversion in particular and to provide control in general. From an epidemiological perspective, that settlement change involving yet further increase in sedentism and population nucleation had calamitous consequences for those native groups in that it enhanced the rapid spread of various pathogens, including those already existing in the New World, such as tuberculosis and treponematosis, as well as newly introduced diseases from the Old World, such as smallpox and measles.

Disease and Nutritional Status in the Georgia Bight

The skeletal pathology most frequently encountered in our study of these skeletal series is periostitis. Less frequently observed is osteomyelitis, a more extensive form of bone infection caused by the introduction of pyogenic (pus-producing) bacteria (Ortner and Putschar 1985). At least some of the lesions associated with periostitis and osteomyelitis may have been treponemal in origin. Indeed, Powell (1990) has reported the probable presence of endemic treponematosis in late prehistoric populations occupying the Georgia coast. Documentary sources suggest that venereal syphilis, another treponemal infection, was also present in the contact populations. In this regard, the Frenchman René Laudonnière observed in late sixteenth-century populations: "Most Indians were found to be diseased by the 'pox,' for they were exceedingly fond of the other sex, calling their female friends 'daughters of the sun'" (from Gatschet 1880:472).

The lesions discussed here are inflammatory responses to a variety of pathological stimuli, most often infection or localized trauma. Due to the nonspecificity of most of the skeletal lesions, however, we have chosen to simply refer to them as nonspecific periostitis, including the rare instances of osteomyelitis.

Because of the presence of incomplete skeletons, we report prevalence of periostitis with reference to skeletal elements rather than to individuals. The use of single skeletal elements in paleopathological study involves a loss of information that is necessary for differential diagnosis and should not be construed as representing prevalence in once-living populations. However, our purpose here is to provide a discussion of the general nature of community health and not an inventory of specific diseases affecting them.

Observations of skeletal lesions entailed recording presence and absence of bone pathology on the major long bones. Pathology ranged from tracks resulting from increased vascularity to virtually complete involvement of the cortical bone with active infection. A large number of individuals in the study series are missing either the left or right skeletal elements. Therefore, in order to maximize the data set, we have combined left and right sides and present prevalence statistics by bone category.

The human remains used in the present investigation are representative of precontact and contact populations from a tribal group in the Georgia Bight called "Guale" by early Spanish explorers. In the middle sixteenth century, the Guale inhabited the coastal zone extending from the North Edisto River to the lower Satilla River in southern Georgia (Jones 1978). After the mission system was established among those populations in 1566, the region was cooccupied by Europeans and native groups until 1680 when the principal outpost at Mission Santa Catalina de Guale on St. Catherines Island, Georgia, was abandoned (Thomas 1987) and relocated immediately south of the present Georgia-Florida border on Amelia Island, Florida (Larsen, Ruff et al. 1992).

For purposes of analysis, we subdivide the skeletal series of the precontact era into two groups: namely, remains from various mortuary localities form a precontact preagricultural group (pre-A.D. 1150) and a precontact agricultural group (A.D. 1150–1550; Larsen 1982). The latter series is mostly represented by remains from the Irene Mound site at the mouth of the Savannah River. The contact sample is represented by the remains of a descendant historic period population recovered from Santa Catalina de Guale de Santa Maria on Amelia Island (A.D. 1686–1702; Larsen et al. 1990).

Health Trends

The results of statistical comparisons between the three groups—precontact preagricultural, precontact agricultural, and contact—reveal a number of temporal trends. Table 15-1 shows the frequency comparisons of periostitis for all adult individuals (females, males, indeterminate sex combined) for each of the three periods. These data indicate that there is a slight increase in frequency of periostitis for the upper limb bones and femur prior to contact that is followed by a slight decrease in frequency for those bones after contact. In contrast to those skeletal elements, the tibia and fibula show a relatively greater increase in frequency prior to contact. However, what is most striking about the comparisons is the marked jump in prevalence for the lower leg bones, especially the tibia. The tibia shows an 11% increase in the precontact agricultural period compared with the precontact preagricultural period; that increase is followed by a 25% increase in the contact period (40% of contact period tibiae from the mission population are so affected).

Analysis for adult (≥ 16 years) females and males separately shows similar trends. Table 15-2 illustrates temporal comparisons for adult females in the three groups. With the exception of the tibia and fibula, the increases in the precontact agricultural group compared with the preagricultural group are slight; there are only minimal differences between the contact and precontact agricultural groups. The only skeletal elements showing statistically significant changes are the lower leg bones. Like the comparison of the total sample, the greatest increases are in the tibia, which shows a 14% increase in the precontact agricultural group followed by a 12% increase in the contact group.

Table 15-1. *Frequency of Periostitis in Precontact Preagricultural (PP), Precontact Agricultural (PA), and Contact (C) Georgia Bight Skeletal Series: Adults (Females, Males, Indeterminate Sex Combined)*

Bone	PP		PA		C		Chi-square[c]
	%[a]	N[b]	%	N	%	N	
Clavicle	1.9	107	4.7	274	3.7	108	—
Humerus	0.5	190	3.2	273	0.0	131	PP/PA
Ulna	0.7	147	3.7	327	2.3	133	—
Radius	0.7	136	4.5	335	3.0	133	PP/PA
Femur	2.1	193	6.8	410	3.5	144	PP/PA
Tibia	4.5	156	15.0	374	40.3	134	PP/PA, PA/C
Fibula	1.7	116	8.3	289	30.9	141	PP/PA, PA/C

[a]Percentage of bones affected by periostitis/osteomyelitis.
[b]Total number of bones examined for presence or absence of periostitis/osteomyelitis.
[c]Comparisons showing statistically significant changes in frequency ($p < 0.05$).

In males, the trends are also straightforward (Table 15-3). Statistically insignificant changes are present for most bones. In sharp contrast to the other long bones, the tibia shows a 12% increase in the precontact agriculturalists compared with the preagricultural hunter-gatherers. In the contact period males, the majority of long bones show either slight increase or even some decrease in frequency. In both the tibia and fibula, however, there are marked increases in skeletal infections—over half of the contact period male tibiae are pathological.

Finally, within each of the three periods, there are few appreciable differences between females and males in the prevalence of periostitis for most of the skeletal elements examined by us (Table 15-4; Figure 15-1). There is an apparent tendency for a slightly lower frequency of periosteal inflammations in precontact agricultural males than females. None of those differences reaches statistical significance, however. Large percentage differences are present between contact period females and males for the tibia and fibula, with males showing considerably higher, statistically significant frequencies of infected tibiae and fibulae than females. In this regard, males have double the number of pathological tibiae of females (52% vs. 28%).

Implications of Decline in Health Status

Periostitis, as represented by proliferative bone remodeling on the external surfaces of long bones, results from nonspecific responses to pathological insults arising from either infection or localized trauma. It is usually a

Table 15-2. *Frequency of Periostitis in Precontact Preagricultural (PP), Precontact Agricultural (PA), and Contact (C) Georgia Bight Skeletal Series: Adult Females*

Bone	PP %[a]	PP N[b]	PA %	PA N	C %	C N	Chi-square[c]
Clavicle	0.0	61	2.9	140	3.6	56	—
Humerus	0.0	106	3.7	190	0.0	68	—
Ulna	1.2	82	3.6	167	2.9	70	—
Radius	0.0	77	4.0	173	4.2	72	—
Femur	1.8	110	7.2	207	6.9	72	—
Tibia	2.4	84	16.0	187	27.7	65	PP/PA, PA/C
Fibula	1.4	74	9.9	152	21.8	55	PP/PA, PA/C

[a]Percentage of bones affected by periostitis/osteomyelitis.
[b]Total number of bones examined for presence or absence of periostitis/osteomyelitis.
[c]Comparisons showing statistically significant changes in frequency ($p < 0.05$).

reaction to or part of pathological developments in the bone underlying the periosteal surface. The lesions result from exposure to the external environment via skin-penetrating wounds, by the spread of infection from adjacent soft tissue, or via the circulatory system from an infection located somewhere else in the body (Ortner and Putschar 1985). We emphasize that in most circumstances the pathological lesions do not lend themselves to diagnosis of specific disease. Thus, they provide a general, albeit crude, indicator of health status in earlier human populations.

Our analysis of precontact and contact era human remains from the Georgia Bight reveals one primary finding. That is, prior to contact there are moderate increases in periostitis that are followed by substantially greater increases during the contact period. Consistent with reports by other researchers, when compared with other skeletal elements, periostitis in late prehistoric and contact period populations in the Eastern Woodlands is highest in the tibia (e.g., Milner 1991; Perzigian et al. 1984). Comparisons with the other reports show a wide range of regional variation in the prevalence of bone infections. Milner (1991), for example, reported frequencies approaching 30% in tibiae from the American Bottom. On the other hand, Lallo and Rose (1979) reported a 67% frequency for Dickson Mounds tibiae. Most investigators have reported prevalence statistics lying somewhere between those two extremes in late prehistoric populations from the Eastern Woodlands (e.g., Eisenberg 1986; Milner and Smith 1990; Perzigian et al. 1984; Rose et al. 1984). It is not clear why the infection rates for the tibia are so much higher than for the other long bones. However, periosteal reactions associated with syphilis show a predilection for the tibia and cranial vault, which—unlike other long bones (e.g., femur)—are not surrounded by large amounts of soft tissue, and thus may be cooler and

Table 15-3. *Frequency of Periostitis in Precontact Preagricultural (PP), Precontact Agricultural (PA), and Contact (C) Georgia Bight Skeletal Series: Adult Males*

Bone	PP %[a]	PP N[b]	PA %	PA N	C %	C N	Chi-square[c]
Clavicle	5.6	36	5.3	114	3.9	51	—
Humerus	2.0	51	3.6	140	0.0	63	—
Ulna	0.0	42	2.3	130	1.6	63	—
Radius	0.0	43	2.9	140	1.6	61	—
Femur	2.0	49	6.4	156	0.0	72	—
Tibia	4.0	50	15.8	146	52.2	69	PP/PA, PA/C
Fibula	0.0	37	5.3	114	40.0	55	PA/C

[a]Percentage of bones affected by periostitis/osteomyelitis.
[b]Total number of bones examined for presence or absence of periostitis/osteomyelitis.
[c]Comparisons showing statistically significant changes in frequency ($p < 0.05$).

more susceptible to infection (Ortner and Putschar 1985). Given the presence of an endemic, nonvenereal form of syphilis in the region prior to contact (see Powell 1990), it is possible that some of the infectious pathology that we document here is due to a specific infectious disease (e.g., endemic syphilis). Regardless of the reasons for our observed pattern of localization of pathology, however, we emphasize that relative to the preagriculturalists in the region, there is an increase in skeletal inflammations.

How, then, can we explain the tremendous increase in the prevalence of skeletal infection during the mission period in Spanish Florida? Aside from potential sampling biases inherent in archaeological human remains (see Wood et al. 1992), there are likely a variety of factors that have to be taken into account. An important factor that we regard as central to any discussion on higher frequency of skeletal pathology during the contact period is the relocation and increased concentration of native populations around mission centers. That change in settlement would have provided conditions conducive to the maintenance and spread of infectious disease. The effects of increased infection rates would likely have been exacerbated by the aforementioned reduction in nutrition. In particular, there is a high degree of synergy between malnutrition and infection (Scrimshaw 1975)—namely, individuals experiencing malnutrition are less resistant to pathogens and are thus rendered more susceptible to infectious disease, and conversely, virtually any infection serves to worsen nutritional status. The relationship between nutrition and infection is synergistic because the consequences of the two acting together are worse than either alone. More specifically, individuals experiencing infectious states frequently show higher basal metabolic rates, which are accompanied by fever and the body's demand for higher intakes of protein and other nutrients for

Table 15-4. *Frequency of Periostitis in Adult Females and Males from Precontact Preagricultural (PP), Precontact Agricultural (PA), and Contact (C) Periods in the Georgia Bight*

	PP		PA		C		
Bone	F[a]	M[b]	F	M	F	M	Chi-square[c]
Clavicle	0.0	5.6	12.9	15.3	23.6	43.9	—
Humerus	0.0	2.0	3.7	3.6	0.0	0.0	—
Ulna	1.2	0.0	3.6	2.3	2.9	1.6	—
Radius	0.0	0.0	4.0	2.9	4.2	1.6	—
Femur	1.8	2.0	7.2	6.4	6.9	0.0	—
Tibia	2.4	4.0	16.0	15.8	27.7	52.2	PA/C
Fibula	1.4	0.0	9.9	5.3	21.8	40.0	PA/C

[a]Percentage of bones affected by periostitis/osteomyelitis in adult females.
[b]Percentage of bones affected by periostitis/osteomyelitis in adult males.
[c]Comparisons showing statistically significant differences in frequency between adult females and males ($p < 0.05$).

the formation of antibodies that fight the infection. Thus, the ability of the body to mitigate infection would be severely hampered by the reduction in nutrition. We argue, therefore, that pathogen virulence would increase in historic period populations, especially as a result of the compromised health status that was linked to poor nutrition.

Lastly, exposure to new pathogens resulting from contact with other populations may also be an important consideration in interpreting increase in the prevalence of periostitis. Accounts from historical records demonstrate the use of native populations from various provinces of Spanish Florida as laborers in regions far from home villages, such as the capital at St. Augustine (e.g., Hann 1988). Those accounts also note the return of the laborers to their home villages and missions once assigned tasks were completed. We suggest that those laborers had been exposed to pathogens, thus providing ideal vectors for the transport of infectious disease back to their home missions and villages. Historical records also inform us that males were used more frequently than females as draft laborers. Indeed, biomechanical study of contact period long bones (Ruff and Larsen 1990) shows that males were more mobile—likely reflecting long-distance travel—than females. Thus, the higher prevalence of skeletal infection in contact period males may point to their relatively greater exposure to novel pathogens or other agents during travel to other localities.

What other evidence suggests that infection was a problem facing contact period populations? One response of the body to a wide range of infections is hypoferremia, or mild iron deficiency. Many microorganisms that invade the body lack iron and thus depend upon iron reserves provided exclusively by

Temporal Sex Differences

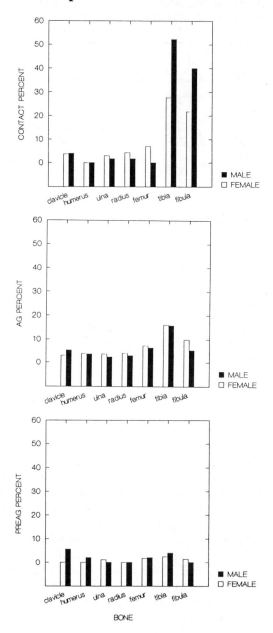

Figure 15-1. *Sex comparisons (female vs. male) for frequency of periostitis in the Georgia Bight. Comparisons of the bar graphs also illustrate the striking contrast between periods, especially between precontact agricultural and contact period tibiae and fibulae.*

the host, the human body. Various studies have shown that reduction of bioavailable iron decreases the risk and/or virulence of a range of bacterial, fungal, and parasitic infections (e.g., Stuart-Macadam 1992). Not surprisingly, in the Georgia Bight contact series there is a marked increase in the frequency of porotic hyperostosis, a pathological condition primarily affecting cranial bones that results from iron deficiency anemia. In the precontact agricultural-ists, for example, only 6% of the crania were affected by the pathology. In the contact crania from Santa Catalina on Amelia Island, the prevalence jumps to 27%; over three-quarters of the individuals less than 16 years of age in the latter series exhibit the pathology (Larsen, Ruff et al. 1992). It is also likely that consumption of maize—a food that inhibits iron absorption—contributed to the increases.

Finally, we note that virtually all the skeletal infections are nearly or com-pletely healed, indicating a high rate of survival of individuals experiencing the circumstances responsible for the skeletal infections. This finding under-scores the adaptability of those populations in the face of decaying environ-mental circumstances.

Conclusions

The presence of periostitis may reflect relative robusticity in the immune response, especially since bone infections indicate that the individual with the lesion survived the initial phase of infection. If the individual had not survived the initial phase, then it is unlikely that there would have been time for the appearance of a bony response prior to death (see also Ortner 1991). Thus, the increased prevalence of skeletal infection in Spanish Florida could be construed as representing an overall improvement in health during the contact period. However, given the overwhelming historical evidence for degeneration of living conditions in native populations, that interpretation seems implausible. Rather, we suggest that an increase in the prevalence of skeletal pathology provides compelling evidence for a general decline in the health and well-being of those populations.

Various evidence indicates that the synergistic relationship between malnu-trition and disease is the key to explaining that decline. Moreover, other miti-gating circumstances, such as increased exposure to newly introduced pathogens, likely contributed to the increases in skeletal pathology. This is not to say that periostitis is a "nutritional disease." Rather, periostitis is an impor-tant indicator of environmental degradation, which also includes nutrition as central to interpreting disease patterns in the past.

Acknowledgments

This paper is a contribution to the La Florida Bioarchaeology Project. We thank D. H. Ubelaker for permission to study the prehistoric human remains housed in the collections of the Smithsonian Institution. We thank David Hurst Thomas, Kenneth W. Hardin, Jerald T. Milanich, and Rebecca Saunders for their cooperation in the completion of excavations on St. Catherines Island, Georgia, and Amelia Island, Florida. Fieldwork on St. Catherines Island was funded by the Edward John Noble Foundation and the St. Catherines Island Foundation. We are indebted to Dr. and Mrs. George H. Dorion of Jacksonville, Florida, for funding the fieldwork at Mission Santa Catalina de Guale de Santa Maria on Amelia Island. Their interest in that research has been instrumental in the success of the project. Lisa Hoshower drew our attention to the quotation from Gatschet (1880) describing "pox" in native populations of Spanish Florida. Analysis of the human remains was funded in part by grants from the National Science Foundation (awards BNS-8406773 and BNS-8703848 to C.S.L.). Thanks are extended to Kristin Sobolik for her invitation to contribute to this volume and to three anonymous reviewers for their comments and suggestions.

References

Eisenberg, L. E.
   1986   *Adaptation in a "Marginal" Mississippian Population from Middle Tennessee: Biocultural Insights from Paleopathology.* Unpublished Ph.D. dissertation, Department of Anthropology, New York University, New York.
Gatschet, A. S.
   1880   The Timucua Language. *Proceedings of the American Philosophical Society* 18:465–502.
Hann, J. H.
   1988   *Apalachee: The Land Between the Rivers.* University Presses of Florida, Gainesville.
Jones, G. D.
   1978   The Ethnohistory of the Guale Coast Through 1684. In *The Anthropology of St. Catherines Island: 1. Natural and Cultural History,* by D. H. Thomas, G. D. Jones, R. S. Durham, and C. S. Larsen, pp. 178–210. Anthropological Papers of the American Museum of Natural History 55 (part 2). New York.
Lallo, J. W., and J. C. Rose
   1979   Patterns of Stress, Disease, and Mortality in Two Prehistoric Populations from North America. *Journal of Human Evolution* 8:323–335.
Larsen, C. S.
   1982   *The Anthropology of St. Catherines Island: 3. Prehistoric Human Biological Adaptation.* Anthropological Papers of the American Museum of Natural History 57 (part 3). New York.
   1987   Bioarchaeological Interpretations of Subsistence Economy and Behavior from Human Skeletal Remains. In *Advances in Archaeological Method and Theory,* vol. 10, edited by M. B. Schiffer, pp. 339–445. Academic Press, San Diego.
Larsen, C. S., C. B. Ruff, M. J. Schoeninger, and D. L. Hutchinson
   1992   Population Decline and Extinction in La Florida. In *Disease and Demography in the Americas: Changing Patterns Before and After 1492,* edited by J. W. Verano and D. H. Ubelaker, pp. 25–39. Smithsonian Institution Press, Washington, D.C.
Larsen, C. S., M. J. Schoeninger, D. L. Hutchinson, K. F. Russell, and C. B. Ruff
   1990   Beyond Demographic Collapse: Biological Adaptation and Change in

Native Populations of La Florida. In *Columbian Consequences, Volume 2: Archaeo-logical and Historical Perspectives on the Spanish Borderlands East*, edited by D. H. Thomas, pp. 409–428. Smithsonian Institution Press, Washington, D.C.

Larsen, C. S., M. J. Schoeninger, N. J. van der Merwe, K. M. Moore, and J. Lee-Thorp
1992   Carbon and Nitrogen Stable Isotopic Signatures of Human Dietary Change in the Georgia Bight. *American Journal of Physical Anthropology* 89:197–214.

Larsen, C. S., R. Shavit, and M. C. Griffin
1991   Dental Caries Evidence for Dietary Change: An Archaeological Context. In *Advances in Dental Anthropology*, edited by M. A. Kelley and C. S. Larsen, pp. 179–202. Wiley-Liss, New York.

Milner, G. R.
1991   Health and Cultural Change in the Late Prehistoric American Bottom, Illinois. In *What Mean These Bones? Studies in Southeastern Bioarchaeology*, edited by M. L. Powell, P. S. Bridges, and A. M. Wagner Mires, pp. 52–69. University of Alabama Press, Tuscaloosa.

Milner, G. R., and V. G. Smith
1990   Oneota Human Skeletal Remains. In *Archaeological Investigations at the Morton Village and Norris Farms 36 Cemetery*, by S. K. Santure, A. D. Harn, and D. Esarey, pp. 111–148. Reports of Investigations No. 45. Illinois State Museum, Springfield.

Ortner, D. J.
1991   Theoretical and Methodological Issues in Paleopathology. In *Human Paleo-pathology: Current Syntheses and Future Options*, edited by D. J. Ortner and A. C. Aufderheide, pp. 5–11. Smithsonian Institution Press, Washington, D.C.

Ortner, D. J., and W. G. J. Putschar
1985   *Identification of Pathological Conditions in Human Skeletal Remains*. Smithson-ian Institution Press, Washington, D.C.

Perzigian, A. J., P. A. Tench, and D. J. Braun
1984   Prehistoric Health in the Ohio River Valley. In *Paleopathology at the Origins of Agriculture*, edited by M. N. Cohen and G. J. Armelagos, pp. 347–366. Aca-demic Press, Orlando.

Powell, M. L.
1990   On the Eve of Conquest: Life and Death at Irene Mound, Georgia. In *The Archaeology of Mission Santa Catalina de Guale: 2. Biocultural Interpretations of a Population in Transition*, edited by C. S. Larsen, pp. 26–35. Anthropological Papers of the American Museum of Natural History No. 68. New York.

Reitz, E. J.
1988   Evidence for Coastal Adaptations in Georgia and South Carolina. *Archae-ology of Eastern North America* 16:137–158.

Reitz, E. J., and C. M. Scarry
1985   *Reconstructing Historic Subsistence, with an Example from Sixteenth-Century Spanish Florida*. Special Publication Series No. 3. Society for Historical Archae-ology, Glassboro, New Jersey.

Rose, J. C., B. A. Burnett, M. S. Nassaney, and M. W. Blaeuer
1984   Paleopathology and the Origins of Maize Agriculture in the Lower Mississippi Valley and Caddoan Culture Areas. In *Paleopathology at the Origins of Agriculture*, edited by M. N. Cohen and G. J. Armelagos, pp. 393–424. Academic Press, Orlando.

Ruff, C. B., and C. S. Larsen
1990   Postcranial Biomechanical Adaptations to Subsistence Strategy Changes on the Georgia Coast. In *The Archaeology of Mission Santa Catalina de Guale: 2.*

234 | *C. S. Larsen and D. E. Harn*

Biocultural Interpretations of a Population in Transition, edited by C. S. Larsen, pp. 94–120. Anthropological Papers of the American Museum of Natural History No. 68. New York.

Ruhl, D. L.
  1990 Spanish Mission Paleoethnobotany and Culture Change: A Survey of the Archaeobotanical Data and Some Speculations on Aboriginal and Spanish Agrarian Interactions in La Florida. In *Columbian Consequences, Volume 2: Archaeological and Historical Perspectives on the Spanish Borderlands East,* edited by D. H. Thomas, pp. 555–580. Smithsonian Institution Press, Washington, D.C.

Scrimshaw, N. S.
  1975 Interactions of Malnutrition and Infection: Advances in Understanding. In *Protein-Calorie Malnutrition,* edited by R. E. Olson, pp. 353–367. Academic Press, New York.

Stuart-Macadam, P.
  1992 Porotic Hyperostosis: A New Perspective. *American Journal of Physical Anthropology* 87:39–47.

Thomas, D. H.
  1987 *The Archaeology of Mission Santa Catalina de Guale: 1. Search and Discovery.* Anthropological Papers of the American Museum of Natural History 63 (part 2). New York.

Thomas, D. H., G. D. Jones, R. S. Durham, and C. S. Larsen
  1978 *The Anthropology of St. Catherines Island: 1. Natural and Cultural History.* Anthropological Papers of the American Museum of Natural History 55 (part 2). New York.

Wood, J. W., G. R. Milner, H. C. Harpending, and K. M. Weiss
  1992 The Osteological Paradox: Problems of Inferring Prehistoric Health from Skeletal Samples. *Current Anthropology* 33:343–370.

16. | "You Are What You Eat"

George J. Armelagos

"You are what you eat." To the anthropologist, this metaphor describes the importance of culture in determining factors that influence individual dietary intake. Each culture's cuisine defines products of the environment that are edible, how food is to be prepared, and social rules about eating (Farb and Armelagos 1981:227–249). To the paleonutritionist, the metaphor is literally true. Many foods have chemical signatures that are incorporated into the skeletal system, and those chemical signals can be read to reveal clues about diet. What is not eaten (if the missing substance is a required nutrient) may be revealed in the bone of an individual as well. If the nutrient is essential to the development of bones or teeth, the formation of those hard tissues may be disrupted. The resulting hard tissue pathology again reveals nutritional information.

While it is beyond our means to define all aspects of cuisine in an archaeological population, there are many features that can be characterized. Paleonutritionists have developed methods that enable them to describe the foods available (the menu), the foods consumed (the diet), and the adequacy of the diet (the nutrition) of prehistoric populations.

Deciphering an ancient menu involves indirect methods such as reconstructing the environment and determining what plants (flora) and animals (fauna) were available as food items. A society rarely consumes all the edible items in its environment. Americans, for example, do not eat insects even though many insects have three times the protein content of beef.

The recent contributions of bioarchaeology and the papers presented in this volume illustrate the advances made in the last three decades in delimiting the menu, defining the diet, and understanding the nutrition of prehistoric populations. In commenting on the chapters presented in this section, I am going to specifically consider the role of pathology and bone chemistry (the analysis of major, minor, and trace minerals and stable isotopes) in dietary and paleonutritional reconstruction.

Dietary and nutritional reconstruction has to be placed in the broader context of adaptation. There is a direct relationship between nutrition and disease

Paleonutrition: The Diet and Health of Prehistoric Americans, edited by Kristin D. Sobolik. Center for Archaeological Investigations, Occasional Paper No. 22. © 1994 by the Board of Trustees, Southern Illinois University. All rights reserved. ISBN 0-88104-078-9.

and between disease and death. Disease and death are not random events, but form discernible patterns. Calvin Wells notes:

> The pattern of disease or injuries that affect any group of people is never a matter of chance. It is invariably the expression of stresses and strains to which they were exposed, a response to everything in their environment and behavior. It reflects their genetic inheritance (which is their internal environment), the climate in which they lived, the soil that gave them sustenance and the animals or plants that shared their homeland. It is influenced by their daily occupation, their habits of diet, their choice of dwelling and clothes, their social structure, even their folklore and mythology [1964:17].

Paleopathologists analyze the bone and artifacts of populations long dead in order to understand their pattern of activity during life. It is paradoxical that the pattern of disease and death gives clues as to how people lived. Paleopathology makes three major contributions to paleonutrition: (1) it delimits the chronology and geography of nutritional deficiency; (2) it reconstructs the dietary lifeway of a society by analyzing patterns of nutritional morbidity and mortality and by measuring the success of a population's adjustment to its environment; and (3) it explores the processes involved in the occurrence of nutritional deficiencies within a population.

The best evidence of disease is the biological remains: mummified tissue and the skeleton itself. The paleopathologist can usually determine the causes of skeletal abnormality. By gross observation of the skeleton, radiographic, chemical, and histological analysis, the cause of the pathological condition can be diagnosed. Having determined the cause of the pathology, the paleopathologist can then analyze the ecological and cultural factors that may have contributed to the disease process.

Recently, Ortner and Aufderheide (1991:1) and Ortner (1991) decried a lack of methodology and theory in paleopathology. They argue that there is no standardized method for describing lesions and little overriding theory to contextualize pathology in prehistoric populations. They seem to imply that there should be some prevailing theoretical perspective that guides paleopathology. I do agree that there is a need to standardize interobserver observation. For example, the evaluation of the severity of a condition such as porotic hyperostosis varies between observer. However, I strongly disagree with Ortner and Aufderheide's interpretation concerning a theoretical perspective that would drive paleopathology research. I believe my differences with them reflect what we mean by *science* and the role that method and theory play in scientific investigation. I see paleopathology as a science capable of testing alternative hypotheses.

A scientific approach to paleopathology can test the validity of a diagnosis and the utility of different methodologies, can evaluate alternative theories on the origin and evolution of a disease, can determine the environmental factors that influence the disease process, and can define the impact of disease on the demographic structure of a population. The papers in this section reflect the richness of a scientific approach to the study of paleopathology.

Given the ability of paleopathology to test alternative hypotheses, it is not surprising that disagreements arise as to the meaning and the implication of pathological conditions. What is surprising is that claims are often made without the scientific evidence to support them. As Goodman (this volume) notes, Neiburger (1990) and Stuart-Macadam (1982, 1992) offer alternative interpretations of osteological and dental lesions without providing the scientific support for their views. Neiburger argues that linear enamel hypoplasia is a poor indicator of diet. Goodman agrees that linear hypoplasia is not a dietary indicator but counters that it is evidence of nutritional inadequacies that may be related to diet, disease or both. Stuart-Macadam claims that porotic hyperostosis is a positively adaptive response of the body to infectious pathogens. Since porotic hyperostosis is an indicator of iron deficiency, Stuart-Macadam suggests that by sequestering iron, anemia is a positive adaptive response to infection.

Goodman effectively dismantles the errors in their thinking, but he questions the adaptive paradigm, since it encourages what he terms "vulgar adaptationism." A researcher, seeing signs of stress and knowing that the human body reacts homeostatically, interprets them as adaptive. As Goodman notes, that interpretation has serious implications because the biological cost of the stressor to the individual or to other levels in the system is ignored. In fact, there is ample evidence as to the cost of pathological conditions such as porotic hyperostosis and enamel hypoplasia. Huss-Ashmore and colleagues (1982) demonstrate that the mortality of individuals with porotic hyperostosis is higher during the first 10 years of life when compared with individuals who show no evidence of the lesion. Furthermore, Mensforth and colleagues (1978) present the statistical evidence of the positive relationship of porotic hyperostosis and periosteal reaction in the Libben population from Ohio. Thus, porotic hyperostosis, rather than conferring protection from infectious pathogens, was directly linked to infection as measured by the periosteal reaction found on the bones of the Libben population.

Nieburger's interpretation of enamel hypoplasia obscures its use as an indicator of nutritional stress and its importance in measuring the consequence of stress. Blakey and Armelagos (1985) demonstrated an increase in the mortality of individuals who in their fetal stage experienced enamel hypoplasia in the development of their deciduous dentition when compared to those who show no indications of enamel defects. Similarly, Goodman and Armelagos (1988) established that adults who were exposed to stressors that produce enamel defects when they were children experienced an increase in mortality as adults.

Paleopathology has the methods and means for testing competing claims. Neiburger and Stuart-Macadam did not avail themselves of the tools to test their hypotheses. Furthermore, I am concerned that Goodman, in response to vulgar adaptationism, questions the value of a concept that is frequently misused. Adaptation has served anthropology well, and we should do what is necessary to clarify its application and expand its use rather than discard it to the intellectual graveyard of outmoded concepts.

Paleopathologists traditionally use deductive methods to reconstruct the factors that cause a disease. While the deductive approach is useful, there are inherent limitations. It is not possible with that method to falsify conclusions. In other words, there are many interpretations that can explain the data, and there is no way to exclude any of them.

There is, however, a methodology that can systematically falsify or exclude alternative hypotheses. Platt (1964) suggests that an inductive approach, which he calls "strong inference," can provide a means for hypothesis testing in science. Platt notes that the roots of strong inference derive from the Baconian approach to experimentation. As early as the late 1870s, T. Chamberlin, a geologist, argued for the multiple-hypothesis testing approach in science. Although inductive inference has been known for many years, it has not penetrated the methodology of paleopathology.

Strong inference could be very effective if applied to problems in paleopathology. It would be the means for transforming the discipline into a science. There are four stages in the development of the strong inference approach: (1) devise alternative hypotheses, (2) devise experiments to exclude one or more of the hypotheses, (3) carry out experiments to get "clean results," and (4) recycle the procedure (Platt 1964:347).

While strong inference is most effectively applied to sciences with experimental possibilities, it can be useful in nonexperimental sciences such as paleopathology. The application to paleopathology does require modification. Since there is no possibility of carrying out experiments to get "clean results," the researcher must rely on comparative analysis for "natural experiments." The studies in Part III provide examples of natural laboratories that can be used for testing hypotheses.

The scientific aspect of the strong inference and the inductive approach can be applied to paleopathology. The model that Goodman (Goodman and Armelagos 1989; Goodman et al. 1984) uses in his paper is an effective tool for demonstrating the levels at which strong inference can be applied. The model provides a systematic framework for the analysis of insults, which cause physiological disruption and potentially affect the individual's and the population's adjustment to the environment.

The impact of stressors on the individual and/or population can be measured in terms of the physiological disruptions that they cause. In an individual, there is a hierarchical biological response to disease. Nutritional deficiencies may initially affect metabolic processes before they affect growth, and growth will be disrupted before there is a loss of muscle or bone. Even with tissue loss, there is a hierarchical response—muscle is lost before bone tissue is catabolized. In dealing with archaeological populations, we are limited to skeletal indicators of disruptions that are the result of severe stressors.

The application of the scientific method using strong inference can be enhanced by the use of multiple stress indicators that exist at different levels of analysis (ecosystem, population, individual, organ, tissue, cell, or chemical constituents of the cell—i.e., collagen and apatite crystals). For example, a dietary deficiency may cause a number of physiological disruptions such as porotic hyperostosis, altered patterns of growth, and lead to premature bone loss. In addition, the same dietary pattern may have different nutritional consequences within a population because segments may be facing quite different risks. Women who are lactating may suffer a greater nutritional crisis from a shortage of calcium and iron than a healthy male of the same age.

In their paper Larsen and Harn provide one of the best examples of how the bioarchaeological approach can be applied to understanding the impact of changes in cultural adaptation on human biology. Working in the Georgia Bight, they show that two major events in the last 4,000 years had an impact on the adaptation of Native American populations. The shift in subsistence from foraging to primary food production and contact with European populations affected their health. Periosteal reactions on bones were used as evidence of infectious lesions and as a measure of changes in health. Because of the taphonomic process, Larsen and Harn had to rely on analysis by skeletal elements (specific bones) rather than on a prevalence of infection among the individuals. As they note, that restriction results in a loss of information. By dividing their sample into a precontact preagricultural group (dated prior to A.D. 1150), a precontact agricultural group, and a contact era population, they were able to measure biocultural changes over time.

The introduction of maize, which was not apparent from floral remains, was a major cultigen and the basis for the agricultural transformation. The changes resulted in the expected pattern of adaptation that includes an increase in sedentism, population size, and social complexity. Larsen and Harn use periostitis as an indicator of environmental degradation. Using the tibia, which is the most frequently involved bone, they found an 11% increase in infectious lesions (from 4.5% to 15%) in the agricultural group. The impact of European contact was even greater, with a 25% increase (40% showed evidence of infection). The Spanish missionization relied on a policy of *reducción*, which concentrated the population through resettlement and increased their potential risk of infectious disease. In addition, through the analysis of stable isotopes of carbon and nitrogen, Larsen and Harn were able to show that maize became a more important dietary item and that there was a decrease in the use of marine resources. This narrowing of the subsistence base has implications for nutrition and infectious disease and reflects the typical pattern with agricultural intensification. The synergy between infection and malnutrition mentioned by Larsen and Harn has been reported in contemporary Third World populations and in other archaeological populations.

One of most interesting aspects of Larsen and Harn's study is the biomechanical analysis of long bones (Ruff 1992) to determine changes in activity and to show the Spanish use of Indians as laborers (males were more mobile than females). Since labor conscription was for a limited period (Worth 1992), Indians returning to their villages would bring back diseases.

Larsen and Harn note that there is an increase in porotic hyperostosis from 8% to 27% in the prehistoric population from Irene Mound during the contact period sample from Santa Catalina. While they show that the increase in porotic hyperostosis could result from a response to infection, they assume that it is caused by a reliance on maize. Their assumption could easily be tested by determining the differences in the levels of the stable carbon isotopes and by testing the association of porotic hyperostosis and periosteal reaction (Mensforth et al. 1978). They do conclude that there was a decline in health with the shift to agriculture and again with European contact.

Ezzo's sample population spans a critical phase in the history of the Southwest (his paper is in Part IV). It provides another opportunity to examine the change in adaptation through time. Grasshopper Pueblo, Arizona (A.D. 1275–1400), was the focus of the University of Arizona Archaeological Field School from 1963 to 1992 and is the source of a large archaeological population of 674 individuals that has been studied extensively. Ezzo uses bone chemistry to provide a unique perspective that complements the extensive data from the previous excavation. The site represents four phases: Establishment, Aggregation, Dispersion, and Abandonment. Eleven elements were analyzed, but barium (Ba) and strontium (Sr) were the only ones considered dietary indicators.

Ezzo also partitions his sample to effectively reveal spatial and temporal differences in diet. Room blocks, he believes, may represent ethnic groups, suggesting that different groups of people at Grasshopper were differentially exploiting resources. Ezzo has also analyzed a subset of stable isotopes of carbon data that suggest changes in diet that may be relevant to questions of abandonment of the site.

While there have been many studies that examine differences among subsets of the population by age and gender, the possibility of studying the variability across space within a site is important. Ezzo shows that in the earlier periods males consumed more meat and cultigens while females ate more wild plant foods. In the later period, the diet of males and females became more similar with both sexes relying on cultigens. However, there was some spatial variability with some groups still relying on significant amounts of wild plant food. The transition to agriculture restricted the number of food types and resulted in an increase in nutritional problems in the late period. From other studies, Ezzo finds that porotic hyperostosis that had been previously analyzed increases in the later period and that there was a decline in subadult health. Unfortunately, he did not link his study to the earlier studies of the paleopathology at the site. It would be very important to see how the chemical indicators link with pathology in individuals.

In their paper Powell and Steele also test a hypothesis that uses a regional comparative approach. They are concerned with the analysis of the adaptation of Paleoindian populations (living between 8500 and 11,000 years B.P.). They specifically examine the role of megafauna and small animals in the diet of those populations. The controversy centers around what Dent (1985) has termed the "received view" and the "revised view" of faunal exploitation. The received view claims that the focal point of Paleoindian adaptation was the megafauna and that climatological changes between 14,000 and 9000 B.P. forced a shift in exploitation to smaller animals. The revised view questions the notion of specialization.

Powell and Steele apply a number of interesting techniques to answer the question of resource exploitation; however, they are seriously hampered by a lack of data. A data set of 10 individuals from eight sites in a region that spans the United States and dates from 8500 to 10,000 years B.P. makes it difficult to generalize. Dental attrition patterns did not show the specialization noted by Turner and Cadien (1969) for Arctic populations. They examine aspects of health and disease, dental attrition, and dental microwear to show that the populations were relying on both plants and animals for their subsistence. While I would applaud Powell and Steele for a model that involves hypothesis testing by pooling populations regionally, their analysis of health, enamel hypoplasia, dental attrition, and microwear is interesting but not conclusive.

Bourque and Krueger's paper examines the regional dietary data from five Gulf of Maine sites to compare conventional methods of dietary reconstruction with those based on stable isotopes from bone. The conventional means of dietary reconstruction include analysis of faunal remains from prehistoric sites and documentary evidence from the early historic site. The authors test the degree of exploitation of maritime resources during the Moorehead phase (4500–3800 B.P.), the Susquehanna tradition (3800–3500 B.P.), the ceramic period (2700–500 B.P.), and the early postcontact period (after 500 B.P.). Bourque (1975, 1976) and Sanger (1975) claim that in the periods following the Moorehead phase there was an abrupt cessation in the exploitation of deep-water maritime resources.

Chemical analysis of bone included the sampling of carbon and nitrogen isotopes from collagen and carbon isotopes from bioapatite. Krueger and Sullivan (1984) developed the rationale for modeling the sources of ^{13}C in bioapatite and gelatin and the implications for dietary reconstruction. That distinction is important since bone collagen may be derived from the protein component of the diet and will thus have a different signature than that revealed by the carbon isotopes in apatite. Bourque and Krueger use source diagrams that denote the expected isotopic composition of the collagen (gelatin) and the bioapatite values from various diets, thus greatly aiding in interpreting the dietary source of the differences in stable isotopes.

Bourque and Krueger use isotopic analysis to assess the vegetal component of the diet because there is a lack of preservation of floral material at the sites. Isotopic analysis even clarifies the faunal reconstruction. For example, faunal analysis suggests that the people of Turner Farm and the Crocker site relied on terrestrial faunal resources such as the cervids while isotopic analysis suggests a marine source for the diet. Bourque and Krueger argue that the terrestrial bias may be related to the differential processing of terrestrial and marine resources. Coastal populations are thought to have seasonally used inland resources.

Ultimately, I agree with Bourque and Krueger's assertion that diet can be revealed through isotopic analysis, but I do not think it worked as well as one might have hoped in their case. Sampling problems prevent an easy characterization of the dietary history of the populations, thus obscuring a definitive answer to the question of marine exploitation during the last 4,500 years. Even though they undertook chemical analysis on a significant sample of available material, the small sample sizes and the extensive variability in some of the samples make it more difficult to characterize the diet of the Gulf of Maine region in any of the periods. The claim that the stable isotope data address issues related to individual diet as compared to the group diet revealed in faunal analysis is true, but given the small sample sizes, the analysis does not provide answers to many of the questions raised. When Bourque and Krueger attempt to explain the "aberrant" individuals from the Moorehead phase, it becomes difficult to evaluate their interpretation objectively. That is, there is no way to falsify any of their alternative hypotheses. The skeletal analysis of the Turner Farm site being completed by Barbian and Magennis (1994) and Shaw's (1988) analysis of the Nevin site population should add to our understanding of the diet and nutrition of those populations.

Reed in his paper examines 52 adults from the Mayan site of Copán—the site of an extensive excavation by Sanders and others. Using stable isotope data, Reed suggests that a major portion of the diet was obtained from C_4 plants, probably maize. Although there are problems with sample size, he suggests that maize consumption may decrease with age. He found no evidence that social status resulted in differential diet. The data according to Reed suggest that males and females had, on the average, different diets, but that difference is confounded by age and/or social status. Finally, Reed's analysis of diet supports evidence that the collapse of the Copán Mayans was related to the effects of agricultural intensification and a degradation of the local ecosystem. Obviously, his conclusion will require presentation of evidence to analyze the relationship of subsistence, technology, and the social system in the abandonment of the site.

Conclusion

Paleonutrition has made great strides in the last decade. The papers in Part III and the volume as a whole attest to the richness of the studies in terms of problem focus, method, and theory. Bioarchaeological samples that span critical phases in a major transition or change in adaptation have been among our most successful tools in studying the biological impact of change. The problems with interobserver error are minimized, and it is easier to control for the factors that affect adaptation and biology. The scientific approach to paleopathology provides the methods for testing hypotheses and theories related to diagnosis, the history and geography of disease, and the role that adaptation plays in the disease process.

References

Barbian, L., and A. Magennis
1994   Appendix 7: The Human Burials from the Turner Farm Site. In *Diversity and Complexity in Prehistoric Maritime Societies: A Gulf of Maine Perspective*, by B. Bourque. Plenum Press, in press.
Blakey, M., and G. J. Armelagos
1985   Deciduous Dentition and Prenatal and Postnatal Stress in Prehistoric Americans from Dickson Mounds. *American Journal of Physical Anthropology* 66:371–380.

Bourque, B. J.
    1975   Comments on the Late Archaic Populations of Central Maine: The View from Turner Farm. *Arctic Anthropology* 12(2):35–45.
    1976   The Turner Farm Site: A Preliminary Report. *Man in the Northeast* 11:21–30.

Dent, R. J.
    1985   Amerinds and the Environment: Myth, Reality, and the Upper Delaware Valley. In *Shawnee Minisink: A Stratified Paleoindian-Archaic Site in the Upper Delaware Valley of Pennsylvania,* edited by C. W. McNett, Jr., pp. 123–163. Academic Press, New York.

Farb, P., and G. J. Armelagos
    1981   *Consuming Passions: The Anthropology of Eating.* Houghton Mifflin, Boston.

Goodman, A. H., and G. J. Armelagos
    1988   Childhood Stress, Cultural Buffering, and Decreased Longevity in Prehistoric Populations. *American Anthropologist* 90:936–944.
    1989   Infant and Childhood Morbidity and Mortality Risks in Archaeological Populations. *World Archaeology* 212:225–243.

Goodman, A. H., D. Martin, G. J. Armelagos, and G. Clark
    1984   Indications of Stress from Bones and Teeth. In *Paleopathology at the Origins of Agriculture,* edited by M. N. Cohen and G. J. Armelagos, pp. 13–49. Academic Press, Orlando.

Huss-Ashmore, R., A. H. Goodman, and G. J. Armelagos
    1982   Nutritional Inferences from Paleopathology. In *Advances in Archaeological Method and Theory,* vol. 5, edited by M. B. Schiffer, pp. 385–473. Academic Press, New York.

Krueger, H. W., and C. H. Sullivan
    1984   *Models for Carbon Isotope Fractionation Between Diet and Bone.* ACS Symposium Series No. 258. Stable Isotopes in Nutrition. American Chemical Society, Washington, D.C.

Mensforth, R. P., C. O. Lovejoy, J. Lallo, and G. J. Armelagos
    1978   The Role of Constitutional Factors, Diet, and Disease in the Etiology of Porotic Hyperostosis and Periosteal Reactions in Prehistoric Infants and Children. *Medical Anthropology* 2(1):1–59.

Nieburger, E.
    1990   Enamel Hypoplasias: Poor Indicator of Dietary Stress. *American Journal of Physical Anthropology* 82:231–232.

Ortner, D. J.
    1991   Theoretical and Methodological Issues in Paleopathology. In *Human Paleopathology: Current Syntheses and Future Options,* edited by D. J. Ortner and A. C. Aufderheide, pp. 5–11. Smithsonian Institution Press, Washington, D.C.

Ortner, D. J., and A. C. Aufderheide
    1991   Introduction. In *Human Paleopathology: Current Syntheses and Future Options,* edited by D. J. Ortner and A. C. Aufderheide, pp. 1–2. Smithsonian Institution Press, Washington, D.C.

Platt, J. R.
    1964   Strong Inference. *Science* 146:347–353.

Ruff, C.
    1992   Biomechanical Analysis of Archaeological Human Skeletal Samples. In *Skeletal Biology of Past Peoples: Research Methods,* edited by A. Katsenberg and S. Saunders, pp. 37–58. Wiley-Liss, New York.

Sanger, D.
    1975   Culture Change as an Adaptive Process in Maine-Maritime Region. *Arctic*

Anthropology 12(2):60–75.

Shaw, L. C.

1988   A Biocultural Evaluation of the Skeletal Population from the Nevin Site, Blue Hill, Maine. *Archaeology of Eastern North America* 16:55–77.

Stuart-Macadam, P.

1982   Porotic Hyperostosis: A New Perspective. *American Journal of Physical Anthropology* 87:39–47.

1992   Porotic Hyperostosis: Changing Interpretations. In *Human Paleopathology: Current Syntheses and Future Options*, edited by D. J. Ortner and A. C. Aufderheide, pp. 36–39. Smithsonian Institution Press, Washington, D.C.

Turner, C. G., II, and J. D. Cadien

1969   Dental Chipping in Aleuts, Eskimos, and Indians. *American Journal of Physical Anthropology* 31:303–310.

Wells, C.

1964   *Bones, Bodies, and Disease.* Thames, London.

Worth, J. E.

1992   *The Timucan Missions of Spanish Florida and the Rebellion of 1656.* Unpublished Ph.D. dissertation, Department of Anthropology, University of Florida, Gainesville.

IV. Integrative Studies

17. Paleonutrition of the Lower Pecos Region of the Chihuahuan Desert

Kristin D. Sobolik

Abstract: This study integrates a variety of dietary and health assemblages to determine the diet of the Archaic occupants of the Lower Pecos region, its nutritional value, and the consequent health of the population. A comprehensive synthesis of the botanical remains from 11 sites, the faunal remains from 17 sites, and the results from the analyses of 359 human coprolites and over 140 human skeletal remains is used to determine the paleonutrition of the population. The analysis reveals that the Lower Pecos populations had access to the nutrients required for a healthy existence. The staples of the population were excellent sources of carbohydrates, protein, and fat. The large variety of supplementary dietary items provided essential amino acids, trace elements, vitamins, and minerals. However, stress, as indicated by growth arrest lines—Harris lines and enamel hypoplasias—was present in the population and may have been nutritionally related.

Introduction

This analysis of the paleonutrition of the Archaic occupants of the Lower Pecos region of the Chihuahuan Desert combines previously analyzed dietary assemblages from the area with newly analyzed dietary assemblages. The database includes botanical remains from 11 sites, faunal remains from 17 sites, 359 analyzed coprolites, and over 140 analyzed human skeletons. After the potential diet of the population was projected, and the possibility of nutritional stress through analyses of the skeletal remains was indicated, a nutritional analysis of the potential diet was conducted to pinpoint and define any deficiencies.

The Lower Pecos region is located on the eastern margin of the Chihuahuan Desert, focusing on the Pecos and Devils rivers and their confluence with the Rio Grande (Figure 17-1). The area centers on southwestern Texas in Val

Paleonutrition: The Diet and Health of Prehistoric Americans, edited by Kristin D. Sobolik. Center for Archaeological Investigations, Occasional Paper No. 22. © 1994 by the Board of Trustees, Southern Illinois University. All rights reserved. ISBN 0-88104-078-9.

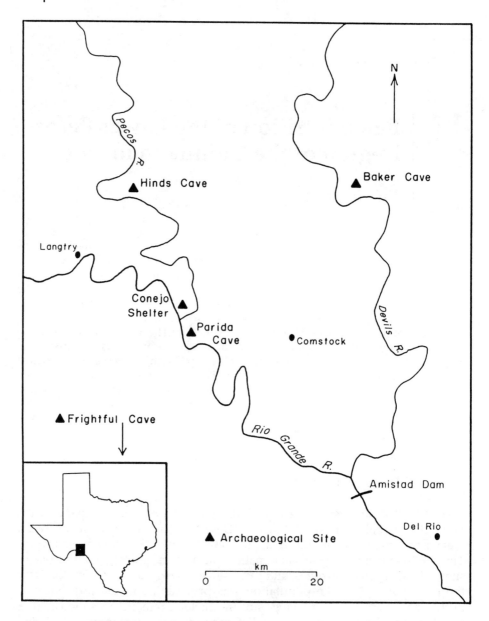

Figure 17-1. *Lower Pecos region.*

Verde County and northern Mexico in Coahuila. The region was occupied by prehistoric populations for approximately 10,000 years (Hester 1988; Shafer 1986, 1988). The environment is mainly semiarid, although the three rivers in the area provided a continuous water supply and supported a diversity of plants and wildlife. The Lower Pecos is dominated by eroded limestone canyons and plateaus, in which are located a large number of rockshelters, solution cavities, and overhangs formed by downcutting in the canyons (Shafer 1988).

The Lower Pecos region has a long-sequenced and highly stratified prehistoric record, mainly resulting from the excellent preservation of the cultural materials that are prevalent in its cave and rockshelter sites, where faunal and botanical remains are abundant. In fact, in a large number of sites the bulk of the fill matrix consists of biological remains. As a result of their ubiquity, faunal and botanical remains have been recovered and analyzed from all time periods in the region.

Coprolites are equally abundant in the dry limestone rockshelters, because the aridity is conducive to preservation, and coprolite analyses have been an important source of information for determining the diet, seasonality, and subsistence patterns of the prehistoric inhabitants of the region. Studies were conducted of 359 coprolite samples, representing a time range of 8,400 years of occupation (Table 17-1). Discussions of the coprolite contents are included in the botanical and faunal sections of this paper.

A small number (approximately 140) of human skeletal and mummified remains have also been found in rockshelters and in vertical and horizontal shaft caves. Rockshelter burials are dated primarily to the late prehistoric period, and shaft cave burials are difficult to date.

Botanical Analysis

Assorted macro- and microbotanical materials have been analyzed from the various sites of the Lower Pecos region, but only a few intensive studies have been conducted. The studies include material from Conejo Shelter (Alexander 1974), Baker Cave (Hester 1983, 1986), and Hinds Cave (Dering 1979; Sobolik 1991). They provide the majority of data for the botanical component of this paleonutritional analysis. The data come from all time periods and from a diverse geographical distribution of occupation, and the results from the studies are easily quantified and can be combined. All coprolite samples from the region were also analyzed for their macrobotanical content, save 11 samples from Parida Cave (Riskind 1970) that were analyzed solely for their pollen content. The most frequently observed dietary botanical items in Lower Pecos sites are listed in Table 17-2.

The most important dietary resources of the prehistoric Lower Pecos populations were the bulbs and leaf bases of the desert succulents, most significantly that of agave (*Agave* sp.), but also including yucca (*Yucca* sp.) and sotol (*Dasylirion* sp.). They contain the highest concentration of nutrients just before they are ready to send up their reproductive stalks. The upper leaves would have been cut from the lower portion, and the central bulblike portion would have been cooked in earthen ovens for about 48 hours to make them edible (Shafer 1986). Burned rock middens formed from the continuous use of the earthen ovens have been observed throughout the Lower Pecos region (Hester 1983; Shafer and Bryant 1977). Much of the succulent bulb was not swallowed,

Table 17-1. *Lower Pecos Coprolite Studies*

Date	Time Period[a]	Location	Sample Size
7500–5000 B.C.[b]	Late Paleoindian	Frightful Cave	15
6280 B.C.[c]	Late Paleoindian	Hinds Cave	29
5500–4800 B.C.[c]	Early Archaic	Hinds Cave	26
4000 B.C.[d]	Early Archaic	Hinds Cave	100
3680–2500 B.C.[e]	Middle Archaic	Hinds Cave	25
2100–600 B.C.[f]	Middle Archaic	Hinds Cave	40
5000–2000 B.C.[b]	Early and Middle Archaic	Frightful Cave	16
2000 B.C.–A.D. 300[b]	Early and Middle Archaic	Frightful Cave	16
500 B.C.–A.D. 800[g]	Late Archaic	Conejo Shelter	43
A.D. 900[h]	Late prehistoric	Baker Cave	38
No dates[i]	—	Parida Cave	11

Sources: [a]Hester (1988); [b]Bryant (1975) and Fry (1976b); [c]Stock (1983); [d]Williams-Dean (1978); [e]Reinhard et al. (1994); [f]Edwards (1990); [g]Bryant (1974); [h]Sobolik (1988); [i]Riskind (1970).

however, and large chunks were chewed continuously until all of the nutritious juice and pulp were extracted. The "quids" were then discarded; teeth indentations are evident on many samples.

All the coprolite studies, except those by Reinhard and colleagues (1994) and Edwards (1990), in which fiber was not quantified or only a small amount of the fiber was quantified, indicated large amounts of fiber in the samples. In some of the studies, epidermal microscopic identifications of the actual fiber types were attempted, and they revealed a predominance of fiber from prickly pear, yucca, agave, and sotol (Sobolik 1988; Williams-Dean 1978).

The pads and fruits of the prickly pear cactus were also important and abundant dietary items. Prickly pear fiber was the most abundant type identified in the coprolites, perhaps because it is one of the easiest to distinguish without the aid of a microscope. Ingestion of prickly pear was also evidenced by the presence in coprolites of glochids, spines and spine bases, and druse crystals that are indicative of the genera *Opuntia* (Jones and Bryant 1992). Prickly pear pads would usually have been ingested after the spines had been

Table 17-2. *Most Frequent Dietary Botanical Items from the Lower Pecos Region*

Item	Scientific Name	Portion Used
Fiber		
Agave	*A. lechuguilla*	Leaf bases
Prickly pear	*Opuntia* sp.	Pads
Yucca	*Yucca* sp.	Leaf bases
Sotol	*Dasylirion* sp.	Leaf bases
Mesquite	*Prosopis* sp.	Pods
Onion	*Allium drummondii*	Bulbs
Seeds and Nuts		
Prickly pear	*Opuntia* sp.	Fruit
Mesquite	*Prosopis* sp.	Beans
Walnut	*Juglans* sp.	Nuts
Acorn	*Quercus* sp.	Nuts
Yucca	*Yucca* sp.	Fruit
Acacia	*Acacia* sp.	Pods and beans
Hackberry	*Celtis* sp.	Berries
Mexican buckeye	*Ugnadia speciosa*	Nuts
Pollen		
Grass	Poaceae	Achenes
Hackberry	*Celtis* sp.	Flowers
Sotol	*Dasylirion* sp.	Flowers
Agave	*Agave* sp.	Flowers
Yucca	*Yucca* sp.	Flowers
Cactus	Cactaceae	Flowers
Mustard	Brassicaceae	Flowers/achenes

Note: Botanical items are presented in order from most to least frequent.

removed, although the coprolite evidence indicates that not all of the spines were removed and that some were ingested. The pads could be roasted or boiled. Whole prickly pear pads have been found in numerous layers from Lower Pecos sites, and it has been suggested that prickly pear pads were used for bedding and flooring material at Hinds Cave (Shafer and Bryant 1977).

Prickly pear seeds were identified in all of the coprolite studies, indicating the importance of ingestion of the prickly pear fruit (tuna). Prickly pear tunas are full of seeds, and it would be difficult to eat a tuna without ingesting them. The tunas were ingested whole, evidenced by whole seeds in the coprolites, or they were ground up and ingested, as suggested by fragmented seeds in the coprolites.

The botanical staples of the population were the desert succulents and prickly pear cactus. Stable carbon isotope analyses of a small sample of human skeletal remains from the Lower Pecos region have also indicated that a major component of the diet was from CAM plants (Huebner 1991). The Archaic population also relied upon a wide variety of other resources to supplement the vegetal staples listed in Table 17-2.

Pollen

Pollen analyses were conducted on 43 coprolite samples from Conejo Shelter (Bryant 1974), 47 from Frightful Cave (Bryant 1975), 165 from Hinds Cave (Edwards 1990; Reinhard et al. 1994; Williams-Dean 1978), 38 from Baker Cave (Sobolik 1988), and 11 from Parida Cave (Riskind 1970). Those studies indicate that prehistoric populations of the region ate a wide variety of flowers or inflorescences (Table 17-2).

The most prevalent pollen types identified as probable dietary items (economic) were *Agave* sp. (agave); Asteraceae pollen of all types, but particularly of the high-spine *(Helianthus, Helenium)* variety; *Dasylirion* sp. (sotol); and Poaceae (grass). Those types were observed in the most samples, although a large variety of pollen types that can be considered economic were actually identified from the coprolite samples.

Faunal Analysis

Faunal remains excavated from rockshelters and caves in the Lower Pecos region are excellently preserved. Some of the remains, even from lower strata, have ligaments still attached, and some of the bones are still "greasy." An example of the faunal spectra present in the Lower Pecos region is provided in Table 17-3, which lists the fauna identified from Baker Cave (for an expanded list of fauna identified from Lower Pecos sites, see Sobolik [1991: Appendix B]). Faunal ingestion is also evidenced by the presence of bone and fur in coprolite samples. Bone was observed in all the coprolite studies, and fur was found in all coprolite samples except those from Conejo Shelter.

Rodents were the most abundant and varied faunal taxa identified in the coprolites and in the excavated site deposits, the most common being packrat (*Neotoma* sp.) and cotton rat (*Sigmodon* sp.). Rodents are usually not considered indicative of prehistoric dietary practices, and rodent bones found in archaeological deposits are usually attributed to noncultural origins. The large number of human coprolite samples that contain rodent remains contradict those assumptions, however (Sobolik 1993). Rodent bones can become deposited in archaeological sites through means other than cultural dietary practices (Andrews and Evans 1983; Bocek 1986; Hoffman and Hays 1987), but the direct evidence of rodent ingestion provided by coprolite contents should force recognition that all rodent remains from archaeological sites are not indicative of contamination (Sobolik 1993).

Table 17-3. *Baker Cave Faunal Remains*

Taxon	MNI[a] (if applicable)	NISP[b]
Vertebrata	—	294
Osteichthyes	—	646
Ictaluridae	23	257
Catostomidae	3	14
Centrarchidae	3	10
Sciaenidae	2	7
Percidae	1	3
Amphibia	1	2
Reptilia		
Testudinata	—	2
Kinosternidae	—	10
Kinosternon sp.	1	4
Sternotherus sp.	1	1
Emydidae	—	4
Terrepene sp.	1	1
Trionychidae		
Trionyx sp.	2	17
Lacertilia	1	1
Serpentes	—	18
Colubridae	1	167
Viperidae	1	14
Aves	—	97
Anatidae	2	4
Cathartidae	1	1
Falco sp.	1	1
Phasianidae	1	6
Colinus sp.	1	1
Columbidae	3	10
Strigidae	1	2
Passeriformes	—	1
Emberizidae	1	1
Mammalia	—	1,737
Leporidae	—	287
Lepus sp.	7	104
Sylvilagus sp.	39	705

Table 17-3.—*Continued*

Taxon	MNI[a] (if applicable)	NISP[b]
Rodentia	—	2
Sciuridae	—	49
Sciurus sp.	2	12
Spermophilus sp.	5	77
Geomyidae	—	19
Geomys sp.	1	3
Pappogeomys sp.	1	1
Thomomys sp.	1	1
Cricetidae	—	121
Sigmodon sp.	1	10
Neotoma sp.	15	71
Erethizontidae		
Erethizon dorsatum	1	3
Carnivora		
Procyonidae	—	1
Procyon lotor	2	8
Bassariscus astutus	1	1
Mustelidae	—	1
Mephitis sp.	1	5
Canidae	—	3
Urocyon cinereoargenteus	4	6
Canis sp.	1	1
Artiodactyla		
Odocoileus sp.	9	110
Antilocapra/ Odocoileus	8	263
Bovidae	—	1
Bison sp.	1	1
Total	120	5,199

Source: Sobolik (1991).
Note: Includes fauna from distrubed areas.
[a]MNI = minimum number of individuals.
[b]NISP = number of identified specimens.

Another abundant faunal resource observed in the sites was rabbit—both jackrabbit (*Lepus* sp.) and cottontail (*Sylvilagus* sp.), with the latter recovered more frequently. Throughout the Archaic period in the southern portion of North America, hunters conducted rabbit drives and corralled rabbits into nets, where they were killed, often with rabbit sticks. Rabbits could also be killed singly with weapons (the atlatl or the bow and arrow) or with traps. Numerous rabbit bones from Lower Pecos sites have been burned and cut, and rabbit fur was used for blankets (Weir 1983).

Fish remains were also abundant, representing 18% of the faunal assemblage analyzed from Baker Cave (Table 17-3). The prevalence of fish remains in the sites indicates the importance of riverine resources to the diet of the Lower Pecos populations, as well as the importance of the three main rivers in the region in comparing the diet of the Lower Pecos population with that of the southern portion of the Chihuahuan Desert.

Deer was also an important resource for the Lower Pecos populations, not necessarily because of the high number of deer killed, but because of the large quantity of protein that one deer can provide in the diet. Deer remains are observed in all of the analyzed sites, although their frequency is low. Artiodactyl remains represent only 6% of the faunal remains from Baker Cave (Table 17-3), and Lord has stated that at Hinds Cave "large grazing and browsing animals were poorly represented within the faunal sample" (1984: 167).

Bison remains have been observed at sites in the Lower Pecos region (Dibble 1967; Lundelius 1984). The remains of long-extinct bison in the basal occupational levels of some sites suggest that big-game hunting may have been an important part of the economy during the Paleoindian period, as it was in the rest of North America. A brief wet interval has been documented at approximately 2500 B.P. in the region (Bryant and Holloway 1985); during that mesic resurgence there was a large-scale kill of modern bison at Bonfire Shelter (Dibble and Lorrain 1968), indicating that the climate was moist enough for bison to move south into the area. Even though bison remains have been recovered from Bonfire Shelter, and more than one kill is indicated (Dibble and Lorrain 1968), they are not prevalent in most Lower Pecos sites. The absence of a large number of bison remains at other sites indicates that they were probably anomalous and did not affect the diet of the population beyond the short-term increase in meat.

Insects

Insects are represented as whole specimens in site deposits and were also observed in the coprolite studies. Most of the insects in the coprolites were probably coprophagous, insects that invade feces when they are still wet. All of the insect remains observed in the Baker Cave coprolites were identified as beetle (Coleoptera) remains from the Ptinidae (spider beetle) and Carabidae (ground beetle) families. The order Coleoptera, especially the family Ptinidae, are known for their preference for burrowing and nesting in animal and plant debris (Spilman 1968). Fly (Diptera) larvae were also observed in coprolites from Hinds Cave (Reinhard et al. 1994; Stock 1983; Williams-Dean 1978) and Baker Cave (Sobolik 1988), and they do not reflect intentional ingestion. However, some of the insect remains may have been eaten as food items. Williams-Dean (1978) suggests that the remains of butterfly larvae (Lepidoptera), beetles (Coleoptera), a millipede (Myriopoda), and grasshoppers from the Hinds Cave coprolites were intentionally ingested.

Parasites

One hundred six coprolites from the Lower Pecos region have been analyzed for parasites. Williams-Dean (1978) analyzed 13 samples; Stock (1983) analyzed 7 samples; and Reinhard and associates (1994) analyzed 96 samples from Hinds Cave and Baker Cave. In those studies only one sample contained endoparasites, an *Enterobius vermicularis* (pinworm) egg from a Hinds Cave sample. This information indicates that the hunter-gatherers of the region were relatively free from endoparasites, a condition expected of most hunter-gatherer populations, as it has been observed that pinworm eggs are present in only 5% of the feces of infected people. If 5% of the analyzed coprolites had contained pinworm eggs, then the entire population would be considered to have been infected (Fry 1976a).

Human Skeletal Remains

Bioarchaeological analyses of the Lower Pecos Archaic period inhabitants have only recently been synthesized and summarized (Hartnady 1988; Powell 1991; Reinhard et al. 1989; Steele and Olive 1989; Turpin et al. 1986). Not all the approximately 148 recovered burials are included in the pathology discussions because only a small number were actually analyzed for pathology (Reinhard et al. 1989). Pathologies associated with the burials are summarized in Table 17-4, but only metabolic and dental disorders are discussed since they occur with sufficient frequency in the population and are more commonly related to nutrition.

A high frequency of Harris lines and enamel hypoplasias indicates that the individuals may have experienced moderate-to-severe nutritional stress. Enamel hypoplasia and Harris lines are growth arrest lines that occur either on the teeth (enamel hypoplasias) or mainly on long bones (Harris lines). Growth arrest lines occur when the growth of an individual has been interrupted, most likely as a result of nutritional deprivation, although infection and disease may also be causes. Growth arrest lines have been attributed to short-term nutritional stress, possibly due to weaning (Clarke and Gindhart 1981) or to seasonal nutritional deprivation (Martin et al. 1985).

Enamel hypoplasias are a strong indicator of weaning stress (Corrucini et al. 1985; Fink and Merbs 1991; Goodman et al. 1987) because their presence on permanent teeth indicates stress that occurred when the individual was an infant or a young child. Basing their inferences upon results of analyses of Seminole Sink remains, Marks and colleagues (1985) suggest that most of the individuals from the Lower Pecos region had enamel hypoplasia by 6–6.5 years of age.

Porotic hyperostosis is also present in Lower Pecos skeletal remains (4%), and Marks and colleagues (1985) observed that 10%–20% of the Seminole Sink

Table 17-4. *Known Pathologies from Lower Pecos Burials*

Pathology	Number of Samples	Percentage
Metabolic disease		
Enamel hypoplasia	6/7	86
Harris lines	1/2	50
Porotic hyperostosis	1/23	4
Cribra orbitalia	0/23	0
Dental disease		
Caries	11/22	50
Abscess	12/22	55
Antemortem tooth loss	19/22	86
Moderate/severe tooth wear	14/22	64
Infectious disease		
Periostitis	2/34	6
Osteomyelitis	0/34	0
Specific insult	0/34	0
Degenerative disease		
Vertebral osteoarthritis	1/17	6
Osteophytosis	6/17	35
Appendicular osteoarthritis	1/17	6
Accidental and aggressive trauma		
Accidental fracture	3/33	14
Parry fracture	0/12	0
Cranial fracture	1/22	5
Projectile wound	0/14	0

Source: Reinhard et al. (1989).
Note: Samples used: Coontail Spin (6 burials); Langtry Creek Burial Cave (6 burials); Conejo Shelter (1 burial); Mummy Shelter (1 burial); Seminole Sink (21 burials); 41 VV 1 (1 burial).

burials indicate porotic hyperostosis. These data suggest that a few people in the population experienced stress that produced porosities of the skull, possibly resulting from iron deficiency anemia or parasitism. The coprolite evidence, however, indicates that parasitism was rare in the Lower Pecos region and suggests that iron deficiency anemia or some other nutritional problem may have been the cause.

The main health problem experienced by the population was dental disease. Caries (50%), abscessing (55%), and antemortem tooth loss (86%) are extremely high, particularly as compared with other hunter-gatherer populations (Marks et al. 1985; Reinhard et al. 1989). This high rate of dental infection indicates that the people were eating a high-carbohydrate diet that caused tooth infection (caries), infection that progressed to gum disease (abscessing) and eventually led to antemortem tooth loss (Hartnady 1988). High-carbohydrate dietary items are succulent fibers, prickly pear fruits, mesquite, acorns, and pecans.

Moderate-to-severe tooth wear is also observed in high frequencies (64%), indicating that the Lower Pecos population ate dietary items that were extremely "hard" and that abraded the teeth. A large portion of the dietary array did contain hard items such as phytoliths and calcium-oxylate crystals from succulents and cacti, nut hulls, seeds, and bones. Coprolite studies indicate that those items were definitely ingested and that in many cases seeds and bones were chewed.

Nutritional Analysis

A healthful diet requires carbohydrates, protein, amino acids, fiber, fat, vitamins, minerals, and trace elements. These substances are directly converted into energy in order to maintain or rebuild body structures or are stored for later use. The nutritional content of the more important food items of the Lower Pecos populations are listed in Table 17-5 (complete tables and a discussion of the nutrients and nutritional analysis of the Lower Pecos diet can be found in Sobolik [1991:Tables 34–40]).

The nutritional analyses of the prominent dietary items (both botanical and faunal) observed in site matrices and coprolite samples indicate that the prehistoric populations had access to dietary nutrients in quantities sufficient for a healthy existence. The dietary staples, those dietary items observed with a high frequency in the sites—carbohydrates, fat, and protein—would provide a significant amount of energy to the diet. Those staples were the desert succulents (most significantly lecheguilla), prickly pear, acorns, mesquite pods, rabbits, fish, and deer. The Lower Pecos region also provided a large variety of supplementary, seasonal dietary items that were ingested by the prehistoric populations. Given the number and variety of dietary items, the population had access to the vitamins, minerals, trace elements, and amino acids necessary to the diet. The water content also provided a significant amount of electrolytes to the diet (Sobolik 1991:252).

Conclusions

The nutritional analysis of the Lower Pecos prehistoric diet indicates that the population had access to the nutrients necessary for a healthy existence. The energy-obtaining nutrients—carbohydrates, fat, and protein— were provided by dietary staples available year-round, including the desert succulents, prickly pear pads, rabbits, rodents, and deer. Trace elements, vitamins, and minerals were obtained from a large variety of supplementary, seasonal dietary items such as fruits, berries, nuts, flowers, and seeds.

Table 17-5. *Nutritional Content of Select Foods*

Food Item	Lipid (g)	Carbohydrate (g)	Protein (g)	Energy (kcal)
Agave[a]	1.1	70	5	310
bulb[a]	0.9	73	3	372
Yucca[a]	1.3	61.6	5.7	349
bulb[a]	1.1	85.7	2.6	363
Mesquite[a]	3.2	46.3	14.7	273
pods[a]	5.1	42.6	40.6	379
Acorns[a]	23.9	40.8	6.2	369
Acorns[a]	31.4	53.6	8.1	509
Prickly pear				
fruit[b]	0.5	9.6	0.7	41
fruit[a]	0.4	7.1	1.0	36
pad[a]	0.4	8.8	1.1	37
pad[c]	0.3	5.6	1.7	27
seeds[a]	17.2	—	16.6	—
seeds[c]	16.0	79.0	1.3	289
Onion[d]	Trace	8.5	0.9	35
Onion[e]	0.2	5.6	1.7	25
Mustard				
seeds[f]	28.8	34.9	24.9	469
Chenopod				
seeds[c]	3.6	33.1	19.1	195
Rabbit[d]	4.0	0	21.9	124
Rabbit[c]	8.0	0	20.4	159
Pigeon[g]	23.8	0	18.5	294
Pigeon[d]	13.2	0	27.8	230
Fish—trout[d]	3.0	0	15.5	89
catfish[h]	7.6	0	15.8	96

Sources: [a]Laferriere (1987); [b]Gebhardt et al. (1982); [c]Winkler (1982); [d]Paul and Southgate (1978); [e]Haytowitz and Matthews (1984); [f]Marsh et al. (1977); [g]Posati (1979); [h]Souci et al. (1981).

Note: Nutritional content evaluated per 100 g of edible portion.

The bioarchaeological data indicate that the population had a high-carbohydrate diet. Caries, abscessing, and antemortem tooth loss are prevalent and were most likely caused by the ingestion of a large quantity of botanical staples, mainly the leaf bases of the desert succulents, mesquite pods, and acorns, all of which have a high-carbohydrate content. The skeletal remains also indicate that the diet was extremely abrasive, contributing to the severe wear patterns observed on the teeth. A large portion of the diet contained abrasive material (i.e., prickly pear seeds, nut shells, bones, and oxylate and silicate crystals).

The skeletal remains also indicate that some members of the population suffered from stress that may have been nutritionally related. Harris lines and enamel hypoplasias are the most prominent of the stress indicators observed in the Lower Pecos samples. A variety of causes can produce such pathologies, but nutritional deficiencies may have contributed substantially to the problem. If the presence of Harris lines and enamel hypoplasias reflects nutritional stress, then the stress was either caused at the time of weaning and/or indicates a short-term seasonal deprivation. Seasonal deprivation would most likely have occurred in the winter months when a variety of dietary items were not available and the population had to rely on a few staples for sustenance. Those staples would not have provided all the nutrients necessary for a balanced diet, and nutritional stress would have occurred. With either seasonal or weaning nutritional stress, most if not all the population would have experienced the stress, and the skeletal remains would indicate as much. The high percentage of samples with enamel hypoplasia (86%) and Harris lines (50%) support this hypothesis.

This study revealed that the diet and nutrition of the prehistoric hunter-gatherers of the Lower Pecos region were relatively good throughout the approximately 10,000 years of occupation in the area. The nutritional quality of the dietary resources was sufficient to support normal growth and development if each member of the population had equal access to the resources year-round. Nutritional stress may have been present in the population, and that stress was most likely evident in the lean winter months when variety in the diet was lacking. Therefore, quantity—not quality—may have produced the nutritional stress.

Acknowledgments

I would like to thank Vaughn M. Bryant, Jr., D. Gentry Steele, and Harry J. Shafer for comments on all aspects of this research. Don S. Rice, Patrice Teltser, and three anonymous reviewers provided useful editorial comments. Stephen Bicknell drafted Figure 17-1. The research was funded in part by the National Science Foundation (BNS-9004064) and Sigma Xi.

References

Alexander, R. K.
1974   *The Archaeology of Conejo Shelter: A Study of Cultural Stability at an Archaic*

Rockshelter Site in Southwestern Texas. Unpublished Ph.D. dissertation, Department of Anthropology, University of Texas, Austin.

Andrews, P., and E. M. N. Evans
1983   Small Mammal Bone Accumulations Produced by Mammalian Carnivores. *Paleobiology* 9(3):289–307.

Bocek, B.
1986   Rodent Ecology and Burrowing Behavior: Predicted Effects on Archaeological Site Formation. *American Antiquity* 51:589–603.

Bryant, V. M., Jr.
1974   Prehistoric Diet in Southwest Texas: The Coprolite Evidence. *American Antiquity* 39:407–420.
1975   Pollen as an Indicator of Prehistoric Diets in Coahuila, Mexico. *Bulletin of the Texas Archeological Society* 46:87–106.

Bryant, V. M., Jr., and R. G. Holloway
1985   A Late-Quaternary Paleoenvironmental Record of Texas: An Overview of the Pollen Evidence. In *Pollen Records of Late-Quaternary North American Sediments*, edited by V. M. Bryant, Jr., and R. G. Holloway, pp. 39–70. American Association of Stratigraphic Palynologists Foundation, Dallas, Texas.

Clarke, S. K., and P. S. Gindhart
1981   Commonality in Peak Age of Early-Childhood Morbidity Across Cultures and Over Time. *Current Anthropology* 22:574–575.

Corrucini, R. S., J. S. Handler, and K. P. Jacobi
1985   Chronological Distribution of Enamel Hypoplasias and Weaning in a Caribbean Slave Population. *Human Biology* 57:699–711.

Dering, J. P.
1979   *Pollen and Plant Macrofossil Vegetation Record Recovered from Hinds Cave, Val Verde County, Texas.* Unpublished Master's thesis, Texas A&M University, College Station.

Dibble, D. S.
1967   *Excavations at Arenosa Shelter, 1965–66.* Texas Archeological Salvage Project. Submitted to National Park Service. Copies available from the Texas Archeological Salvage Project, University of Texas, Austin.

Dibble, D. S., and E. R. Lorrain
1968   *Survey and Test Excavations at Amistad Reservoir, 1964–1965.* Texas Archeological Salvage Project Survey Reports No. 3. University of Texas, Austin.

Edwards, S. K.
1990   *Investigations of Late Archaic Coprolites: Pollen and Macrofossil Remains from Hinds Cave (41VV456), Val Verde County, Texas.* Unpublished Master's thesis, Texas A&M University, College Station.

Fink, T. M., and C. F. Merbs
1991   Hohokam Paleonutrition and Paleopathology: A Search for Correlates. *The Kiva* 56:293–318.

Fry, G. F.
1976a   *Analysis of Prehistoric Coprolites from Utah.* Anthropology Papers No. 97. University of Utah, Salt Lake City.
1976b   Human Coprolites from Frightful Cave (CM 68) Coahuila, Mexico. Paper presented at the 40th Annual Meeting of the Society for American Archaeology.

Gebhardt, S. E., R. Cutrufelli, and R. H. Matthews
1982   *Composition of Foods: Fruits and Fruit Juices; Raw, Processed, Prepared.* Agriculture Handbook No. 8–9. United States Department of Agriculture, Washington, D.C.

Goodman, A. H., L. H. Allen, G. P. Hernandez, A. Amador, L. V. Arriola, A. Chavez, and G. H. Pelto
  1987   Age at Development of Enamel Hypoplasias in Mexican Children. *American Journal of Physical Anthropology* 72:7–19.
Hartnady, P. W.
  1988   *Premature Molar Tooth Loss in the Archaic Trans-Pecos Region of South Texas.* Unpublished Master's thesis, Department of Anthropology, University of Arkansas, Fayetteville.
Haytowitz, D. G., and R. H. Matthews
  1984   *Composition of Foods: Vegetables and Vegetable Products; Raw, Processed, Prepared.* Agriculture Handbook No. 8–11. United States Department of Agriculture, Washington, D.C.
Hester, T. R.
  1983   Late Paleo-Indian Occupations at Baker Cave, Southwestern Texas. *Bulletin of the Texas Archeological Society* 53:101–119.
  1986   Baker Cave: A Rich Archaeological Record. In *Ancient Texas: Rock Art and Lifeways along the Lower Pecos,* edited by H. J. Shafer, pp. 84–87. Texas Monthly Press, Austin.
  1988   Chronological Framework for Lower Pecos Prehistory. *Bulletin of the Texas Archeological Society* 59:53–64.
Hoffman, R., and C. Hays
  1987   The Eastern Wood Rat *(Neotoma floridana)* as a Taphonomic Factor in Archaeological Sites. *Journal of Archaeological Science* 14:325–337.
Huebner, J. A.
  1991   Cactus for Dinner, Again! An Isotopic Analysis of Late Archaic Diet in the Lower Pecos Region of Texas. In *Papers on Lower Pecos Prehistory,* edited by S. A. Turpin, pp. 175–190. Studies in Archeology No. 8. Texas Archeological Research Laboratory, University of Texas, Austin.
Jones, J. G., and V. M. Bryant, Jr.
  1992   Phytolith Taxonomy in Selected Species of Texas Cacti. In *Phytolith Systematics: Emerging Issues,* edited by G. Rapp and S. Mulholland, pp. 215–239. Plenum Press, New York.
Laferriere, J. E.
  1987   NUTRICOMP Database Program. Department of Botany, Washington State University, Pullman.
Lord, K. J.
  1984   *The Zooarchaeology of Hinds Cave (41 VV 456).* Unpublished Ph.D. dissertation, Department of Anthropology, University of Texas, Austin.
Lundelius, E. L.
  1984   A Late Pleistocene Mammalian Fauna from Cueva Quebrada, Val Verde County, Texas. *Carnegie Museum of Natural History Special Publication* 8:456–481.
Marks, M. K., J. C. Rose, and E. L. Buie
  1985   Bioarcheology of Seminole Sink. In *Seminole Sink: Excavation of a Vertical Shaft Tomb, Val Verde County, Texas,* edited by S. A. Turpin, pp. 99–152. Texas Archeological Survey Research Report No. 93. University of Texas, Austin.
Marsh, A. C., M. K. Moss, and E. W. Murphy
  1977   *Composition of Foods: Spices and Herbs; Raw, Processed, Prepared.* Agriculture Handbook No. 8–2. United States Department of Agriculture, Washington, D.C.
Martin, D. L., A. H. Goodman, and G. J. Armelagos
  1985   Skeletal Pathologies as Indicators of Quality and Quantity of Diet. In *The Analysis of Prehistoric Diets,* edited by R. I. Gilbert, Jr., and J. H. Mielke, pp. 227–

280. Academic Press, Orlando.

Paul, A. A., and D. A. T. Southgate
1978   *McCance and Widdowson's: The Composition of Foods.* 4th ed. MRC Special Report No. 297. Elsevier/North-Holland Biomedical Press, Lund, Sweden.

Posati, L. P.
1979   *Composition of Foods: Poultry Products; Raw, Processed, Prepared.* Agriculture Handbook No. 8–5. United States Department of Agriculture, Washington, D.C.

Powell, J. F.
1991   Human Skeletal Remains from Skyline Shelter (41VV930), Val Verde County, Texas. In *Papers on Lower Pecos Prehistory,* edited by S. A. Turpin, pp. 149–173. Studies in Archeology No. 8. Texas Archeological Research Laboratory, University of Texas, Austin.

Reinhard, K. J., J. G. Jones, and R. P. Barros
1994   A Bioarchaeological Survey of the Lower Pecos Region, Western Texas. In *Health and Disease in the Prehistoric Southwest II,* edited by S. Rhine and R. T. Steinbock. Maxwell Museum, University of New Mexico, Albuquerque, in press.

Reinhard, K. J., B. W. Olive, and D. G. Steele
1989   Bioarcheological Synthesis. In *From the Gulf to the Rio Grande: Human Adaptation in Central, South, and Lower Pecos Texas,* edited by T. R. Hester, S. L. Black, D. G. Steele, B. W. Olive, A. A. Fox, K. J. Reinhard, and L. Bement, pp. 93–114. Research Series No. 33. Arkansas Archeological Survey, Fayetteville.

Riskind, D. H.
1970   Pollen Analysis of Human Coprolites from Parida Cave. In *Archaeological Excavations at Parida Cave, Val Verde County, Texas,* edited by R. K. Alexander, pp. 89–101. Papers of the Texas Archeological Salvage Project No. 19. University of Texas, Austin.

Shafer, H. J.
1986   *Ancient Texans: Rock Art and Lifeways along the Lower Pecos.* Texas Monthly Press, Austin.
1988   The Prehistoric Legacy of the Lower Pecos Region of Texas. *Bulletin of the Texas Archeological Society* 59:23–52.

Shafer, H. J., and V. M. Bryant, Jr.
1977   *Archaeological and Botanical Studies at Hinds Cave, Val Verde, County, Texas.* Annual Report to the National Science Foundation.

Sobolik, K. D.
1988   *The Prehistoric Diet and Subsistence of the Lower Pecos Region, as Reflected in Coprolites from Baker Cave, Val Verde County, Texas.* Studies in Archeology No. 7. Texas Archeological Research Laboratory, University of Texas, Austin.
1991   *Paleonutrition of the Lower Pecos Region of the Chihuahuan Desert.* Unpublished Ph.D. dissertation, Department of Anthropology, Texas A&M University, College Station.
1993   Direct Evidence for the Importance of Small Animals to Prehistoric Diets: A Review of Coprolite Studies. *North American Archaeologist* 14(3):227–244.

Souci, S. W., W. Fachman, and H. Kraut
1981   *Food Composition and Nutritional Tables 1981/82.* Wissenschaftliche Verlagsgesellschaft, Stuttgart.

Spilman, T. J.
1968   Two New Species of Niptus from North American Caves (Coleoptera: Ptinidae). *The Southwestern Naturalist* 13(2):193–200.

Steele, D. G., and B. W. Olive
1989   Bioarcheology of Region 3 Study Area. In *From the Gulf to the Rio Grande:*

Human Adaptation in Central, South, and Lower Pecos Texas, by T. R. Hester, S. L. Black, D. G. Steele, B. W. Olive, A. A. Fox, K. J. Reinhard, and L. Bement, pp. 93–114. Research Series No. 33. Arkansas Archeological Survey, Fayetteville.

Stock, J. A.
  1983   *The Prehistoric Diet of Hinds Cave (41 VV 456), Val Verde County, Texas: The Coprolite Evidence.* Unpublished Master's thesis, Department of Anthropology, Texas A&M University, College Station.

Turpin, S. A., M. Hennenberg, and D. H. Riskind
  1986   Late Archaic Mortuary Practices of the Lower Pecos River Region, Southwest Texas. *Plains Anthropologist* 31:295–315.

Weir, G. H.
  1983   Analysis of Mammalian Hair and Plant Fibers in Cordage from a Texas Archaic Shelter. *Bulletin of the Texas Archeological Society* 53:131–149.

Williams-Dean, G. J.
  1978   *Ethnobotany and Cultural Ecology of Prehistoric Man in Southwest Texas.* Unpublished Ph.D. dissertation, Department of Anthropology, Texas A&M University, College Station.

Winkler, B. A.
  1982   *Wild Plant Foods of the Desert Gatherers of West Texas, New Mexico, and Northern Mexico: Some Nutritional Values.* Unpublished Master's thesis, Department of Anthropology, University of Texas, Austin.

18. Paleonutrition at Grasshopper Pueblo, Arizona

Joseph A. Ezzo

Abstract: Prehistoric diet and nutritional status at Grasshopper Pueblo, Arizona (A.D. 1275–1400), is considered in terms of bone chemistry data supplemented by pathological, paleobotanical, and faunal data. Changes in diet through time indicate greater dependence on maize and less on hunting and collected wild plant foods. While the diet in general was probably adequate in calories, and in most nutrients, the data suggest possible marginal intakes and perhaps deficiencies in calcium, iron, and protein. Dietary and nutritional stress most likely contributed to the abandonment of the site and the region circa A.D. 1400.

Introduction

This study considers the diet and nutritional status of a prehistoric Southwestern population in light of bone chemistry, paleobotanical, faunal, and, to a lesser extent, pathological data. Dietary change through time and access space at Grasshopper Pueblo have been inferred to be significant adaptations in the history of the pueblo. Nutritional aspects of such variability may contribute to our understanding of human adaptations at the site.

Grasshopper Pueblo is a fourteenth-century 500-room masonry pueblo site located on the Salt River drainage in the White Mountains of east-central Arizona at an altitude of 6,000 ft (1,829 m; Holbrook and Graves 1982; Longacre and Graves 1982). The site was the focus of excavation and field research of the University of Arizona Archaeological Field School from 1963 to 1992. The Grasshopper Plateau features both woodland and grassland communities. Upland stands of ponderosa pine *(Pinus ponderosa)*, pinyon *(Pinus edulis)*, and juniper *(Juniperus)* highlight the landscape (Longacre and Graves 1982). Grasslands and shrub communities are located in the valley bottoms (Longacre and Graves 1982), and most resemble the Plains Grassland Formation (Holbrook and Graves 1982:Table 2.1). The annual precipitation in the

Paleonutrition: The Diet and Health of Prehistoric Americans, edited by Kristin D. Sobolik. Center for Archaeological Investigations, Occasional Paper No. 22. © 1994 by the Board of Trustees, Southern Illinois University. All rights reserved. ISBN 0-88104-078-9.

region is approximately 20 in (475 cm); the rainy season occurs in July and August with additional moisture coming from winter snows (Longacre and Graves 1982). No data are available for length of growing seasons in the immediate vicinity of Grasshopper Pueblo, but climatological data for adjacent regions indicate an average of 120–130 frost-free days per year (Tuggle et al. 1984). At the time of occupation of the site the surrounding woodland was thicker than at present, although intensive human utilization of the forest did lead to a significant thinning during the pueblo's occupation (Holbrook 1982).

Soils in the Grasshopper region are generally poorly developed, with no Class I soils in evidence. Approximately 85% of the soils of Classes II–IV are located within a 3 mi (5 km) radius of Grasshopper Pueblo (Tuggle et al. 1984:Figure 1). Class II soils are alluvial material and include Lynx Loam (derived from sandstone) and Tours Silt Loam (derived from limestone, sandstone, and shale).

The site is characteristic of a period of population aggregation in the Transition Zone. Prior to the initial settling of the site occurring around A.D. 1275 (all dates based on tree-ring data), the settlement pattern of the Grasshopper region was one of scattered, small pueblos ranging in size from 5 to 21 rooms (Reid 1989). Aggregation occurred fairly rapidly as locals and newly arrived immigrants reorganized into large pueblos; by A.D. 1350, 10 sites in the Grasshopper region contained 80 or more rooms, and the region housed 1,800 pueblo rooms, compared to 200 rooms 75 years earlier (Reid and Tuggle 1988). During the 1320s, smaller, less accessible sites such as Canyon Creek Pueblo (Haury 1934) and Red Rock House were constructed as population reached a maximum, and niche-filling occurred as newly formed households budded off from the large pueblos and new immigrants to the area settled at smaller sites (Reid 1989). Maximum population was probably reached at Grasshopper Pueblo around A.D. 1330 at 600 to 700 individuals. Shortly thereafter the pueblo's population began to decline; the occupation of the site lasted until about A.D. 1400, when both site and region were abandoned (Dean and Robinson 1982; Graves 1991; Reid 1989). For purposes of discussing the dynamics of pueblo growth, aggregation, and decline, four stages of occupation have been delineated for Grasshopper Pueblo: the Establishment stage (1275–1300), the Aggregation stage (1300–1330), and the Dispersion-Abandonment stages (A.D. 1330–1400), which overlap in time (Reid 1989).

Grasshopper Pueblo consists of 3 major room blocks; 3 rectangular plazas (associated with each of the room blocks); 10 smaller, outlying blocks of rooms; and 15 smaller habitation units (Longacre and Graves 1982; Longacre and Reid 1974). The three primary room blocks (designated Room Blocks 1, 2, and 3) contain nearly 300 of the site's room spaces and consist of full-walled one- and two-story rooms (Figure 18-1); the range of tree-ring dates for each of them indicates initial construction at roughly the same time (the last quarter of the thirteenth century) and an occupation length spanning the entire period of occupation for the pueblo (Dean and Robinson 1982; Graves 1991). Rooms in the outliers tend to be low-walled structures, often containing only three walls; they date to the late stage of occupation and may have been occupied

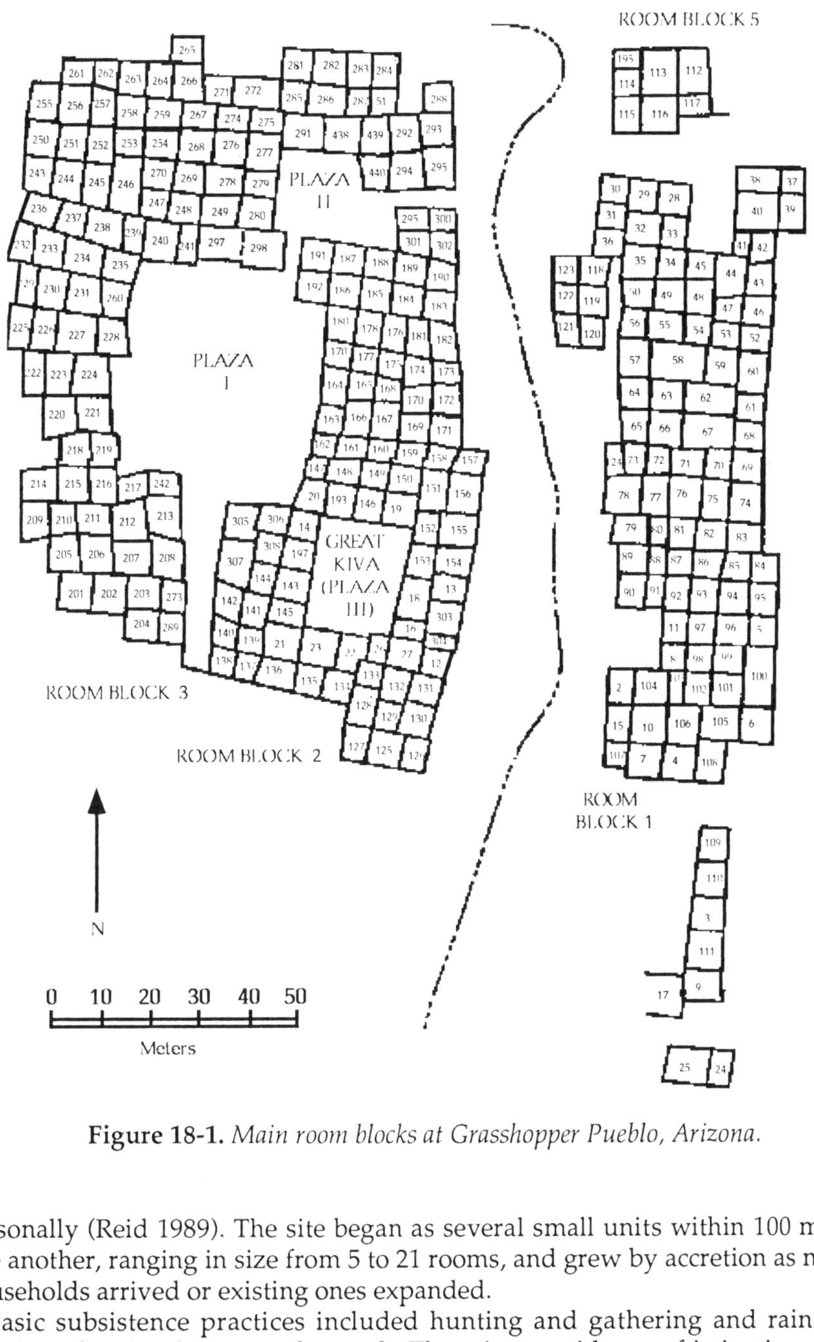

Figure 18-1. *Main room blocks at Grasshopper Pueblo, Arizona.*

seasonally (Reid 1989). The site began as several small units within 100 m of one another, ranging in size from 5 to 21 rooms, and grew by accretion as new households arrived or existing ones expanded.

Basic subsistence practices included hunting and gathering and rainfall farming of maize, beans, and squash. There is no evidence of irrigation and very little evidence of land modifications in order to increase agricultural productivity. According to Olsen (1990), mule deer *(Odocoileus hemionus)* was the most important hunted game, supplemented by rabbit, squirrel, and turkey. Wild plant foods included walnuts (more common in the early occupation of the site [McComas 1981]), pinyon nuts, juniper berries, manzanita, cholla, prickly pear, amaranth, tansy mustard, grapes, and sunflower (Bohrer 1982). Through time, hunting and gathering declined in importance, and cultigens, particularly maize, became increasingly significant in the diet (Table 18-1).

Distinctive social groups, possibly of different ethnic origins, have been identified at Grasshopper Pueblo on the basis of architecture, spatial distribution of decorated ceramics, cranial deformation, and diet (Birkby 1982; Ezzo 1991, 1992; Reid et al. 1989; Reid and Whittlesey 1982). Room Block 1 inhabitants, for example, relied more heavily on foraging, particularly wild plant food gathering, than did the inhabitants of Room Block 2 or 3. The ultimate abandonment of Grasshopper coincides with an overall depopulation of the Transition Zone in the early fifteen century (Reid 1989). The reasons are not wholly clear, but food stress appears to be in evidence at Grasshopper and was likely one cause of relocation to other regions.

The Database

Between 1963 and 1978 the field school excavated 674 individuals in 664 distinct burial loci; 231 individuals are of reproductive age or older. Age, sex, and burial location of individuals are presented in Tables 18-2 and 18-3. I sampled all but one (Burial 228, which consisted of cranial fragments only) in September 1990 and analyzed them for 11 elements (Al, Ba, Ca, Fe, K, Mg, Mn, Na, P, Sr, Zn) via ICP-AES as part of a dissertation project on dietary change and variability at Grasshopper Pueblo (Ezzo 1991). A subset ($n = 54$) was selected by stratified random sampling and analyzed for stable carbon isotope ratios via mass spectroscopy. The midshafts of long bones, primarily the femur, were sampled because cortical bone is less subject to diagenesis (postmortem chemical alteration) than trabecular bone (Grupe 1988; Price 1989; Sillen 1989).

The results of the elemental analysis are presented as ratios following Ezzo (1992). Barium (Ba) and strontium (Sr) were the only elements considered as potential paleodietary indicators (see Elias et al. [1982] and Storey [1961] for the physiological basis). The units of analysis for the elemental data are the ratios of strontium and barium to calcium (Sr/Ca and Ba/Ca; formula = Sr $(Ba)_{parts\ per\ million\ (ppm)}/Ca_{ppm} \times 1000$). The rationale for reanalyzing this data set using ratios derives from the fact that although the calcium values of H5 all fell within the 95% confidence level (Ezzo 1991:Appendix 5), the overall range was broader than the precision of the instrument. Thus, the elemental values for some samples are considered to be distorted as a result of analytical error. Using the ratios of strontium and barium to calcium normalizes the values. In addition, the ratio data can reduce the effects of some minor cases of diagenesis (for example, dual enrichment of calcium and strontium by carbonates). The presentation of the stable isotope data (Figures 18-2 and 18-3) utilizes a bivariate model developed by Krueger and Sullivan (1984).

The results of the analysis permitted a series of inferences (Ezzo 1991, 1992).

Table 18-1. *Ranking of Grasshopper Pueblo Food Resources*

First Order	Second Order	Third Order	Fourth Order
		Establishment-Aggregation Stages	
Maize	Beans, squash	Nuts, manzanita, mule deer, juniper berries, cholla, prickly pear	Amaranth, tansy mustard, grapes, sunflower, rabbit, turkey
		Dispersion-Abandonment Stages	
Maize	Beans (?), squash (?)	Manzanita, juniper berries	Mule deer, amaranth, prickly pear, cholla, grapes, sunflower, tansy mustard, rabbit, turkey

First, dietary change occurred through time at Grasshopper Pueblo, and dietary variability across space was evident. Second, while diets did not vary according to age or associations to grave goods of any sort, they did vary according to sex. During the Establishment-Aggregation stages, males tended to consume more meat and cultigens than did females, who in turn consumed greater amounts of wild plant foods (Figures 18-2 through 18-7). Most likely hunting was primarily a male activity, gathering a female activity and with both sexes participating in farming.

During the Dispersion-Abandonment stages, however, male and female diets become virtually indistinguishable on the whole; greater emphasis was placed on consumption of cultigens, particularly maize, and less on hunted and collected foods. The shift to a greater reliance on a C4 plant source (in this case, maize) is borne out quite clearly by the stable isotope data (Figures 18-2 and 18-3). Spatially it appears that the diets of Room Block 1 inhabitants contained more wild plant foods, while those of Room Block 2 and 3 inhabitants were more oriented toward agriculture. Despite the trend toward homogenization of diets in the Dispersion-Abandonment stages, there is still spatially discrete variability, as some household or kin groups apparently continued to supplement their diets with significant amounts of wild plant foods. That is particularly evident in the northeast corner of Room Block 1 and the southeast corner of Room Block 2 (Ezzo 1992:Figures 20 and 21).

Nutritional Status: Potential Nutrient Deficiencies

The diet of the Grasshopper inhabitants probably provided adequate caloric intake of the most part as well as adequate nutrient intake of

Table 18-2. *Age and Sex Distribution of Grasshopper Pueblo Adults*

	Males	Females	Indeterminant
Age Range			
14–20	10	14	3
20–29	21	35	—
30–39	24	36[a]	1
40–49	22	33	—
50+	6	16	—
Indeterminant	4	3	3
Total	87	137[a]	7

[a]Includes Burial 228.

vitamins, carbohydrates, fat, fiber, and all minerals with the exception of calcium and iron. In addition, adequate protein intakes, particularly late in the occupation once hunting had declined, may have been problematic. Adequate calcium intake is often a problem in areas where milk and milk products are not part of the diet. Maize, the Grasshopper staple, has virtually no calcium, which is why barium and strontium levels in maize-based diets ought to be significantly lower than in vegetable diets based on plants that are richer mineral sources. Beans, however, are potentially very good calcium sources, averaging better than 150 mg/100 g edible portion (Nutrition Monitoring Division 1986; Wolfe et al. 1985); amaranth has similar levels, and prickly pear, cholla, and walnuts are also good sources. However, the fact that well over 500 mg of calcium is needed in the diet daily, and that the absorption of calcium is reduced by phytates (which are abundant in maize, less so in beans [Thorn et al. 1983]), makes the task of consuming adequate calcium a problem in such diets. The major technological innovation that compensates for that inadequacy in the traditional American Southwest involves mixing maize with lime ash in various way to enhance its mineral content (Greenhouse 1981; Katz et al. 1974; Kuhnlein 1981; Kuhnlein and Calloway 1977, 1979; Kuhnlein et al. 1977; Wolfe et al. 1985). According to Kuhnlein (1981) and to Calloway and colleagues (1974), fine grinding of maize using limestone manos and metates can enhance calcium value more than tenfold, while preparing with lime ash can enhance the calcium content more than a hundredfold. From a bone chemistry standpoint, such processing would result in increased strontium and barium levels. Whether those practices occurred at Grasshopper Pueblo is impossible to say. Limestone is the dominant bedrock in the region. However, most of the Grasshopper grinding implements are of local quartzite, which contains virtually no calcium. Further, there is no evidence of the practice of making lime ash at the site, although the slab-lined hearths from a number of room floors may well have served that purpose. I hypothesize that calcium status is reflected somewhat in barium and

Table 18-3. *Location of Adult Burials by Sex*

Location	Males	Females	Total
Room Block 1	13	127[a]	240
Room Block 2	15	30[a]	45
Room Block 3	14	7	21
Outliers	1	7	8
Great Kiva (Plaza III)	11	16	27
Plaza I	8	4	12
Plaza II	2	7	9
Extramural	23	39	62
Total	87	137[a]	224

[a]Includes Burial 228.

strontium values of bones and that higher values would indicate more calcium in the diet. Those individuals with high barium and strontium are primarily women whom I have interpreted as having subsisted more substantially on wild plant food resources than others with lower barium and strontium values. Perhaps higher intakes of nuts, seeds, prickly pear, cholla, amaranth, and possibly cultivated beans on their part led to better calcium status.

Iron presents many of the same problems as calcium; fiber and phytates greatly reduce its absorption, and it is not found in maize. Again, major sources are meat, nuts, and beans. The source of iron in plants is nonheme, which is generally poorly absorbed. Certain nutrients, such as ascorbic acid and protein, tend to enhance iron absorption. The predominant form of iron in meat is heme, which is better absorbed than nonheme. Iron-deficiency anemia was probably a fairly common occurrence at Grasshopper, particularly among children and pregnant and lactating women. Pathological data at Grasshopper indicate that porotic hyperostosis and cribra orbitalia were prevalent in both the Establishment-Aggregation stages and the Dispersion-Abandonment stages at the site; both of them are symptomatic of iron-deficiency anemia (Berry 1983; Hinkes 1983). Mixing maize with lime ash does significantly improve the iron content of the resulting food (Greenhouse 1981; Kuhnlein 1981).

In terms of protein, Maize is most limiting in the amino acids tryptophan and lysine, and thus diets based on maize often result in marginal protein intake (Robson 1974). Arroyave (1975) reports a Biological Value of corn of 95% (complete protein sources have a value of $\geq$ 100%). To get an adequate amount of tryptophan (the more limiting of the two amino acids), one must either consume a food richer in tryptophan than maize along with the maize or eat proportionally more maize. For example, if one were to derive all of the daily protein required for an adult (about 60 g) from maize, the amount of maize needed to be consumed would be as follows:

$$(60/9.4 \text{ g})/(.92)(.95) \times 100 = 730 \text{ g/day (about 25.5 oz)}$$

where 9.4 is the number of grams of protein in 100 g of corn (Nutrition Monitoring Division 1989a), .92 is an estimate of efficiency of protein absorption (Steele and Harper 1990), and .95 is the Biological Value of corn. That amount of maize consumption would provide nearly 2,700 calories, or 100% of the daily energy needed for a reference 70-kg adult male. That is, of course, not a feasible dietary practice. The lack of minerals and the vitamin niacin in maize would quickly create severe nutrient deficiencies.

A far more successful means of utilizing protein from maize is to mix it with beans. The tryptophan and lysine levels in beans compensate for the low levels in maize, while the limiting amino acid in beans, methionine, is compensated for by adequate levels in maize. Thus, when consumed together, maize and beans form a complete protein. Bressani and colleagues (1962) modeled that relationship and found that optimum growth of rats occurred when the relative contribution of protein from maize:beans was 40:60, and optimum efficiency of protein utilization occurred when the two sources contributed equally. The latter situation results in a ratio of maize to beans of 72:28 by weight. Beans tend to be 20%–25% protein by weight (Nabhan et al. 1985; Nutrition Monitoring Division 1986; Wolfe et al. 1985). To obtain adequate protein from maize and beans, the following equation can be used:

$$(60 \text{ g})/(.72)(9.4 \text{ g})(.28)(22.5 \text{ g}) \times 100 = 460 \text{ g (16 oz)}$$
maize contribution = 331 g (11.6 oz)
beans contribution = 129 g (4.4 oz)

The caloric value of the mixture would be approximately 360 kcals/100 g, or 1,650 kcals for 460 g. Such a mixture of maize and beans would promote healthier eating habits than a more monotonous diet of maize. In addition to providing improvements in protein quality and energetic efficiency, beans are also a valuable source of fat, niacin, folacin, calcium, phosphorus, magnesium, and iron. Other good plant protein sources are nuts and seeds.

The richest source of protein in the Grasshopper diet, however, would have been meat. The amount of meat consumed is impossible to calculate, although the bone chemistry and carbon isotope ratio values suggest it constituted less than half the diet by weight. The data also indicate males had somewhat greater access to meat than females during the Establishment-Aggregation stages, and possibly throughout the site's occupation. Cooked deer and wild rabbit provide as much protein as beans on a weight basis, but they are complete protein sources. In energetic terms, however, they provided considerable less per weight unit (160–180 kcals/100 g [Nutrition Monitoring Division 1989b]). The reduction of meat consumption in the late period of occupation at Grasshopper Pueblo would have probably made the task of meeting protein needs, especially for children, quite difficult. For adults, consumption of adequate calories per day often provides enough protein in the diet so that deficiency is not a problem (Torun and Viteri 1988). Berry (1983) notes the increase of dental disease through time at Grasshopper, suggesting a decrease

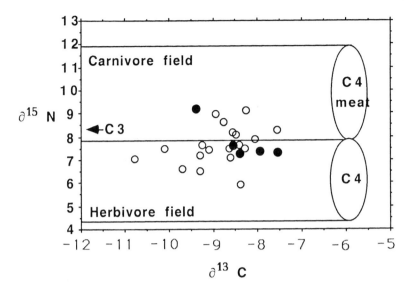

Figure 18-2. *Stable carbon and nitrogen isotope ratios for males: Establishment-Aggregation stages vs. Dispersion-Abandonment stages. Superimposed model is from Krueger and Sullivan (1984). For Figures 18-2 and 18-3, circles are individual isotopic ratios for the Establishment-Aggregation stages, dots for the Dispersion-Abandonment stages.*

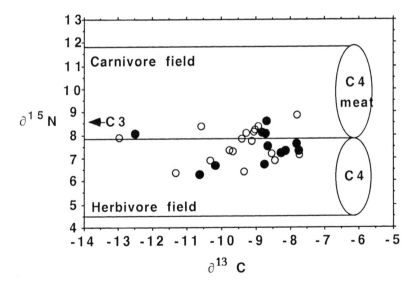

Figure 18-3. *Stable carbon and nitrogen isotope ratios for females: Establishment-Aggregation stages vs. Dispersion-Abandonment stages.*

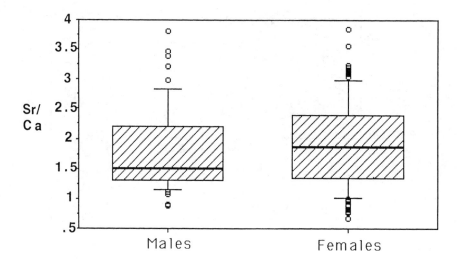

Figure 18-4. *Sr/Ca: Establishment-Aggregation stages, males vs. females. For Figures 18-4 through 18-7, broad lines represent mean; boxes include all values contained in 90th percentile; whiskers represent 2-sigma range; circles beyond whiskers are individual values that fall outside the 2-sigma range.*

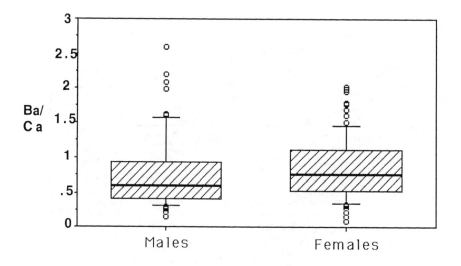

Figure 18-5. *Ba/Ca: Establishment-Aggregation stages, males vs. females.*

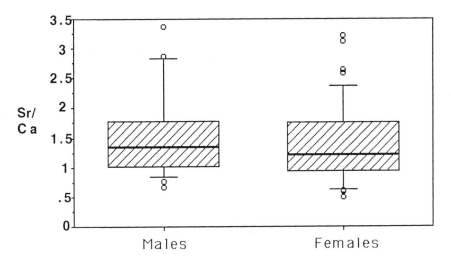

Figure 18-6. *Sr/Ca: Dispersion-Abandonment stages, males vs. females.*

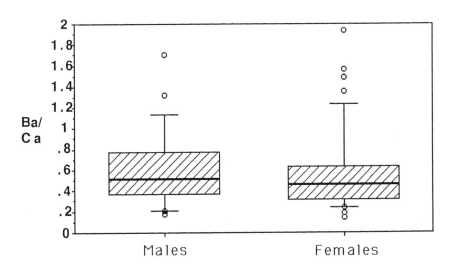

Figure 18-7. *Ba/Ca: Dispersion-Abandonment stages, males vs. females.*

in protein consumption and a concomitant increase in the consumption of starchy foods. For children protein is needed for the additional function of growth, and adequate caloric intake, particularly in a diet based on starch, can often be insufficient in protein, resulting in kwashiorkor (Naismith 1973). A decline in subadult health is supported by increased evidence of stress markers through time at the site (Hinkes 1983). It is therefore likely that if more reliance on maize and less on meat (and possibly beans as well) was the rule in the late period, the health of children would probably have been affected more adversely than adults.

Conclusions

The transition to an agricultural subsistence strategy based on a starchy staple functioned to restrict the number of food types consumed by Grasshopper Pueblo residents in the late period of occupation at the site. The potential nutritional problems discussed above would thus have been more acute in the last period. Coupled with an extended period of aridity after A.D. 1325 (Dean and Robinson 1982) and reduction of forest resources, they would have created considerable food stress that was buffered by increased mobility, caching of food in relatively inaccessible areas, reduction in household size, and, ultimately, migration out of the region (Ciolek-Torrello and Reid 1974; Ezzo 1991, 1992; Reid 1978).

I suggest that elemental and isotopic data, when combined with faunal, paleobotanical, and pathological data, allow insights into prehistoric diets that cannot otherwise be obtained. Furthermore, the bone chemistry data may also provide additional information on nutritional status, particularly in the case of the overall calcium status of a population. That possibility underscores the potential importance of integrating bone chemistry analysis into the research protocol on human burials, particularly regarding issues such as diet and health in antiquity.

References

Arroyave, G.
   1975   Amino Acid Requirement and Age. In *Protein-Calorie Malnutrition*, edited by R. L. Olson, pp. 1–18. Academic Press, New York.
Berry, D. R.
   1983   *Disease and Climatological Relationship among Pueblo III–Pueblo IV Anasazi of the Colorado Plateau.* Unpublished Ph.D. dissertation, Department of Anthropology, University of California, Los Angeles.
Birkby, W. H.
   1982   Biosocial Interpretations from Cranial Nonmetric Traits of Grasshopper Pueblo Skeletal Remains. In *Multidisciplinary Research at Grasshopper Pueblo, Arizona*, edited by W. A. Longacre, S. J. Holbrook, and M. W. Graves, pp. 36–41. Anthropological Papers No. 40. University of Arizona, Tucson.
Bohrer, V. L.
   1982   Plant Remains from Rooms at Grasshopper Pueblo. In *Multidisciplinary*

Research at Grasshopper Pueblo, Arizona, edited by W. A. Longacre, S. J. Holbrook, and M. W. Graves, pp. 97–105. Anthropological Papers No. 40. University of Arizona, Tucson.

Bressani, R., A. T. Valiente, and C. E. Tejada
1962   All-Vegetable Protein Mixtures for Human Feeding VI: The Value of Combination of Lime-treated Corn and Cooked Black Beans. *Journal of Food Science* 27:394–400.

Calloway, D. H., R. D. Giauque, and F. M. Costa
1974   The Superior Mineral Content of Some American Indian Foods in Comparison to Federally Donated Counterpart Commodities. *Ecology of Food and Nutrition* 3:203–211.

Ciolek-Torrello, R. S., and J. J. Reid
1974   Changes in Household Size at Grasshopper. *The Kiva* 40:39–47.

Dean, J. S., and W. J. Robinson
1982   Dendrochronology of Grasshopper Pueblo. In *Multidisciplinary Research at Grasshopper Pueblo, Arizona,* edited by W. A. Longacre, S. J. Holbrook, and M. W. Graves, pp. 46–60. Anthropological Papers No. 40. University of Arizona, Tucson.

Elias, R. W., Y. Hirao, and C. C. Patterson
1982   The Circumvention of the Natural Biopurification of Calcium Nutrient Pathways by Atmospheric Inputs of Industrial Lead. *Geochimica et Cosmochimica Acta* 46:2561–2580.

Ezzo, J. A.
1991   *Dietary Change at Grasshopper Pueblo, Arizona: The Evidence from Bone Chemistry Analysis.* Unpublished Ph. D. dissertation, Department of Anthropology, University of Wisconsin, Madison.
1992   Dietary Change and Variability at Grasshopper Pueblo, Arizona. *Journal of Anthropological Archaeology* 11:219–289.

Graves, M. W.
1991   Estimating Ring Loss on Tree-ring Specimens from East-Central Arizona: Implications for Prehistoric Pueblo Growth at Grasshopper Ruin. *Journal of Quantitative Anthropology* 3:83–115.

Greenhouse, R.
1981   Preparation Effects on Iron and Calcium in Traditional Pima Foods. *Ecology of Food and Nutrition* 10:221–225.

Grupe, G.
1988   Impact of the Choice of Bone Samples on Trace Element Data in Excavated Human Skeletons. *Journal of Archaeological Science* 15:123–129.

Haury, E. W.
1934   The Canyon Creek Ruin and Cliffdwellings of the Sierra Ancha. *Medallion Papers* No. 14. Gila Pueblo, Globe, New Mexico.

Hinkes, M. J.
1983   *Skeletal Evidence of Stress in Subadults: Trying to Come of Age at Grasshopper Pueblo.* Unpublished Ph. D. dissertation, Department of Anthropology, University of Arizona, Tucson.

Holbrook, S. J.
1982   The Prehistoric Local Environment of Grasshopper Pueblo, Arizona. *Journal of Field Archaeology* 9:207–215.

Holbrook, S. J., and M. W. Graves
1982   Modern Environment of the Grasshopper Region. In *Multidisciplinary*

Research at Grasshopper Pueblo, Arizona, edited by W. A. Longacre, S. J. Holbrook, and M. W. Graves, pp. 5–11. Anthropological Papers No. 40. University of Arizona, Tucson.

Katz, S. H., M. L. Hediger, and L. A. Valleroy
 1974   Traditional Maize Processing in the New World. *Science* 184:765–773.

Krueger, H. W., and C. H. Sullivan
 1984   Models for Carbon Isotope Fractionation Between Diet and Bone. In *Stable Isotopes in Nutrition,* edited by J. R. Turnland and P. E. Johnson, pp. 205–220. American Chemical Society, Washington, D.C.

Kuhnlein, H. V.
 1981   Dietary Mineral Ecology of the Hopi. *Journal of Ethnobiology* 1:84–94.

Kuhnlein, H. V., and D. H. Calloway
 1977   Contemporary Hopi Food Intake Patterns. *Ecology of Food and Nutrition* 6:159–173.
 1979   Adventitious Mineral Elements in Hopi Indian Diets. *Journal of Food Science* 44:282–285.

Kuhnlein, H. V., R. D. Calloway, and D. H. Calloway
 1977   Minerals in Human Teeth: Differences Between Preindustrial and Contemporary Hopi Indians. *American Journal of Clinical Nutrition* 30:863–866.

Longacre, W. A., and M. W. Graves
 1982   Multidisciplinary Studies at Grasshopper Pueblo. In *Multidisciplinary Research at Grasshopper Pueblo, Arizona,* edited by W. A. Longacre, S. J. Holbrook, and M. W. Graves, pp. 1–4. Anthropological Papers No. 40. University of Arizona, Tucson.

Longacre, W. A., and J. J. Reid
 1974   The University of Arizona Archaeological Fieldschool at Grasshopper: Eleven Years of Multidisciplinary Research and Teaching. *The Kiva* 40:3–38.

McComas, M.
 1981   Archaeobotany at Grasshopper Pueblo. Paper presented at the 46th Annual Meeting of the Society for American Archaeology, San Diego.

Nabhan, G. P., C. W. Weber, and J. W. Berry
 1985   Variations in Composition of Hopi Indian Beans. *Ecology of Food and Nutrition* 16:135–152.

Naismith, D. J.
 1973   Kwahiorkor in Western Nigeria: A Study of Traditional Weaning Foods, with Particular Reference to Energy and Linoleic Acid. *British Journal of Nutrition* 30:657–665.

Nutrition Monitoring Division
 1986   *Composition of Foods: Legumes and Legume Products.* United States Department of Agriculture, Washington, D.C.
 1989a *Composition of Foods: Cereal Grains and Pasta.* United States Department of Agriculture, Washington, D.C.
 1989b *Composition of Foods: Lamb, Veal, and Game Products.* United States Department of Agriculture, Washington, D.C.

Olsen, J. W.
 1990   *Vertebrate Faunal Remains from Grasshopper Pueblo, Arizona.* Anthropological Papers No. 75. Museum of Anthropology, University of Michigan, Ann Arbor.

Price, T. D.
 1989   Multielement Studies of Diagenesis in Prehistoric Bone. In *The Chemistry of Prehistoric Human Bone,* edited by T. D. Price, pp. 126–154. Cambridge SAR, Cambridge.

Reid, J. J.
  1978   Response to Stress at Grasshopper Pueblo, Arizona. In *Discovering Past Behavior: Experiments in the Archaeology of the American Southwest*, edited by P. Grebinger, pp. 195–228. Gordon and Breach, New York.
  1989   A Grasshopper Perspective on the Mogollon of the Arizona Mountains. In *Dynamics of Southwestern Prehistory*, edited by L. S. Cordell and G. J. Gumerman, pp. 65–98. School of American Research Advanced Seminar. Smithsonian Institution, Washington, D.C.
Reid, J. J., M. B. Schiffer, S. M. Whittlesey, M. J. Hinkes, A. P. Sullivan III, C. E. Downum, W. A. Longacre, and H. D. Tuggle
  1989   Perception and Interpretation in Contemporary Southwestern Archaeology: Comments on Cordell, Upham, and Brock. *American Antiquity* 54:802–814.
Reid, J. J., and H. D. Tuggle
  1988   Settlement Pattern and System in the Late Prehistory of the Grasshopper Region, Arizona. Paper presented at the conference "From Pueblo to Apache: The People of the White Mountains," Grasshopper, Arizona.
Reid, J. J., and S. M. Whittlesey
  1982   Households at Grasshopper Pueblo. *American Behavioral Scientist* 25:687–703.
Robson, J. R. K.
  1974   The Ecology of Malnutrition in a Rural Community in Tanzania. *Ecology of Food and Nutrition* 3:61–72.
Sillen, A.
  1989   Diagenesis of the Inorganic Phase of Cortical Bone. In *The Chemistry of Prehistoric Human Bone*, edited by T. D. Price, pp. 211–229. Cambridge SAR, Cambridge.
Steele, R. D., and A. E. Harper
  1990   Proteins and Amino Acids. In *Present Knowledge in Nutrition* (5th ed.), edited by M. L. Brown, pp. 67–79. International Life Science Institute, Washington, D.C.
Storey, E.
  1961   Strontium "Rickets": Bone, Calcium, and Strontium Changes. *Australian Annals of Medicine* 10:213–222.
Thorn, K. A., A. M. Tinsley, C. W. Weber, and J. W. Berry
  1983   Antinutritional Factors in Legumes of the Sonoran Desert. *Ecology of Food and Nutrition* 13:251–256.
Torun, B., and F. E. Viteri
  1988   Protein-Energy Malnutrition. In *Modern Nutrition in Health and Disease* (7th ed.), edited by M. E. Shils and V. R. Young, pp. 746–773. Lea and Febiger, Philadelphia.
Tuggle, H. D., J. J. Reid, and R. C. Cole
  1984   Fourteenth Century Mogollon Agriculture in the Grasshopper Region of Arizona. In *Prehistoric Agricultural Strategies in the Southwest*, edited by S. K. Fish and P. R. Fish, pp. 101–110. Anthropological Research Papers No. 33. Arizona State University, Tempe.
Wolfe, W. S., C. W. Weber, and K. D. Arviso
  1985   Use and Nutrient Composition of Traditional Navajo Foods. *Ecology of Food and Nutrition* 17:323–344.

19. | Food, Diet, and Population at Arroyo Hondo Pueblo

Wilma Wetterstrom

Abstract: Arroyo Hondo Pueblo, a fourteenth-century community located near Santa Fe, New Mexico, had a population of 400 to 600 people through much of its 125-year life span. Its food base, estimated from archaeological, ecological, and ethnographic data, was marginal at best. As a result of frequent droughts the community probably suffered from periodic food shortages, especially during the drought of 1335–1345. During extended droughts, infants and young children, the most vulnerable members of the population, would have died from malnutrition and infectious diseases at especially high rates. Those losses could have had a dramatic impact on the population's demographic patterns, as estimated from hypothetical populations. As the cohort born during severe droughts reached maturity, there would have been relatively fewer adults and a higher ratio of dependents to producers, with important consequences for the functioning of the community. The shortage of adults may have prompted the community to follow more flexible forms of social organization and to develop more productive methods of farming.

Introduction

We often hear the expression "You are what you eat." If this metaphor applies to the individual, can it apply to an entire society? Does a society over a long period reflect the quality of its food supplies? There is good evidence to suggest a link between diet and demography (Buikstra and Mielke 1985:361) but not many archaeological examples. Arroyo Hondo Pueblo, the subject of a major excavation by the School of American Research, offered an opportunity to look at such relationships in a prehistoric community.

Arroyo Hondo Pueblo was established near Santa Fe, New Mexico, about

Paleonutrition: The Diet and Health of Prehistoric Americans, edited by Kristin D. Sobolik. Center for Archaeological Investigations, Occasional Paper No. 22. © 1994 by the Board of Trustees, Southern Illinois University. All rights reserved. ISBN 0-88104-078-9.

A.D. 1300 toward the end of a period of Pueblo expansion in the Northern Rio Grande region. Arroyo Hondo's settlers initially enjoyed moist conditions, which had encouraged Puebloan expansion, but the rains began to diminish in the 1330s. For the rest of the century the inhabitants who remained at Arroyo Hondo endured a roller coaster climate—dry spells relieved by occasional brief moist periods. Finally severe drought struck much of the Southwest early in the fifteenth century, forcing Arroyo Hondo Pueblo and other communities in marginal locations to retreat to major watercourses.

Located where agriculture was barely feasible under even the best conditions, the people of Arroyo Hondo Pueblo must have suffered deprivation and hardship for nearly a century once the moist phase ended. In this study I try to assess the pueblo's food resources, how they were affected during dry phases, how the resulting diet in turn affected nutritional status and death rates, and finally how demographic patterns were altered. Lacking direct evidence bearing on those issues, I used an indirect method employing a variety of ecological and ethnographic data, combined with boundary calculations, model, and inference. The picture that emerges from the analysis is of a pueblo beset by infectious disease and malnutrition suffering large losses of young children during drought periods. Those losses in turn plagued the demographic patterns for at least 30 years, with important implications for the functioning of the community. Archaeological data from Arroyo Hondo Pueblo unfortunately are too scant to verify that reconstruction. Nonetheless it offers insights into how climate, diet, and demography might have been linked in the past.

Arroyo Hondo Pueblo: Ecological Setting and History

Arroyo Hondo Pueblo sits on a high plateau overlooking the deep Arroyo Hondo canyon, near a perennial spring. The narrow canyon offered relatively fertile and well-watered soils, while the piedmont above could have been dry-farmed when precipitation was above the mean. The pueblo is located in a pinyon-juniper woodland that is closely bounded by the adjacent vegetational zones of a ponderosa-pine forest to the east and a short grass plain to the west. Both zones offered a variety of wild plant resources and game that were an important part of the diet.

The climate, documented in remarkable detail by Rose, Dean and Robinson's (1981) dendroclimatological study, was never exceptionally lush. Mean annual rainfall for the period A.D. 985 to 1970 was only 338.8 mm with a standard deviation of 54.9 mm. The variation is small in absolute terms but highly significant since average rainfall is so low that a difference of literally a few inches stands between a good crop and barren fields.

During Arroyo Hondo Pueblo's first 30 years, which Rose and colleagues (1981) identified as a moist phase, the community expanded rapidly. By 1330 it reached its maximum size, 1000 rooms, although not all of them were in use at that time. With the onset of drought in 1335 the pueblo began a decline. A small population inhabited the village until 1370 when the community saw some new growth. After 1410 the pueblo once again went into decline and by 1425 it was totally abandoned never to be reoccupied (Schwartz 1986:xv, xvii).

I have estimated that the population was probably somewhere between 400 and 600 people during the early years. After that it never exceeded 400 and may have varied between 200 and 300. The estimates, which are explained in detail elsewhere (Wetterstrom 1986:42–46), are based on architectural evidence from the site, ethnographic data on Pueblo household size, and the carrying capacity of the region.

Food Resources at Arroyo Hondo

My goal in estimating Arroyo Hondo's food resources was to determine how much food the pueblo might reasonably have produced. Under favorable conditions were food supplies abundant or merely adequate? My estimates suggest that even during good times the pueblo lived on the edge with meager surpluses (Table 19-1). The steps involved in estimating Arroyo Hondo's food resources are briefly explained below, although in the interests of space much of the detail is omitted (consult Wetterstrom [1986:46–86] for a full account).

Following a well-trodden path in archaeology, I began by first assembling a list of the pueblo's food resources from archaeological data: pollen, fauna, and macroflora (Bohrer 1986; Lang and Harris 1984; Wetterstrom 1986). Since the roster of preserved remains is never a complete inventory of diet and may also include nonfood items, I modified the list in light of ethnographic data from the historic Pueblos of the Rio Grande.

For the next step, determining how much food could have been produced at Arroyo Hondo, I turned to ecological data, boundary calculations, and guesswork. The single most important component in the estimate is the maize (*Zea mays*) crop because as Arroyo Hondo's staple food, it would have contributed the bulk of the diet. Throughout the world people in traditional societies usually derive 70% to 80% of their calories from starchy staples (Gaulin and Konner 1977:48–51). In the Southwest the residents of San Juan Pueblo depended on grain crops for over 70% of their diet at the turn of the century (Ford 1968:158).

The first step in estimating maize crops was calculating the amount of land the Arroyo Hondoans might have cultivated. New Mexico Soil Conservation Service maps show the distribution of various soils in the Arroyo Hondo area. Vita-Finzi and Higgs (1970; Higgs and Vita-Finzi 1972:31–32) offer clues as to how much of the lands might have been cultivated. On the basis of ethnographic data, they concluded that the maximum distance farmers go to their fields is 5 km, but they rarely walk any more than 3 or 4 km. Moreover, farmers use the land within 1 km of their homes most intensively, with use declining as distance increases. Following Vita-Finzi and Higgs's (1970; Higgs 1975; Higgs and Vita-Finzi 1972) procedures for "site catchment analysis," I drew a series of concentric circles on a map at distances of 1, 2, 3, and 4 km from Arroyo Hondo Pueblo, adjusting the circles to take into account features in the

Table 19-1. *Summary of the Estimated Harvests of Arroyo Hondo Pueblo's Food Resources*

Food		Percentage
Common Name	Latin Name	
Maize	*Zea mays*	50–70 (average year)
		75–100 (wet year)
Bean	*Phaseolus vulgaris*	0.9–3.3 (average year)
		1.4–1.7 (wet year)
Weed seed	*Amaranthus* sp.	2.5–15.0 (weed seed collective total)
	Chenopodium sp.	
	Cleome sp.	
	Cycloloma sp.	
	Physalis sp.	
	Portulaca oleraceae	
Pinyon nut	*Pinus edulis*	5.0–15.0
Prickly pear	*Opuntia* spp.	0.4–6.6
Yucca fruit	*Yucca baccata*	1.0–13.6
Deer	*Odocoileus hemionus*	10.0
Turkey	*Meleagris gallopavo*	
	merriami	1.0
Rabbit	*Sylvilagus audoboni*	1.1–1.5
	Lepus californicus	
	texianus	0.5
Antelope	*Antilocapra*	
	americana	1.1–1.5
Total		71.8 (average year with lowest yields)
		137.9 (wet year with highest yields)

Note: Estimates are expressed as a percentage of the total annual caloric requirement for a population of 400 people.

landscape that would affect travel time (Wetterstrom 1986:Figure 2). Using soil maps that Kelley (1980:49–55) prepared for the Arroyo Hondo area, I then determined the acreage of arable land within the canyon and on the piedmont at a distance of 1 to 4 km from the pueblo.

As a next step in assessing Arroyo Hondo's foods, I calculated the maize crops that would have been raised on those lands within each of the zones, using yield figures of 500, 600, and 700 kg per hectare, which are based on ethnographic and experimental data. San Juan Pueblo at the turn of the century raised an average of 667 kg of maize per hectare in irrigated fields (Ford 1968:156). On the Rio Grande, near Albuquerque, chapalote corn, similar to the variety raised at Arroyo Hondo, yielded the equivalent of 750 kg per hectare in a small experimental plot (Wetterstrom 1986:47). Arroyo Hondo's yields were almost certainly lower than these figures since the growing season was shorter, the temperatures were cooler, the soils poorer, and water supplies probably less ample.

To relate the maize crops to the pueblo's food needs, the values for each of the zones were then converted to calories and drawn as bar graphs with cumulative values for 1 to 4 km from the pueblo marked on the bars (Figure 19-1). The group of bars on the left shows combined totals for canyon and piedmont, which could have been produced only during exceptionally moist years. The bars on the right give caloric totals for canyon lands, which were probably the only soils cultivated during periods of poor or average rainfall.

The dashed lines drawn horizontally across the figure represent estimated annual caloric needs for populations of from 200 to 800 people. Lines representing 75% of the total annual caloric requirement are also shown. The energy requirement was estimated to be 2,000 calories per person per day, a figure based on Food and Agriculture Organization and World Health Organization (1973) formulas for populations in developing nations (Wetterstrom 1986:Appendix A).

The bar graphs suggest that there was adequate land for 600 or possibly even 800 people when both canyon and piedmont soils were farmed. But in light of the fact that some of the land must have been left fallow, soils were not sufficient for more than 400 to 600 people, unless Arroyo Hondoans cultivated fields far from the pueblo.

How much land Arroyo Hondoans actually cultivated is a matter of inference and guesswork. Ethnographic data offer some clues. Pueblos in the early twentieth century farmed an average of 0.4 to 0.7 hectare per person (Ford 1968:156; Lange 1968:11, 438). But they may have cultivated more than prehistoric farmers since they also raised various Old World crops along with their traditional foods. If Arroyo Hondoans tilled less than did historic Pueblos, say 0.3 hectare per person, the harvests probably would have been adequate, representing from between 75% to more than 100% of the annual caloric requirement. For small populations adequate lands for that level of cultivation could have been found in the canyon and on the piedmont. For example, a community of 400 raising 0.3 hectare per person would have cultivated 120 hectares, which encompasses nearly all the arable land on the piedmont and canyon up to 2 km from the pueblo, with enough additional land within a reasonable distance to allow for fallowing. A community of 600 would have cultivated 180 hectares, which would require slightly less than all the arable land within 3 km of the pueblo and still leave soils for fallowing within walking distance.

Within reach of the pueblo during moist phases, there was adequate land to produce a substantial share of the diet, but Arroyo Hondo's maize stores probably never held much surplus. The maize stocks would have dwindled after seed corn was set aside and storage losses took their toll. Even the people of San Juan Pueblo, living on the Rio Grande River where water was ample and the growing season longer, never succeeded in raising any more than a month's surplus despite their stated goal of storing a two-year food supply (Ford 1968:161–162).

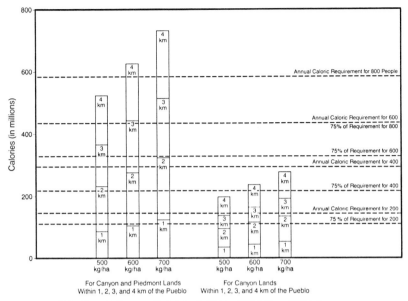

Figure 19-1. *Food needs of Arroyo Hondo Pueblo compared with estimated maize yields.*

Food stores would have been even less adequate during periods of average rainfall or drought. There was an overwhelming disparity between moist and dry phases, with the tillable acreage drastically reduced to the narrow canyon when rainfall was at or below the mean. Only a small population of 400 or fewer could have found adequate land in the canyon to support themselves. With a yield of 600 kg per hectare, the crops grown in the canyon within 4 km of the pueblo would have totaled slightly more than 75% of the annual caloric requirement for 400 people, before seed corn and storage losses were taken into account. But with that much land under cultivation, there would have been little land for fallowing without going down the canyon some distance. Larger groups would have found themselves pushing farther and farther away from the village in search of farmland. The larger the community, the more vulnerable and precarious it would have been during periods of average or below-average precipitation.

Beans *(Phaseolus vulgaris)* and squash *(Cucurbita pepo)* supplemented maize, but their contributions were probably small and would not have significantly improved the pueblo's lot during dry periods. The squash, a warm-weather plant highly sensitive to cold (Harrington and Minges 1954:146), would not have grown well because of late spring frost. Bean crops were probably small as well if the ethnographic evidence is any guide. Historic Pueblos, who all regarded beans as an important food, raised few; the harvests amounted to only 2% to 5% of the maize crop by weight (Ford 1968:158; Lange 1968:438; White 1962:106). If Arroyo Hondoans raised comparable amounts, beans would have contributed 0.9% to 4.7% of the diet, a small caloric contribution but an important source of protein.

Some 16 different species of wild plants also supplemented the Arroyo Hondo diet. It was impossible to calculate those resources with any precision, but I tried to at least estimate the potential range of available wild plant foods. To what extent could the wild plants supplement the staple? I used the same basic procedure in estimating most of the wild plant foods: yield figures came from published ecological data or harvesting trials. I then estimated how much was available to Arroyo Hondo Pueblo, taking into account these factors: acreage of land left uncultivated and neighboring pueblos to the north and south that would have restricted the size of collecting territories. That estimate was followed by an estimate of how large an area might have been combed and how much time Arroyo Hondoans might have spent gathering. The combined total of these estimates, expressed as a percentage of the pueblo's annual caloric requirement, ranges from about 9% to 50% of the caloric needs for a population of 400 (Table 19-1). The high figure could probably have been achieved only under exceptional conditions during moist years with Arroyo Hondoans foraging intensively. More likely the harvests were closer to the lower estimate. Neither the yield nor density of those plants would have been great enough in that semiarid region to provide a significant share of the diet for 400 villagers. After all, foragers are able to support themselves in comparable environments following two strategies not available to Arroyo Hondoans: low population density and mobility (Lee 1968).

Most of the meat in the Arroyo Hondoans' diet came from mule deer (*Odocoileus hemionus*) with hares (*Lepus californicus texianus*), rabbits (*Sylvilagus audobonii*), and turkeys (*Meleagrus gallopavo merriami*) providing a small but reliable contribution. A variety of small animals, such as the ground squirrel, were also exploited. The annual "harvests" of meat were estimated using data on game densities and seasonal population changes along with ethnographic accounts of hunting patterns. It was assumed that Arroyo Hondo hunters culled only a portion of a game population's "excess individuals," that is, the proportion of the population most likely to die within the course of a year. Mule deer, the largest source of meat, was estimated to contribute from 7% to over 10% of the diet for a community of 400. Antelope contributed a meager 1% because it ranged widely and was difficult to hunt. Turkeys, hares, and rabbits probably contributed less than 2% of the diet.

The sum of all these food estimates, about 70% to 140% of caloric needs, may be off the mark, given that they are based on numerous assumptions and little hard data. But if they have underestimated the food resources, they probably are not far below the actual totals. The largest share of the estimate, the maize crop, is based on the most reliable data, including yields, distribution of arable soils, and limitations on nonmechanized farming. Large quantities of food could not have been coaxed from the environment, even under exceptional conditions. The Arroyo Hondoans, like the people of San Juan Pueblo, probably produced no more than a month's surplus of food, if even that. They would not have been well cushioned for dry periods or other natural calamities.

Major Food Shortages

The real difficulties started about 1335 for Arroyo Hondo when the rains began to fail. Initially the harvests on the piedmont would have been poor. After repeated crop failures, Arroyo Hondoans would have been forced to abandon those fields altogether and plant all their crops in the narrow canyon. There they probably saw crop yields decline as the water table, springs, and headwaters all dwindled. Arroyo Hondoans may have tried to compensate by collecting more intensively, but their efforts may not have been well rewarded. Over the course of several years, the entire area would have gradually become desiccated as plant and animal resources dwindled. Some of the wild crops may have failed entirely or have fallen off drastically. Arroyo Hondoans may have ended up with only the hardiest wild plants, such as prickly pear, and they may have turned to starvation foods such as leaf fibers, roots, and the inner bark of trees. Animal populations probably declined with the loss of their food and cover. Mule deer are especially susceptible to environmental conditions; when food is limited, fertility drops and a large share of young arrive stillborn (Klein 1970:32–33). As a result Arroyo Hondo hunters may have taken fewer deer and may have tried to compensate with a greater range of animals.

As conditions grew worse after each succeeding year, Arroyo Hondoans may have turned to other mechanisms in addition to more intensive collecting and farming. A common pattern for communities struggling with food stress is to adopt more inclusive responses involving larger groups (Minnis 1981:23). Arroyo Hondo may have worked more cooperatively to allocate the scarce canyon lands, to pool resources, and to encourage households to produce a surplus for communal storage. On the other hand, if the situation became desperate, the social organization may have disintegrated, as has also been observed among communities suffering from famine (Sahlins 1972:214). We may have no archaeological evidence for either response, but it is clear that some families took an out by simply abandoning the pueblo. It appears that only a small population remained at the pueblo between 1340 and 1370, perhaps later to be joined by new immigrants (Schwartz l986:xv).

As families fled Arroyo Hondo in the l340s, the remaining inhabitants would still have had a hard time making a living, although the shortages might not have been so acute. With fewer mouths to feed the limited resources would have gone farther, but the stragglers had to eke out a living from a much-reduced resource base, offering far fewer plant and animal resources than in the past. With fields restricted to the Arroyo Hondo canyon, land would have been at a premium while yields may have dropped as a result of drought. Even during the brief moist phases, such as 1370–1375, Arroyo Hondoans may not have attempted dry farming on the piedmont because it seemed too risky.

Diet and Health During Lean Times

After 1330 undernutrition and specific nutritional deficiencies were probably common at Arroyo Hondo as a result of food shortages. Although everyone would have endured a poor diet, young children under five would have suffered the most severe consequences. Young children and infants are far more vulnerable than are older individuals to nutritional deficiencies, especially to protein calorie malnutrition (PCM or protein energy malnutrition), which is a major health problem for toddlers in much of the developing world today (Behar 1968; Gopolan 1975). They are more likely to develop infectious diseases as a result of malnutrition and are more likely to die from one or a combination of these (Scrimshaw et al. 1968:16). As a result they are the most sensitive barometers of a community's nutritional status.

Young children are also likely to have an enormous impact on demographic patterns since they often contribute a large share to death. For example, in a sample of contemporary nonindustrialized societies, which offer a useful analogy to prehistoric agriculturalists, young children represented 35% to 65% of total mortality (Patwardhan 1964). Children under five can also exhibit wide ranges in their death rates, thereby having a great impact on demographic patterns.

At Arroyo Hondo PCM and related infectious disease were probably a constant threat to young children. During the best of times toddlers' diets were almost certainly marginal, but after 1330 when everyone had problems finding enough to eat, toddlers may have been especially shortchanged on calories. As a result, rates of PCM, infectious disease, and death probably peaked during the depths of extended droughts.

Modeling the Demographic Effects of Drought

We can gain insights into the impact of these deaths on demographic patterns by examining how hypothetical populations are affected over time by deaths in the youngest age classes. For this purpose three tables were prepared using, in part, figures from three of the model life tables that Weiss (1973) developed for anthropological demographic work. Weiss's generalized models attempt to describe the underlying demographic features of the populations with which anthropologists and archaeologists work. Based on data from skeletal, historic, contemporary, and other anthropological populations, the life tables describe the mortality and longevity experiences of a population by age class. The tables can be used to explore how a change in one parameter might affect the others, as will be done below.

The three model life tables selected from Weiss's work span a range of adult and juvenile mortality patterns characteristic of nonindustrialized societies. They represent two extremes of mortality experience and a middle value that seems to best characterize the Arroyo Hondo population based on the skeletal data (Palkovich 1980:34). They include populations in which either 30% or 50% of the population survives to age 15 and the life expectancy after 15 is 20 or 30 years.

Using those models I experimented with different death rates, plugging in new values for the under-five age group in Weiss's tables. My goal was to find out what would happen to the population later on if mortality were increased to 40%, 50%, and so on up to 80% in that age group. How would the shape of the population be changed by those excess deaths? After substituting new toddler mortality values in Weiss's tables, I calculated the new survivorship at age five and then continued calculating for each succeeding interval using Weiss's figures. It was assumed that after age five death rates returned to the "normal" values given in Weiss's table. That assumption seemed reasonable since the survivors, after reaching five, would no longer have been as vulnerable as the youngest age groups, and their death rates would have dropped accordingly. Moreover, there is evidence from modern nonindustrialized societies that survivors fare as well as their age mates (Martorell et al. 1978:149). The next step in modeling Arroyo Hondo's demographic patterns was to determine the total population of adults aged 15 to 50 and to compare those figures with the original values to determine the percentage lost to the population for each case.

I found that the percentage lost varies with juvenile mortality and adult life expectancy. Populations with high juvenile mortality are more strongly affected than those with lower levels, and the percentage of loss also increases as the adult life expectancy declines. But the pattern is the same for the three model cases: a small increase in toddler deaths has negligible effect, whereas a mortality rate of 50% to 60% produces a significant dip in the adult population. Thus a drought's effect depended on its length and severity. A short dry spell resulting in a small increase in deaths among young children, even for five years, would have created only a minor, quickly absorbed perturbation in the population size. A large increase in deaths during one or two years would have been similarly damped. On the other hand, an extended and severe drought could have had a dramatic impact on the population. If the death rates reached 50% to 60% for the youngest age groups during a five-year dry period, the future adult population could have been reduced roughly 10% to 15%, and the loss could have been as high as 25% if toddler mortality increased to 80%. The Arroyo Hondo area endured four dry phases after 1335—1335–1345, 1360–1370, 1375–1380, and 1394–1400—that were long enough to have had an impact on demographic patterns through malnutrition and death.

Testing the Reconstruction

Unfortunately, the archaeological evidence for this reconstruction is murky. On the one hand, there are signs of food stress after 1335 and high death rates among young children related to malnutrition. But the evidence cannot be dated precisely and conclusively attributed to dry periods.

The faunal remains suggest that Arroyo Hondo hunters tried to compensate for food shortages after 1330 by traveling farther in pursuit of game, by hunting longer, and by stalking a greater range of species (Lang and Harris

1984:51–52, 55, 59, 63). They began hunting deer in the off-season, August through January, when the animals were concentrated in the higher foothills and mountains. Previously they had hunted only in the spring, when deer came down to lower elevations and did not have to be stalked great distances. Hunters also began using species that they had hardly touched during the pueblo's early years: prairie dogs, tree squirrels of the montane forest, and a greater range of birds, all of which would have required much additional effort for relatively small returns.

The most compelling evidence for malnutrition and food shortages comes from skeletal remains. The 108 burials from the period 1300 to 1370 showed a demographic pattern similar to Weiss's tables for nonindustrialized societies, but mortality rates were exceptionally high among infants and young children. Only about 40% of the population survived to age 15, and the age group 0–5 years accounted for roughly 42% of all deaths (Palkovich 1980:31–37). Four forms of skeletal pathology associated with nutritional deficiencies—cribra orbitalia, generalized porosity, porotic hyperostosis, and endocranial lesions—were especially common in the youngest age classes. Palkovich concluded that "malnutrition, acting in combination with infectious disease, was at least partially responsible for the high level of mortality among infants at Arroyo Hondo" (1980:47). Unfortunately, since the skeletons cannot be precisely dated, the deaths and pathologies cannot be correlated with drought.

Conclusions

Without "hard" evidence this reconstruction must remain unproven, though highly plausible. Still, the estimates of resources, though far from precise, highlight the problems of making a living in the Arroyo Hondo area and make a case for food shortages, particularly during dry periods. Moreover, the demographic models indicate that if the shortages had led to additional deaths among young children, they could have affected population patterns with a "baby bust" that would have followed the survivors through their lifetimes.

Such population fluctuations could have had far-reaching consequences for the Pueblos. Once the childhood survivors of drought reached adulthood, the community would have suffered from a drop in the number of young adults. As a result, the dependency ratio would have shifted; each productive adult would have supported a larger share of elderly, infirm, and young than in the past. The deficit of adults might have caused economic hardship for many households, prompting them to turn to a wider range of kinsmen for support. As a result, new residence patterns might have appeared. At the same time the community might have tried to intensify agriculture and find additional ways to make a living.

The shortage of appropriate personnel probably strained the community's social, political, and religious organization. Faced with a dearth of adults, Arroyo Hondoans had to be flexible about marriage rules, about the personnel who filled ceremonial and political positions, and about how responsibilities and privileges were distributed across the community. As old rules were bent and broken, new forms of social organization would have gradually emerged. If the community originally had a flexible, bilateral form of organization, similar to that of contemporary Rio Grande Pueblos (Eggan 1972:293), the population fluctuations would have reinforced it. Had the system been more rigid, it probably would have broken down as Arroyo Hondoans tried to adapt to varying numbers and deficits of adults. From this reconstruction it seems highly probable that the Puebloan communities that emerged from this period of turmoil in the Northern Rio Grande were a product of what they ate.

Acknowledgments

This research was carried out in conjunction with the School of American Research's project at Arroyo Hondo Pueblo, headed by Douglas W. Schwartz, SAR director, and supported by National Science Foundation grants. I am grateful to Dr. Schwartz for inviting me to work at Arroyo Hondo and for his support and encouragement throughout the project. I also thank the Arroyo Hondo field crew and the SAR staff, who provided help and support in innumerable ways. In addition, I owe a great debt of gratitude to Dr. Richard I. Ford, an ever-helpful critic and unflagging source of moral support during the early phase of this work, which constituted my Ph.D. dissertation at the University of Michigan.

References

Behar, M.
1968   Prevalence of Malnutrition among Preschool Children of Developing Countries. In *Malnutrition, Learning, and Behavior*, edited by N. S. Scrimshaw and J. Gordon, pp. 30–41. MIT Press, Cambridge, Massachusetts.

Bohrer, V. L.
1986   The Ethnobotanical Pollen Record at Arroyo Hondo Pueblo. In *Food, Diet, and Population at Prehistoric Arroyo Hondo Pueblo, New Mexico,* by W. Wetterstrom with additional reports by V. L. Bohrer and R. W. Lang, pp. 187–250. Arroyo Hondo Archaeological Series, vol. 6. School of American Research Press, Santa Fe.

Buikstra, J. E., and J. H. Mielke
1985   Demography, Diet, and Health. In *The Analysis of Prehistoric Diets*, edited by R. L. Gilbert, Jr., and J. H. Mielke, pp. 359–422. Academic Press, Orlando.

Eggan, F.
1972   Summary. In *New Perspectives on the Pueblos*, edited by A. Ortiz., pp. 287–305. University of New Mexico Press, Albuquerque.

Food and Agriculture Organization (FAO) and World Health Organization (WHO)
1973   *Energy and Protein Requirements. Report of a Joint FAO/WHO ad hoc Expert Committee.* Food and Agriculture Organization Nutrition Meeting Series No. 52, World Health Organization Technical Report Series No. 522. Rome, Italy.

Ford, R. I.
1968   *An Ecological Analysis Involving the Population of San Pueblo, New Mexico.*

Unpublished Ph.D. dissertation. Department of Anthropology, University of Michigan, Ann Arbor.

Gaulin, S. J. C., and M. Konner
1977   On the Natural Diet of Primates Including Humans. In *Malnutrition and the Brain*, vol. 1, edited by R. J. Wurtman and J. J. Wurtman, pp. 1–86. Raven Press, New York.

Gopolan, C.
1975   Protein vs. Calories in the Treatment of Protein-Calorie Malnutrition: Metabolic and Population Studies in India. In *Protein Calorie Malnutrition*, edited by R. E. Olson, pp. 343–351. Academic Press, New York.

Harrington, J. P., and P. A. Minges
1954   *Vegetable Seed Germination*. University of California Agriculture Experiment Service Mimeograph.

Higgs, E. S.
1975   Appendix A: Site Catchment Analysis: A Concise Guide to Field Methods. In *Paleoeconomy*, edited by E. S. Higgs, pp. 223–234. Cambridge University Press, Cambridge.

Higgs, E. S., and C. Vita-Finzi
1972   Prehistoric Economies: A Territorial Approach. In *Papers in Economic Prehistory*, edited by E. S. Higgs, pp. 29–36. Cambridge University Press, Cambridge.

Kelley, N. E.
1980   *The Contemporary Ecology of Arroyo Hondo, New Mexico*. Arroyo Hondo Archaeological Series, vol. 1. School of American Research Press, Santa Fe.

Klein, D. R.
1970   Food Selection by North American Deer and Their Response to Over Utilization of Preferred Plant Species. In *Animal Populations in Relation to Their Food Resources*, edited by A. Watson, pp. 25–44. British Ecological Society Symposium No. 10. Blackwell Scientific, Oxford.

Lang, R. W., and A. H. Harris
1984   *The Faunal Remains from Arroyo Hondo Pueblo, New Mexico: A Study in Short-Term Subsistence Change*. Arroyo Hondo Archaeological Series, vol. 5. School of American Research Press, Santa Fe.

Lange, C. H.
1968   *Cochiti: A New Mexico Pueblo, Past and Present*. Reprinted. Arcturus Books. Originally published 1959, Southern Illinois University Press, Carbondale.

Lee, R. B.
1968   What Hunters Do for a Living or How to Make Out on Scarce Resources. In *Man the Hunter*, edited by R. Lee and I. DeVore, pp. 30–46. Aldine, Chicago.

Martorell, R., A. Lechtig, C. Yarbrough, H. Delgado, and R. E. Klein
1978   Small Stature in Developing Nations: Its Causes and Implications. In *Progress in Human Nutrition*, vol. 2, edited by S. Margen and R. A. Ogar, pp. 142–158. Avi Publishing, Westport, Connecticut.

Minnis, P.
1981   *Economic and Organizational Response to Food Stress by Non-Stratified Societies: An Example from Prehistoric New Mexico*. Unpublished Ph.D. dissertation, Department of Anthropology, University of Michigan, Ann Arbor.

Palkovich, A. M.
1980   *Pueblo Population and Society: The Arroyo Hondo Skeletal and Mortuary Remains*. Arroyo Hondo Archaeological Series, vol. 3. School of American Research Press, Santa Fe.

Patwardhan, V. N.
  1964   Protein-Calorie Deficiency Disease: Public Health Aspects. In *Proceedings of the Sixth International Congress of Nutrition*, edited by C. F. Mills and R. Passmore, pp. 310–323. E. and S. Livingstone, Edinburgh.
Rose, M. R., J. S. Dean, and W. J. Robinson
  1981   *The Past Climate of Arroyo Hondo, New Mexico, Reconstructed from Tree Rings*. Arroyo Hondo Archaeological Series, vol. 4. School of American Research Press, Santa Fe.
Sahlins, M.
  1972   *Stone Age Economics*. Aldine, Chicago.
Schwartz, D. W.
  1986   Forward. In *Food, Diet, and Population at Prehistoric Arroyo Hondo Pueblo, New Mexico*, by W. Wetterstrom, pp. ix–xix. Arroyo Hondo Archaeological Series, vol. 6. School of American Research Press, Santa Fe.
Scrimshaw, N., C. E. Taylor, and J. E. Gordon
  1968   *Interactions of Nutrition and Infection*. World Health Organization, Rome.
Vita-Finzi, C., and E. S. Higgs
  1970   Prehistoric Economy in the Mount Carmel Area: Site Catchment Analysis. *Proceedings of the Prehistoric Society* 36:1–37.
Weiss, K. M.
  1973   *Demographic Models for Anthropology*. SAA Memoirs No. 27. Society for American Archaeology, Washington, D.C.
Wetterstrom, W.
  1986   *Food, Diet, and Population at Prehistoric Arroyo Hondo, Pueblo, New Mexico*. Arroyo Hondo Archaeological Series, vol. 6. School of American Research Press, Santa Fe.
White, L. A.
  1962   *The Pueblo of Zia, New Mexico*. Bureau of American Ethnology Bulletin No. 184. Smithsonian Institution, Washington, D.C.

20. Paleonutrition: Implications for Contemporary Native Americans

Barrett P. Brenton

Abstract: This paper presents the implications and applications of paleo-nutrition research for contemporary Native Americans. Paleonutrition-ists must recognize the need for an applied dimension to their research and must foster a dialogue with contemporary Native American groups that provides insight into factors that have affected their diet and health in the past and that continue to do so today. I call attention to that issue by presenting a set of guidelines and recommendations for initiating communication with Native Americans. An example of ongoing research with the Hopi of northeast Arizona will present my own involvement in the discussion.

Introduction

With the Columbian Quincentennial (celebration and/or memo-rial?) behind us, it is especially appropriate to recognize the contributions that archaeological research can make toward understanding diachronic change in the social, political, economic, and biological status of Native Americans. I wrote this paper under the premise that little of the information generated by archaeologists is disseminated to the people whose past is being studied. However, studies in paleonutrition are in the unique position of being able to provide a time depth, via interpretations of the archaeological record, to issues that have affected Native American diet and health.

Even though the focus of the conference was on the paleonutrition of prehistoric Americans, we must also consider the vital role paleonutrition can play in understanding the historic nutrition of Native Americans. Indeed, since the contact period a rapid change in the diet and health of Native Americans has taken place. In this case, the archaeological record is valuable in expanding an understanding that might otherwise be lessened from cultur-ally or politically biased historic documents and/or oral histories. Together,

Paleonutrition: The Diet and Health of Prehistoric Americans, edited by Kristin D. Sobolik. Center for Archaeological Investigations, Occasional Paper No. 22. © 1994 by the Board of Trustees, Southern Illinois University. All rights reserved. ISBN 0-88104-078-9.

a prehistoric, historic, and contemporary perspective on diet and health is most useful in understanding issues confronting the well-being of Native Americans.

I specifically want to explore the implications and applications of paleonutrition research for contemporary Native Americans in order to generate discussion among archaeologists and biological anthropologists about their responsibilities to Native Americans. The judgement of whether that suggestion is too didactic or naive will be left to the readers. However, such thoughts do not release readers from confronting the issues by reentrenching themselves in their own self-awareness.

I do not wish to manipulate Euramerican guilt for past treatment of Native Americans as a justification for applying paleonutrition research. That incentive should come from the continued realization of a humanistic archaeology (Ford 1973; Trigger 1990). We have to recognize that our "Western" scientific perspectives often differ from an array of traditional views expressed by various Native American groups (McGhee 1989). Those views are not static, but as with all dimensions of culture, they are constantly changing. The restructuring of Native American identity, especially the Pan-Indian movement, has puzzled many archaeologists who expect to find some static and consistent way to deal with Native American groups (Trigger 1990). Yet, at the same time we must recognize that Native Americans are very much a part of our society. That contradictory juncture creates a platform for accommodating the application of archaeological knowledge.

I am not an archaeologist who has suddenly discovered applied anthropology; rather, I am an applied anthropologist doing archaeological and contemporary research and questioning why archaeology is not applied to contemporary issues. With that said, I in no way want to lessen the importance of the completed and ongoing applied research undertaken by archaeologists. However, I do ask them to become more vocal in catalyzing an active position of applying archaeological research. Working in and with Native American communities forces us to confront a number of our own assumptions and assumptions that Native Americans have about us (Wax 1991; Weibel-Orlando 1990); such is the dilemma of any cross-cultural research.

To facilitate such a discussion, I begin with some comments on the relations between Native Americans and archaeologists. Then, I provide a set of guidelines and recommendations for making paleonutrition research more relevant to issues concerning contemporary Native Americans by identifying the types of paleonutrition data that might be applied. Finally, a discussion of my research with the Hopi in northern Arizona in part highlights my ongoing negotiation with one Native American group concerning a diachronic perspective on diet and health.

We should recognize that the implications of paleonutrition research are what we make of them through our analyses, interpretations, and most importantly, their dissemination. The relevance of this is related to what categories of information are applicable to contemporary issues and how those categories are decided upon. Here, relevance is tied to sets of culturally constructed categories relating diet to health—all of course contingent upon a continually changing understanding of diet and health, which alters our own perceptions and interpretations of the past. Paleonutritionists must come to terms with the issues of relevance and interpretation with Native Americans and generate action and even activism with respect to applying their data.

Relations Between Native Americans and Archaeologists

What is the context of the relationship between archaeologists and Native Americans? Initially, we have to admit that applying archaeological knowledge to the needs of contemporary populations, especially Native Americans, has not been a strong point of the discipline. Information used for land claims, the protection of sacred sites, and general public education strives in that direction (Johnson 1973; McGhee 1989; Sprague 1974; Trigger 1980, 1990; Winter 1980). Indeed, within the last 10 years or so many Native American groups have begun their own archaeology programs with their own research agendas (Adams 1984; Ferguson 1984). In many cases, however, efforts have been viewed more as a reconstruction of the past for political gains, fulfilling legal obligations and site preservation, than as a sincere interest in contemporary Native American issues. "It is far easier, cheaper and apparently equally soothing of tender consciences for non-native North Americans to support native rights in the cultural sphere than to render economic and political justice to native people" (Trigger 1990:779).

In a discussion on archaeology and the image of the American Indian, Trigger (1980) has suggested that nineteenth-century scholars viewed Indians as static, simple, and incapable of developmental changes during the past. During the early twentieth century, scholars focused on creating chronologies and the classification of artifact types. Emphasis was placed on the role of diffusion and migration, which gave little or no credit to the creativity of Native Americans or to the voicing of their contemporary concerns. With the developments of a processual archaeology, or the New Archaeology, since the middle of this century the Indians' past has been seen

> as a convenient laboratory for testing general hypotheses about socio-cultural development and human behavior . . . simply a more intellectualized manifestation of the lack of sympathetic concern for native peoples that in the past has permitted archaeologists to disparage their cultural achievements, excavate their cemeteries, and display Indian skeletons in museums without taking thought for the feelings of living native peoples [Trigger 1980:671].

Trigger reminds us that "the New Archaeology has provided, and will continue to provide, valuable insights into the significance of archaeological data" (1980:672). But he adds that "if prehistoric archaeology is to become socially more significant, it must learn to regard the past of North America's native peoples as a subject worthy of study in its own right, rather than as a means to an end" (1980:671). I might add that reconsiderations of our implicit and explicit research goals and actions as archaeologists, central to many postprocessual debates, have provided some insight into how these issues might be confronted. One way in which this critique manifests itself is through a reexamination of the reseacher's own cultural biases, but there again, efforts toward an effective application have been slow.

I am not advocating that researchers engaging in paleonutrition studies alter their research agendas to the point of losing a focus on scientific rigor and the accumulation of knowledge (see Hill 1991). We must realize the distinction between methodological developments—especially in paleonutrition—provided by processual archaeology and the use of those methods in different theoretical contexts. I believe that we must rethink the goals of our research agendas in the face of whose common past we are trying to reconstruct and to what ends. Our goals should be sensitive to and include other forms of understanding and interpretation beyond a strictly Western positivistic model. The reburial issue has forced all archaeologists to critically reconfigure their own research agendas.

Avoiding the epistemological eddy of reburial (Echo-Hawk 1992; Zimmerman 1992), it will suffice to say that negotiating cultural constructs and contexts is difficult and requires a great deal of time, effort, and patience. When ethical responsibilities are couched in expectations of cultural anthropology, we have to ask ourselves if cultural anthropologists today would dare go into the field without fully defining the terms of their research and without stressing a commitment to providing a full report and application of their findings to the people with whom they work. The answer is no. The ethical responsibilities of archaeologists to the people whose past they research should be no less.

Recommendations for Applying Paleonutrition Studies to Contemporary Native American Issues

It is not my intent to fully outline how archaeologists and Native Americans can develop better working relations and seek common grounds (for further discussion on this issue see, for example, Adams [1984]; Cheek and Keel [1984]; Echo-Hawk [1992]; Ferguson [1984]; Goldstein and Kintigh [1990]; Johnson [1973] ; Leone and Potter [1992]; McGhee [1989]; Meighan [1984]; Sprague [1974]; Trigger [1980, 1990]; Winter [1980]; Zimmerman [1992]). I will, however, consider the role and application of paleonutritional data in these discussions.

None of the following six groupings of recommendations for applying paleonutrition studies to contemporary Native American issues are mutually exclusive. In fact, many suggestions could be cross-referenced. For the sake of brevity many basic ethical considerations will not be repeated from one recommendation to the next. Although these recommendations stress the integration of paleonutrition research, they could be generally applied to any research context and to some degree do exist in the idealized world of a good working relationship between Native Americans and researchers.

Many readers will have had negative or indifferent experiences in applying their research; others will have met with success. I am still optimistic that archaeologists can make a contribution to the welfare of all indigenous peoples. We must remember that the first step in implementing any of these recommendations is contingent upon opening a dialogue with a Native American group, which is often the most difficult step to work through and is often initially unsuccessful. In addition, a primary concern should be an active search for Native Americans to be employed as consultants and archaeological researchers in the research process and its application.

Recommendations for applying paleonutrition studies are as follows:

> 1. When formulating a research project, initiate communication with Native Americans that incorporates their own culturally specific archaeological research agendas as a primary goal. Goals should specify how that agenda could provide information from paleonutrition studies that would be applicable to contemporary diet and health issues. This action should take place with various Native American groups in a region, regardless of any direct-historical relationships between the groups and the archaeological context within which you are working. Discussions only for the sake of fulfilling legal obligations should not end the process and commitment.
> 2. If a project is already underway, invite local Native Americans to sites to discuss whether they think the information you are gaining is useful. Discuss specifically what kinds of diet and health information would be useful to them. If arrangements for a visitation of sites is not possible, provide groups with an update of your progress and goals.
> 3. If a project has been completed, even if it was decades ago, contact local Native American groups and involve them in the reinterpretation of data from sites. Stress what contributions can be made from dietary and health data provided through the paleonutrition research.
> 4. Compile regional and longitudinal data relating long-term diachronic change in diet and health among prehistoric and historic populations and apply that information to contemporary issues. Present the information to Native American groups in both technical and nontechnical reports and through direct discussions and presentations.
> 5. In order to effectively integrate paleonutrition and historical-nutrition studies into a contemporary setting, be in contact with Indian-related health programs and services to understand or become familiar with the scope of problems. In fact, part of the project should incorporate diet and health studies assessing the needs of contemporary Native Americans.

The overall applied and active contributions of paleonutrition to contemporary issues can target various groups:

> 1. Local Native American groups with or without direct-historical association to an archaeological context.

2. Regional Native American groups with or without direct-historical association to an archaeological context.
3. Native North Americans in general (Pan-Indian).
4. Indigenous peoples in the New World.
5. Indigenous peoples in the world.
6. Global issues of diet and health affecting all people.

How Paleonutrition Studies Might Be Applied to Contemporary Native American Issues of Diet and Health

This section briefly explores some of the types of paleonutrition data that might be applied to contemporary Native American issues of diet and health. The list is of course in no way exhaustive. Initially, contributions are subdivided into different categories of paleonutrition research, ending with a discussion on their integration.

Archaeobotany and Paleoethnobotany

Researchers should highlight the range and diversity of plants recovered in archaeological contexts, considering how they were utilized or that they were at least present for food and medicine in the past. Archaeobotanical interpretations can be compared with ethnohistoric and contemporary knowledge of plant use. Such comparisons may provide incentives to continue using the plant resources or to revitalize their former use in a contemporary context by reinstating traditional gathering/collecting areas. The time depth of plant use may provide a direct-historical relationship with Native American groups and aid in the preservation of areas or ecological zones in which the resources grow, grew, or were grown.

The nutritional or medicinal value of these plants, recognized in both "western scientific" and "traditional" terms, could be integrated into educational programs emphasizing the value of traditional foods for a healthier diet and the use of medicinal plants for ameliorating specific health problems. The point of reference for comparison, however, should be the diet-related health problems encountered with contemporary diets and an integration of traditional and western models of health care. Although not the focus of this discussion, the use of plants for industrial and ceremonial purposes (e.g., fibers, dyes, fuel, building materials, tools) should also be considered.

Zooarchaeology and Paleoethnozoology

Many applications of animal products would be similar to those discussed for plants, including areas traditionally used for hunting game and the nutritional value of specific animal products (e.g., Speth 1983). One should also include the economic importance of animal pests (e.g., rodent and insects) on decreasing crop yields, increasing storage loss, and affecting the nutritional value of foods. Again, although not the focus of this discussion, the use of animal products for industrial and ceremonial purposes (e.g., fibers, feathers, skin, fuel, building materials, tools) should also be considered.

Skeletal Biology, Paleopathology, and Coprolite Studies

The analysis of skeletal remains is of course the most controversial as well as the most directly insightful means we have of reconstructing past diets and health. Studies in paleodemography can give us information pertaining to past populations and their composition (age, sex, mortality rates, and so forth). When we combine them with paleopathology, we can begin to understand the epidemiology of both infectious disease and diet-related health problems in the past. This is especially important in the context of historic contact and the spread and related destruction of Old World diseases and foods.

Paleopathology, when combined with chemical analyses of bone for dietary reconstruction, provides insight into some diet-related health problems with direct application to contemporary Native Americans, whereas coprolite studies provide us with the most direct interpretations or evidence of past diets and perhaps medicinal use. Some skeletal biologists/paleopathologists have applied their analyses to issues relevant to contemporary peoples. Most notable are dental caries, enamel hypoplasias, osteoporosis, and forensic medicine. However, with the exception of Gregg (Birkby and Gregg 1975), little of that information has been made directly relevant to contemporary Native American diet and health issues.

Integrated Studies

The reconstruction of paleodiets and an understanding of paleonutrition can take place only with the integration of the above research and associated data. The integration of that information provides a diachronic baseline for understanding change and the foundation for applying interpretations of the past to contemporary issues. For example, conditions that affected the past diet and health of Native Americans, as interpreted through an examination of the archaeological record, can be applied in contexts where similar conditions are producing similar effects today. That application might encompass insights into the political, economic, and sociocultural dimensions of the past projected onto the present.

An important juncture for the integration can be the correlation of food-processing activities in the past, their effect on the nutritional value of foods, and the relationship to corresponding indicators of health. Such an application can highlight the advantage of many traditional methods of food processing. This effort involves a commitment to understanding the role of food processing in the past (Stahl 1989; Wing and Brown 1979). However, paleonutritionists must go beyond just strictly citing analogies from food science and play an active role in experimentation and analyses of processes more closely related to the archaeological context in which they are working

(Brenton 1984, 1988, 1990) as so many European scholars have done. The production of that information could be applied to contemporary issues of appropriate technology for indigenous peoples as well.

Case Study: Negotiating and Applying Paleonutrition Research to Issues Affecting Contemporary Hopi Diet and Health

My research with the Hopi has sought to integrate prehistoric, historic, and contemporary perspectives on diet and health with issues affecting them. The scope of the project is to document change in Hopi foodways and health. Since the application of that research is still underway I can only provide a progress report and suggest what directions the project might take in its present form.

Initially, I contacted the director of the Cultural Preservation Office of the Hopi tribe to inform him of my research interests and to begin arbitrating the conditions of my research. My proposal was then brought before the Hopi Tribe's Resource Committee and the Tribal Chairman, and they approved a permit to conduct research. Since only about half the communities sent representatives to the Tribal Council, in protest of its agendas, I contacted community boards in various villages to ensure further cooperation.

My proposed research was met with mixed reactions that varied from not being allowed to speak, to being told to go elsewhere, to being informed that only Hopis can decide issues of cultural preservation, to being given unanimous approval. I made it clear that the information on changes in Hopi diet and health that I gained would be shared with the community through the distribution of information pamphlets, given to each household, and by presentation of my findings at an open community meeting. Specified publication of the information would not take place without the consent of the community board. Similar information would be distributed for use in the local schools.

After receiving approval from some villages, I then proceeded to go house-to-house conducting interviews with the informed consent of each participant/consultant. It was also imperative that I keep communication open with various agencies responsible for Hopi well-being, to aid in assessing diet-related health problems—for example, constantly informing and discussing the terms of my research with the Hopi Health Department and Indian Health Services.

Surveys conducted in communities on all three Hopi mesas included an assessment and identification of microbial, insect, and rodent pest loss during storage; changes and variation in the knowledge and terminology of traditional methods of food processing and traditional foods; nutritional analyses and experimental food processing of stored and alkali-processed corn products; dietary surveys of elementary school students and Hopi women; and Hopi attitudes toward changing patterns of agriculture, the use of traditional foods, and diet and health.

The ethnoarchaeological and experimental dimensions of that research are being applied to interpret the diachronic dimensions of Hopi diet and health. The temporal perspective has been provided through research on historical photos and documents related to Hopi economy, food, and health. In addition, I have been trying to understand both the historic and prehistoric archaeological contexts of mobility, changing architecture, food-processing technology, subsistence, diet, health, and demography of Hopi antecedents on the Colorado Plateau. That research has encompassed a review and compilation of paleonutrition data from numerous studies done in the region. Most notable are the Awatovi, Walpi, and Homolovi excavations and the Black Mesa project. My own research has included surveying a number of unrecorded isolated granaries and storage areas from Pueblo time periods and various archaeological sites on Hopi lands.

The dissemination of that information will involve, as did gaining permission to do the research, further input from the Hopi. As we are finding out more and more worldwide, traditional foods and diets are often health promoting. That is, of course, no surprise to the Hopi. It is a prophesy that a loss in the traditional culture, like foodways, will lead to a decrease in the quality of Hopi life and health. The need to maintain traditional foodways as a way of resisting that change is very much based in Hopi identity. The reality of a rapid decrease in the use of traditional foods and an increase in diet-related health problems forms a complex state of events and contradictions.

The process of changing Hopi diet and health over time has been an issue of negotiation and synthesis. Archaeological evidence from Hopi sites spanning the prehistoric and Spanish mission period demonstrate a rapid introduction and integration of Old World foods into the Hopi diet (e.g., apricots, peaches, watermelon, sheep/goats; Adams 1989). That trend continued during the nineteenth and twentieth centuries with the introduction of industrially processed foods (e.g., canned meats and fruit, refined flour, sugar, coffee). The political economic consequence of centuries of assimilation has been an almost complete transition from a subsistence economy to a cash economy. The result has been a decrease in the production and use of traditional Hopi foods. It should be noted that many of the Old World foods introduced early on are now incorporated as traditional foods. Therefore, we must bear in mind that what is traditional changes within and between each passing generation.

What then are the applications of paleonutrition studies to Hopi needs? Primarily, the information is a baseline for understanding diachronic change in diet and health within an environmental and cultural context (at least as defined by the archaeologist). That perspective can then be used to address contemporary diet-related health problems. For example, the rapid increase in diabetes among the Hopi is not only related to a change in the type of foods being eaten over time but also includes the ways they have been processed and prepared. In addition, research that has included an ethnoarchaeological and experimental component has helped to define contemporary problems in diet and health, from both a biological and a political economic perspective. Finally, I recognized that my inquiries about Hopi foodways in and of themselves catalyzed an interest around issues of the loss of traditional foodways and diet and health problems among the Hopi.

An optimistic vision that arises over time is that the knowledge of traditional Hopi diets is still a part of being Hopi, however symbolic that expression may be. The maintenance of that indigenous knowledge system will allow future generations to tap into it for reinterpretations of the Hopi diet. The rapid increase in health problems for each succeeding generation of Hopi youth will out of necessity lead the Hopi to confront the role of their traditional diet and the diachronic change that has taken place. We should then apply paleonutritional data from a Western scientific perspective to those discussions.

Conclusions

I have provided a set of recommendations for making archaeological research more relevant to contemporary Native American issues through the application of paleonutrition studies to issues of diet and health. A discussion of my own research is only a preliminary progress report. Discussions with the Hopi have begun, and some phases of the research have been completed while others continue; however, the application of that knowledge is still to be realized

Applying paleonutrition studies is particularly beneficial when they are combined with contemporary studies to develop an educational curriculum. Most Native Americans, like the Hopi, have their own history and realize the recent changes in their diet and health, especially those concerning the increased incidence of diabetes and obesity. The usefulness of the information that we can provide as paleonutritionists lies in its ability to give a tangible context and reference point, over time, of change. If anything, that information can help individuals, today or in the future, remember and revitalize their traditional diet and foods.

Ultimately the information must be viewed as pertinent to advancing Native American self-determination, so crucial to a disenfranchised people. As ideal as this sounds, in the end, Native Americans will be the ones who decide how diet and health affect their well-being and what traditions will be maintained. We can only hold up the mirror to reflect those changes.

What then are the implications and applications of paleonutrition research for contemporary Native Americans? Again, my primary goal in asking that question has been to generate discussion among archaeologists and biological anthropologists about their responsibilities to Native Americans. In turn, this paper is really a call for a continued development of a humanistic archaeology. Only with an active relationship between archaeologists and Native Americans will the implications and applications of the research be defined.

For the Hopi, as with many native peoples, the knowledge and use of traditional foods is rapidly disappearing, with a concomitant increase in diet-related disease. Yet in the face of adversity, the Hopi still actively engage in negotiations of change while holding onto an impressive base of traditional knowledge—slowly fading into symbolic expression with the passing of each cycle of Hopi ritual.

Acknowledgments

I would like to express my gratitude to all Hopi past and present for their patience and understanding in tolerating the research of yet another anthropologist. I know that I will never be able to give back as much as I have been given. A global thanks to all those individuals who have politely helped me with my esoteric inquiries, including Blythe Roveland, Mary Ann Levine, Brenda Baker, Ann Marie Mires, Sol Katz, and Jim Hahn. Additional thanks go to my dissertation committee—Brooke Thomas, George Armelagos, and Peter Pellet—and to the three anonymous reviewers and Kristin Sobolik, whose useful editorial comments reflected the need for this type of research. The research was funded in part by a Wenner-Gren Foundation Predoctoral Grant and a University of Massachusetts-Amherst Graduate Fellowship.

References

Adams, E. C.
  1984   Archaeology and the Native American: A Case at Hopi. In *Ethics and Archaeology*, edited by E. L. Green, pp. 236–242. The Free Press, New York.
  1989   Passive Resistance: Hopi Responses to Spanish Contact and Conquest. In *Columbian Consequences, Volume 1: Archaeological and Historical Perspectives on the Spanish Borderlands West*, edited by D. H. Thomas, pp. 77–91. Smithsonian Institution, Washington, D.C.
Birkby, W. H., and J. B. Gregg
  1975   Otosclerotic Stapedial Foodplate Fixation in an 18th Century Burial. *American Journal of Physical Anthropology* 42:81.
Brenton, B. P.
  1984   *Preliminary Investigations in the Nutritional Significance of Indian Maize Processing*. Unpublished Bachelor of Arts thesis, Department of Anthropology, University of Nebraska, Lincoln.
  1988   Fermented Foods in New World Prehistory: North America. In *Diet and Subsistence: Current Archaeological Perspectives*, edited by B. V. Kennedy and G. M. LeMoine, 329–337. Proceedings of the 19th Annual Chacmool Conference, Archaeological Association of the University of Calgary, Calgary, Alberta.
  1990   Mycotoxin Analyses of Stored Barley from Iron Age-Type Pits: Implications for Human Health and Nutrition (Abstract). *American Journal of Physical Anthropology* 81:199.
Cheek, A. L., and B. C. Keel
  1984   Value Conflicts in Osteo-Archaeology. In *Ethics and Archaeology*, edited by E. L. Green, pp. 194–207. The Free Press, New York.
Echo-Hawk, W. (guest editor)
  1992   Special Edition: Repatriation of American Indian Remains. *American Indian Culture and Research Journal* 16(2).
Ferguson, T. J.
  1984   Archaeological Ethics and Values in a Tribal Cultural Resource Management Program at the Pueblo of Zuni. In *Ethics and Archaeology*, edited by E. L. Green, pp. 224–235. The Free Press, New York.
Ford, R. I.
  1973   Archeology Serving Humanity. In *Research and Theory in Current Archeology*,

edited by C. L. Redman, pp. 83–93. John Wiley & Sons, New York.
Goldstein, L., and K. Kintigh
   1990   Ethics and the Reburial Controversy. *American Antiquity* 55:585–591.
Hill, J. N.
   1991   Archaeology and the Accumulation of Knowledge. In *Processual and Postprocessual Archaeologies: Multiple Ways of Knowing the Past*, edited by R. W. Preucel, pp. 42–53. Occasional Paper No. 10. Center for Archaeological Investigations, Southern Illinois University, Carbondale.
Johnson, E.
   1973   Professional Responsibilities and the American Indian. *American Antiquity* 38:129–130.
Leone, M. P., and P. B. Potter, Jr.
   1992   Legitimation and the Classification of Archaeological Sites. *American Antiquity* 57:137–145.
McGhee, R.
   1989   Who Owns Prehistory? The Bering Land Bridge Dilemma. *Canadian Journal of Archaeology* 13:13–20.
Meighan, C. W.
   1984   Archaeology: Science or Sacrilege. In *Ethics and Archaeology*, edited by E. L. Green, pp. 208–223. The Free Press, New York.
Speth, J. D.
   1983   *Bison Kills and Bone Counts: Decision Making by Ancient Hunters*. University of Chicago Press, Chicago.
Sprague, R.
   1974   American Indians and American Archaeology. *American Antiquity* 39:1–2.
Stahl, A. B.
   1989   Plant-Food Processing: Implications for Dietary Quality. In *Foraging and Farming: The Evolution of Plant Exploitation*, edited by D. R. Harris and G. C. Hillman, pp. 171–194. Unwin Hyman, London.
Trigger, B. G.
   1980   Archaeology and the Image of the American Indian. *American Antiquity* 45:662–676.
   1990   The 1990s: North American Archaeology with a Human Face? *Antiquity* 64:778–787.
Wax, M. L.
   1991   The Ethics of Research in American Indian Communities. *American Indian Quarterly* 15:431–456.
Weibel-Orlando, J. (guest editor)
   1990   Anthropologists and American Indians. *Practicing Anthropology* 12(2).
Wing, E. S., and A. B. Brown
   1979   *Paleonutrition: Method and Theory in Prehistoric Foodways*. Academic Press, New York.
Winter, J. C.
   1980   Indian Heritage Preservation and Archaeologists. *American Antiquity* 45:121–131.
Zimmerman, L. J.
   1992   Archaeology, Reburial and the Tactics of a Discipline's Self-Delusion. *American Indian Culture and Research Journal* 16(2):37–56.

V. Summary and Conclusions

21. The Past, Present, and Future of Paleonutritional Research

Elizabeth S. Wing

Introduction

Research on human subsistence in the past and its consequence, human nutrition, has escalated since the second half of this century, resulting in many new and innovative techniques that have been brought to bear on that important subject. The interest in paleonutrition has been driven by a concern for a better understanding of what fuels societies and by a desire to document the range in foods consumed by our species. Our broad diet is an attribute that is at least in part responsible for the distribution of people throughout the world.

Despite the great breadth of the human diet, the specific foodways practiced by each culture are finely tuned, and specific patterns of consumption are conservative cultural traits. The breadth of the human diet, the specialized techniques required to identify dietary components from archaeological refuse and those incorporated in human bone, and the evidence of nutritional inadequacy in human remains require an interdisciplinary approach. The interdisciplinary nature of that research teases apart the evidence for past diets, and the challenge that is now being met is to integrate those data to define the components of a diet and to judge its adequacy.

Past History of the Development of Paleonutrition

Although interest in past subsistence extends back a long time, research on aspects of the subject accelerated exponentially from the 1950s to the present. The major advances in dietary reconstruction based upon the refuse from past meals, both garbage and feces, and in the interpretation of the consequences of diet as seen in human remains occurred from the 1950s through the 1970s. In the 1970s and 1980s major advances in the techniques

Paleonutrition: The Diet and Health of Prehistoric Americans, edited by Kristin D. Sobolik. Center for Archaeological Investigations, Occasional Paper No. 22. © 1994 by the Board of Trustees, Southern Illinois University. All rights reserved. ISBN 0-88104-078-9.

that measure the relative concentration of the trace elements and stable isotopes of bone and the association of those bone constituents with diet were achieved. Those advances have set the stage for the focus of some of the research questions posed today and so well illustrated by the papers published in this volume.

Present Emphasis

Ground truthing is being vigorously pursued in all aspects of dietary reconstruction—driven by the need for more precise understanding of factors altering the record such as bone diagenesis in bone chemistry and taphonomic losses in archaeobiological data. Such examination should be expected in an emerging field of study where the data are subject to great variation in their prehistoric conditions, deposit in archaeological context, losses through environmental factors, recovery by archaeologists, and analysis by specialists.

I will use experience from zooarchaeology to describe just two ways that ground truthing is resulting in a changed perspective of the archaeological record and the prehistoric way of life that record reveals. Zooarchaeology can provide information on only one aspect of past subsistence—that of animal protein, an essential nutritive component of the diet. Better understanding of the implications of animal remains for past diet are important for integrating those data with other complimentary data in a reconstruction of human nutrition and health. Similar approaches are being undertaken in all aspects of dietary reconstruction (Price 1989; Sillen and Armelagos 1991; Sillen et al. 1989) and are exemplified by a number of papers in this volume. In this concluding paper I will discuss ways to account for differential loss of faunal remains and alternate ways to estimate potential meat weight as reflected by the faunal remains.

That faunal remains are differentially lost through taphonomic factors is well known. However, when studies of faunal remains are reported, the unspoken assumption is usually that they reflect elements that were deposited in approximately the proportion in which each faunal component was used. An experiment designed to track losses of refuse caused by scavenging domestic dogs documented profound losses of skeletal material (Walters 1984). Only 3% of the bones that were discarded were subsequently recovered after six months. Similar results have been reported (Wheeler and Jones 1989:61–64). Not only was there a great overall loss of bone, but the remains of smaller animals were lost at a greater rate than the bones of larger animals. An experiment designed to investigate the magnitude of refuse losses resulting from scavengers in the absence of domestic dogs and cats was conducted on islands along the Gulf Coast of Florida (Wing and Quitmyer 1992). The losses of faunal remains were not as great as those experienced when dogs were the predominant scavengers. Nevertheless, substantial bias in the faunal assemblage did result with no loss of shellfish (primarily oyster not counting symbionts) and at least a 37% (minimum numbers of individuals of cooked and filleted carcasses) loss of fishes.

Another aspect of the experiment conducted on the Gulf Coast islands was a comparison between the accuracy in the number of identified specimens (NISP) and minimum number of individuals (MNI) in reflecting the relative abundance of the species represented in the faunal assemblage. The experimental results indicated that MNI more closely reflected the complex of animals deposited. The reason is that when scavengers take hold of a discarded carcass, the grasped portion is pulled off the site, leaving behind a fragmentary representative of the individual. In this experiment, the recovered NISP was only 29% of the fish deposited, whereas the MNI was 58%.

Many other confounding factors affect faunal assemblages. Taphonomic loss resulting from other factors such as mechanical damage has been a major concern of zooarchaeologists (Marean 1991), and a number of attempts have been made to gauge the intensity of that loss and the resulting bias related to bone density. Different taphonomic factors would be expected to have critical affects under different conditions. The further step to adjust estimates of past diets for the effects of bone destruction is not usually taken.

Alternative methods of quantifying potential meat contribution by the animals represented in the faunal assemblage can also provide different perspectives on the contribution of the various components of the diet. We know that losses occurred, as just described. We also know that some animals, which were consumed, would not leave any identifiable vestige in the site because they were entirely consumed and refuse was deposited off the site. Based on ethnographic evidence, some entire animals were consumed by the occupants of the site, and others, usually large animals, were shared in the larger community, or where markets operated, only a portion of a larger carcass was purchased. Traditionally, faunal analysts have assumed that the entire carcass of each individual represented at the site was consumed (White 1953). However, taking some of the other alternative assumptions into account requires that this method be paired with another to present a broader range of estimates.

This approach has two parts, and the objective is to provide a minimum and a maximum estimate of the potential relative contribution of each animal. Clearly the samples must be of adequate size and be recovered by sieving with fine-gauge screens (Payne 1972). The maximum estimate would be a modification of the method proposed by White (1953). The modification involves the use of allometric relationships for estimating individual weight. Such relationships, derived from the live weights and skeletal dimensions, are the basis of least squares formulas that can be used for more accurate estimates of individual biomass (or meat weight). This is particularly important in work with remains of fishes and molluscs because prehistoric fishing may have concentrated on fishing in the nursery grounds and the fishes may all be juveniles and therefore much smaller than the size reported in the literature for the species. The other extreme is also possible. Individuals of some species found in archaeological contexts are larger than their modern counterparts (Hales and Reitz 1992). Both extremes are of interest from the standpoint of the biology of exploited species, prehistoric technology, and diet reconstruction.

The maximum meat weight method assumes that the meat from each individual animal represented in a sample was entirely eaten, but another possibility exists if we assume that only the meat around those parts of animal carcasses represented in the sample was consumed. The minimum estimate would be based on the correlation between the weight of the excavated bone or shell and body or meat weight. The accuracy of such estimates is a problem because bone may be either leached and lighter than it was when deposited or it may be mineralized and therefore heavier. Relatively, however, bone from the same context experienced the same environmental forces and would be altered proportionally the same. If the relationships between bone or shell weight and total body weight (muscle weight) are used, an approximate minimum estimate can be derived.

Comparisons between the maximum and minimum estimates reveal shared carcasses and an objective way of interpreting animals that were not important in the diet. To illustrate this approach, data can be used from a prehistoric site at Kings Bay (Poisonberry Area Feature 22) on the southeastern coast of Georgia in which deer and coastal fishes predominated in the vertebrate assemblage excavated from an oyster midden (Wing and Quitmyer 1985; Figures 21-1 and 21-2). The two methods of estimating biomass (or meat weight) give contrasting impressions of the relative importance of the faunal components. If one assumes that an entire deer represented by two bones in the sample from Kings Bay was consumed, deer would be estimated to have contributed in a major way, 25%, to the diet. However, it is also possible that those two bones were associated with the portion of the deer acquired by the disposers of the refuse and that the many small fishes, which constitute 51% of the estimated meat weight, provided the bulk of the protein, at least from vertebrates (Figure 21-1).

These estimates can then be further modified to reflect some of the differential losses to scavengers, and they would further increase the relative contribution of fish to as much as 70% of the animal protein portion of the diet (Figure 21-2). Just as these calculations suggest that fish were more important to the diet than they at first appear, others have demonstrated that by closer examination of the Hohokam (Szuter, this volume) and the Anasazi (Cummings, this volume) diets were broader and in many respects different than originally thought. Independent evidence, such as might come from bone chemical analysis, can enhance our interpretation of past reality. These two approaches—faunal analysis and bone chemistry—applied to data from the coast of Maine have provided the opportunity to evaluate the shortcomings of each method (Bourque and Krueger, this volume).

This discussion has revolved around subsistence, including foods and menu, but equally important to investigations of paleonutrition is an assessment of the nutritional health of the individuals in a population. Larsen and Harn (this volume) have used the incidence of periostitis in three time periods in the southeastern United States as a measure of nutritional adequacy. Their approach is based on the synergistic relationship between diet and disease and is in some ways comparable to the modern use of E. coli to gauge contamination of water. Other symptoms of dietary stress and consequent poor

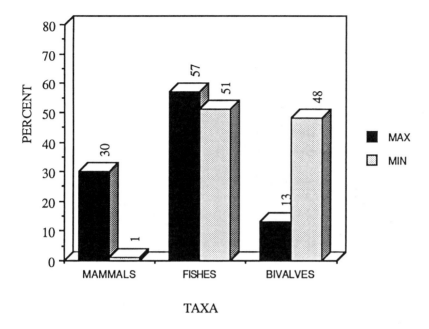

Figure 21-1. *Maximum and minimum estimates of meat weights. Major faunal components of the Poisonberry site at Kings Bay, Georgia, illustrate the differences between the two basic assumptions of meat contribution. Each pair may be viewed as the ends of the probable range of contributed meat.*

health are seen in demographic changes. The demography at Arroyo Hondo Pueblo as affected by loss of productivity of the catchment area resulting from drought conditions is another convincing argument by Wetterstrom (this volume) for nutritional inadequacy. In all of these studies an interdisciplinary approach is the most fruitful.

One of the greatest challenges in paleonutrition is the integration of a wide range of data relating to diet and health. That challenge is already being met, as illustrated in this volume (Sobolik, Fritz, and Crane and Carr). The advice by Fritz to "integrate as many types of subsistence information as possible" is well taken. Historic documents augment interpretation of the archaeological data. In the absence of applicable documents or representations of diet and health, such information must be entirely derived from archaeological data. Those data are, of course, viewed with an understanding of contemporary characteristics of diet such as its conservatism and the establishment of traditional cuisines, social connotations of food, food preparation methods, impact of deficiencies on health, and faunal and floral uses for food by people with widely different economies. Data derived from the full array of archaeological

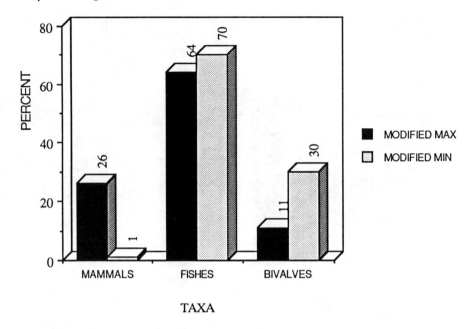

Figure 21-2. *Meat estimates modified by loss to scavengers. This graph is the same as Figure 21-1 except that the experimentally derived extent of losses to scavengers is calculated.*

remains by specialists in fields as different as chemistry, zoology, botany, and physical anthropology must continue to devise ways in which their evidences for diet and health can be integrated to provide a fuller picture of past conditions.

Another, but related, issue raised by Brenton (this volume) is the dissemination of the results of paleonutritional studies to the public. In his case, he has been involved with the Hopi community from the inception of his research. In general, I think the research discussed at the conference on paleonutrition and presented in this volume is of interest to a wide audience. It remains an important challenge to us all to make our research results widely available for their basic interest and their applied value.

Challenges for the Future

Many other challenges remain for achieving a full understanding of past subsistence and nutrition. Clearly, we must continue to improve techniques and strategies for integrating data that provide evidence for what was consumed and the state of health maintained. In addition, we must set our sights on the dynamics of the access to food within a family and community, the development of a cuisine, the maximization of nutrition through scheduled exploitation and food preparation, and the impact of human food extraction on the populations that were exploited and that shared the ecosystem with our species.

We are quite successful in defining what the major food items are in a past diet. We can also discern periodic stress in a growing child that may be the result of food shortages. To truly approach issues of paleonutrition, however, we must address many of the details of diet and health that we take for granted in our daily lives: how food is distributed among members of a family and within the community and whether differential access to food is related to status, gender, or age differences. In their papers Reed and Gumerman have come to grips with data demonstrating such inequalities in food access. Which foods are used for feasting, which foods are taboo, and when special foods are either part of a celebration or are denied also need to be demonstrated for fuller reconstruction of past foodways.

The manner in which foods are prepared and consumed follows precise rules. Such rules undoubtedly existed in the past as they do today, and perhaps they can be reconstructed under special circumstances. The details may be most easily detected in historic sites for which documents exist and in which varied food implements are preserved. Historic sites may then serve as models for interpretation of prehistoric evidence.

The development of a cuisine undoubtedly involved a relatively long period of experimentation with combinations of foods that imparted greater nutritional benefits than those gained from individual items. Tracing the special preparation of foods that required detoxification, special preparation to enhance the amino acid balance, or methods used in preservation would also illustrate ways that people could extract special nutrients and protect themselves against periods of food scarcity. All of this information would provide a better picture of the varied ways people have coped with the basic need for nourishment.

The other perspective of human subsistence that continues to be a research challenge is how human exploitation has affected the other organisms in the environment and has resulted in landscape changes (Szuter, this volume). Persistent and intensive exploitation of a plant or animal will have an effect on its distribution, abundance, size range, and morphological characteristics. Even the efforts to promote the growth of a favorable species by "selective encouragement" can affect its abundance and may ultimately lead to its domestication (Smith 1987). This perspective views our species as an active force in the environment that should be taken into account in an understanding of nature as it exists.

Conferences such as the one that served as the basis for this volume are a forum for specialists in different aspects of paleonutrition to report progress and formulate challenges still to be met. Such interaction provides better understanding of the constraints experienced by other specialists in meeting their research goals and therefore in effectively contributing to the interdisciplinary research effort.

Great progress in paleonutrition has been achieved in the past three decades, but for it to progress along the same trajectory, the close cooperation of interdisciplinary team efforts must be fostered. Few people can master all the specialized fields that have an impact on the reconstruction of the nutrition of a past population. That reconstruction requires detailed knowledge of plant and animal anatomy, ecology, and distribution; human anatomy, nutrition, and pathology; tools related to hunting, gathering, and food preparation; pollen and phytolith identification; and chemical and microbiological analyses. It is an awesome task to master the identification and interpretation of the diverse lines of evidence upon which an understanding of the paleonutrition of a people is based. Therefore, studies are performed more commonly by a team of specialists—i. e., zooarchaeologists, paleoethnobotanists, and physical anthropologists (biological anthropologists).

For each specialist to contribute meaningfully to the integration of the diverse data sets, he or she must have some appreciation of the nature of all relevant lines of evidence and must be fully incorporated at all levels of archaeological programs. If all members of the team work closely together and have the opportunity to discuss their findings throughout the course of the study, each of them can be alerted to finds that have broad implications and should signal changes in other data sets.

Those most able to collaborate effectively should have an understanding of both the potentials and the limitations of the contribution of each data set to the reconstruction of paleonutrition. We continue to find data relating to subsistence in appendices because integration has not been achieved. Integration must be more than simply combining the information from various lines of investigation; it can come about only through the close collaboration of all those involved in attempting to reconstruct the diet and health of prehistoric peoples.

Acknowledgments

I am, as always, most indebted to my students for their diligence in pushing forward the frontiers of zooarchaeological research and sharing their thoughts. Thanks also to Jane Buikstra for her thoughtful comments on the draft of this paper.

References

Hales, L. S., Jr., and E. J. Reitz
   1992   Historic Changes in Age and Growth of Atlantic Croaker *Micropogonias undulatus* (Perciformes: Sciaenidae). *Journal of Archaeological Science* 19(1):73–99.
Marean, C. W.
   1991   Measuring the Post-depositional Destruction of Bone in Archaeological Assemblages. *Journal of Archaeological Science* 18(6):677–694.
Payne, S.
   1972   Partial Recovery and Sample Bias: The Results from Some Sieving Exper-

iments. In *Papers in Economic Prehistory*, edited by E. S. Higgs, pp. 49–64. Cambridge University Press, Cambridge.

Price, T. D. (editor)
1989   *The Chemistry of Prehistoric Human Bone*. Cambridge University Press, Cambridge.

Sillen, A., and G. Armelagos
1991   Introduction to This Issue. *Journal of Archaeological Science* 18(3):225–226.

Sillen, A., J. C. Sealy, and N. van der Merwe
1989   Chemistry and Paleodietary Research: No More Easy Answers. *American Antiquity* 54:504–512.

Smith, B. D.
1987   The Independent Domestication of Indigenous Seed-bearing Plants in Eastern North America. In *Emergent Horticultural Economies of the Eastern Woodlands*, edited by W. F. Keegan, pp. 3–47. Occasional Paper No. 7. Center for Archaeological Investigations, Southern Illinois University, Carbondale.

Walters, I.
1984   Gone to the Dogs: A Study of Bone Attrition at a Central Australian Campsite. *Mankind* 14(5):389–400.

Wheeler, A., and A. K. G. Jones
1989   *Fishes*. Cambridge University Press, Cambridge.

White, T. E.
1953   A Method of Calculating the Dietary Percentages of Various Food Animals Utilized by Aboriginal Peoples. *American Antiquity* 18:396–398.

Wing, E. S., and I. R. Quitmyer
1985   Screen Size for Optimal Data Recovery: A Case Study. In *Aboriginal Subsistence and Settlement Archaeology of the Kings Bay Locality*, edited by W. H. Adams, pp. 49–58. Reports of Investigations No. 2. Department of Anthropology, University of Florida, Gainesville.
1992   A Modern Midden Experiment. In *Culture and Environment in the Domain of the Calusa*, edited by W. H. Marquardt, pp. 367–373. Monograph No. 1. Institute of Archaeology and Paleoenvironmental Studies, Gainesville, Florida.

Contributors

George J. Armelagos is professor of anthropology at Emory University and has taught at the University of Massachusetts and the University of Florida. His research has focused on diet and disease in human adaptation. He has coauthored and coedited a number of bioarchaeological volumes and has published over 100 articles and presented over 125 papers at professional scientific meetings. He has been president of the American Association of Physical Anthropologists and the Northeast Anthropological Association and chair of the Biological Anthropology unit of the American Anthropological Association.

Bruce J. Bourque is chief archaeologist at the Maine State Museum and lecturer in anthropology at Bates College. His research interests focus on northeastern North America. Most of his fieldwork has been conducted on the central Maine coast, especially Penobscot Bay, where he has worked since 1969. His interests in paleo-dietary research arise from the wealth of organic remains recovered from coastal shell middens.

Barrett P. Brenton is a doctoral candidate and instructor in anthropology at the University of Massachusetts-Amherst. His research interests include the biocultural evolution of food-processing technology and its effect on diet and health, indigenous knowledge systems, and appropriate food-storage technology. Currently he is working with the Hopi of northeastern Arizona on documenting traditional methods of food processing and the effects of diet-related health problems among Native Americans.

Vaughn M. Bryant, Jr., is director of the Palynology Laboratory and department head of anthropology at Texas A&M University. He has been active in the field of palynology for over 25 years and is best known for his research in the reconstruction of prehistoric diet, archaeological palynology, and pollen work in paleoenvironmental reconstructions of Quaternary sediments. Currently he and his graduate students are conducting research in forensic palynology, entomopalynology, and melissopalynology.

H. Sorayya Carr is research fellow in the Department of Archaeology at Boston University. She is a zooarchaeologist specializing in the analysis of materials from the Maya Lowlands. She has served as a consultant to several archaeological projects in the Maya area and has also conducted research in the southcentral Plains region of the United States. Her interests include the economic and ideological roles of animals in past complex societies and contemporary ethnozoology.

Cathy J. Crane is a doctoral candidate at Southern Methodist University, specializing in archaeobotany and palynology. Her interests include subsistence and paleoenvironmental reconstructions, and she has served as a consultant to archaeological projects in the Maya Lowlands and in the southeastern United States. She has also done archaeological fieldwork in Colorado, New Mexico, Texas, and Illinois.

Linda Scott Cummings is director of PaleoResearch Laboratories in Golden, Colorado, and an adjunct professor in the Department of Anthropology at Colorado

State University. She has over 22 years' experience in paleoenvironmental, subsistence, and paleonutritional research approached through the identification of pollen, phytoliths, and macrofloral remains. Her current research focuses on identification of and nutritional evaluation of the diet of the Anasazi in the American Southwest and the early Christians in Nubia.

Joseph A. Ezzo is a project director for Statistical Research, Inc., in Tucson. His primary geographical interests are southwestern and North American prehistory, and his topical interests include paleonutrition, bone chemistry analysis, archaeometry, prehistoric social organization, and subsistence strategies.

Gayle J. Fritz is assistant professor in anthropology at Washington University. Since 1988 her primary archaeological fieldwork and paleoethnobotanical analyses have dealt with late prehistoric sites in the lower Mississippi River valley and with early Caddoan sites in Oklahoma, Texas, and Arkansas. Her interests include subsistence continuity and change, the creation of anthropogenic environments, agricultural evolution, and the relationship between diet and sociopolitical complexity.

Alan H. Goodman is dean and associate professor of biological anthropology in the School of Natural Science, Hampshire College. He is vice president of the Council of Nutritional Anthropologists, a contributing editor to *Nutrition Reviews*, and book review editor of *Medical Anthropology Quarterly*. He specializes in nutritional and medical anthropology and is currently engaged in ethnonutritional studies in Mexico, Egypt, and Guatemala.

George Gumerman IV is teaching in the Department of Anthropology at Northern Arizona University. His main research focus is understanding subsistence variation between socioeconomic groups by examining political economy and ideology. He is specifically interested in Andean complex societies and has also conducted research in the American Southwest, the Great Basin, and California.

Dawn E. Harn is a bioarchaeologist in the Illinois State Museum's Quaternary Studies Program. She has conducted research on human remains from prehistoric and historic archaeological sites in central Illinois and from the coastal region of Florida.

Harold W. Krueger was trained as a geologist at the University of Minnesota and Massachusetts Institute of Technology, specializing in isotope geochemistry. He was one of the founders of Geochron Laboratories in 1960 and has operated the company since then, providing K-Ar and ^{14}C age determinations and a variety of other isotopic analyses to clients worldwide. Recently he has become interested in the developing field of isotope studies relating to diet, and his work has focused primarily on developing improved and new techniques for interpreting diets from isotopic data and developing more quantitative models for use in those interpretations.

Clark Spencer Larsen is associate professor in the Department of Anthropology and research associate in the Research Laboratories of Anthropology at the University of North Carolina and research associate in anthropology at the American Museum of Natural History. He has worked extensively with archaeological human remains and is currently engaged in a long-term study of biocultural adaptation in native New World populations, including dietary and nutritional changes in postcontact groups that inhabited Spanish Florida.

Joseph F. Powell is currently a doctoral student in the Department of Anthropology, Texas A&M University. Specializing in dental anthropology and human skeletal biology, his research is focused on quantitative variation and biological relationships among Paleoindian and early Archaic populations in North America.

David M. Reed is a doctoral candidate in the Department of Anthropology at The Pennsylvania State University. His research focuses on complex societies in the Americas. He specializes in quantitative methods in archaeology, with particular interests in the statistical and chemical analysis of material remains. He has performed paleodietary analyses of specimens from Copán (Honduras), Iximche (Guatemala), Pennsylvania, West Virginia, and Georgia.

Kate Aasen Rylander currently analyzes packrat middens for the United States Geological Survey at the Desert Laboratory in Tucson. Her research interests include both the reconstruction of past vegetation and climate in western North America using palynological and macrofloral study and the identification of prehistoric Anasazi subsistence practices through the microscopic examination of botanical remains.

Kristin D. Sobolik is assistant professor of anthropology and Quaternary Studies at the University of Maine. Her interests include Archaic populations of the southern North American deserts and adaptations to desertic environments. She specializes in paleonutrition, zooarchaeology, paleoethnobotany, and coprolite analyses.

D. Gentry Steele is professor of anthropology at Texas A&M University with interests in North American human paleobiology and zooarchaeology. He is coauthor of *The Anatomy and Biology of the Human Skeleton* and coeditor of *Method and Theory for Investigating the Peopling of the Americas*. His publications have primarily been on the human biology and ecology of North American hunters and gatherers.

Bonnie W. Styles is director of sciences for the Illinois State Museum and has archaeological field experience in the southwestern and midwestern United States. A specialist in zooarchaeology, she has identified and analyzed faunal remains from over 30 prehistoric archaeological sites in the Midwest and Southeast and has published reports on such archaeological topics as faunal exploitation, human subsistence practices, and paleoecology.

Mark Q. Sutton is associate professor of anthropology in the Department of Sociology and Anthropology, California State University, Bakersfield. His interests include the prehistory of California and the Great Basin, particularly the Mojave Desert; linguistic prehistory; human and cultural ecology; entomophagy; and hunter-gatherer theory.

Christine R. Szuter is a specialist in the zooarchaeology of the American Southwest. She is author of *Hunting by Prehistoric Horticulturalists in the American Southwest* and numerous articles on the relationship between prehistoric people and animal use. Her research interests include the relationship between hunting and anthropogenic environmental change, prehistoric subsistence strategies, the role of women and children in hunting, and the social dimensions of meat in the diet.

Wilma Wetterstrom is an associate at the Botanical Museum at Harvard University. Her main interests are plants, farming practices, and diet in ancient societies. She has carried out fieldwork in the American Southwest and Southeast but is currently focusing on the Mediterranean region and Africa with projects in Egypt, Syria, Spain, and Madagascar.

Elizabeth S. Wing is a curator at the Florida Museum of Natural History. Major long-term projects include study of the prehistoric exploitation of coastal resources in the southeastern United States and circum Caribbean area, the origin and spread of domestic animals in the Andes, and plant and animal use by colonists of the West Indian island chain. Throughout her work emphasis is placed on improvement of zooarchaeological methods and integration of data from all classes of biological remains in archaeological contexts.